lonely planet

# ELECTRIC VEHICLE ROAD TRIPS

## USA & CANADA

# Contents

## EASTERN USA



## CANADA

BUF9745

# Introduction

This book sets out to expand horizons across the USA and Canada for owners of electric vehicles. It's also for the try-before-you-buy experimenters, who can do so by renting an EV to enjoy a road trip along any of the 60 routes our team of authors and cartographers have plotted in these pages. And it's for the not-quite-convinced-yet – read on to find out how steadily growing charger infrastructure and the ever improving battery range of new EVs now make an impressive mix of cities, landscapes and experiences accessible.

## WHAT EXACTLY IS AN EV?

An EV (electric vehicle) or BEV (battery electric vehicle) is a car, van or truck with a battery pack in place of a fuel tank, and an electric motor (or motors) in place of the internal combustion engine (ICE) in a vehicle fueled by gasoline or diesel. The routes covered in this book are also suitable for plug-in hybrid electric vehicles (PHEVs) – these have a small electric motor with a battery pack that can be topped up by a charger, matched to an ICE to extend range.

Responses to the climate crisis are driving the transition from ICE vehicles to EVs. For instance, in 2021 the US Federal Government set a goal for half of all new vehicles sold in 2030 to be "zero emissions."

While the roll out of EVs is expanding and the technology used to propel them is also fast developing, the EV itself is not a recent invention. The first practical electric automobiles arrived in the 1890s and soon became as popular as the primitive gasoline-fueled contraptions of the time. Only with the immense expansion of road networks through the 1920s did the longer range of ICE vehicles allow them to dominate. But now a second dawn for the EV has arrived.

## ADVANTAGES TO EVS

Drive an EV and you'll have the happy experience of traveling in near silence, while releasing zero carbon dioxide and other emissions "curbside" from a tailpipe. The greater the proportion of electricity produced from renewable sources that is used to charge an EV, the lower that EV's overall environmental impact becomes.

In most cases you'll pay much less to charge your EV than you would to fuel an ICE equivalent. Some large US and Canadian cities are assessing low emission zones that might restrict entry by ICE vehicles but not EVs. And in many places, EVs are now allowed to drive in HOV (high occupancy vehicle) lanes even with only a driver on board, have discounted tolls or parking, and use dedicated spaces in parking lots.

## CHOOSING AN EV

EVs come in greatly varied shapes and sizes, from the Mini Hardtop Cooper SE to the spacious Cadillac Lyriq SUV, via the well-established Hyundai Kona Electric and the Tesla Model 3. They vary in speed (and cost) from the compact Chevrolet Bolt to the Porsche Taycan sports car.

While some small, older-generation EVs have a range limited to perhaps 100 miles (160km), most can now manage between 150 and 300 miles (240km to 480km) – with high-end models like the luxurious Mercedes EQS topping 450 miles (720km). We've made sure that even an EV with a modest range will be suitable for driving the majority of the road trips covered in this book.

# Getting to know EVs

The roll out of electric vehicles is ongoing across the US and Canada. In many places there is fast-growing charger infrastructure, while ever-evolving technology is improving the experience of owning or renting an EV. But still there's room for confusion, especially if you're new to EVs and hope to plan a road trip in one. This might be brought about by inconsistencies in regulations between different states or even cities, in how EVs of different types are equipped, or in how they need charging. To follow are some essential tips to ease you in.

**Connecting up** EVs have a J1772 (Type 1), CCS (incorporating a J1772) or Tesla Combo connector that allows them to charge using AC (alternating current), Level 1 at around 1kW–1.8kW (kilowatts) or Level 2 up to a maximum of 19.2kW. Many EVs have either a CCS or (rarer now) CHAdeMO socket for fast Level 3 charging using DC (direct current), from 50kW to 360kW.

**AC charging** The slowest way to charge an EV is to use a home-charging cable to connect to a regular 110/120 volt electrical socket. This is a method car manufacturers tend to term as for emergency use only, given it's so slow (overnight likely won't be enough to fully charge) and you'll need to carefully check if the electrical circuit is safe to use for this purpose – if in doubt, don't. At accommodations, offer to pay for any electricity used. A more usual way to charge your vehicle is to use the AC charging cable that comes with every EV and allows you to charge at a Level 2, 208-240 volt EV-specific AC charging station, such as might be fitted where you're staying. You plug one end of the cable into the vehicle and the other into the charger (unless it has a fixed cable), then pay to start the charge. While slow 3kW–3.7kW charge stations still exist, versions around 7.6kW are more prevalent across North America. They're great to use for destination charging during a longer rest or overnight stay, as it can take several hours to charge the battery to 80–100%. 19.2kW Level 2 stations are a faster option in places, but are only if your EV supports that AC charge rate – many have a maximum of 11kW.

**DC charging** Level 3 chargers are less numerous than AC stations, but they're multiplying quickly and are fantastic to use while on the road. Such DC stations are increasingly found as public chargers and along highway corridors, and always have a cable of their own. You often activate them by first paying, and then plug into the CCS, CHAdeMO or Tesla Combo connector of your vehicle. DC stations offer speeds from 50kW to 360kW (soon to be more), although the charging speed can fluctuate. It depends on the amount of kWs your vehicle can handle, as well as battery temperature and whether other EVs are charging at the same station. DC stations are best used for topping up on the go, as you'll find you rarely need to charge to more than 80% of battery capacity. Expect to be on the road again in 15 to 45 minutes, depending on your charging speed.

**Finding a charger** Flick through the entries in this book and you'll spot linking themes to the charger locations mentioned at quite varied destinations. Along with at certain gas stations, highway rest stops and major stores, they tend to also appear in clusters at spots you'll likely enjoy pausing at for a while – environmentally-minded accommodations; national park offices; malls, larger museums, amusement parks and restaurants; and public parking lots at the edge of walkable city neighborhoods.

**Apps for route planning** One of the easiest ways to find charging stations on the road is to use Google Maps and search for "EV charger/nearby" in your area. The results will tell you the number of chargers, their speed and the plug type(s) needed at the location. There are also several apps that allow you to input your vehicle's details for customized route planning recommendations. An example is the Chargeway app, covering the US and Canada. This can apply filters for just the charger types your EV can use, and factor in outside temperature and your present level of battery charge to set out the best charging stops en route to your destination – also advising on amenities near suggested chargers. In the US and Canada, use of Tesla Superchargers has been opened up for drivers of other brands of EV, so long as they have a CCS connector and use Tesla's app to search for and pay at suitable sites.

**Paying for charging** This isn't entirely as straightforward as getting out your (virtual) wallet. Although many charging stations will simply accept a credit card or have a QR code that you can use to easily pay online, plenty also must be activated through a dedicated app, or RFID – a card or fob equipped with radio-frequency identification technology. That is why it's recommended to download some apps before your trip or even to take delivery of payment cards, for instance from major charger companies such as Chargepoint, EVGo, Electrify America and Electrify Canada. On your road trip, bring a credit card and make sure you have enough storage space and data on your smartphone (plus if you're traveling from abroad, roaming enabled) to be able to download local apps.

**Battery capacity** The principle of charging the battery is not quite like filling up a gas tank. EV drivers usually keep their battery charge in the zone between 20% and 80% full. The theory goes that it's always good to have a little battery charge left in case your expected charger of choice proves unavailable (think long lines due to demand, or technical malfunctions) – and in unfamiliar places, remember to keep your battery charged up to a level that will cause no issue if the next charger station on your route isn't working. On the other hand, a battery fills up more slowly when it's almost full, so the last 20% takes longer. Consider it like inflating a tire: the last bit takes the most effort. To disconnect after charging, unlock your vehicle and remove the cable – sometimes you'll need to swipe your card again as well.

**Charging etiquette** If you leave your car charging, set a timer, such as on your phone, to remind you when it will be fully charged (you can see how long you have left to go on the vehicle's display). It's considered bad manners to leave your EV plugged in after completing a charge, and doing so can also cost you if the charging station has idle fees. Parking your vehicle in a dedicated EV parking space fitted with a charger but you then not using it to charge up is, of course, a big no-no. And if you arrive at a charging station and there's a line, be sure to patiently wait your turn.

**Terrain and weather** EVs can handle similar terrain and weather conditions to equivalent ICE vehicles, but it's good to be aware of circumstances that might reduce their range. When your vehicle's battery is cold, its performance is limited – so many EVs have systems to warm the battery up... but these drain power. The same goes for heating the vehicle's interior. Using air-conditioning or cooling the batteries also drains power, though less than is lost by heating. Your EV will use more power when driving into a strong headwind or when driving up an incline – also, the faster you drive, of course the more energy you'll expend. If your EV has an eco-mode, this can be used to eke the most out of its range, but know that it can limit the vehicle's acceleration and the effectiveness of its air-conditioning. EVs have regenerative braking – in mountainous areas, when driving downhill stretches, you can expect to get back around a third of the power that was lost on climbs. If there are enough chargers along the route, try not to charge up to 100% in the mountains or you'll wear your brakes faster, because you won't be able to use regenerative braking when the battery is full.

**Renting an EV** Most car-rental companies across the USA and Canada now offer EVs, albeit not yet evenly distributed. Always check with a rental company how best to charge an EV you're booking from them, both in the state or province you'll pick it up from and in any others that you're planning to drive through. They can often also advise on or provide methods of payment, and explain local regulations that might be advantageous to EV drivers. If you're eager to save time throughout your road trip, consider renting an EV that supports at least 75kW of fast Level 3 DC charging.

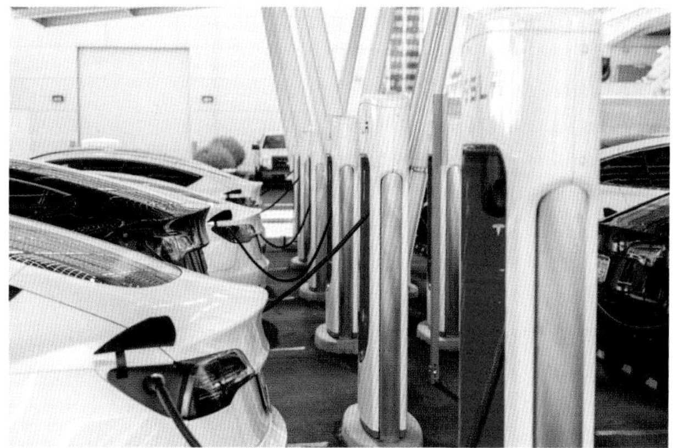

## How to use this book

Orange plug icons appear on every map in this book. These show where clusters of chargers can be found along each route covered, typically the fastest chargers available in the area. We've designed these routes so the places we recommend you stop for a charge (often overnight) are appealing in their own right. The gaps between clusters of chargers are paced so you won't feel pressure to always fully recharge at each, or you'll have options if one is closed. The tips for accommodations in "plan & prepare" panels explain where you'll find chargers either on site or very close by, so you can top up overnight and banish range anxiety as you set out the next day. Many people contributed to this book (their names are listed on p304); they are a mix of experienced electric vehicle early adopters and newcomers, and bring with them first-hand knowledge of the greatly varied driving environments described here – from high-altitude passes to urban streets and meandering coastal roads. They share their expertise on underlying themes, too; look for insights on outdoor activities, wildlife, history, art, culture, food and (we're assuming the help of a designated driver) drink. Each route's description includes the total distance you can expect to cover and the amount of time to allow for enjoying that road trip at an unhurried pace. You'll also find highlight experiences and directions mentioned throughout. The map with each entry gives an overview of the route to follow, along with suggested stopping off points. While you'll likely make use of your EV's satellite navigation system or a smartphone's mapping apps, the maps in this book will reassure of the manageable scale of routes and their suitability for EVs.

# WESTERN USA

**Below:** discover Seattle's coffee culture at the city's renowned roasteries
**Right:** False Creek waterfont and Burrard Bridge, Vancouver

➔ **Distance: 333 miles (536km)**

➔ **Duration: 4-6 days**

# Vancouver to Portland

**BRITISH COLUMBIA, WASHINGTON & OREGON**

This Pacific Northwest EV journey heads from outdoor-oriented Vancouver and across the border to Washington State's farm county, the food and art hubs of Seattle and Tacoma and into eclectic Portland.

Before getting in your EV, explore Vancouver's mix of urban and outdoor attractions. Visit the Vancouver Art Gallery, the Bill Reid Gallery of Northwest Coast Art – which highlights Indigenous artists from the region – and Granville Island's art studios and popular food market. Trails crisscross the temperate-zone rainforest in expansive Stanley Park; rent a bike and circle the seawall to see the ever-popular totem poles and enjoy primo views of downtown and the North Shore mountains.

## TO THE BORDER & BEYOND

Consider topping up your battery's charge, then have your passport handy as you start your drive south, leaving Vancouver on Hwy 99, which takes you to the US–Canadian border in under an hour. Over on the Washington side, the road becomes I-5, which you'll follow to Bellingham, a good place for a quick stop. Camber Coffee roasts the beans that they serve in their airy café here, a quick stroll from downtown chargers.

South of Bellingham, follow Chuckanut Dr (Hwy 11) along the Pacific Coast and head into the agricultural Skagit Valley, a hotspot for local food. Detour into the tiny conjoined communities of Bow-Edison to stop at Samish Oyster Bar and Shellfish Market for fresh

## Plan & prepare

### Tips for EV drivers

Vancouver has one of Canada's highest adoption rates for zero-emission vehicles, with EV chargers available throughout the city. BC Hydro (electricvehicles.bchydro.com) supplies many of the province's speedier charging stations. Along I-5 through Washington and Oregon, the West Coast Electric Hwy (westcoastgreenhighway.com) provides fast charging stations. In Seattle, the ongoing City Light's Curbside Electric Vehicle Charging program is installing public Level 2 chargers. Portland has 100-plus charging stations.

### Where to stay

Hotels with onsite chargers abound. Downtown Vancouver options include the Douglas or JW Marriott in the Parq Vancouver complex (parqvancouver.com), and three Fairmont properties (fairmont.com). In downtown Seattle, there's luxurious Hotel 1000 and mid-range Hilton Motif (both hilton.com), and boutique Kimpton Hotel Monaco (monaco-seattle.com). In Portland, try Provenance Hotels' (provenancehotels.com) Dossier and Hotel deLuxe, or Hotel Eastland (hoteleastlund.com) on the east side.

### When to go

While you can do this road trip at any time of year, you'll typically have the mildest, driest weather between May and October. July and August are the Pacific Northwest's warmest months, but they're also the busiest with visitors; May to June and September to October can be less crowded alternatives. While it can snow in winter, you're more likely to see rain, especially November through February. March and April can still be drizzly, but early spring flowers add color to the damp days.

### Further info

Destination British Columbia (destinationbc.ca), Washington State Tourism (stateofwatourism.com) and Travel Oregon (traveloregon.com) offer regional overviews. Destination Vancouver (destinationvancouver.com), Visit Bellingham (bellingham.org), Visit Seattle (visitseattle.org), Travel Tacoma (traveltacoma.com) and Travel Portland (travelportland.com) provide city planning tips. Visit Skagit Valley (visitskagitvalley.com) and Woodinville Wine Country (woodinvillewinecountry.com) have further useful info.

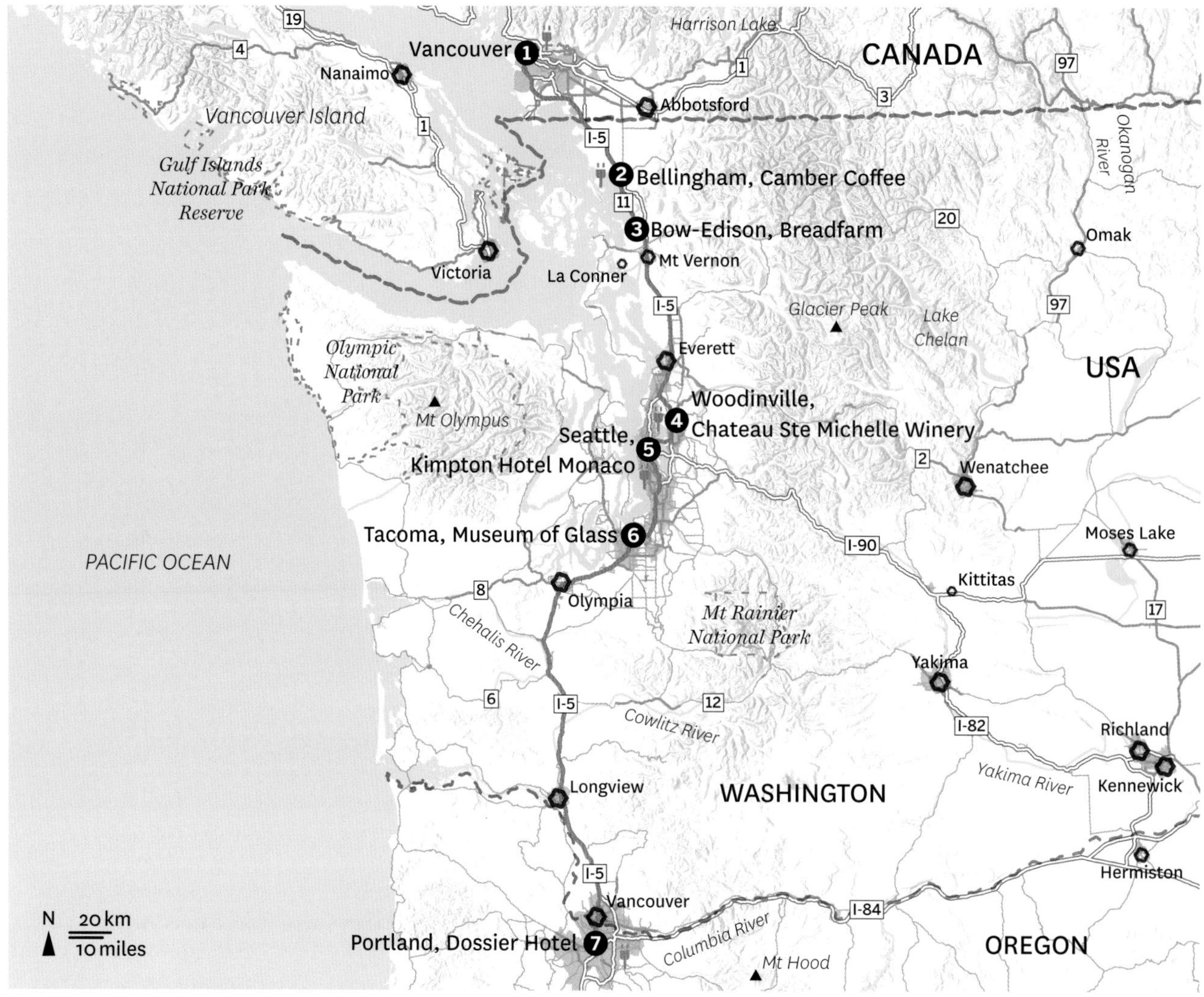


seafood or pick up creamy aged Ladysmith and other cheeses crafted at Samish Bay Cheese, which pair well with the fresh-baked breads (or tasty pastries) from the Breadfarm. Terramar Brewing not only produces beer, cider and liquor, but makes creative pizzas and salads. If you have time, rent a bike in Mt Vernon or La Conner and pedal the mostly flat farm roads. When you return to I-5 and continue south, the surroundings become increasingly urban as you approach Seattle, the Pacific Northwest's largest city.

## ROCKIN' & CAFFEINATING IN SEATTLE

Before reaching Seattle, detour east on I-405 to Woodinville, 65 miles (105km) from Bow-Edison, where 130-plus Washington State wineries have tasting rooms or wine shops. Visit small, woman-owned wineries such as Damsel Cellars, or major producers including Chateau Ste Michelle, with EV charging stations nearby.

Thirty minutes south of Woodinville, park up while you check out Seattle's city-center attractions, from the food vendors at Pike Place Market to the contemporary works at the Seattle Art Museum. Just north of downtown, the Seattle Center complex includes more attractions: Chihuly Garden & Glass, an amazing glass-art collection highlighting the shimmering works of renowned creator Dale Chihuly; the 605ft-tall (184m) Space Needle, with vistas across the city; and the Museum of Pop Culture, a Frank Gehry–designed building where exhibits span rock 'n' roll, film and video gaming.

On downtown's south side, the International District is also worth exploring. Wing Luke Museum highlights the culture and history of the region's Asian Americans, Native Hawaiians and Pacific Islanders, and offers neighborhood walking tours. You don't have to be waiting for a train to check out the cool art gallery that's tucked away on the upper level of Seattle's Gilded Age

## City of glass

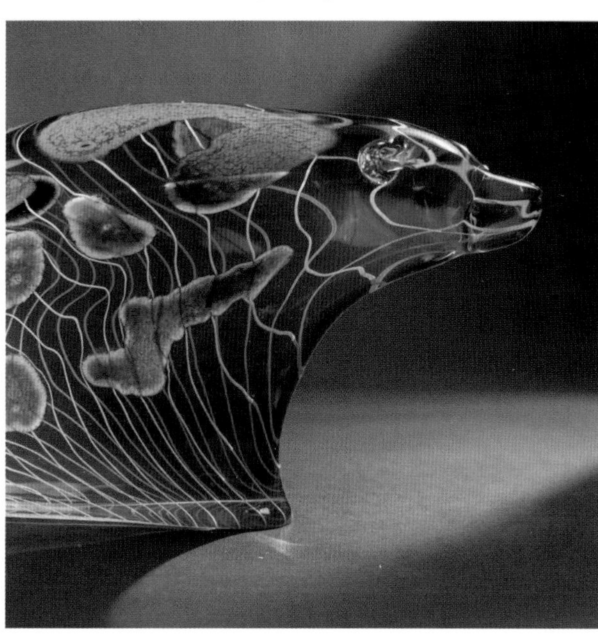

The fact that 400-plus glass artists currently work in the Pacific Northwest is thanks in part to Dale Chihuly. The Tacoma-born glass maestro has been credited with putting Seattle's glass scene on the art map – beginning in 1971, when he co-founded Pilchuck Glass School, a training ground for the region's glass creators. While big-hitters like Chihuly Garden & Glass and Tacoma's Museum of Glass offer major glass-art exhibitions, many smaller Seattle venues highlight works by more diverse artists. Worthy places to check out include Stonington Gallery near Pioneer Square, which regularly features Indigenous artists like Preston Singletary, Raven Skyriver and Dan Friday; the Traver and Vetri galleries downtown both mount changing glass-art shows. Seattle Glassblowing Studio has a small gallery and store showcasing local artists, plus a Hot Shop offering glassblowing classes. The best time to see what's new in Seattle glass art is during Refract Seattle Glass Experience (refractseattle.org), an annual festival (usually October) with open-studio events, glassblowing demos and workshops, and gala parties. Want to check out Seattle's glass artists before you hit the road? Netflix series *Blown Away* features several local glass creators.

**Clockwise from top left:** vineyard at Woodinville's Chateau Ste Michelle; *Salish Sea Bear*, by Dan Friday; the city's Pike Place Market

## Portland's food carts

Plenty of US cities have food trucks, where you can get a quick and inexpensive bite to eat, but Portland takes things to a whole new level. Hundreds of food carts, as they're known here, have set up shop across the city, most clustered into so-called pods, which are essentially food-cart mini-malls, where you can sample the dishes from many different vendors – often representing a variety of diverse cultures – in a single location.

So how do you find the food? Food Carts Portland (foodcartsportland.com) is a useful online guide to local food trucks, and Travel Portland (travelportland.com) can direct you to popular food-cart pods. A few local favorites include Nong's Khao Man Gai, for flavorful Thai-style chicken and rice; Bing Mi, serving moreish Northern Chinese *jianbing* (an omelet-like crepe); and Matt's BBQ for fine brisket, smoked turkey and pulled pork.

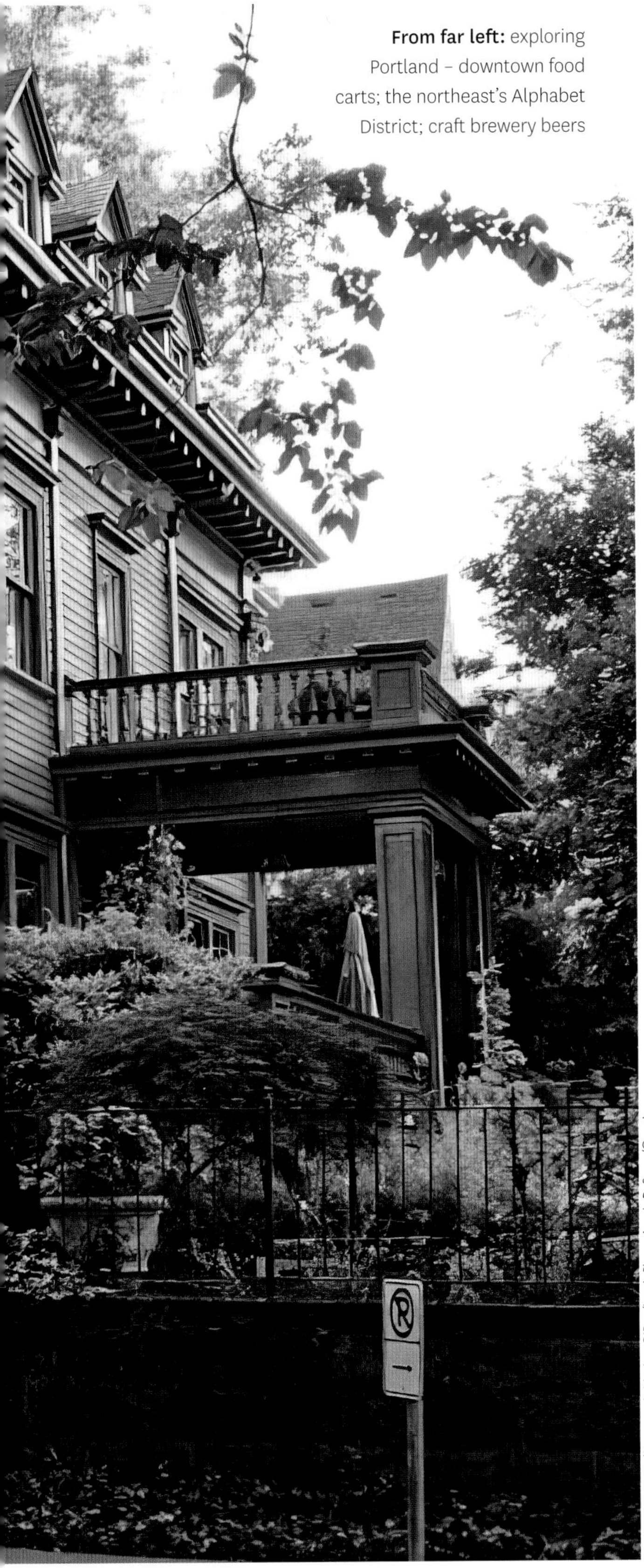

**From far left:** exploring Portland – downtown food carts; the northeast's Alphabet District; craft brewery beers

© Iris van den Broek/Shutterstock; Meghan O'Dea/Lonely Planet; Angelo DeSantis/Getty Images

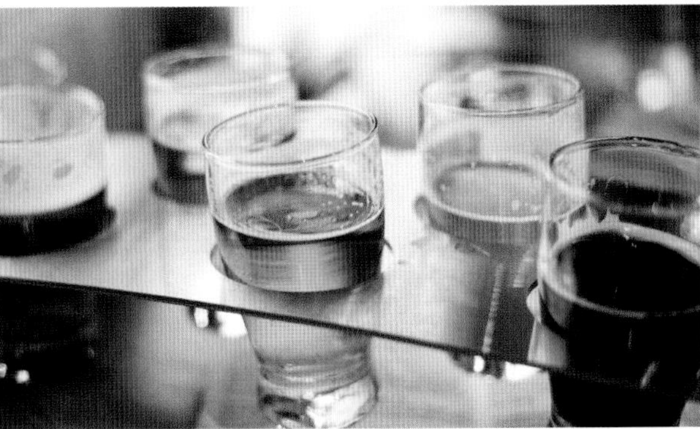

King Street Station. Nearby, sample rice-and-chicken *arroz caldo* and *buko* (coconut) pie paired with a purple-yam (*ube*) latte at Filipino bakeshop-café Hood Famous, or pick up a *kare-pan* (curry bread) or cream-filled *malasada* doughnut at Fuji Bakery. While many coffee drinkers make a pilgrimage to the original Starbucks near Pike Place, the Starbucks Reserve Roastery on Capitol Hill is a more intriguing space for your caffeine hit: book a tour or a tasting, or simply enjoy an espresso or a coffee cocktail. If you want a heartier meal, take your pick from Capitol Hill's many great restaurants.

Leaving Seattle on I-5, it's 35 miles (56km) south to Tacoma, with another first-rate glass-art attraction. The Museum of Glass exhibits work by local and international artists, and you can watch glassblowers creating colorful artworks in the Hot Shop theater. From Tacoma, the I-5 takes you straight to Portland in about 2½ hours.

## ALL ABOUT NEIGHBORHOODS

Portland's most interesting places are its quirky neighborhoods, from the stylish Pearl District to the funky Southeast, where you can hang out over coffee and all sorts of contemporary cuisine. Don't miss grazing through the city's food-cart pods, clusters of to-go eateries dispensing deliciously eclectic cuisine – we've picked out some favorites in the sidebar. To see and sample what grows hereabouts, visit Portland Farmers Market at Portland State University, open Saturdays year-round.

The Portland Art Museum features works by Pacific Northwest artists, including Native American creators. Portland earns its "Rose City" moniker at the International Rose Test Garden, where some 610 varieties bloom; the nearby Portland Japanese Garden is another tranquil outdoor space – if you've shopped at massive Powell's City of Books, Portland's bibliophile magnet, it's the ideal place to find a quiet corner and turn some pages. EV parked up for an overnight stay, toast the conclusion of your road trip with a beer at one of Portland's numerous craft breweries, or a tasting tour of the dozen liquor makers on the city's Distillery Row.

**Below:** take a crash-course in all things apple at the Washington Apple Commission Visitors Center, Wenatchee
**Right:** driving the Loop along Rte 20 as it shimmies through the North Cascade Mountains

**Distance: 440 miles (708km)**

**Duration: 5 days**

# The Cascade Loop

**WASHINGTON**

Rugged and partly inaccessible for half the year, this National Scenic Byway marries the Wild West with brawny mountains, apple orchards and quirky towns doused with the spirit of Bavaria.

Designated a National Scenic Byway in 2021, the Cascade Loop has been developed by Washington State authorities as an EV-friendly route, liberally scattered with charging stations. The best place to jump onto it is Everett, 30 miles (48km) north of Seattle, where Hwy 2 crosses the I-5, paralleling the Skykomish River as it climbs west toward Stevens Pass, at 4061ft (1238m), accessible year-round thanks to a popular day-use ski area.

## GERMANY TO THE WILD WEST

Beyond Stevens Pass, the foliage folds from cedars and hemlocks to pine and larch as the road descends through the steep-sided Tumwater Canyon to Leavenworth, a German-style town with quaint *fachwerk* (timber-beamed) houses etched against an appropriately alpine backdrop.

The road east of Leavenworth marks one of the most abrupt scenery switches in the state as you lurch from pseudo-Germany into roadtrippy Americana amid bald hills, fruit orchards and the wide, snaking Columbia River. Fruit stands enliven the highway as you approach Wenatchee, self-proclaimed "Apple Capital of the World." On the way into town, stop by the Washington Apple Commission Visitors Center to wise up on the merits of fuji over honeycrisp.

## Plan & prepare

### Tips for EV drivers

Tesla Superchargers can be found in Everett, Leavenworth, Entiat (near Chelan) and Burlington. Slower chargers are common in even the smallest communities. The longest gap between chargers is 56 miles (90km) just east of Stevens Pass. Bear in mind that the long climbs to Stevens Pass on Hwy 2 and Washington Pass on Rte 20 will suck extra energy from your battery.

### Where to stay

The German-themed Enzian Inn (enzianinn.com) in Leavenworth has multiple swimming pools, an elegant grand piano in its lobby, and an owner who serenades guests on an alphorn over breakfast. A long-established stop on any Washington road trip, deluxe Sun Mountain Lodge (sunmountainlodge.com), 10 miles (16km) west of Winthrop, is a self-contained hilltop haven with its own trail network. Across the Cascade Mountains, the assemblage of floating cabins at Ross Lake Resort (rosslakeresort.com) once formed a logging camp.

### When to go

The section of Rte 20 between the Ross Dam and Methow Valley is closed from late November to late April (exact dates vary) due to heavy snowfall and avalanche danger. This effectively blocks the loop in winter, making it impossible to complete in its entirety. The drive is at its best in the spring and summer when fruit stands are piled high and outdoor activities are refreshingly accessible. Don't write off early autumn, when Leavenworth celebrates its Teutonic-flavored Oktoberfest.

### Further info

The official website of the Cascade Loop drive (cascadeloop.com) has multiple suggestions for EV charging and route-planning: the loop was specially developed between 2012 and 2015 with EVs in mind. Seattle, with several EV rental outlets, is an obvious gateway city, although Vancouver in Canada, 78 miles (125km) north of Burlington, is another option. You'll need a passport to cross the US–Canadian border. It's a short ferry ride from Clinton in southern Whidbey Island back to the US mainland.

## Bavarian Leavenworth

Germany? In the Pacific Northwest? It's easy to assume that someone must have slipped something strong into your coffee as you drive expectantly into Leavenworth, a former lumber town surrounded by alpine-esque mountains that underwent a Bavarian-themed revamp in the 1960s when an economic downturn threatened to put it permanently out of business. Trading tree-felling for timber-beamed houses and sawdust for flowerboxes, Leavenworth eloquently reinvented itself as a quintessential Romantic Road–style village, with beer and bratwurst served against a pretty *Sound of Music* backdrop. A stroll amid the gabled houses of Front St, past restaurants and shops overseen by dirndl-wearing attendants, is an essential Cascade Loop experience. Herein lurk yodeling accordionists, cheesemakers and a museum dedicated to an esoteric collection of nutcrackers. Beyond the suds and lederhosen, Leavenworth is also a hub for adventurous mountain pursuits. The adjacent Alpine Lakes Wilderness offers hiking aplenty (including a segment of the long-distance Pacific Crest trail), plus daredevil singletrack mountain biking. It's also one of the top 10 areas for rock-climbing in the US. Closer to town, whitewater rafting lures the brave.

**Above:** Leavenworth, a slice of Bavaria in the Pacific Northwest
**Opposite, from left:** the road through Washington Pass; Wild West–styled Winthrop

Hwy 97A plies the west side of the Columbia River to lakeside Chelan, another potential overnight stop that's ripe for boat tours, kayaking excursions and waterside wineries. Then rejoin Hwy 97 and coax your EV north through the grand coulees of the Columbia River Valley to Pateros and take Rte 153 as far as Twisp, where Rte 20 branches left toward Winthrop, another preplanned theme-town that switched from mining to tourism in the 1960s. Remodeled to look like a Wild West cowboy settlement, Winthrop's John Wayne touches feel grittily realistic: wooden shopfronts hide a genuine frontier spirit, succinctly catalogued at the local Shafer Historical Museum.

### HEADING BACK OVER THE CASCADES

West of Winthrop, Rte 20 enters the bucolic Methow Valley, scattered with dusty bike- and horse-riding trails, before ascending the North Cascade Mountains. This part of Rte 20 is a major engineering feat crowned by 5477ft (1669m) Washington Pass, with fine views of the Liberty Bell Mountains' Early Winters Spires. Eleven miles (18km) further on, a deceptively tough 7 mile (11km) out-and-back trail up to Easy Pass gives sweeping vistas of of Mt Logan and the Fisher Basin.

### LOGAN AND THE FISHER BASIN

Heading west, you'll enter the Ross Lake National Recreation Area, where three huge dams supply Seattle with electricity. The wilderness here is some of the rawest outside Alaska. Ross Lake stretches north into Canada and shelters an isolated floating resort.

Past the beaches and boat launch of Diablo Lake, head west in your EV alongside the narrow Gorge Reservoir, stopping in tiny Newhalem to explore national park hiking opportunities at the North Cascades Visitor Center.

The Skagit River maintains a constant presence as you glide on through Rockport, looking out for rafters and raptors. The river is a winter hunting ground for some 600 or so bald eagles, which feed on spawning salmon between November and March.

You could end the drive in Burlington, in the heart of the Skagit Valley, but consider pressing on through pastoral Whidbey Island to see the charming Coupeville, one of the state's oldest towns; and the pioneering farming memorabilia at Ebey's Landing National Historical Reserve.

N
20 km
10 miles
Mt Baker
Ross Lake
Ross Lake Resort
Baker Lake
Newhalem, North Cascades Visitor Center
Methow River
Winthrop, Shafer Historical Museum
Washington Pass
Burlington
Skagit River
Rockport
Cascade River
Twisp
WASHINGTON
Suiattle River
Sauk River
Ebey's Landing National Historical Reserve
Glacier Peak
Whidbey Island
Marysville
Lake Chelan
White River
Everett
Clinton
Chelan
Skykomish River
Shoreline
Entiat
Redmond
Leavenworth, Enzian Inn
Sammamish
Seattle
Alpine Lakes Wilderness
Renton
Burien
Wenatchee, Washington Apple Commission Visitors Center
Kent
Cedar River
Little Kachess Lake
I-5
I-90
20
530
153
97
97A
525
9
2
203
18
3
28

**Below:** the waterfront at Victorian-era Port Townsend
**Right:** on the road through Olympic National Park

- **Distance: 450 miles (724km)**
- **Duration: 4 days**

# Olympic Peninsula loop

**WASHINGTON**

Plunge into primeval rainforest on the slopes of the Olympic Mountains, hiking to hot springs, beachcombing along remote shores and goggling at some of the biggest trees on Earth.

Rule of life: if there's a ferry, take it. There are multiple ways to get from Seattle to the Olympic Peninsula, but none as pleasant as the Seattle–Bremerton car ferry. Park your EV on deck and sail across the Puget Sound, watching the Seattle skyline grow smaller as you cruise the tidal straits of the Kitsap Peninsula to the naval-base town of Bremerton. If you're lucky, you might even spot a whale breaching the dark gray waters.

## PORT TOWNSEND TO PORT ANGELES

Roll off the ferry and head north 50 miles (80km) to Port Townsend. A Victorian-era seaport on the far northeast tip of the Olympic Peninsula, Port Townsend has an arty vibe and is a beachcomber favorite for its sea-glass-studded shores overlooking the Strait of Juan de Fuca. It's also got a reasonable, though not always super-fast, charging infrastructure, and makes a pleasant overnight stop.

Another 30 miles (48km) southwest is Sequim, the "Lavender Capital of North America." A geographical quirk means this coastal village gets dramatically less rain than the rest of the (famously soggy) peninsula, allowing for acres of fragrant purple fields each summer. Just west, Port Angeles has the bulk of the area's fast chargers; nearby Granny's Cafe makes a good stop for diner fare.

## Plan & prepare

### Tips for EV drivers

For a rural area, the Olympic Peninsula is well supplied with chargers. The towns along the eastern and northern shores of the peninsula have plenty of Level 2 and occasional Level 3 chargers. Things are sparser on the west coast, so do plan to charge overnight at one of the lodges. Much of this trip is within Olympic National Park; the National Park Service website (nps.gov; search "EV charging map") maintains its own real-time list of available chargers.

### Where to stay

The National Park Service (nps.gov) maintains four lodges within Olympic National Park. Sol Duc Hot Springs Resort (closed November to March) and year-round Kalaloch Lodge are on the route described here, and have chargers. Camping in the park is an option too, if you don't need to charge overnight. Many coastal towns cater to travelers, with inns, motels and resorts – such as the Ravenscroft Inn, Port Townsend (ravenscroftinn.com), and the Ocean Crest Resort, Moclips (oceancrestresort.com).

### When to go

High summer – July and August – is the best moment to visit the park. This is the driest time of year, and the warmest, though it's still sometimes chilly – nights can drop to as low as 45°F (7°C); by July, the snows that blanket upper-elevation trails should be melted. Snow starts as early as October, and the wet season lasts through spring.

### Further info

The Bremerton–Seattle car ferry leaves every two hours or so and is first-come, first-served. Be aware that roads on the peninsula are narrow and winding, so a 30-mile (48km) drive could easily take an hour or more. The national park itself is $30 per vehicle to enter; pay online or at any visitor center. Parking lots at popular trailheads can fill up by mid-morning, and booking ahead for lodges and campsites is a must.

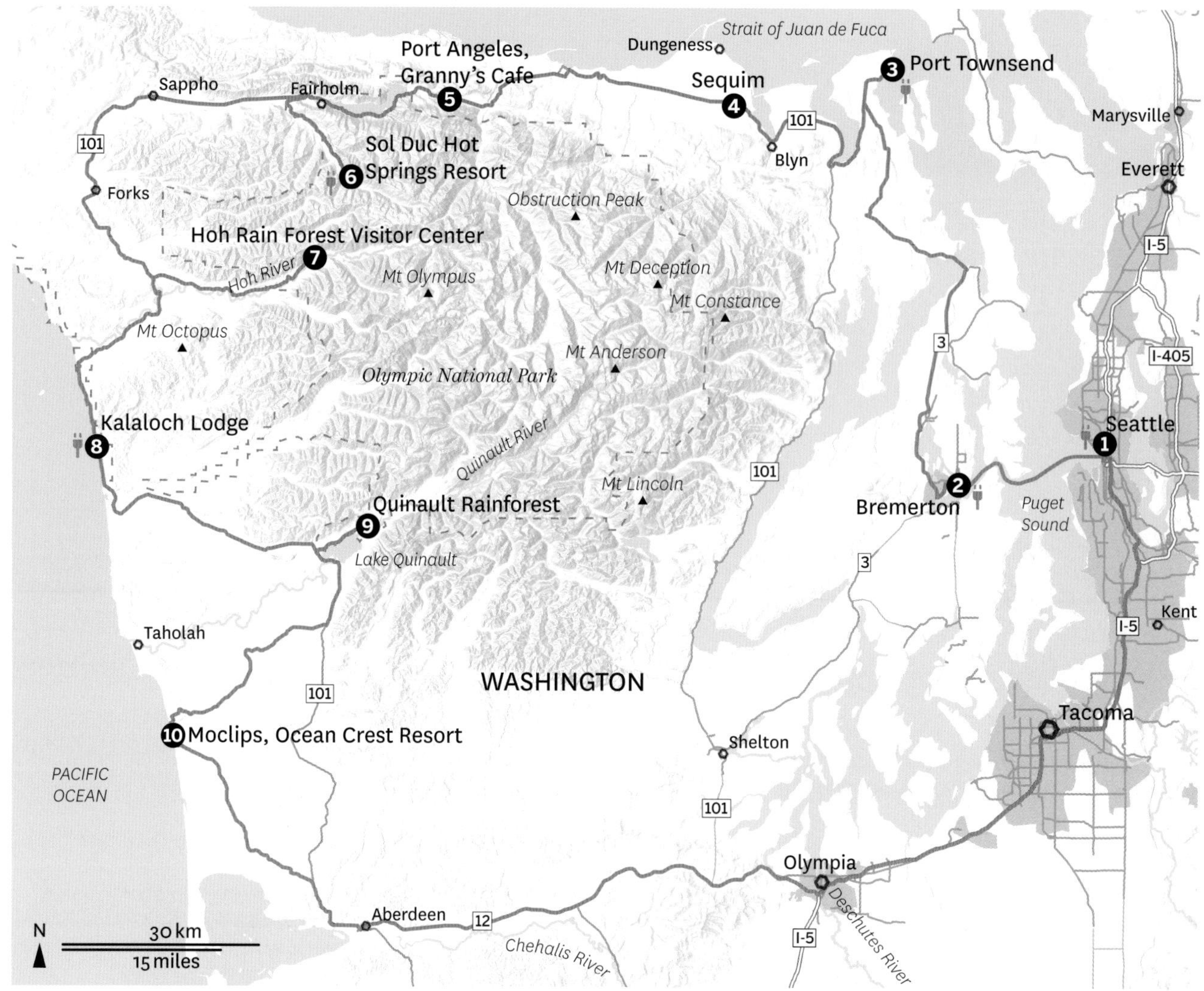


INTO OLYMPIC NATIONAL PARK

Follow the Olympic Hwy (Rte 101) southwest, shoreside along Lake Crescent then south through the spruce forest into Olympic National Park. From late September to November, look for coho salmon running the cascades of the Sol Duc River from a viewing platform just off Sol Duc Road. A bit further along is the trailhead to Ancient Groves, a 0.6-mile (1km) loop through old-growth forest with mossy canyon views. Spend the night soaking in natural mineral springs and sleeping at rustic Sol Duc Hot Springs Resort (there's a Level 2 charger), then do another hike in the morning – the 2.6-mile (4.2km) Mink Lake Trail passes through fir and hemlock forest, along slopes blooming with trillium and anemones.

Retrace your drive back to the Olympic Hwy and continue counterclockwise 28 miles (45km) to Forks, famously the setting of the *Twilight* series. It's another 31 miles (50km) inland to the Hoh Rain Forest. This is perhaps the pinnacle of the trip – a moss-shrouded cathedral of spruce, cedar and fir, every nook and cranny pullulating with ferns and lichens and mushrooms. Some 140in (360cm) of rain annually make this one of the greenest places on Earth, and its remoteness makes it one of the quietest too – a small red stone in the midst of the forest marks a symbolic "one square inch of silence."

Head back down the coast for 40 miles (64km) to overnight at Kalaloch Lodge, with rooms and cabins (and EV chargers) along the crashing gray Pacific. In the morning, get in a hike through the lush, ancient Quinault Rainforest, about 34 miles (55km) inland – don't miss the world's biggest Sitka spruce, more than 58ft (17.7m) wide and 191ft (58.2m) tall. Then return to the southwest coast for more beach strolls. Eat at the Ocean Crest Resort in Moclips – the clam chowder is rightly famous – then stay overnight before heading back to Seattle via Tacoma.

## Wildlife of the Olympic Peninsula

Olympic National Park and its surrounds teem with wildlife. The Strait of Juan de Fuca is a major migration path for orcas and gray whales during the spring and fall: take a half-day whale-watching tour from Port Townsend or Port Angeles. Humpbacks can often be seen on the peninsula's northwestern tip, around Neah Bay, in June through November. Kalaloch, Rialto and Shi Shi beaches are other good whale-spotting sites along the northwest coast. Also look out for dolphins, otters, sea lions and seals. In September and October coho salmon jump through the rapids of the Sol Duc River; in spring, steelheads do the same. The peninsula's most impressive – but potentially most dangerous – land animals are black bears, which can frequently be seen in the backcountry, especially at dawn and dusk: always carry bear spray when backcountry hiking or camping. Also active at dusk and dawn are Roosevelt elk, which graze in the valleys and rainforests. Keep eyes peeled, too, for cartoonishly cute marmots, small furry rodents that waddle among the rocks at high elevations. As for birds, bald eagles, northern pygmy owls and black oystercatchers are among the must-spot list.

**Clockwise from top left:** Hoh Rain Forest, Olympic National Park; spawning coho salmon running the Sol Duc River; spotting orcas in the Strait of Juan de Fuca

**Below:** visit Tillamook Creamery for cones and a history of local cheesemaking
**Right:** vivid color on the road through Samuel H Boardman State Scenic Corridor

**Distance: 377 miles (607km)**

**Duration: 7 days**

# Pacific Coast, Astoria to Crescent City

**OREGON**

A procession of lighthouses, sea stacks, wild beaches and old-growth forests line the Oregon coast, an outdoor playground that encourages hiking, biking, kayaking and thorough relaxation.

There's an end-of-the-world feeling along the Oregon coast: the ocean views are cinematic, the air pristine and the grandeur of nature makes you feel quite insignificant in comparison to it all. It's a place where you can hike through forests home to 1000-year-old trees, surf giant rollers or soak up the sounds on windswept beaches and dramatic headlands as whales lumber by.

## PORTLAND TO THE OREGON DUNES

Start your EV adventure in Astoria, the first US settlement on the west coast and the location for 1985 hit movie *The Goonies*. Astoria was named after millionaire John Jacob Astor, who established a trading post here in 1811. Many historic houses survive, and chic art galleries and boutiques line the streets. Around 25 miles (40km) south, at lively Cannon Beach, the 235ft-high (72m) Haystack Rock sits on a wide expanse of sand, waterfalls pour over low cliffs and sea mist rises in a plume. Rent a board and catch some surf, or walk through pristine forest to hidden coves and blustery promontories in Ecola State Park.

At Tillamook, 40 miles (64km) south, drop into the Blue Heron French Cheese Company to pick up gourmet cheeses, charcuterie and seafood, or head for the more commercial Tillamook Creamery to recharge your EV

## Plan & prepare

### Tips for EV drivers

The Oregon coast is well serviced by EV infrastructure and you shouldn't have to travel more than 50 miles (80km) between chargers at any point; however, in places, there can be longer breaks between fast chargers so it's worth planning ahead. Also be sure to check individual charger locations, as some hotels and motels reserve their chargers for patrons only.

### Where to stay

Stay at the Cannery Pier Hotel & Spa (cannerypierhotel.com) in Astoria, which sits at the tip of the pier, its large, modern rooms overlooking the water. Alternatively, the Overleaf Lodge & Spa (overleaflodge.com) in Yachats has spacious rooms with ocean views, or you could escape from it all at secluded Tu Tu' Tun Lodge (tututun.com) on the Rogue River near Brookings, where a stay comes with the chance to spot deer, elk, beavers, eagles and osprey.

### When to go

The Oregon coast is sublime year-round but if you're planning outdoor activities such as hiking, camping or watersports, May to September make the best moment to visit. You'll also find plenty of festivals at this time of year, from artists' open studios and county fairs to birding events, farmers markets and the popular Oregon Coast Music Festival, which takes place in Coos Bay during the last two weeks of July.

### Further info

All 363 miles (584km) of the Oregon coast have been public land since 1913, a move which led to it being dubbed the "People's Coast." Dozens of state parks protect the coastline and along with hiking, biking and watersports, birding is hugely popular. Tillamook Bay and Boiler Bay are prime spots for viewing waterfowl and shorebirds including black oystercatchers, red-throated loons, tufted puffins, rhinoceros auklets, cormorants, guillemots and murrelets. Spring and fall are good times to visit for birding.

## Whale-watching along the Oregon coast

Twice a year, every year, about 18,000 gray whales make their way along the Oregon coast on their migration between the warm lagoons of Mexico's Baja California and the cold waters of the Bering Sea off Alaska. A journey of about 6000 miles (9656km), it is the longest migration of any mammal. You can spot whales from numerous points along the coast, with the highest concentration of sightings between mid-December and mid-January when about 30 whales pass per hour on their southbound migration. They return to the north between late March and mid-June. As gray whales are bottom feeders, sucking and filtering sediment from the sea floor, they need to stay in shallower waters, making them relatively easy to spot. Some 200 whales stay resident along the coast all summer. The Whale Watching Center in Depoe Bay is open year-round and is a good place to find out more about these creatures, while Whale Watch Week, held in late-December and again in late-March, sees volunteers stationed at 17 sites along the coast to help visitors spot the whales. For more information see orwhalewatch.org.

**Clockwise from top left:** pounding surf at Cape Kiwanda; migrating gray whale along the Oregon coastline; Haystack Rock at Cannon Beach

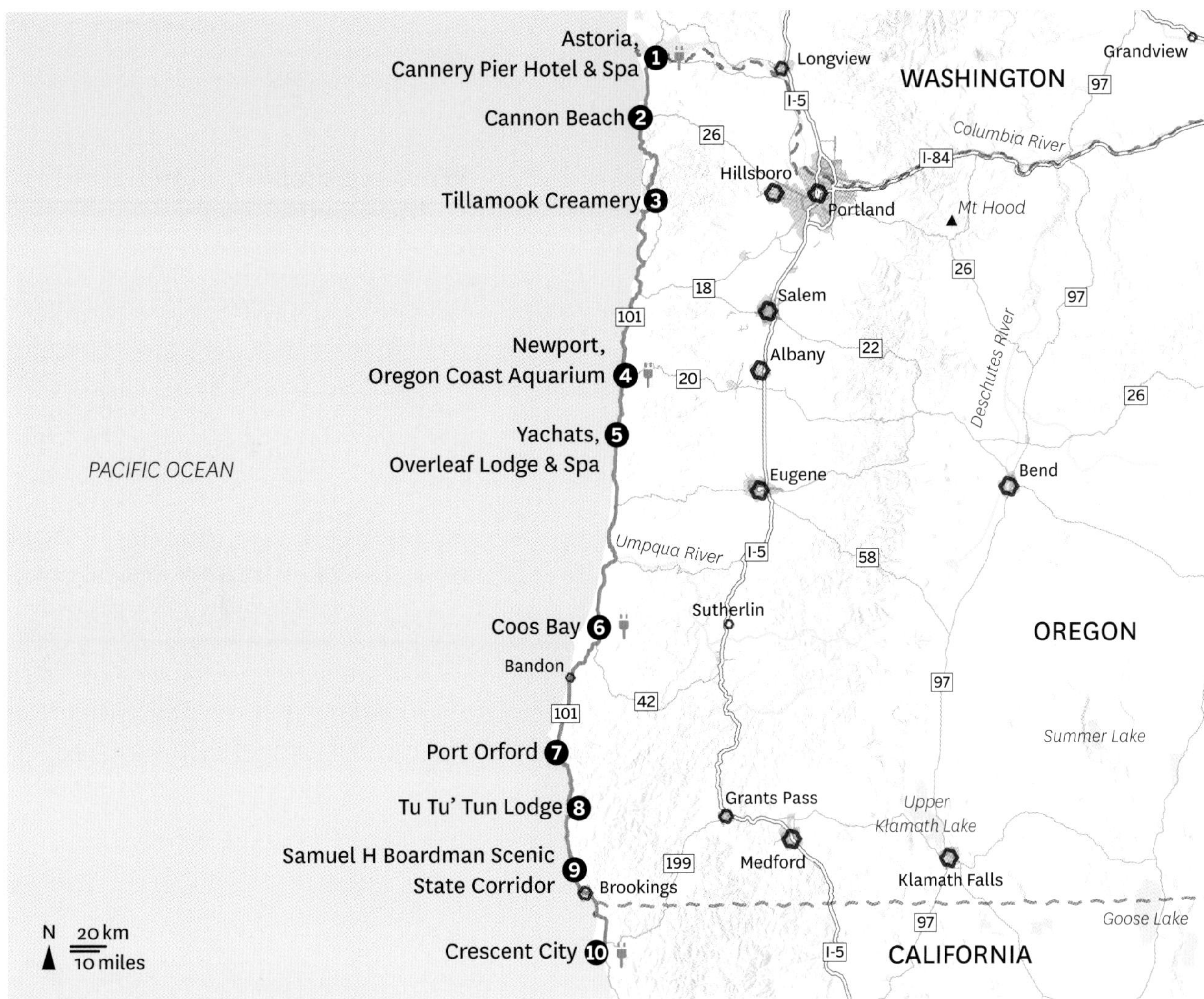


while you learn about about the history of cheesemaking here, which dates back to the 1890s. Detour off Hwy 101 towards Netarts for a slow but stunning coastal route past Cape Lookout and Cape Kiwanda to busy Newport, home to the perennially popular underwater tunnels of the Oregon Coast Aquarium.

South of Newport, Yachats (ya-hots) marks the start of a glorious stretch of coastline pounded by crashing surf. Stop off at Cape Perpetua Overlook to ramble through the forest or watch water explode through the volcanic rocks at Devil's Churn and Cook's Chasm. Driving on, it's 24 miles (39km) south to Florence and the start of the vast expanse of the Oregon Dunes. Stretching around 40 miles (64km) along the coast, the dunes reach 500ft high (152m) in places and extend up to 3 miles (5km) inland.

## COOS BAY TO CRESCENT CITY

Recharge the car in Coos Bay while you visit the Coos Art Museum or head on to charming Bandon to plug in your EV while you stroll around the Old Town, fortify yourself with the catch of the day at Tony's Crab Shack, or observe the seals and sea lions by the beach.

Set by a natural harbor between two state parks, the fishing town and artists' enclave of Port Orford offers some of the Oregon coastline's most scenic views; hike Humbug Mountain through old-growth cedar forest for some of the best. Back in town, you can wander the art galleries, take a guided kayak tour or dine with ocean views at Redfish.

It's a 40-mile (64km) drive south to the glorious Samuel H Boardman State Scenic Corridor, where giant Sitka spruce give way to panoramic viewpoints, rock bridges, hiking trails and tidal pools. The money shot is at the Natural Bridge Viewpoint, where rock arches are framed by trees set against the backdrop of crashing surf. From Brookings, it's just a 26-mile (42km) drive south over the state border to Crescent City.

**Below:** streetcar in the Castro, San Francisco
**Right:** Bixby Creek Bridge along the Big Sur coast

**Distance: 612 miles (985km)**

**Duration: 10-14 days**

# San Francisco to San Diego

**CALIFORNIA**

Winding down the Pacific Coast Highway, this classic drive links California's charismatic cities with seaside towns, cliffs and coves, redwood forests and a host of historic sites, all accessible by EV.

Made famous by countless movies, books and TV series, California's coast may seem uncannily familiar, even for a first-time visitor. Its soft sandy beaches, rugged cliffs and charming towns and cities have lured Hollywood A-listers, literary legends, surfer dudes and the merely monied for as long as anyone can remember. Allow as much time as possible to wind your way along the coast in your EV: you'll be slowed by a string of state parks, stands of redwoods, blustery headlands with views that go on forever, and rickety old wooden piers where the fish tacos and crab-stuffed sandwiches taste like heaven.

## SAN FRANCISCO & THE NORTH COAST

Boho, non-conforming San Francisco is a creative hub with a hedonistic vibe and generous heart. Just wandering its hilly streets or hopping on and off one of its vintage cable cars offers rewards aplenty, with museums, galleries, fantastic food and eclectic shops wherever you go. Tick off its most famous sights by walking across the Golden Gate Bridge, getting your bearings from Coit Tower or seeking out the row of colorful Victorian-era "Painted Lady" houses. The Powell-Hyde cable car gives views of the bay and Alcatraz; Chinatown offers temples, tea houses

## Plan & prepare

### Tips for EV drivers

You can rent an EV at San Francisco International Airport, though if you're planning a one-way rental, shop around to try to avoid incurring additional fees. EV charging infrastructure is extensive across California and you'll generally have no problem finding places to recharge – except for more remote stretches of the scenic coastal highway, such as along Big Sur and in the Santa Monica Mountains, where you'll want to plan ahead.

### Where to stay

The Nantucket Whale Inn (nantucketwhaleinn.com) in the heart of lively Half Moon Bay is a historic inn with contemporary styling, while further south, Ventana Big Sur (ventanabigsur.com) has a choice of rustic-luxury rooms, suites and tent cabins tucked among a redwood forest above the crashing sea. For cinematic history, head for the landmark Montecito Inn (montecitoinn.com), built by Charlie Chaplin and friends and once the height of Californian fashion. All three have chargers onsite or within a short walk.

### When to go

May, June, September and October are great times to visit California, with warm weather and lots of activities but fewer crowds. Southern California is mild year-round but winters in the north can be cool, wet and foggy, though you'll have a good chance of spotting gray whales migrating southwards between November and February. July to September is the hottest and busiest time, but you'll find lots of festivals in full flow – including San Diego's massive Comic Con in late July.

### Further info

Parking is hard to find and expensive in California's major cities: do your research, book lodgings with parking and expect to use public transport. If visiting in winter, coastal fog is a serious concern at times, and winter rains can also cause mudslides and rockfalls – drive with caution and check road conditions (via roads.dot.ca.gov). If you're visiting the California wineries, ensure you have a designated driver to get you back to your lodgings.

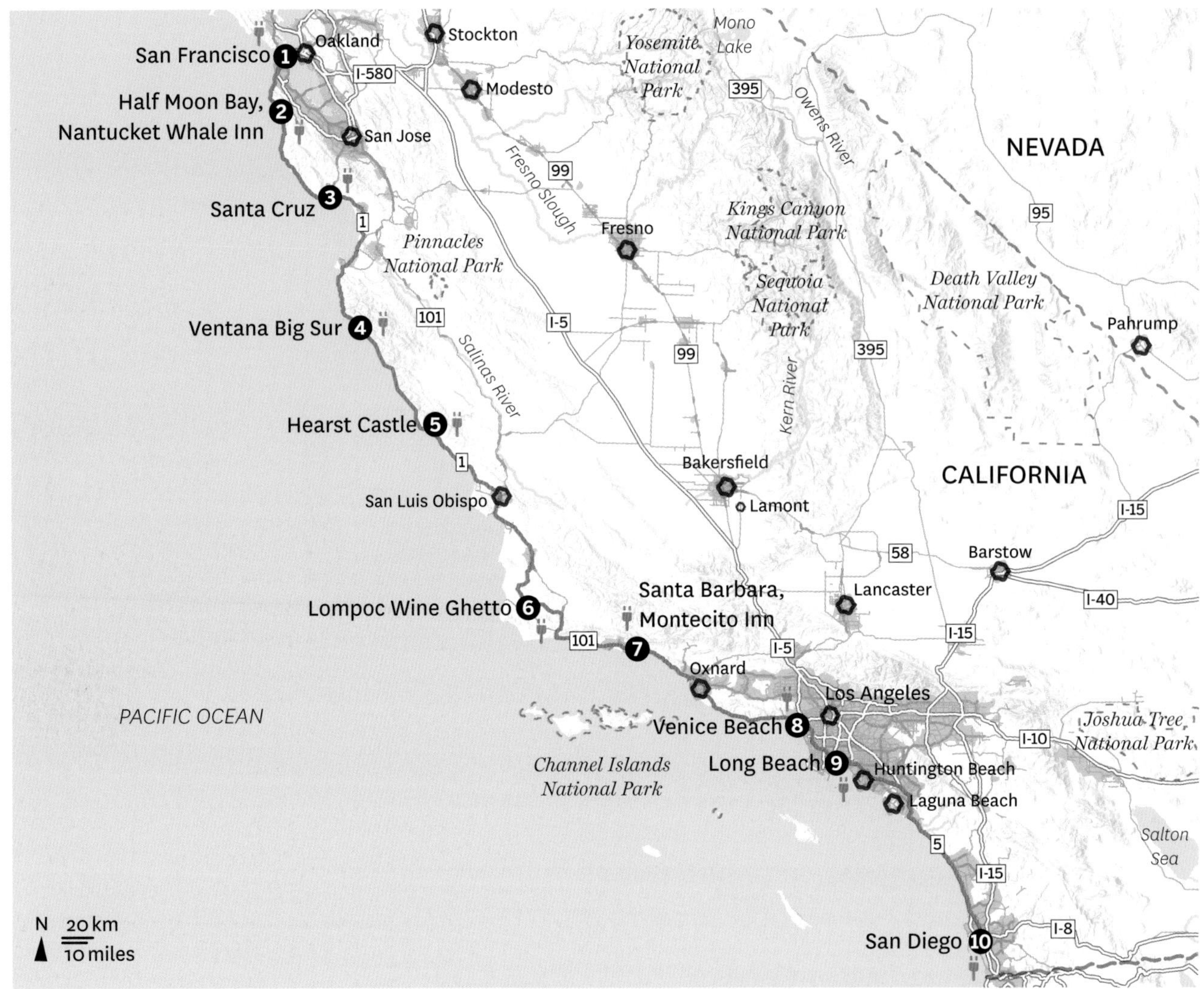


and markets; and literary history comes alive at the Beat Museum and City Lights Bookstore.

Leaving the city behind, ease out onto the snaking Pacific Coast Highway, heading 30 miles (48km) south to Half Moon Bay for big-wave surf, sweeping ocean vistas and the start of a road trip straight from the silver screen. Stop off at Wilder Ranch State Park for walking trails along coastal cliffs, then recharge in boho Santa Cruz as you stroll the retro boardwalk with its old-school amusements.

## THE WINELANDS & BIG SUR

It's a scenic drive south to Monterey, where John Steinbeck wrote some of his most famous works – but it's the art galleries, boutiques and farmers markets of Carmel-by-the-Sea, 4 miles (6km) on, that are a bigger draw today. This hub of the wine-producing Carmel Valley also has a host of tasting rooms (designated driver again required) and a self-guided Wine Walk to point you round them. Heading on south, legendary Big Sur tops wild cliffs and storm-bashed beaches that appear even more majestic thanks to the silence of your EV. Redwoods, waterfalls and scenic lookouts litter the state parks along the way, and while the views at Garrapata and Julia Pfeiffer Burns are cinematic, it's oft-snapped Bixby Creek Bridge that brings an overwhelming sense of déjà vu.

Stately Hearst Castle gives a complete change of pace, its sumptuous rooms filled with priceless antiques and gilt-framed Old Masters. Built by newspaper magnate William Randolph Hearst, this opulent hilltop mansion was once the haunt of Hollywood stars, literary legends and the political elite. Continuing on, historic architecture, excellent restaurants and wine-tasting rooms may encourage you to linger in hip, laid-back San Luis Obispo, 42 miles (67km) south; or head on to Lompoc, to recharge while you sip cool-climate Chardonnay and Pinot Noir in the tasting rooms at the Lompoc Wine Ghetto.

## California's Galápagos

A wild and rugged landscape of canyons and caves, blustery peaks, tidepools and kelp forests, California's Channel Islands National Park feels a world away from the densely populated coast. The islands have been isolated from the mainland since the last ice age and are home to about 150 plant and animal species found nowhere else on Earth. Visitors can spot whales, dolphins and porpoises on the hour-long journey from the mainland, then set out on foot along quiet trails to remote headlands, pristine beaches and mountain lookouts. Alternatively, book ahead and plan to kayak, snorkel or paddleboard through crystalline waters teeming with brightly colored fish. Whatever you do, you can't miss the national park's most famous inhabitant, the cute and wily island fox, which is about the size of a housecat. Five of the islands are open to the public: Santa Cruz and Anacapa are served by Island Packers boats year-round, and a more limited schedule runs to the outer islands March through November. Boats leave from Ventura but plan ahead: the islands have no shops, cell phone service or gear rental. See the National Park Service site (nps.gov) for more information.

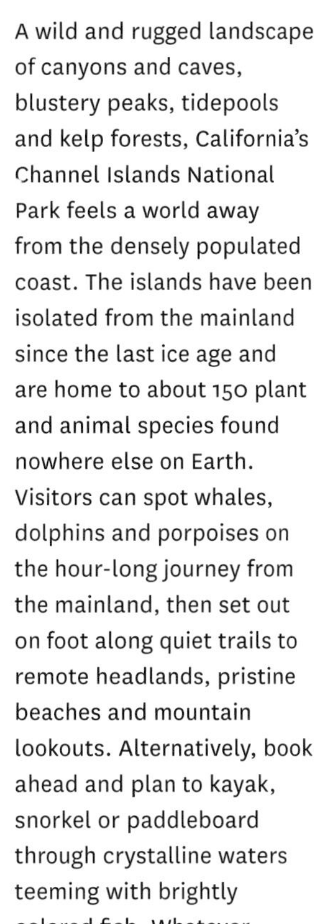

**Clockwise from top left:** Hearst Castle; colorful anemones off Anacapa Island, Channel Islands National Park; the Pacific Coast at Big Sur

## Take to the seas

Fancy setting sail in a replica 16th-century galleon? You can at the San Diego Maritime Museum (sdmaritime.org), where the collection of tall ships, steamboats and submarines includes active craft that regularly make passenger trips. After you've checked out the fine collection of artifacts and clambered around historic ships like the *Star of India*, an 1863 iron-hulled square-rigger that plied the route between England and India, you can take to the water. Options include an exhilarating high-speed naval history tour on a Swift Boat or a half-day cruise on the *Californian*, a replica 1850s tall ship. For talks on archaeology and Spanish seafaring history as well as immersive sailing, cartography and navigation lessons, multiday trips are available aboard a replica of the *San Salvador*, a 16th-century galleon that brought Juan Rodriguez Cabrillo (the first European explorer to set foot here) to San Diego.

**From far left:** HMS *Surprise* and the *Star of India*, San Diego Maritime Museum; surf's up at Huntington Beach; Venice's Boardwalk

## THE SOUTH COAST

With a swath of beautiful beaches, affluent Santa Barbara, 55 miles (88km) south, lures its visitors with sunshine and sand, a pier, beautiful Old Mission and fresh-off-the-boat seafood. Driving on, the coastal highway is squeezed dramatically between the sea and the Santa Monica Mountains, the mansions of the rich and famous overlooking the waterfront at Malibu. Stop off at the Getty Villa Museum for Greek and Roman antiquities, or wind between palm-lined beaches and eucalyptus hills into Santa Monica, where the traditional pier marks the end of famed Route 66. Browse the farmers market or stroll eclectic Main St; if you're planning to sneak inland to LA, leave the car and take the tram instead.

Heading south, Santa Monica segues seamlessly into Venice, a beachside community that embraces every stereotype of the Californian coast. Bronzed bodybuilders strut their stuff at Muscle Beach, rollerbladers whizz by and skateboarders carve, grind and flip round the skate park. Once you've done the Boardwalk, stroll along the Venice Canals to slick Abbot Kinney Blvd for boutiques, bars and restaurants. From here, a string of beach towns unfurls along the coast – take your pick from Long Beach, with its high-tech aquarium and absorbing Museum of Latin American Art; "Surf City USA" Huntington Beach; chic yachtie haven Newport; or affluent Laguna Beach, with its many art galleries.

Breezing into mellow San Diego, 72 miles (116km) south, your oceanfront odyssey comes to an end, but it's worth planning a few days here to explore Balboa Park's gorgeous gardens and museums, downtown's buzzy Gaslamp Quarter and arguably the nation's best Mexican food in Barrio Logan. Top it all with a drive out to Coronado's white-sand beaches, for an end-of-trip sundowner overlooking the rolling waves.

**Below:** morning mist rolls over a Santa Rosa farmstead **Right:** Sonoma County winelands

**Distance: 483 miles (777km)**

**Duration: 5-7 days**

# Santa Rosa to Santa Barbara

**CALIFORNIA**

California's winelands offer rich rewards for EV roadtrippers: a hedonistic getaway of sunny days, spectacular scenery, exceptional wine and the chance to learn about sustainability in the industry as you go.

Wandering from the sun-kissed hills of Napa and Sonoma through the giant redwoods and twisting mountain roads of Santa Cruz to the historic charms of Paso Robles, this route takes in just a handful of California's 4700-odd wineries. These historic, family-owned estates and boutique operations generally share a vision, however, for a greener, fairer way of producing fine wines while looking after their people and their land for generations to come.

Start your trip in laid-back Santa Rosa, a thriving hub surrounded by mountains and rolling hills. Sonoma County is a world leader in biodynamic and organic winemaking and you can learn all about it at Hamel Family Wines, just 17 miles (27km) to the south. At this small-scale producer known for its limited-production, high-quality wines, tours of the vineyards cover everything from the importance of their volcanic soils to dry-farming philosophy (relying on natural rainfall only). With a designated driver alongside, don't miss a chance to sample their reserve series Cabernet Sauvignons.

Alternatively, continue to the nearby Napa Valley, home to about 40% of all certified sustainable wineries in California. Leave your EV to charge as you explore the Saintsbury Winery, a great place to sip Chardonnay or

## Plan & prepare

### Tips for EV drivers

EV infrastructure in California is rapidly expanding and you should have no problem finding chargers along this route. EV drivers can use carpool lanes even if they're the only occupant, but you'll need to apply for a sticker from the DMV (Department of Motor Vehicles). EVs also qualify for reduced tolls on many roads and bridges if you add your sticker to your FasTrak (bayareafastrak.org) account. Note, however, that benefits are likely to be phased out.

### Where to stay

Within Napa's Tuscan-inspired Meritage Resort (meritageresort.com), each room has a patio or balcony overlooking the surrounding hills and vineyards. Hotel Los Gatos (hotellosgatos.com) in the Santa Cruz Mountains channels a Mediterranean vibe and its pool is a godsend after a hot day's driving. Santa Barbara's Hotel Californian (hotelcalifornian.com) offers a winning mix of Spanish colonial and North African styling, and an unbeatable location next to the beach and Stearns Wharf. The latter two options have fast chargers.

### When to go

Although you can visit most vineyards year-round, the most impressive time to wander between the vines is from mid-August until late September, when the harvest buzz grips the estates. You'll get warm, sunny days and lots of activity but also crowded tasting rooms at the larger wineries, so it's a good time to seek out more boutique operations. It's also worth timing a visit to coincide with Festival Napa Valley in July or the Sonoma Harvest Music Festival in the fall.

### Further info

The legal BAC (blood alcohol concentration) limit for adult drivers in California is 0.08%, so carefully track any drinking, or ideally nominate a designated driver. Otherwise, plan your trip around your lodgings and take local tours to wineries so you don't have to drive. All alcohol in your vehicle must be kept in the trunk.

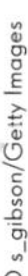

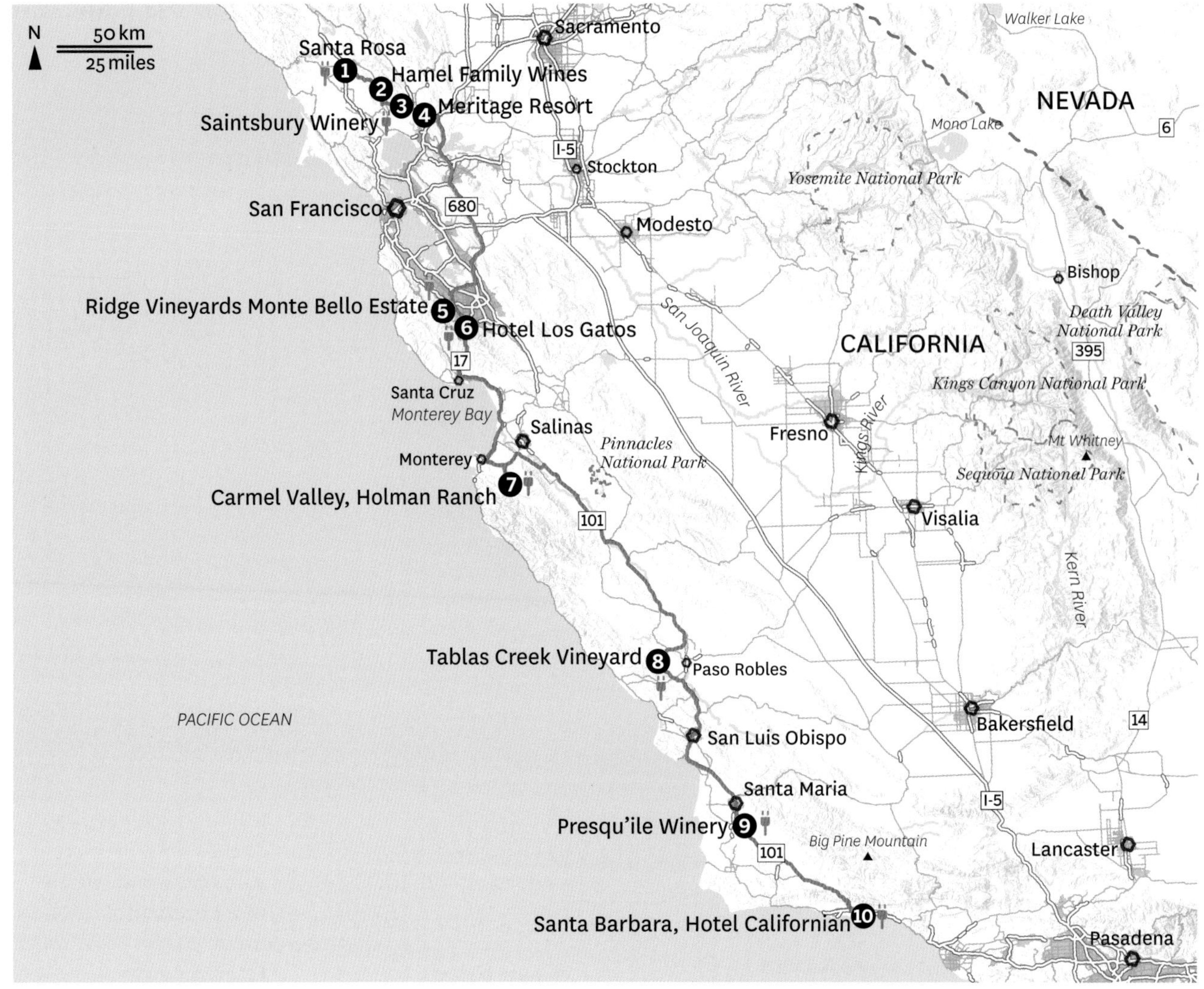


Pinot Noir in the English gardens and learn about the finer details of wine aging and clonal selection.

## SKIRTING THE BAYS

Back on the road and heading south about 90 miles (145km), past San Francisco Bay, you'll find Ridge Vineyards Monte Bello Estate, which produced its first wines back in 1885. Here, Old World winemaking techniques combine with organic and regenerative practises to make Ridge a highly respected name – its Monte Bello Chardonnay is one of California's best whites. Plan ahead and combine a visit with a concert at nearby Mountain Winery, another history-rich landmark with a scenic outdoor amphitheater.

It's a winding 92-mile (148km) drive, skirting Monterey Bay, to the Carmel Valley's Holman Ranch, a historic vineyard producing award-winning wines. Using Burgundian winegrowing techniques and holistic, low-intervention land practises, they make the most of cool coastal fogs and warm valley days. For an immersive experience, come for an evening tour followed by dinner and an overnight stay. Although there's no onsite charger, Carmel Valley Village, a three-minute drive away, has public charging stations.

## PASO ROBLES TO SANTA BARBARA

In Paso Robles, an up-and-coming wine region known for its boutique wineries, recharge as you visit Tablas Creek Vineyard, an organic winery known for its regenerative farming techniques. Having won multiple Green Medals – the Californian wine community's highest honor for sustainability – it's a great place to learn about the industry's challenges and solutions on a vineyard tour. Look out for the estate's flagship Esprit de Tablas wines.

About 70 miles (113km) south, the Presqu'ile Winery just outside Santa Maria is a family-owned estate known

for its cool-climate Pinot Noir, Chardonnay and Syrah. You can charge your EV while you tour the vineyards on horseback, enjoy a food-and-wine tour, or a wine tasting overlooking the San Rafael Mountains. From here, it's about 60 miles (96km) into Santa Barbara – where you can pick up the Urban Wine Trail, visit the Old Mission or just laze on the beach.

## What's the difference? Organic, biodynamic and sustainable wines

About 60% of Californian wines have some kind of sustainability mark, but there are so many different accreditation schemes it can be difficult telling them apart. Organic wines are grown with restrictions on synthetic chemicals, GMOs (genetically modified organisms) and sulfites (at least in the USA) throughout the production process. Biodynamic farming goes a step further, taking the whole ecosystem into consideration. In addition to growing and processing grapes on organic principles, key considerations include soil health and planting schedules. You'll often find planting, pruning and harvesting aligned with the lunar calendar; and ducks, sheep or horses roaming freely through the vines to reduce pests and fertilize the soil. Certified sustainable wine is not always organic, but the production process takes an even broader range of factors into consideration. Alongside soil health and biodiversity, key concerns include water and energy consumption, social responsibility and economic feasibility. Regenerative farming builds on this philosophy and aims not just to work in harmony with nature but to improve soil conditions, enhance biodiversity and enrich local communities. Visit sipcertified.org for more on Californian certifications.

**Clockwise from top left:** Ridge Vineyards Monte Bello Estate; grapes on the vine, Napa Valley; checking on the Pinot Noir, Sonoma County

**Below:** Point Reyes Lighthouse
**Right:** San Francisco's Golden Gate Bridge at the golden hour

**Distance: 400 miles (644km)**

**Duration: 3-5 days**

# San Francisco to Crescent City

**CALIFORNIA**

The tallest trees on Earth and the cool coastal conditions in which they thrive are the centerpieces of a nature-lover's EV tour of Northern California's redwood parks and shoreside towns.

In the 1850s, more than 3125 sq miles (8094 sq km) of redwood – a conifer considered the tallest in the world – forest covered Northern California, with individual trees reaching ages of around 2000 years and heights of up to 367ft (112m), the equivalent of a 35-story building. Today, just 5% of the original forest remains, largely protected by parks such as the Redwood National and State Parks, where ocean fog hydrates the trees and the understory is filled with blooming rhododendron. It's the pinnacle of tree-hugging to take a walk among them, and the drive along legendary Hwy 1 that gets you there from San Francisco also takes in arty towns, verdant vineyards, vast beaches ripe for combing, and chances to spot sea lions and migrating whales. Prepare to stop a lot.

## COMBING THE COAST

Leaving San Francisco via the Golden Gate Bridge, pick up Hwy 1 in the northern direction of Point Reyes National Seashore, where you can stretch your legs while peering into tidepools filled with sea stars and anemones, or watching baby elephant seals play in the shallows. Charge up in nearby Point Reyes Station, perhaps while scarfing down some local Tomales Bay oysters in the garden of Cafe Reyes.

## Plan & prepare

### Tips for EV drivers

California has both the highest level of electric vehicle registrations of any US state, and the most charging stations in the country. Renting an EV is easier than in many other places, too – you'll find them at major car rental companies in San Francisco. Still, charging stations tend to cluster in major population centers, which excludes the northernmost counties of California, so keep a closer eye on your battery once you're north of Sonoma County.

### Where to stay

In Tomales Bay, the delight of staying in the waterfront cottages built on stilts at Nick's Cove (nickscove.com) is dining on fresh oysters at its acclaimed restaurant. Just south of Mendocino, you'll hear waves crashing from your room in the Craftsman-style mansion at Elk Cove Inn & Spa (elkcoveinn.com). In tiny Orick, in the Redwood National and State Parks' south end, the Roosevelt Base Camp (rooseveltbasecamp.com) is a smartly redesigned motel named for the local elk. All options have chargers onsite or nearby.

### When to go

Northern California is popular year-round, though crowds tend to thin near the national park where the California oak woodlands give way to a moist climate. Temperatures in the redwood coast stay mild throughout the year, though winters are cool and often rainy; 60in to 80in (152cm to 203cm) of rain falls annually October through April. In summer, coastal fog seeps into the forests, allowing the redwoods to thrive.

### Further info

Many navigation apps will direct you from San Francisco via highways to the north, but stick to Hwy 1 for the most scenic, albeit slower, route. Once you reach the redwood parks, you won't want to miss hiking in the forests of giants, but the park system also maintains a series of scenic drives that are worth taking when your legs need a break. Search for "redwood drives" at nps.gov for more info.

After a night in a waterfront cottage at Nick's Cove – and more bivalves – continue to Bodega Bay for birdwatching along the Pacific Coast migration route or a stroll on expansive Portuguese Beach. Moving on, replenish your car's battery exploring Mendocino – a photogenic village on a bluff overlooking the churning ocean, where gorgeously maintained Victorian buildings are filled with galleries, shops and restaurants – then check into the Elk Cove Inn & Spa, just south of town, for riveting views of sea stacks and passing whales from the gardens.

## INTO THE WOODS

Hwy 1 heads inland north of Rockport to link up with Hwy 101, which skirts Humboldt Redwoods State Park. The parallel Avenue of the Giants road offers an opportunity to weave slowly amid the soaring trees. Charge up over halibut and chips at Eureka's Lost Coast Brewery & Café, and take a stroll around the mural-covered downtown.

Hwy 101 rejoins the coast for views that whiplash from sand dunes on one side to redwood forests and lagoons on the other before you reach Redwood National and State Parks, which run about 50 miles (80km) in length, with the 101 as the main artery through a series of preserves jointly managed by the state and federal governments. Near Orick, stop at the Thomas H Kuchel Visitor Center to search for migrating gray whales in November, December, March and April. But above all, this is the place to hike. Look for the three-mile Cathedral Trees Trail to make your acquaintance with giants such as the Big Tree, one of the largest, some 1500 years old.

There are a number of lovely drives in the parks, including the 10-mile (16km) Newton B Drury Scenic Parkway north of Orick; keep your eyes peeled for grazing elk. There are no EV chargers in the parks, but they are readily accessible in the gateway towns of Orick, Klamath and Crescent City, where you might choose to stay awhile.

## Drive-thru or drive through?

Carving a road through a massive tree seems like such a bad idea today, but during the 1930s, when the environmental movement was a relative whisper, drive-thru trees on private land in California's redwood region became popular novelties. The last three remaining specimens reside here, including the popular Chandelier Tree in Leggett. A giant officially listed at 315ft (96m) high (though other reports have it at 276ft/84m), it's named for the symmetrical branches about a third of the way up the trunk. Another 45 miles (72km) north in Myers Flat, the Shrine Tree is a "chimney tree," hollowed out by fire over a century ago and further widened by its owner to allow cars to pass through. Despite their kitschy popularity, today's approach to tree tourism is far more hands-off, and the best way to navigate redwoods is to drive around them. Conservation of the old-growth forests is a key concern: the Redwoods Rising program (savetheredwoods.org) aims to restore some 188 sq miles (486 sq km) of state and national park forests over 30-plus years, using selective planting and thinning to allow the redwoods room to grow to their full potential.

**Clockwise from top left:** Avenue of the Giants, Humboldt Redwoods State Park; Leggett's Chandelier drive-thru tree; Tomales Bay, Point Reyes National Seashore

**Below:** topping up at a Tesla Supercharger station, San Francisco
**Right:** paddleboarding the crystal waters of Lake Tahoe

➔ **Distance: 244 miles (393km)**

➔ **Duration: 7 days**

# San Francisco to Lake Tahoe

**CALIFORNIA**

Winding from Pacific sunsets through urban joie de vivre, wine-country sophistication and Gold Rush–era history to craggy mountain peaks, this route offers ample opportunity for EV adventures.

Set on a hilly peninsula surrounded by water on three sides, San Francisco has always pushed the boundaries. From hippies to high society, it's a city that beats to its own drum and does so with devilish charm. Start with a trawl through the vast collection at the San Francisco Museum of Modern Art, then make your way to the perennially popular Fisherman's Wharf to hop on the boat to Alcatraz. A stroll down the waterfront brings you to the Ferry Building, a gourmet hub where chefs, farmers and families come to sample some of California's best street food. Nearby, hop on a cable car up over Nob Hill for a classic city experience and sweeping views.

## WINE & GOLD

Take to the road and head for liberal Berkeley, 14 miles (23km) northeast. Founded in 1868, the University of California, Berkeley, is widely considered the world's top public university, with 35 Nobel Prize winners to its name. Join a free walking tour or ride to the tip of the Campanile for a bird's eye view.

Heading north towards the Napa Valley, stop off at the stately Domaine Carneros. Modeled on a French chateau, the estate is best known for its sparkling wines and Pinot Noir. Join a tour then make for nearby Napa, where you

## Plan & prepare

### Tips for EV drivers

You can rent an EV at San Francisco International Airport as well as downtown, but one-way rentals incur extra fees. EV infrastructure is advanced across the state and at the time of writing (rules may change) EV drivers qualify for some concessions, such as being allowed to use carpool lanes if displaying a sticker from the DMV (Department of Motor Vehicles; dmv.ca.gov), and reduced tolls if you have a FasTrak account (bayareafastrak.org) and add the sticker details.

### Where to stay

The central riverfront location and choice of rooms make the Napa River Inn (napariverinn.com) a good base for the Napa Valley. The Kimpton Sawyer Hotel (sawyerhotel.com) in downtown Sacramento has sleek and stylish rooms along with a rooftop terrace and pool, while the huge rooms at Basecamp Tahoe South (basecamptahoesouth.com) give access to a brewery and beer garden, private beach and hot tub. All these lodgings have onsite EV chargers.

### When to go

There's year-round interest at every stop along this route, but June and September may just bring the best combination of weather and quiet roads. Late June sees outrageous celebrations at Pride in San Francisco; high summer and the September harvest mean heavy traffic around the Napa Valley. Winter snows pull the crowds to Tahoe from late November to late April, when the area's dozen or so ski resorts jump into action.

### Further info

It's no surprise to learn that traffic is bad in San Francisco, and finding parking even worse. If you're renting an EV, don't pick it up until you're ready to leave town. The San Francisco Visitor Passport allows for unlimited travel on public transit for one, three or seven consecutive days. Download and book on the MuniMobile app, the city's official ticketing app, for the best deals.

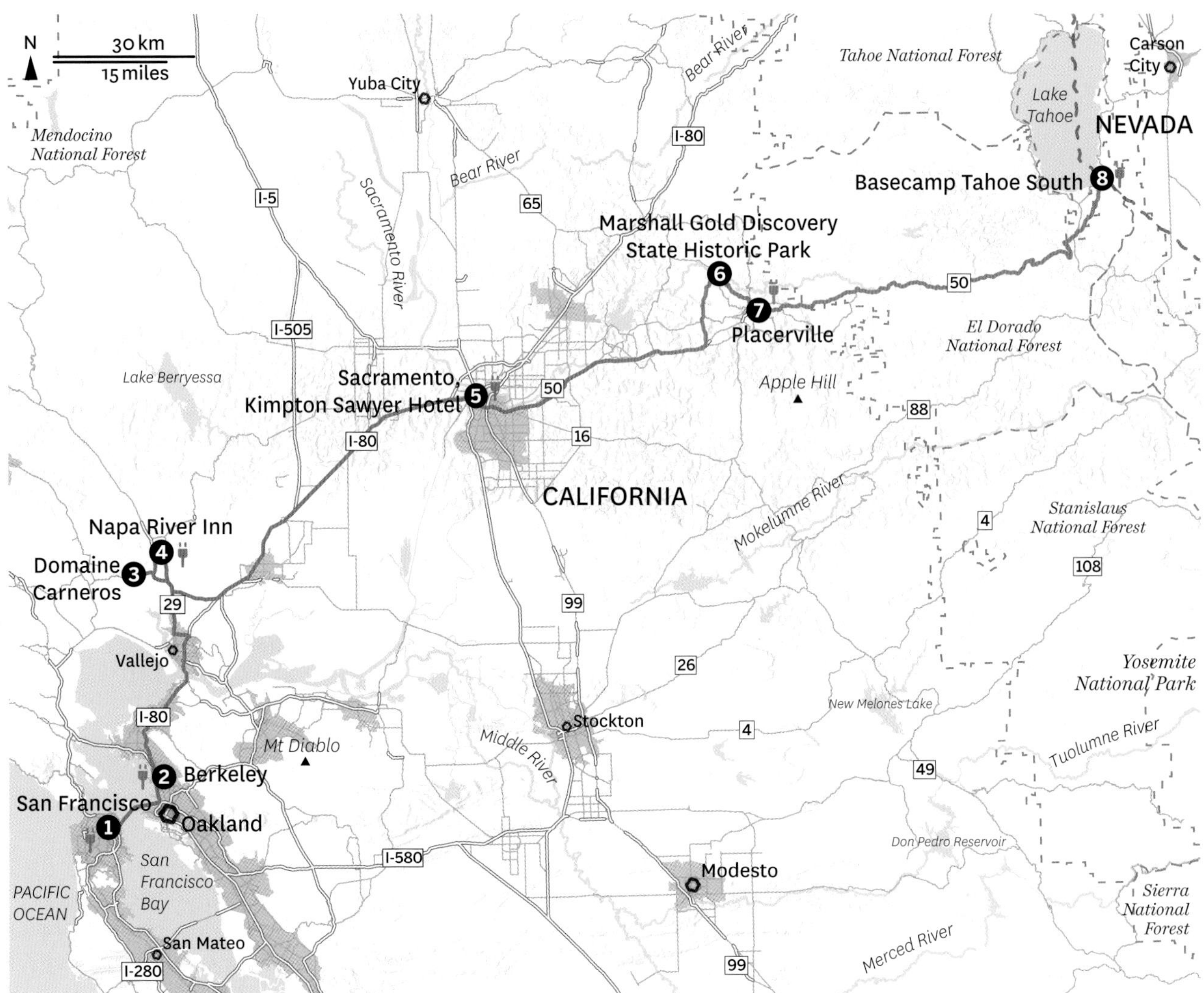


can recharge as you explore the Oxbow Public Market, an epicurean delight dishing up all sorts of seasonal foods from oysters and latkes to sushi, empanadas and pizza.

From Napa, it's 63 miles (101km) to state capital Sacramento, a buzzy urban hub built around a network of green spaces. Recharge as you explore the Capitol Building and its gorgeous grounds, then hit the streets to wander between vintage shops and bookstores, craft breweries and farmers markets.

Continuing into the Sierra Nevada foothills, it's a 46-mile (74km) drive to the Marshall Gold Discovery State Historic Park; the California Gold Rush began here in 1848, when James W Marshall noticed flecks of gold in the water. News of his discovery soon spread and hundreds of thousands flocked to the mountains to try their luck. Nearby Placerville has plenty of period buildings and a choice of local wineries and wine cellars to visit, including Rucksack Cellars and its sister vineyard Madroña.

## LAKE TAHOE

Heading east through the Eldorado National Forest, it's 68 miles (109km) up into the Sierra Nevada to the sparkling topaz waters of Lake Tahoe. Set against snowcapped peaks, the clear water and alpine-esque forests are a hotspot for hikers, climbers and kayakers. South Lake Tahoe is the most developed part of the lake, but the gondola at Heavenly takes you high into the hills for walking trails with panoramic views.

Alternatively, head 12 miles (19km) west to Emerald Bay State Park, where a narrow blue-green inlet is flanked by pine trees and topped by Vikingsholm Castle, a Nordic-style mansion dating back to the 1920s.

For the committed, it's a scenic 72-mile (116km) drive around the lake, weaving through thick forests past rocky coves, sandy beaches and granite cliffs, though you may just wish to stop and gaze at the rugged peaks and their mirror-like reflections instead.

## Hikes around Lake Tahoe

Dubbed one of the most spectacular hikes in the world, the 165-mile (266km) Tahoe Rim Trail circumnavigates the lake and offers views of alpine lakes and meadows, high-altitude waterfalls and the shimmering blue waters of the lake below. Luckily, you don't have to do it all. It's divided into 14 different day hikes and, for far-reaching views, the Relay Peak Hike can't be beaten. It's a strenuous 10-mile (16km) round-trip that takes you to the highest point on the Rim Trail for views of azure waters and chiseled peaks. Start at the Mt Rose trailhead. For something less strenuous, the Echo Lakes Trail threads up to two hidden lakes where you can swim with stunning views and even take a water taxi back to where you started. Not for the fainthearted, but requiring no previous climbing experience, the Tahoe Via Ferrata is an assisted climbing activity that uses ladders, steps and bridges to help you access some of the region's most ambitious terrain. The three courses weave between granite towers, up near-vertical slopes and along narrow ledges for astounding views and a major hit of adrenaline.

**Clockwise from top left:** Napa Valley vineyards; hiking the Tahoe Rim Trail; epicurian delights at Napa's Oxbow Public Market

**Below:** Lake Tahoe's Emerald Bay
**Right:** on the road through Death Valley National Park

**Distance: 494 miles (795km)**

**Duration: 4-5 days**

# Lake Tahoe to Las Vegas via Death Valley

**CALIFORNIA & NEVADA**

Drive down California's backbone and into Nevada on a road trip of superlatives (highest; lowest; hottest...) that takes you from Lake Tahoe's shores to the Las Vegas Strip.

The Pacific Coast and big cities like LA and San Francisco hog the limelight in California, but the Golden State has a quieter, equally scenic side that mostly follows Rte 395, east of the Sierra Nevada mountains and into the Silver State.

## FROM LAKE TO LAKE TO LAKE

The drive begins at lovely Lake Tahoe, right on the California–Nevada border. The water here is the second-deepest in the country (after Oregon's Crater Lake), reaching 1645ft (501m), and there are myriad activities to enjoy on and around it. But there's a lot to pack in to day one's drive so bid farewell to South Lake Tahoe and pick up Rte 395; it's often single-lane but is generally not busy.

After two hours you approach Dog Town, where a left turn on to Rte 270 leads to Bodie, one of California's best-preserved ghost towns (note the last few miles are unpaved). When gold was discovered here in 1859, a lawless boomtown sprang up with a population of 10,000 – and 65 saloons to water them. Once the gold disappeared, the town was abandoned, and today some 200 buildings are preserved in a state of "arrested decay."

Retrace your route and continue south to Mono Inn in Lee Vining, a top spot for food with enticing views of

## Plan & prepare

### Tips for EV drivers

South Lake Tahoe and Las Vegas have dozens of charging stations, some of them free. Elsewhere, despite the small size of many of the towns on this drive, there are plenty of chargers, including Superchargers, that will help you get around with no range anxiety. That said, given the heat and sometimes uphill driving, plug in regularly when the opportunity presents itself, especially before and in Death Valley.

### Where to stay

Mammoth Lakes has accommodations for all budgets – including Tamarack Lodge (tamaracklodge.com), whose rustic cabins have an enviable lakeside setting close to chargers. In Lone Pine, the Whitney Portal Hostel and Hotel (mountwhitneyportal.com) is run by the people who own the store and offers dorms or motel-style rooms – ask for one with mountain views. The best base in Death Valley is the Oasis in Furnace Creek (oasisatdeathvalley.com), two hotels in one sharing six charging stations.

### When to go

Late spring or fall are the perfect times for this trip: temperatures are warm but manageable, and everywhere is open but not too busy. Hiking is at its most greenery-filled in spring. Summers can be hot, ferociously so in Death Valley, but if seeing whether the world's highest temperature record will be broken appeals, visit then. Winter sees snow at high elevations (Bodie and Mt Whitney) and chilly conditions even in Death Valley, so is best avoided.

### Further info

Reno Tahoe Rental Car (renotahoerentalcar.com) at the airport in South Lake Tahoe has lots of electric vehicles to rent, including 4WD if you feel like getting off the main roads. Rte 395 itself is toll free, but note that entering Death Valley National Park means paying the $30 per car fee. You can pay on arrival (no cash) or online before you get there (at nps.gov).

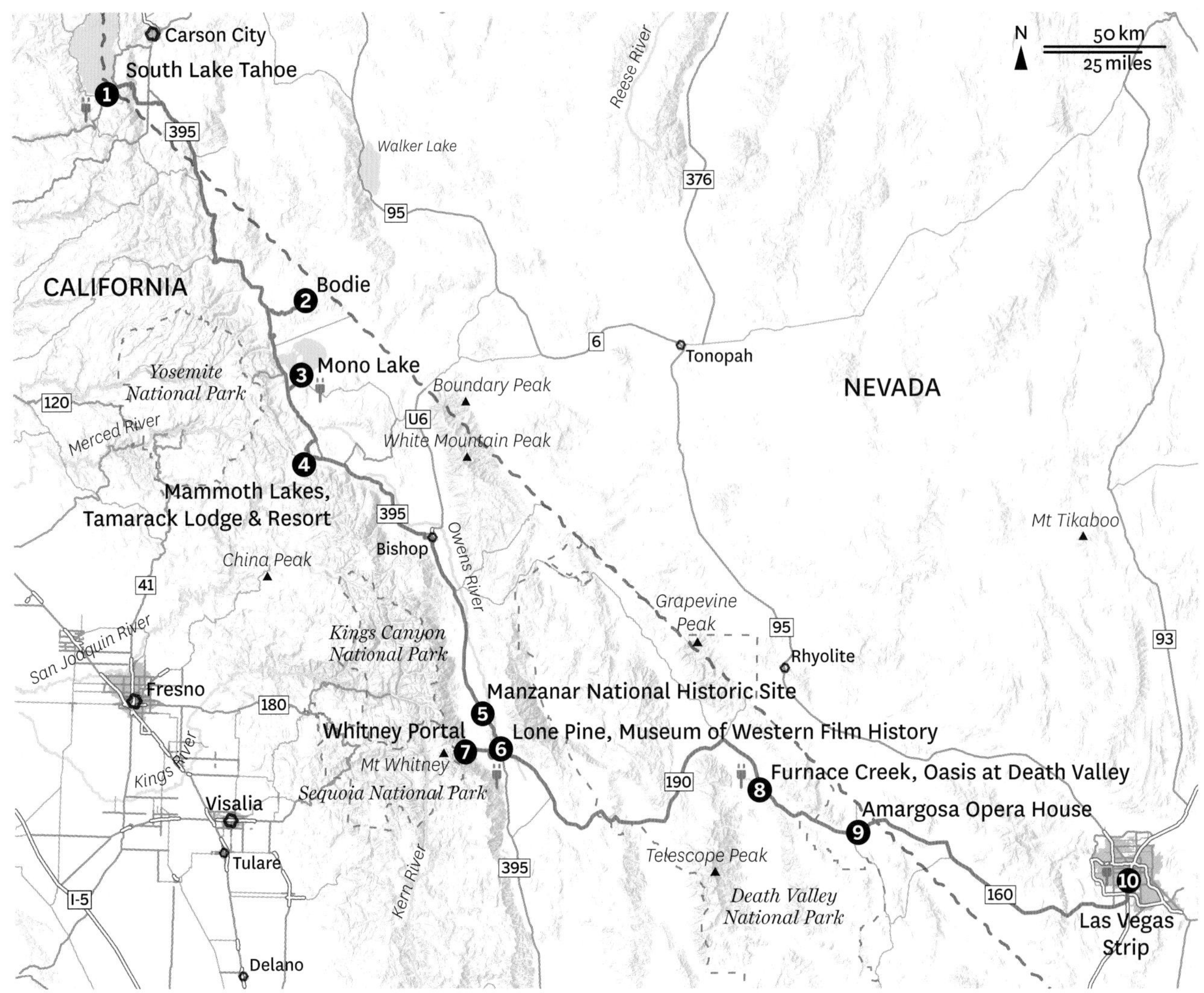


your next stop, Mono Lake. At the lakeshore's South Tufa Area, explore otherworldly towers of tufa – limestone formations that dot the water here. If visiting in fall you'll see millions of migratory birds feasting on the lake's shrimp. Photos taken, it's a 40-minute drive to Mammoth Lakes for more wonderful water and plenty of good sleeping options.

## MOUNTAIN HIGH

While your EV charges, spend the next morning enjoying lakeside strolling before a detour to Minaret Vista, which provides stunning views of the Sierra Nevada; these same views would have been stunning for very different reasons when 19th-century settlers were confronted by them.

Back on Rte 395, it's 100 miles (160km) to Lone Pine, but stop just before this small town for a history lesson at Manzanar National Historic Site, an internment camp where 10,000 Japanese Americans were held during WWII. In Lone Pine itself, plug in the car and visit the Museum of Western Film History. Over 400 movies (and commercials) have been made around Lone Pine and the museum has fascinating exhibits from many – and not just Westerns, despite the name. Drive from the museum into the Alabama Hills, the setting for dozens of those movies, along Whitney Portal Rd, whose name gives a clue to your destination. The drive itself is breathtaking, but it's the peak at the top, Mt Whitney, that is your goal. The highest mountain in the Lower 48 tops out at 14,505ft (4421m) and is a relatively straightforward climb – if you've secured your all-important permit (see sidebar). Climbing or not, the tiny settlement of Whitney Portal is a pleasant (and pleasantly cool when it's hot below) place to meander, and the store here serves up big portions of hearty food, perfect if the mountain air gives you an appetite. Stay overnight in Lone Pine, preferably at a place with Sierra views for sunset and sunrise spectacles.

## Climbing Mt Whitney

If you're tempted to climb Mt Whitney, here are a few tips for bagging the Lower 48's highest mountain. First, secure an elusive but absolutely necessary permit, which you can buy in advance online (at recreation.gov). You'll need to decide which permit you require (the day permit means hiking up and back in one long but doable day; the overnight permit allows multiday trips); and apply between February 1 and March 1 and hope you get one (any remaining permits are released on April 22). The fee is $15. Permit in hand, the hardest part is behind you as climbing Mt Whitney is relatively straightforward – the main requirement is being fit. The hike starts in Whitney Portal, at 8300ft (2530m), and climbs a further 6200ft (1890m) over 11 miles (17.7km). If attempting it in one day, leave at sunrise, pack a flashlight for descending in the dark, and bear in mind the altitude. Snow is likely outside July to September. The trail itself, opened in 1904, was used by mules to carry scientific equipment up the peak for tests. Your reward at the top is a large, flat summit giving unmatched views across California and beyond.

**Clockwise from top left:** Lone Pine's Museum of Western Film History; eye-stretching views on the Mt Whitney climb; tufa formations at Mono Lake

## The fastest boomtown in the west

All over California and Nevada, the gold rush that lasted from the 19th century into the 20th saw the rise and fall of boomtowns like Bodie. None though had a shorter lifespan than Rhyolite. It was established in 1905, after two prospectors found gold in the area; the good times were all over by 1911 when the mine closed. Yet over six short years Rhyolite spawned hotels, a school, electric street lighting, a stock exchange, an opera house and the usual raucous saloons. It also had a three-story building that cost a reputed $90,000 to construct, and a home built from 50,000 beer bottles because good wood was scarce. Today Rhyolite is a ghost town whose remains (including the bottle house) draw the curious. If you're one of them, detour 38 miles (61km) north from Furnace Creek in Death Valley to visit.

**From far left:** Rhyolite, Nevada; stargazing at Badwater Basin, Death Valley National Park; Amargosa Opera House

## INTO THE VALLEY OF DEATH

From the highest point in the contiguous US it's just over 80 miles (129km) east to the lowest. And what an 80 miles, because on day three you and your trusty EV are heading into Death Valley, which not only has the lowest point in North America – Badwater Basin, 282ft (86m) below sea level – but has also recorded the highest temperature on Earth, a fearsome 134°F (56.6°C). Make sure your car has been fully charged in Lone Pine – you'll be using a lot of air-con – and drive gently. Death Valley National Park has several highlights, including Zabriskie Point, where erosion-carved rocks ripple across the landscape; and Dante's View, where lower temperatures and the chance to spot Mt Whitney again await. To give you and your EV a rest, overnight in Furnace Creek.

Day four is all about swapping big landscapes for bright lights as you leave California and head into neighboring Nevada. Just before the state border, pull over at the highly unexpected Amargosa Opera House. Created by dancer Marta Becket after her car broke down here in 1967, it's a surreal and popular venue still. Come for a show (book in advance) or take a tour.

From small-scale entertainment it's 90 miles (145km) to one of the world's entertainment capitals, Las Vegas. Arrive at sunset and cruise along the (in)famous Strip as the neon comes on and the crowds throng the sidewalks. Stop by the Bellagio for spectacular water-and-music fountain shows; swap four wheels for a gondolier on the canals at the Venetian; dive into the aptly named Bacchanal buffet at Caesars Palace; and visit one of the museums (yes, museums in Vegas) covering topics including neon signs, the mob and atom bombs.

**Below:** LA's storied Hollywood Boulevard
**Right:** Chevrolet Bolt EV in Joshua Tree National Park

**Distance: 294 miles (473km)**

**Duration: 3-4 days**

# LA to Joshua Tree National Park

**CALIFORNIA**

Highbrow culture, urban grit, desert luxury and the great outdoors – all accessible by EV on this classic drive from LA to the wild, barren landscapes of the high Californian desert.

A city of dreams and dreamers, LA melds cosmopolitan sophistication with raw ambition, a rich history and cutting-edge design. Leave your EV at your hotel and walk the streets of historic El Pueblo or lively Chinatown, join art fans at the Broad and Moca Grand, or head to Hollywood for star-studded sidewalks and studio tours or slick Beverley Hills to visit the compelling Museum of Tolerance.

## OLD-WORLD ELEGANCE, WILD WEST TOWNS

Heading east in your EV, it's just 15 miles (24km) to affluent Pasadena, at the foot of the San Gabriel Mountains. Its heritage architecture, chic boutiques and Old Town charm feel a world away from LA. Visit the Gamble House, a 1908 Arts and Crafts masterpiece considered one of America's most architecturally significant homes; or the art collection and colorful themed gardens at renowned Huntington Library. Recharge in Riverside, 50 miles (80km) away, as you pause for a margarita on the tree-shaded terrace of the Mission Inn, a bewitching Spanish Revival–style property that oozes old-world glamour. The hotel museum charts the mixed fortunes of this landmark building, which takes up a whole city block.

# Plan & prepare

## Tips for EV drivers

You can hire an EV at Los Angeles International Airport and in downtown LA. EV infrastructure along this route is well developed everywhere except inside Joshua Tree National Park. Plan to charge up before you enter the park. Bear in mind that high summer temperatures will affect your range as your EV tries to keep itself and the cabin cool. Equally, the cold winter nights in the high desert will also affect your battery range, so plan accordingly.

## Where to stay

The gorgeous Mission Inn (missioninn.com) in Riverside makes a fabulous overnight stay in historic surroundings. For poolside relaxation and spa treatments, stop over at the O Spa + Resort (theospahotsprings.com) in Desert Hot Springs, which has rooms loosely designed on celebrity styles. In Twentynine Palms, El Rancho Dolores (motelerd.com) has simple modern rooms, some with kitchenettes or patios, and a seasonal outdoor pool. All have chargers onsite or within a short walk.

## When to go

April sees the world descend on Palm Springs for the Coachella Festival. June to September offers sunny days, snow-free mountain passes and, in LA, the quirky Cinespia outdoor cinema events set among the tombs of silver-screen greats in the Hollywood Forever Cemetery. However, summer in the high desert is swelteringly hot and dry. Spring and fall are better bets, particularly if you plan to hike. Desert wildflowers bloom February through April and cacti from April to June.

## Further info

Traffic in LA is notorious: use the Metro buses and trains to travel between downtown sights, and if you value your time, don't attempt to leave or return to LA during the morning or evening rush hour. Cell signal is weak across much of the Joshua Tree National Park, so download your maps in advance or pick up a paper version at the entrance. Bring plenty of water when hiking, whatever time of year, but especially in summer.

## Desert Queen Ranch

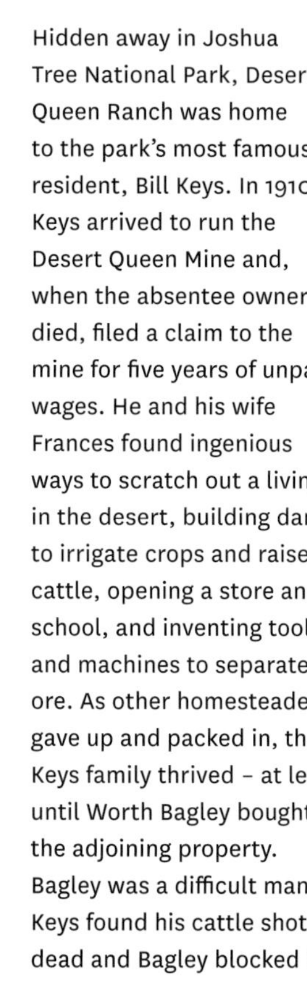

Hidden away in Joshua Tree National Park, Desert Queen Ranch was home to the park's most famous resident, Bill Keys. In 1910, Keys arrived to run the Desert Queen Mine and, when the absentee owner died, filed a claim to the mine for five years of unpaid wages. He and his wife Frances found ingenious ways to scratch out a living in the desert, building dams to irrigate crops and raise cattle, opening a store and a school, and inventing tools and machines to separate ore. As other homesteaders gave up and packed in, the Keys family thrived – at least until Worth Bagley bought the adjoining property. Bagley was a difficult man; Keys found his cattle shot dead and Bagley blocked his access routes to his land. In May 1943, Bagley ambushed Keys but in the resulting shootout Bagley wound up dead. Keys was convicted of manslaughter but a long campaign by Frances and acquaintance Erle Stanley Gardner, the *Perry Mason* author, eventually got him released with a full pardon. You can join a 90-minute ranger-led tour of the Desert Queen Ranch to hear more about Keys' story. Book ahead (via nps.gov).

**Clockwise from top left:** Spanish Revival style at the Mission Inn, Riverside; Desert Queen Ranch; heady views from the top station of Palm Springs Aerial Tramway

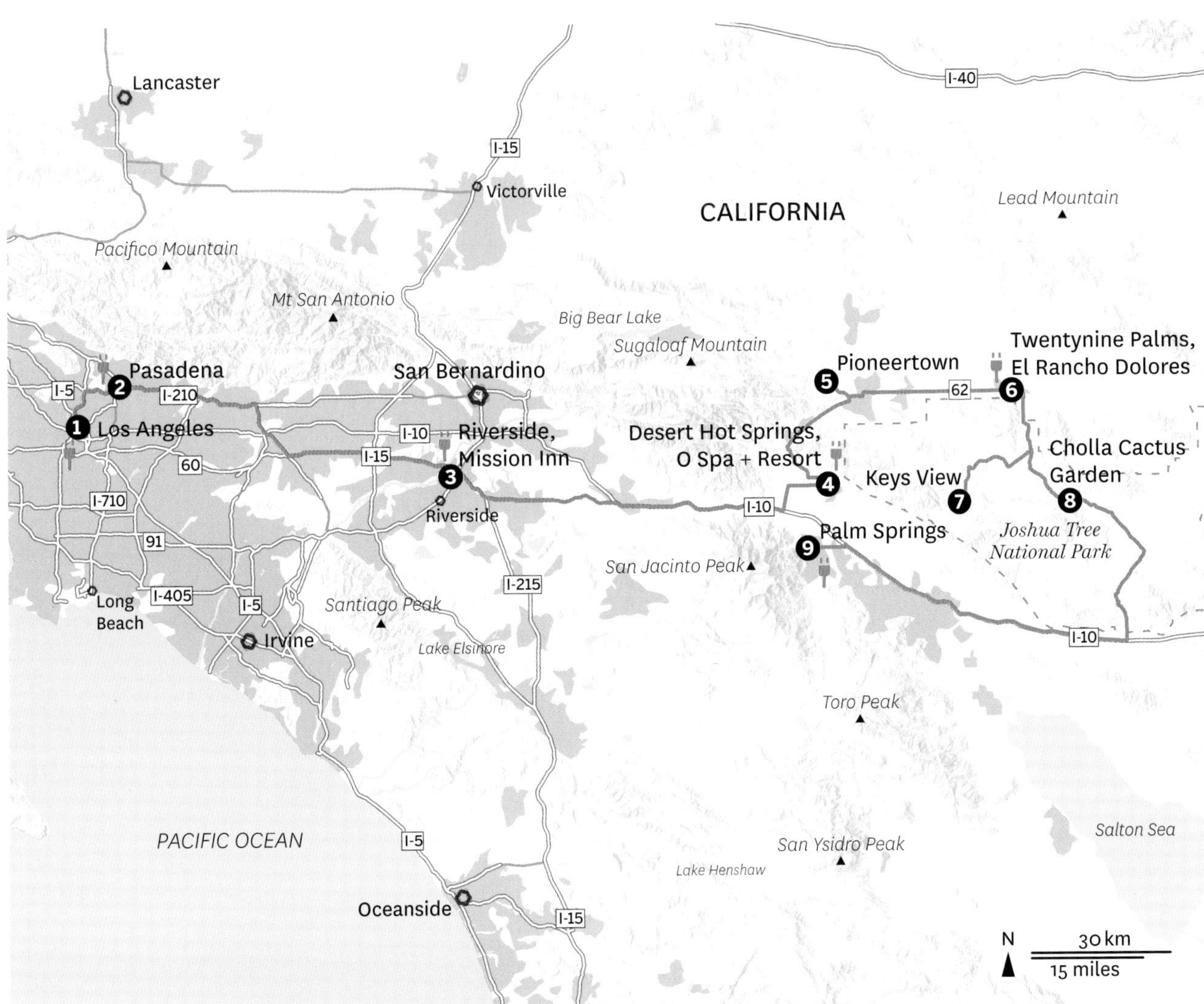


It's 59 winding miles (95km) through the mountains then north along Hwy 62 to the steep-sided Big Morongo Canyon, a lush oasis between the Mojave and Colorado deserts. Stop to walk the trails and see some of the 247 bird species that rest or nest here, then detour in your EV to Pioneertown, a fully functioning movie production set with an 1880s theme, staged gunfights and old-time saloons, before arriving at Joshua Tree National Park.

## HIGH DESERT TO PARTY CITY

The stark, raw beauty of the high desert, its sculptural cacti, dramatic rock formations and endless vistas, make Joshua Tree a beguiling place to visit. At sunset, Keys View, 19 miles (30km) from the west entrance, is one of the most spectacular outlooks. Set on the crest of the Little San Bernardino Mountains at 5185ft (1580m), it towers above the plunging Coachella Valley and San Andreas Fault below. Linger after sundown and see the sky light up in a wondrous diamond-studded show. Further east, climbers flock to Jumbo Rocks, also a good place to hike or scramble over the massive boulders of this otherworldly landscape; Arch Rock is a much-photographed formation reached on an easy hike from Twin Tanks. Before leaving the park, stop to walk the Cholla Cactus Garden, which showcases the desert's surprisingly diverse plant life.

Once a glamorous hideaway for the Rat Pack, heady Palm Springs, 46 miles (74km) away, is a hipster hangout whose mid-century-modern bars and hotels host the state's best pool parties. Hop on a guided tour of modernist showpiece Sunnylands, or get out to Indian Canyons for hiking along red-rock canyons to fan-palm groves and scenic lookouts. Then end your trip by taking the Palm Springs Aerial Tramway up through five vegetation zones to the pine-filled Mt San Jacinto State Park, for a sweeping overview of the surrounding desert.

**Below:** hiking Zion's vertigo-inducing Angels Landing Trail
**Right:** looking down on Zion Canyon from the Angels Landing Trail

**Distance: 500 miles (804km)**

**Duration: 14 days**

# Mighty Five national parks

**UTAH**

Wind your EV around Utah's "Mighty Five" national parks, where nature went wild and magnificent canyons, delicate arches, mesas, spires and buttes litter the red rocks of the sun-scorched earth.

Alternately serene, savage and sublime, Utah's national parks are home to some of the most awe-inspiring landscapes on Earth. With endless walking trails and scenic detours begging to be explored, more cinematic lookouts than you could possibly count and a growing sense of nature's grandeur with every corner turned, it's worth leaving as much time as you possibly can to do this drive.

## ZION TO BRYCE

Start your journey in Springdale, a park town full of galleries and artisan shops all set against a backdrop of deep-red mountains in Zion National Park. From here, you can access a wide variety of hikes, from easy strolls along the lush banks of the Virgin River to strenuous hikes such as the Angels Landing Trail, which runs along a vertigo-inducing route with sheer drop-offs and phenomenal views. Map out your plans at the Zion Canyon Visitor Center, where staff can also advise on quieter trails to walk in the busy summer months.

Leave the park following the Zion–Mt Carmel Hwy, an engineering marvel that winds up tight switchbacks to the scorched slickrock of the dramatic Checkerboard Mesa. Shaped by wind, rain, rivers and frost over

# Plan & prepare

### Tips for EV drivers

Although this route has a good selection of EV chargers, many accommodations only allow charging for patrons. To avoid an issue, call ahead and check. If you're traveling between October and April, bear in mind that nights are seriously cold in the desert. This may cause range loss, as will the changes in altitude along these high-desert roads, so make sure you factor this in and allow for a greater safety margin than usual.

### Where to stay

Fancy an overnight stay in a historic log cabin with breathtaking views? Head for Zion Lodge (zionlodge.com), where the traditional cabins have fireplaces and porches or balconies. In Torrey, close to Capitol Reef, the Cougar Ridge Lodge (cougarridge.com) has villas with plenty of local character, while in Moab the Gonzo Inn (gonzoinn.com) is a condo-style boutique hotel with desert-chic rooms. All properties have EV charging onsite.

### When to go

Spring and fall are easily the best times to visit the parks. Warm days and quieter trails make hiking and sightseeing more pleasant, and hotel prices can drop by up to 50%. If you do intend to drive the route between April and September, expect to meet a lot of other travelers along the trails, in the visitor centers and on the roads – and plan well ahead as park lodges and hotels nearby often get booked up months in advance.

### Further info

There are numerous state parks and national monuments that make easy side-trips along this route. With entrance fees to each park at $30-$35, it's worth buying a Southeast Utah Parks Pass ($55; stateparks.utah.gov) that gives a year's entry to Arches, Canyonlands and Natural Bridges National Monument; or better still, an America the Beautiful National Park Pass ($80; store.usgs.gov) which gives a year's entry to all US national parks, forests and monuments.

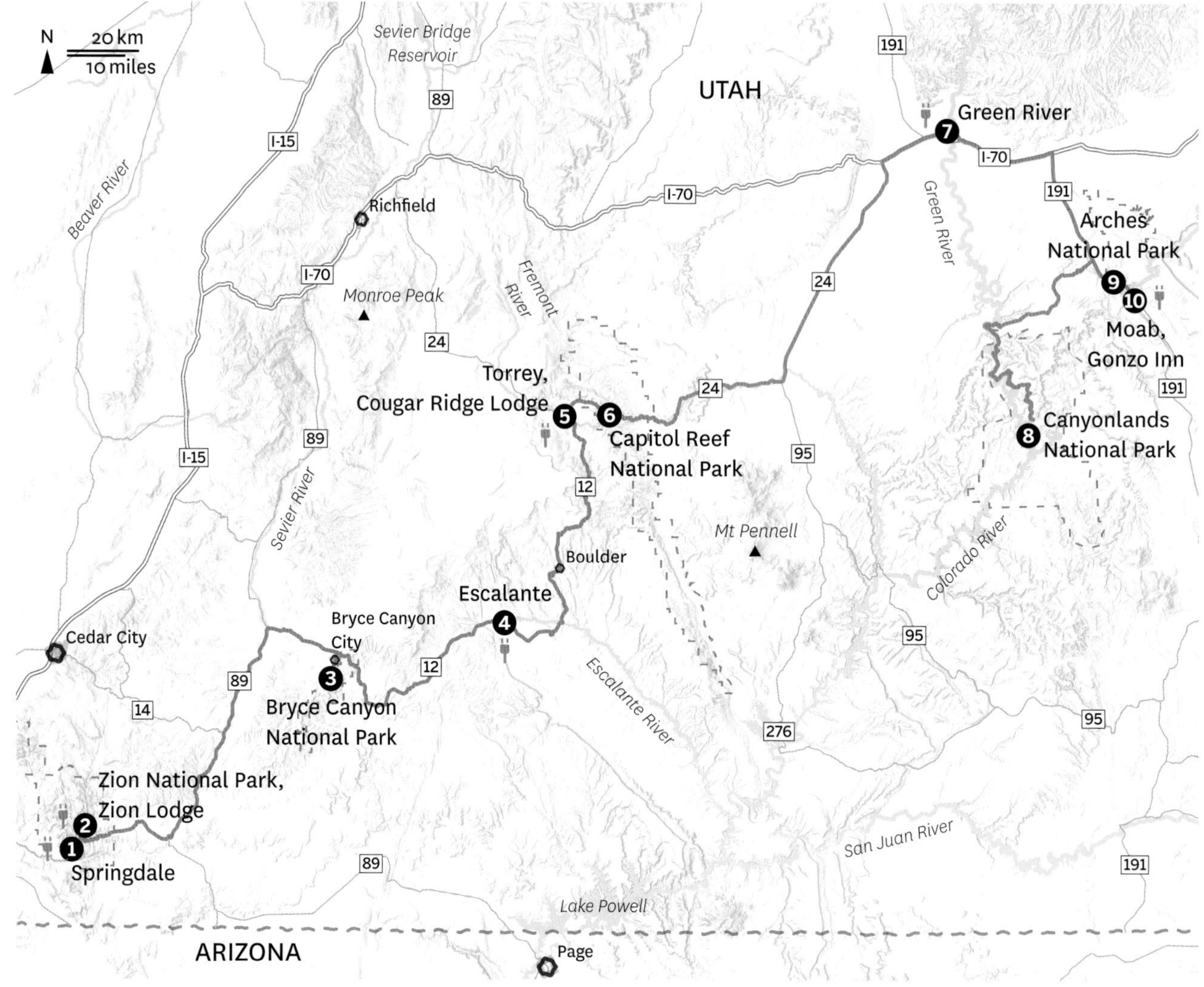


millennia, this wild landscape was immortalized by Maynard Dixon, a Great Depression–era painter whose home and studio can be visited in Mt Carmel. Further on, at Red Canyon, thread your EV between the intensely red monoliths that flank the road and stop to walk the short Arches Trail, which passes 15 rock arches.

From here, it's just 9 miles (14km) to Bryce Canyon National Park, where the pastel pinks and oranges of the stately hoodoos are sculpted into pleated folds like an unearthly pipe organ. To reduce congestion (as well as noise and air pollution in the case of vehicles other than EVs), visitors are encouraged to take the shuttle bus from Bryce Canyon City, where you can leave your EV to charge. The shuttle, which runs from April to October, is free and passes the park's most popular overlooks and trailheads, allowing you to walk among the spindles and spires by taking one trail down to the fragrant desert floor and another back up.

## THROUGH THE CANYONS TO MOAB

From Bryce Canyon City, Scenic Byway 12 winds its way east through rugged canyonland to the towns of Escalante, Boulder and Torrey, all offering EV chargers on this 106-mile (170km) stretch of the drive. If you need to stop, the Escalante Interagency Visitor Center has a wealth of information on the geology and ecosystems of the area as well as all nearby public lands, and can give useful tips on quieter hikes hereabouts. In Boulder, the Anasazi State Park Museum delves into the history of an Ancestral Puebloan (Anasazi) village, once one of the largest communities west of the Colorado River. Between Escalante and Torrey, sculpted slickrock, narrow ridge-backs and a steep ascent over Boulder Mountain await.

Recharge overnight in the small pioneer town of Torrey, which also makes a great base for exploring nearby Capitol Reef National Park, where wondrous rock formations combine with pioneer history. Underrated

## Screen darlings

Millions of years of geologic history combined with erosion by wind, rain, ice and snow have created Utah's otherworldly landscapes, which have long provided a stunning backdrop for the film industry. The first Westerns were filmed here in the 1920s and since then, the cliffs, arches, spires, buttes and canyons have played a leading role in Hollywood history. Zion's deep red cliffs and lush river canyons starred in *Butch Cassidy and the Sundance Kid* and *Romancing the Stone*, Bryce Canyon appeared in arthouse classic *Koyaanisqatsi*, Arches made appearances in *Hulk* and *Indiana Jones and the Last Crusade*, while Canyonlands and Arches National Parks were settings for HBO's *Westworld*. One of the most memorable films made in Utah, however, was 1991 feminist road-movie thriller *Thelma & Louise*, much of which was shot in Canyonlands and Arches National Parks. The movie's iconic final scene, however, was filmed just southwest of Moab, at Fossil Point in Dead Horse Point State Park – where you'll also find numerous fossilized dinosaur bones – but you'll need to hike in or have a high-clearance 4WD to get there.

**Clockwise from top left:** a host of hoodoos in Bryce Canyon National Park; looking through the North Window, Arches National Park; cruising Utah's canyonland along Scenic Byway 12

## Leave No Trace

Utah's magnificent parks are some of the most popular in the country, but with all that footfall, the very landscapes travelers come to see are under threat from visitor behavior. "Leave No Trace" principles should always be followed to minimize your impact. This means visiting at quieter times, checking closures and conditions in advance, leaving all you find and never approaching wildlife. On the trails, stick to established paths and walk single-file in the middle of the path. Pack out all your trash – and yep, this includes food scraps and toilet paper. Bury human waste, camp on durable surfaces and only light a fire if absolutely necessary. Wildfires have become a major problem in recent years; if you light a fire, do so in an established fire ring, keep it small, and make sure it's completely extinguished before you move on.

**From far left:** a quiet moment along Zion's Angels Landing Trail; discover little-visited arches and ravishing red-rock views in Capitol Reef



and consequently less crowded than Utah's other national parks, Capitol Reef's deep canyons, colorful cliffs and 65-million-year-old Waterpocket Fold are just as impressive as anything you'll see elsewhere. Hike the Hickman Bridge Trail to arrive at a giant natural bridge and memorable canyon views.

From Torrey, it's 105 miles (169km) to Green River, the next EV charging point and a great place to go on a river-running trip on the Green or Colorado Rivers. Choose from tranquil day trips or multiday whitewater excursions that combine rafting through sheer-faced canyons and hiking remote trails. Base yourself in Green River, or head on about 50 miles (80km) to Moab, adventure capital of the region, from where Canyonlands and Arches National Parks are within easy reach.

## CANYONLANDS & ARCHES NATIONAL PARKS

Exploring the elemental landscapes of Canyonlands National Park, you'll be surrounded by buttes and mesas, rock fins and arches, craggy spires, needles, craters and sheer-walled river gorges. This high-desert wilderness is an untamed wonder where the hiking, rafting and stargazing are unmatched. The scenic drive to Grand View Point passes numerous overlooks and trailheads before finishing at the lip of the mesa, while the Needles District inspires wonder with its orange and white sandstone spires soaring to the sky.

Nearby Arches National Park wows with more than 2000 rock arches that frame red-desert landscapes and snowy peaks. Many of the arches can be reached on paved walking trails, but it's worth arriving early or late to avoid the crowds. The much-photographed Delicate Arch, Landscape Arch and Balanced Rock have become social media darlings, but join a ranger-led hike to the narrow canyons and pleated fins of the Fiery Furnace and you'll find Insta-worthy images all of your own.

**Below:** Desert Botanical Garden, Phoenix
**Right:** taking in the vastness of the Grand Canyon

➜ **Distance: 325 miles (523km)**

➜ **Duration: 7 days**

# Phoenix to the Grand Canyon

**ARIZONA**

Combining Wild West history, historic saloons, charming towns and glorious hiking set among a whole load of canyons, buttes and red-rock wonder, this is one epic all-American EV drive.

A desert metropolis growing at a hefty rate, Phoenix is a buzzing cultural hub with a host of museums, a thriving food scene and lots of great entertainment. Learn about Indigenous culture from the perspective of elders and traditional knowledge-keepers at the Heard Museum; see how Arizona's incredible landscapes have been captured by artists over the centuries at the Phoenix Art Museum; and visit the Desert Botanical Garden to bone up on the plant life you'll see on your road trip. Roosevelt Row has bars, galleries, indie shops and great street art, but for good food, head to La Santisima for contemporary Mexican, or to local legend Durant's, an old-school steakhouse.

## MINING HISTORY

Leaving Phoenix, drive your EV along Hwy 60 for about 50 miles (80km) to reach Wickenburg, a town with a decidedly Old West air. Traditional storefronts herald saddle shops and general stores, the jail tree – a 200-year-old mesquite – still stands, and the Desert Caballeros Western Museum displays artwork celebrating the West. If you have the time, a 12-mile (19km) side-trip to the Vulture City Ghost Town offers a glimpse of life in what was once Arizona's most productive gold mine.

## Plan & prepare

### Tips for EV drivers

You can pick up an EV rental at Phoenix airport but you'll need to plan a return journey to drop it back. EV infrastructure is good across Arizona and there are many free charging stations. However, the state gets incredibly hot in summer, and high temperatures can reduce your battery range, not least because of the energy used to keep the cabin cool. Park in the shade – your battery will thank you.

### Where to stay

There's no EV charger, but Rancho de los Caballeros (ranchodeloscaballeros.com) outside Wickenburg gives an unmissable taste of the Wild West: join in rodeo experiences, sunset cookouts, and penning, roping and barrel-racing lessons. Charger-equipped options include Sedona's Amara Resort & Spa (amararesort.com), with superb views and spacious, contemporary rooms; for old-world charm and the location of a lifetime, try El Tovar Hotel (grandcanyonlodges.com), a 1905-built wooden lodge on the rim of the Grand Canyon.

### When to go

Driving this route in spring or fall allows you to avoid the summer heat and crowds – temperatures are far more pleasant for hiking, and parking lots at popular destinations are less likely to be full. Time a visit for October and you can catch Phoenix's Arizona State Fair which lures huge crowds to its rodeo, livestock displays, pie-eating competitions and live performances.

### Further info

In summer, avoid the wait at the Grand Canyon entrance gates and the battle for parking in Grand Canyon Village by leaving your EV at the National Geographic Visitor Center in Tusayan and hopping on the shuttle into the park from there. While at the center, nip in to see the jaw-dropping Grand Canyon: *Rivers of Time* IMAX film which chronicles the canyon's history, geology and mythology over the course of its formation.

## The Grand Canyon, past and present

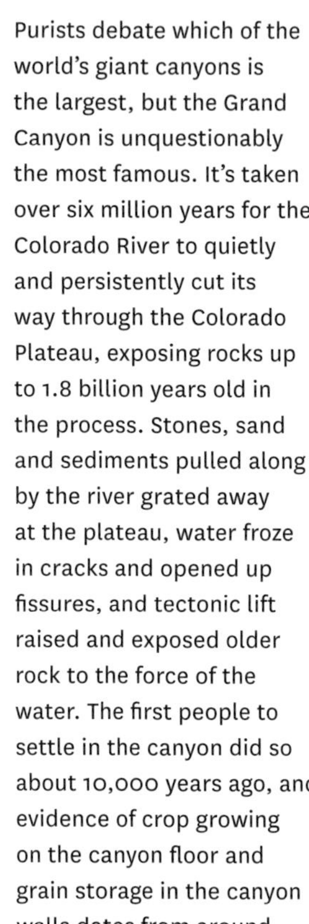

Purists debate which of the world's giant canyons is the largest, but the Grand Canyon is unquestionably the most famous. It's taken over six million years for the Colorado River to quietly and persistently cut its way through the Colorado Plateau, exposing rocks up to 1.8 billion years old in the process. Stones, sand and sediments pulled along by the river grated away at the plateau, water froze in cracks and opened up fissures, and tectonic lift raised and exposed older rock to the force of the water. The first people to settle in the canyon did so about 10,000 years ago, and evidence of crop growing on the canyon floor and grain storage in the canyon walls dates from around 1000 years ago. Everything changed in 1963, however, when the dam at Glen Canyon was completed, altering the river's water temperature and preventing spring runoffs from bringing new sediment to the canyon's beaches and sandbars. The Grand Canyon's fragile ecosystem remains under threat, with non-native species thriving. Its health, however, is just one of many competing demands on an already overburdened water system in a hot and arid state.

**Clockwise from top left:** sunset from Cathedral Rock, Sedona; bird's eye view of the Glen Canyon Dam; winding through boho Jerome

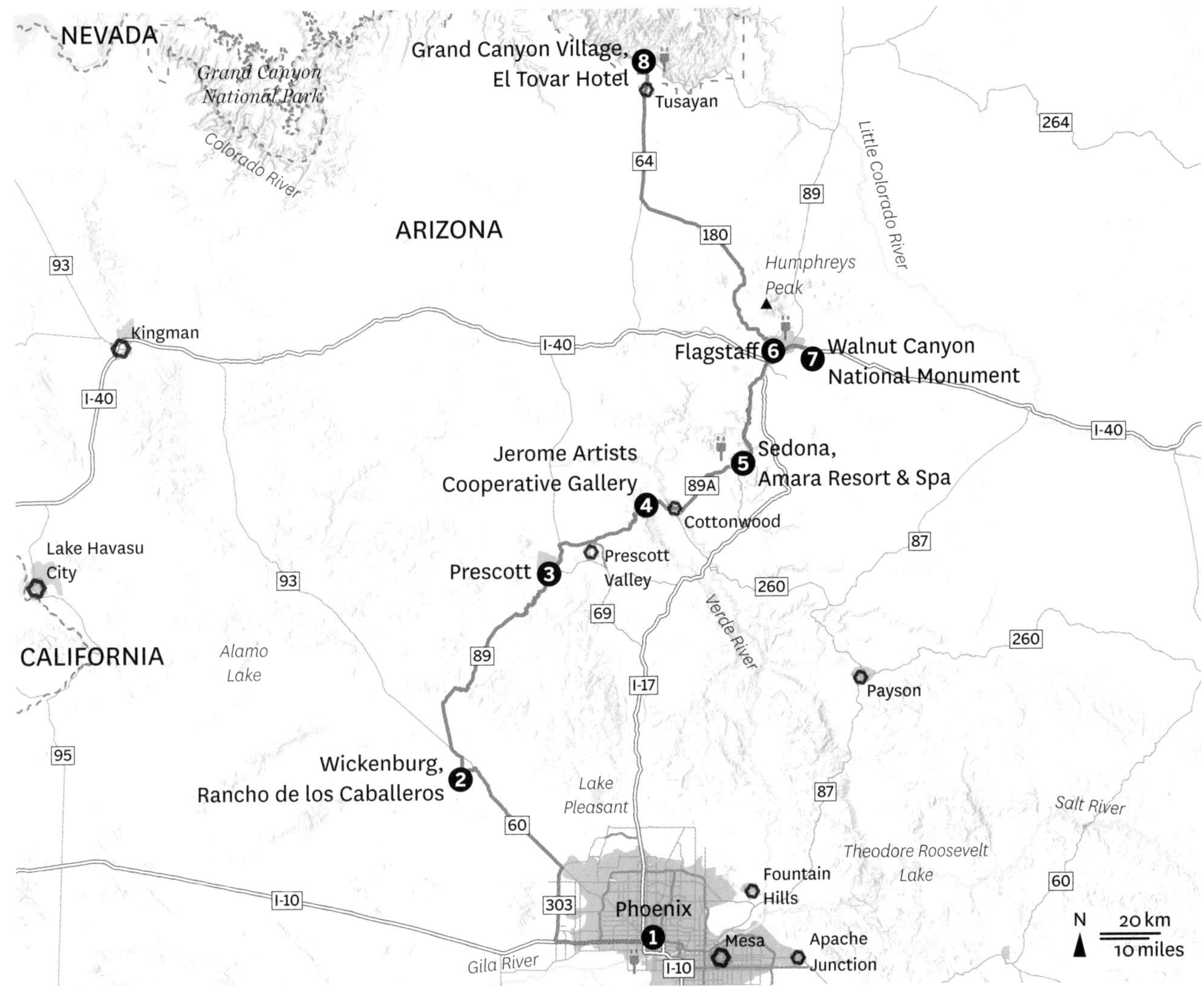


The road north from Wickenburg climbs steeply up into the Weaver Mountains to Prescott, 59 miles (95km) away. The town's Victorian-era downtown area comprises more than 500 historic buildings, including a strip of old saloons known as Whiskey Row. If you need to clear your head or stretch your legs after a visit, Thumb Butte just west of town offers good views; to the north, the scenic Granite Dells, a system of exposed bedrock and granite boulders, promises plenty of options for trail walking.

EV passengers will delight in the sweeping views on the twisty road north through the Mingus Mountains as you approach boho Jerome. During its heyday in the 1800s, residents' debauchery earned it the moniker of the "Wickedest Town in the West"; bust followed boom, but Jerome was joyfully brought back to life in the 1960s by an influx of hippies attracted by cheap property prices. Today, galleries, cafes, bars, boutique stores and wine-tasting rooms line the town's steep streets. Check out the Jerome Artists Cooperative Gallery for local creations or venture on to Tuzigoot National Monument east of Clarkdale, where you can explore a prehistoric pueblo built by the Sinagua people and enjoy sweeping views of the Verde Valley.

## RED-ROCK COUNTRY

Winding through red rock sculpted into magnificent shapes, the road leads on about 27 miles (43km) into Sedona, where the power of the local landscape has long attracted New Age spiritualists, healers and artists. It's a glorious, if busy, place to wander and you'll find galleries, crystal shops, outdoor sculptures and cafes at every turn. To feel the power of the Earth's deepest energies, head just south of town to Cathedral Rock Vortex at sunset, for sweeping views of sandstone outcrops glowing deep red and orange in the evening light.

## Water into wine

Fancy abandoning your car and floating downriver to a wine tasting? You can do just that at Alcantara Vineyards (alcantaravineyard.com), a sustainably farmed winery near Cottonwood. Kayak down the Verde River to the confluence with Oak Creek, then meander back through the vines learning about sustainable viticulture, irrigation and varietals. Alternatively, you could combine kayaking with e-biking through the estate before ending with a wine tasting and food pairing. Stand-up paddleboarding, yoga, and even SUP yoga are all possible here, as are horseback tours of the estate, which venture a little further afield for panoramic views of the river valley and Mingus Mountain. A key part of the operation here is maintaining the health of the river and of water sources, with work continuing with other local organizations on reducing erosion and restoring water flow while supporting local wildlife.

**From far left:** kayaking the Verde River; seeing the sights by balloon from Sedona; sunrise over the Grand Canyon

North of Sedona along Hwy 89A, Oak Creek Canyon is an oasis where vibrant green foliage contrasts with the deep-red rocks, and swimming holes entice you to linger. From here, it's about 25 miles (40km) to laid-back Flagstaff, with its historic downtown and scenic setting at the foot of Humphreys Peak. Flagstaff was designated the world's first International Dark Sky City in 2001, and it would be remiss not to visit Lowell Observatory, where Pluto was first spotted. Alternatively, follow the Flagstaff Ale Trail for a tour of the city's many microbreweries; venture out to Coconino National Forest to hike through aspen groves and ponderosa pines; or visit Walnut Canyon National Monument to see the remains of cliff dwellings built by the Sinagua people over 1000 years ago.

North of Flagstaff, drive your EV along Hwy 180, soaking up the views of the San Francisco Peaks as you go. It's about 90 miles (145km) to the Grand Canyon, with the excitement building with every passing mile.

## THE "BIG DITCH"

Nothing quite prepares you for your first sight of the Grand Canyon. The scale, intricacy and subtle tonal changes of this natural wonder are truly breathtaking: ridges, spires and mesas stretch in multicolored layers as far as the eye can see. You'll get background information on the canyon's history at the visitor center, which also lists talks, guided walks and activities available on the day of your visit. Free shuttle buses run between viewpoints and trailheads along the canyon rim, but walk even a short distance from the drop-off points and you'll quickly lose the crowds. Another good tactic is to rise early – buses start at 4am – and see the canyon at sunrise in all its glory. For hiking, the Hermit or Grandview Trails are generally quieter but also narrower and steeper, so are only suitable for more experienced hikers.

**Below:** dolphins along the Nā Pali Coast
**Right:** Waimea, the "Grand Canyon" of Kaua'i

**Distance: 140 miles (225km)**

**Duration: 3 days**

# Kaua'i loop

**HAWAI'I**

Taking in glorious beaches and tropical gardens, a full loop by EV around Kaua'i – arguably the Hawaiian archipelago's most beautiful island – is only interrupted by its most remarkable sight: the Nā Pali Coast.

EV rental collected at Lihue Airport, head north on Rte 56, aka Kuhio Hwy. Destination? The highlights of Kaua'i's north coast. After 25 miles (40km), look for the "Kīlauea Lighthouse" sign and take a right.

## NORTH COAST WONDERS

A short drive brings you to Kīlauea Point National Wildlife Refuge, where the century-old lighthouse commands spectacular ocean views. Look for passing dolphins and whales (winter only), and birdlife in abundance on the cliffs. Legs stretched, it's back in the car for a 20-minute cruise to overnight option, Hanalei Beach. This long crescent of sand offers swimming, snorkeling and surfing. Take a sunset stroll along the pier, but don't go to bed late: you'll need to be up early for day two, as there's a lot to see and your first stop, the Kalalau Trail, gets very busy, very quickly. Parking at the trailhead is limited – avoid weekends – but the reward for an early start is one of the most magnificent walks on Earth. This is your first glimpse of the awesome Nā Pali Coast, and if the steeply undulating hike doesn't leave you breathless, the views will. The first 2 miles (3km) are open to everyone, but beyond Hanakapi'ai Beach, it's permit holders only. Everyone needs an advance hiking and parking

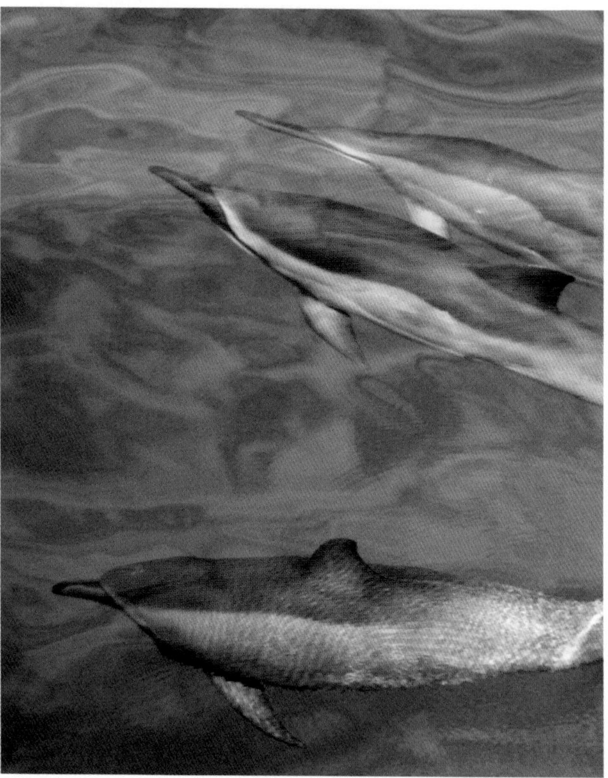

© [photographer credit, partly cut off] / Getty Images

## Plan & prepare

### Tips for EV drivers

See Hawaii EV (hawaiiev.org/ev-rentals) for tips on archipelago-wide EV rental options. Distances between places of interest are short on this drive and there are charging stations available at or near most stops. Very handily, charging is available at the West Kaua'i Heritage Center, at the turnoff for the uphill drive to Waimea Canyon State Park, where you can learn about local culture while your car recharges.

### Where to stay

Hanalei Colony Resort (hcr.com) has an oceanfront setting for its traditionally styled suites and is just a couple of miles west of Hanalei Beach and east of the Kalalau Trail, giving you a head start on other hikers. Swaying palm trees, brightly colored rooms and a cool beachside bar-restaurant make Kauai Shores (kauaishoreshotel.com) a firm favorite on the east coast; it has chargers onsite and nearby, and there are several good eating and drinking options within short walking distance.

### When to go

Though it's a tropical island, with warm weather year-round, Kaua'i does have seasons, kind of, that will determine the best time to go. Winter (November to March) equals rainy season, so if hiking is high on your to-do list then note that trails can be muddy and sometimes impassable – but waterfalls are at their best. In summer/dry season, sunshine is plentiful but so are the crowds, and parking at the island's natural charms – and enjoying them in tranquility – is trickier.

### Further info

Lihue is the main airport on the island and there are EV rental options available from the usual companies, plus local specialists such as Aloha Rents (aloharents.com). A volunteer organization, KauaiEV (kauaiev.org), has lots of useful information including PlugShare, which lists island EV owners who are happy for visitors to charge with them. A state-funded program launched by Hawai'i Energy aims to expand the island chain's public charging network substantially in coming years.

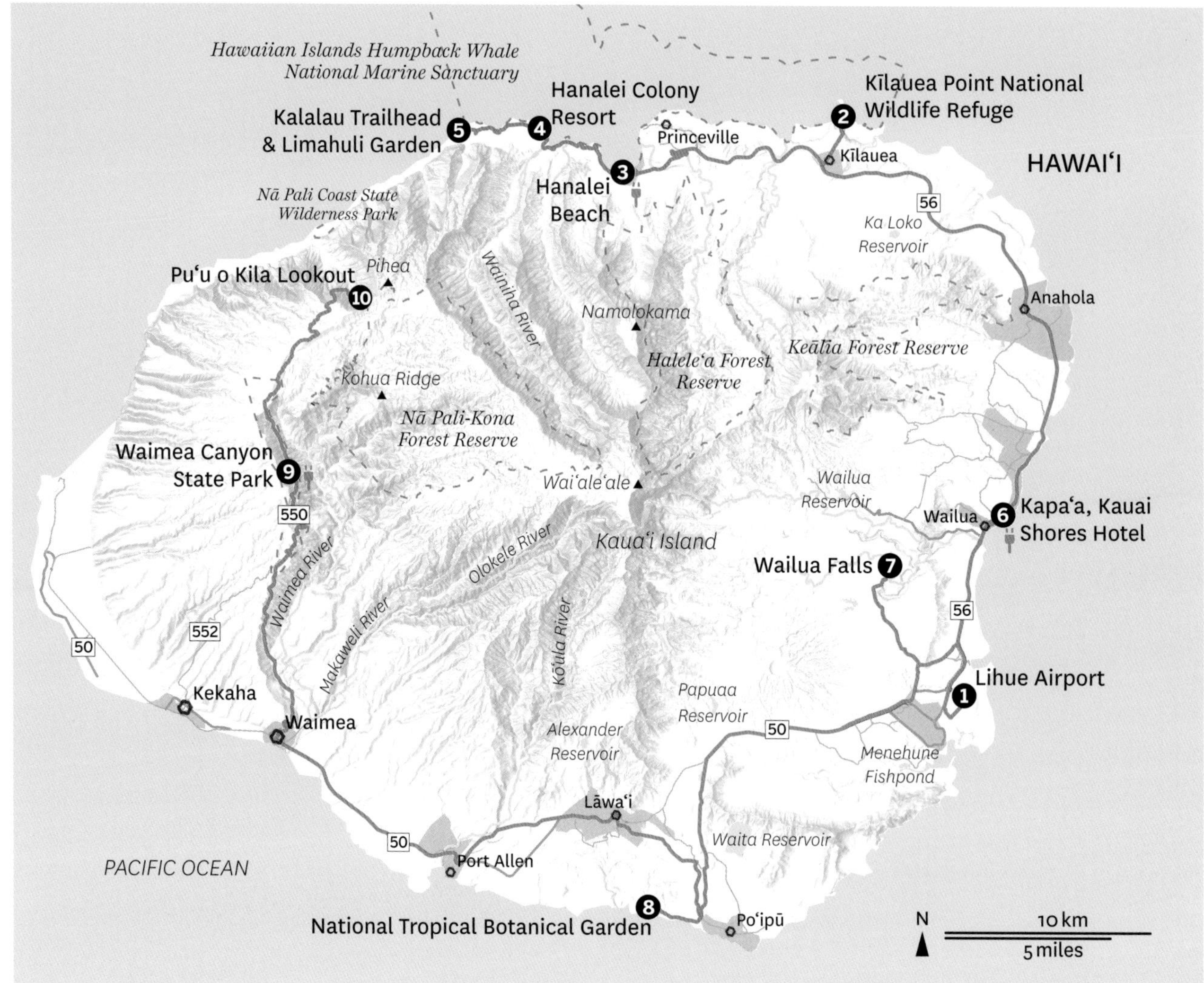


reservation, however (see opposite page). Tear yourself away and find your second wind to visit Limahuli Garden, a short walk east of the trailhead. Follow the self-guided tour past unique plant species and enjoy more ocean views, then double back towards your second overnight location in Kapaʻa, Kauaʻi's largest town, pausing at beaches along the way.

## SOUTHERN SHOWSTOPPERS

With you and your EV recharged, double back on Rte 56 in the morning and follow Rte 583 inland to Wailua Falls. You won't have this popular, tall (officially 80ft/24m; after rain, much higher) cascade to yourself – another early start will mean easier parking and the chance to see the falls' famous morning rainbows.

It's an easy 18 miles (29km) on Rte 50 towards Kauaʻi's south coast. Break the journey at the National Tropical Botanical Garden, really two gardens, Allerton and McBryde, where more fantastic flora awaits. Allerton sits above a pretty beach; McBryde is further inland and has rare endemic species and the second waterfall of the day.

Continuing west, turn off Rte 50 onto Rte 550 and begin a scenic climb towards Waimea Canyon State Park. On an island of such great natural beauty, this canyon only misses out on the number-one spot because of the Nā Pali Coast. But second place never looked better. Kauaʻi's "Grand Canyon" has several viewpoints, plus trails for extended exploration.

A 20-minute drive leads to your final stop – and we've saved the best for last. The two lookouts at the road's end, Kalalau and Puʻu o Kila, leave many lost for words. From them, the huge, jagged, vegetation-clad cliffs of the Nā Pali Coast dramatically drop 4000ft (1220m) into the Pacific with inexpressibly beautiful results. Stroll a section of the Pihea Trail for different angles and spend as long as you can taking in this natural wonder.

## The Kalalau Trail

Can't get enough of the Nā Pali Coast? Who could blame you. Luckily there are several ways to experience its majesty beyond picturesque lookouts. Whether doing the Kalalau Trail's permit-free (but day-reservation needed) stretch or the full, permit-required 22-mile (35.5km) round-trip hike, you need to book as far in advance as possible – see kalalautrail.com for details. The full hike is not easy, but it's the best up-close way to enjoy the coast. You'll cross five valleys, carpeted in endemic plants, have views of cliffs seen by few other humans, and get to camp at Kalalau Beach at the end, where Ho'ole'a Falls provides a celebratory shower. For a more leisurely perusal of the coast, boats sail there from Hanalei and Port Allen (south coast). Several companies offer cruises (sunset sailings are very popular) on which you can snorkel and swim, plus have a good chance of spotting dolphins, turtles and, sometimes, whales. A buffet lunch or dinner is generally included. For once-in-a-lifetime, blow-the-budget, Jurassic-Park-evoking (it was filmed here) views, take a helicopter flight and spot hikers on the beach at the end of the Kalalau Trail way below.

**Clockwise from top left:** endemic ōhi'a lehua tree in flower; look for green turtles on a boat cruise to Kalalau Beach; Wailua Falls

**Below:** lava flow from Kīlauea, one of the Big Island's three active volcanoes
**Right:** astronomical observatories atop Mauna Kea

**Distance: 221 miles (356km)**

**Duration: 2-3 days**

# Big Island southern loop

**HAWAI'I**

Active volcanoes, a globally important peak, historical sights and a hub town with plenty of character are the stars of this circular route around the "Big Island" of Hawai'i.

The island of Hawai'i offers an array of wow-inducing sights to tempt you away from the beach and into your EV. Start in the multicultural town of Hilo to charge up and stroll elegant Lili'uokalani Park, a Japanese garden named after Hawai'i's last queen, with ocean views and impressive trees. Stop by the daily Hilo Farmers Market to stock up on road-trip supplies, then head southwest out of town on Rte 11, aka the Belt Rd.

## SEE ELEMENTAL FORCES AT WORK

After 30 miles (48km) look for signs to Kīlauea Visitor Center, entry point to Volcanoes National Park. Check the latest conditions (volcanic activity can close sections of road) and then take your pick of the many options, all amazing, on offer here. Hike the Crater Rim Trail to Kīlauea Overlook for a view of lava and steam shooting out of one of the world's most active volcanoes. Then drive Chain of Craters Rd until it reaches the Pacific and Hōlei Sea Arch, stopping along the way to enter Nāhuku (Thurston Lava Tube); walk the Kīlauea Iki Trail across a solidified-lava lake; and marvel at the Pu'uloa Petroglyphs, some 23,000 ancient carvings.

Mind blown by Earth's intimidating power, pick up the Belt Rd again, driving on 80 miles (129km) west to

## Plan & prepare

### Tips for EV drivers

It's smart to mostly plug in your car whenever a charger is available as the island of Hawai'i has its EV facilities gathered in clusters. In downtown Hilo and in Kailua-Kona there are plenty of chargers, some free, but between stops things get sparse. There are a couple of options on Rte 11 (the Belt Rd) between Volcanoes National Park and the west coast, but currently nothing on the road to Mauna Kea. See Hawaii EV (hawaiiev.org/ev-rentals) for tips on EV rental options.

### Where to stay

A night in Hilo before and after the trip means you can explore this diverse town in depth. For ocean views and resort facilities, try Grand Naniloa (grandnaniloahilo.com) or Hilo Hawaiian (castleresorts.com), both close to Lili'uokalani Park and with chargers onsite or nearby. Kailua-Kona has abundant condo rentals – book one near Magic Sands Beach, the island's top spot for surfing and bodyboarding. To stay within Volcanoes National Park, book a room, cabin or camping site at Volcano House (hawaiivolcanohouse.com).

### When to go

The island of Hawai'i sits in the tropics so the weather is warm year-round. Hilo and the east coast can be damp; west is best for sunny conditions; and if you're heading to Mauna Kea, especially if going to the summit, bring warm layers as it can be literally freezing at the top. Christmas/New Year and June through August are when accommodation prices peak and attractions get very busy – avoid if possible.

### Further info

EV drivers currently have a few perks when visiting Hawai'i: at parking meters and in state-run facilities across the island, parking is free for electric vehicles; plus any parking lot with over 100 spaces is required to have at least one space set aside for an EV and equipped with a charger. An intriguing fact: the first car ever seen in Hawai'i, back in 1899, was powered by electricity.

## The Big Island that's getting bigger

Tens of millions of years ago, all of the islands in the Hawaiian archipelago rose from the sea thanks to intense volcanic activity generated by the Pacific tectonic plate. The chain's namesake island formed to become the group's largest, but not content with already taking up around 62% of all Hawai'i's landmass, the Big Island just keeps growing. And that's because of the five volcanoes that produced the island – Kohala, Mauna Kea, Hualālai, Mauna Loa, Kīlauea – three (Hualālai, Mauna Loa and Kīlauea) are still active, spewing lava and adding to the island's size. The latter two sit within Hawai'i Volcanoes National Park, and Kīlauea, one of the most active volcanoes in the world, gives scientists a wonderful opportunity to study Earth's geological forces while giving visitors the equally wonderful opportunity to stand open-mouthed as bursts of fire and smoke emerge from cracks in the landscape. Despite hostile-looking terrain, the park is also home to unique flora and fauna, including the island's only native mammal, the endangered Hawaiian hoary bat, and the lava-defying 'ae fern, often the first plant to appear after an eruption.

**Clockwise from top left:** snorkeling at Kealakekua Bay, where Captain Cook met his end in 1779; remarkable views to active Mauna Loa volcano; extinct craters aplenty from the sacred summit of Mauna Kea

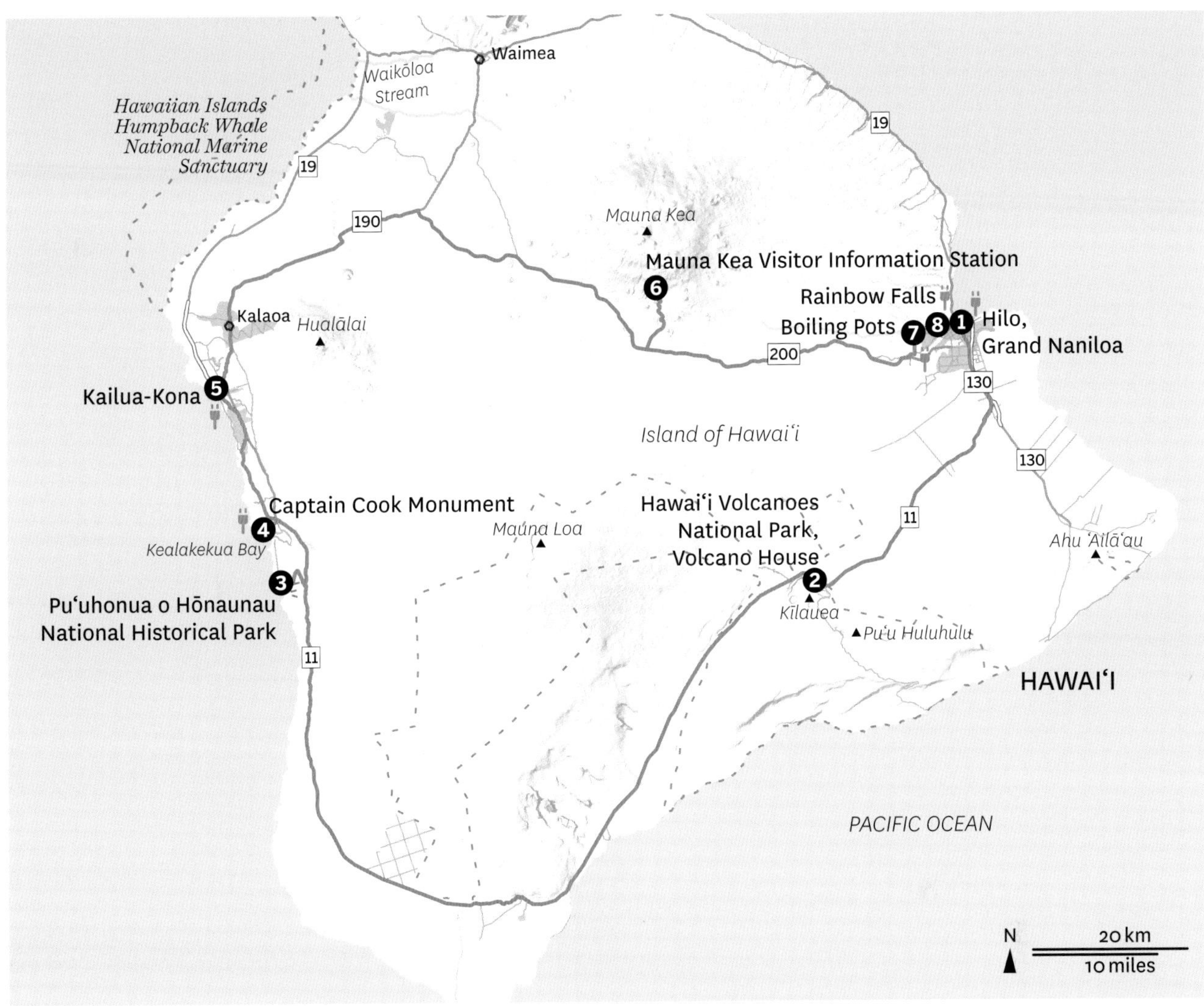


Pu'uhonua o Hōnaunau National Historical Park. This important site for Hawaiians has a half-mile (1km) walking route past wooden *ki'i* (deity images) to the Pu'uhonua, a place of refuge for any *kapu* (sacred laws) breaker, and the Royal Grounds, where *ali'i* (chiefs) once lived.

## THE WORLD'S TALLEST MOUNTAIN?

Just 10 miles (16km) north lies another historically significant location – Kealakekua Bay, where Captain Cook was killed in 1779 by Hawaiians. The exact reasons for the British explorer's death remain unclear, but theft and attempted kidnapping were involved. Today, the spot is marked by a 27ft-high (8m) white obelisk, visible from across the bay or reached by a steep walk from a trailhead just off the Belt Rd; there's excellent snorkeling in the waters below the monument.

Continuing north, you reach Kailua-Kona, a good if commercial overnight option, where the road turns inland towards your last but one destination, Mauna Kea. This active volcano is the tallest mountain in the world if you measure its height from the seabed, from where it reaches 33,500ft (10,211m), making it almost 4500ft (1372m) higher than Everest. Debatable superlatives aside, Mauna Kea is an awesome sight, sacred to Hawaiians and crowned by international astronomical observatories which take advantage of the air's clarity (you're above 40% of the Earth's atmosphere) to gaze deep into space.

If you're in a 4WD then the summit and its unsurpassed views are yours for the taking (until 30 minutes after sunset at least). But for a less adventurous drive (the road to the top is wheel-clenchingly steep) and some stargazing of your own, check out the Visitor Information Station, accessible to any vehicle. From here it's a scenic 35 miles (56km) back to Hilo on Rte 200; just before town, pause at the Boiling Pots and Rainbow Falls for a final dose of Hawaiian natural wonder.

# CENTRAL USA

**Below:** bull elk in Yellowstone National Park
**Right:** mountain driving on the Beartooth Hwy

**Distance: 335 miles (539km)**

**Duration: 5-7 days**

# Billings to Idaho Falls via Yellowstone

**MONTANA & IDAHO**

Roadtrip by EV through a landscape of epic grandeur, where snowcapped peaks give way to explosive geysers and bubbling mudpots, and the wild terrain sustains elk, bison and bear.

A ring of sandstone cliffs surrounds chilled-out Billings, Montana's largest city and a magnet for hikers, bikers and climbers who disperse into the wild and return for its down-to-earth welcome and unpretentious style. Billings is known as "Montana's Trailhead," and 50 miles (80km) of trails start right here.

## THE BEARTOOTH TO YELLOWSTONE

Heading southwest, it's 63 miles (101km) to the historic town of Red Lodge at the base of the Beartooth Mountains. Recharge while you lunch at PREROGATIvE Kitchen, then take in some local art at the Carbon County Arts Guild. Back in your EV, the legendary Beartooth Hwy climbs steeply out of town, winding around hairpin bends in a glaciated valley. This 68-mile (109km) stunner is one of America's most beautiful drives, with plenty of pull-outs and short trails so you can stop and admire the views as you go. Rising above the tree line, the tundra opens up as you climb to Beartooth Pass at 10,947ft (3337m). Weaving down the far side, you'll come to a lake-littered plateau set against a backdrop of snow-clad peaks.

Cooke City, a former mining camp beloved by Ernest Hemingway, marks the end of the highway. Hemingway spent five summers here, declaring that the one-street

## Plan & prepare

### Tips for EV drivers

This route includes a lot of steep inclines that will strain your battery, though you'll make some of this energy up with regenerative braking on the descents. The terrain can make it hard to predict your range, so allow leeway in your calculations. Chargers are scattered regularly along this route, but often at hotels and motels – check ahead to see if they're available for non-guests to use.

### Where to stay

The Yodeler Motel (yodelermotel.com) in Red Lodge has Bavarian-themed decor, a good choice of rooms and a hot tub onsite. You'll find a similarly rustic vibe at the Three Bear Lodge (threebearlodge.com) in West Yellowstone, where reclaimed wood and dark colors combine in the spacious rooms. In Idaho Falls, the Residence Inn (marriott.com) has sleek, modern suites with full kitchens. All options have chargers onsite or nearby.

### When to go

The Beartooth Hwy usually opens in late May and stays open until early October. Check the National Park Service website (nps.gov) for up-to-date details. Expect lots of bikers enjoying the switchbacks in mid-July when they amass for the Beartooth Rally. In fall, the mountain forests put on a great show of color and the elk rut makes for extra-special wildlife viewing.

### Further info

Cell service can be patchy in places on this route, especially along the Beartooth Hwy and in remote settlements such as Cooke City. Bring or buy a paper map or download your route in advance to avoid problems. Winter temperatures persist along much of this route into May and June, and return by late September. Pack warm clothes and expect the possibility of snow, especially on high passes.

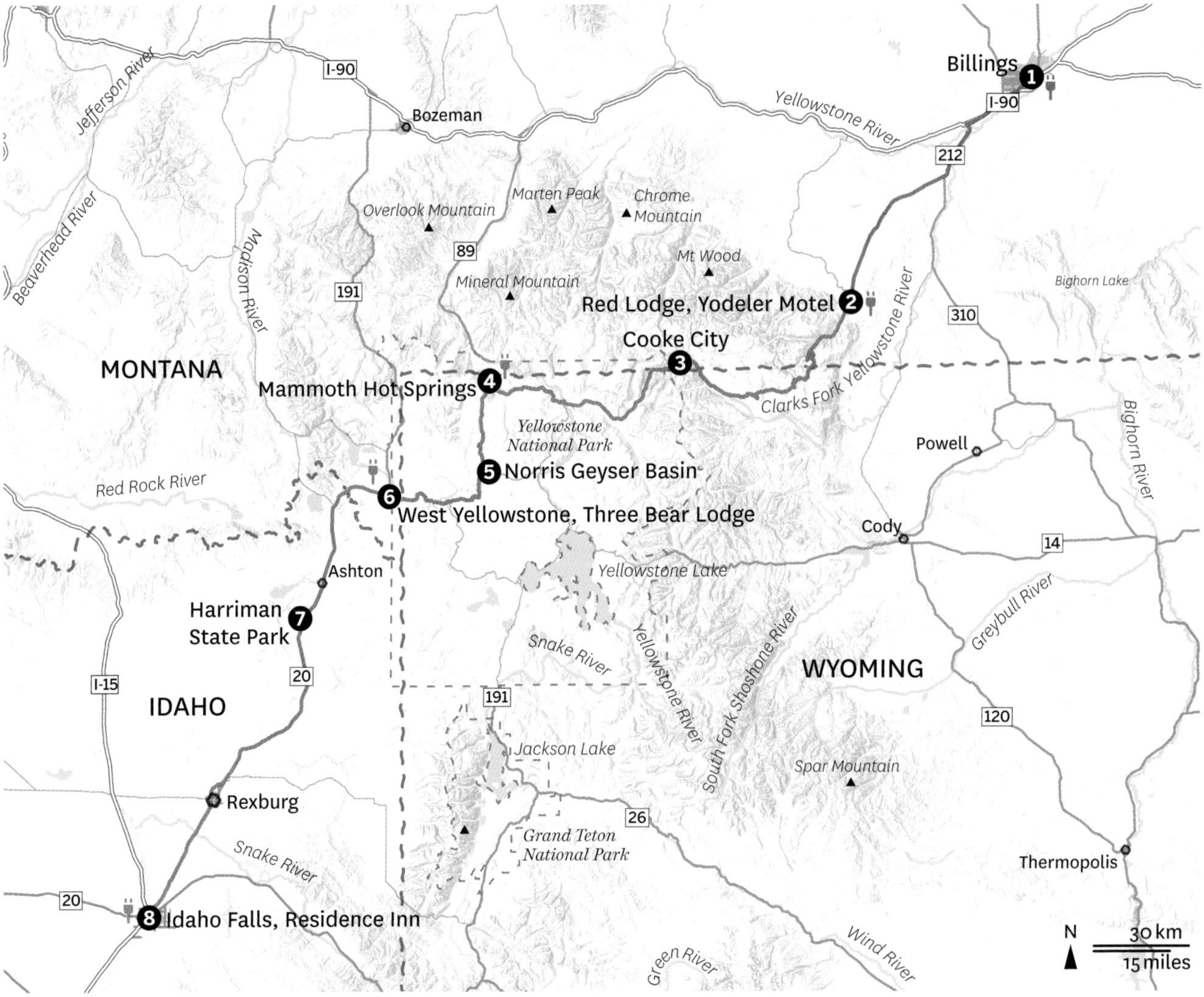

town rivaled Paris and Madrid as a location for his work. Take a peek at the Cooke City General Store, from where he sent off his manuscripts.

Just 4 miles (6km) on you'll enter Yellowstone National Park and the Lamar Valley, a region known as the "Serengeti of North America." Drive through late in the day and you're likely to spot bison, elk and possibly wolves, bears or coyotes. Pull into Mammoth to recharge the car and take the scenic loop around the ledges, pools and travertine terraces of the Mammoth Hot Springs. Like a giant, otherworldly fountain, hot water pours over these white- and pastel-colored geothermal shelves, depositing more dissolved limestone as it cools.

From Mammoth, it's a scenic 20-mile (32km) drive to Norris but it's worth stopping to walk the short trail to Sheepeater Cliffs, where hexagonal basalt columns are stacked like organ pipes. At Norris Geyser Basin, Steamboat – the world's tallest active geyser – is the big attraction. Spewing hot water 300ft (91m) into the air, it's just one of many geysers, fumaroles, hot springs and mudpots here, from Black Growler to Whale's Mouth.

## MADISON TO IDAHO FALLS

Look out for elk and bison as you drive 14 miles (23km) southwest to Madison Junction, stopping to see the bubbling mudpools at Artist Paintpots, and the scenic Gibbon Falls, before heading west and leaving the park at busy West Yellowstone. This regional hub offers guided tours, its own dude ranch and a rescue center for problem bears, so there's plenty to do, but you'll find quieter trails around Hebgen and Quake Lakes to the north.

Continuing south, it's 108 miles (174km) to Idaho Falls; en route, there's quiet hiking, biking or horseback riding at Harriman State Park, and chargers at Island Park, Ashton and Rexburg. Ririe's Heise Hot Springs makes a relaxing stop before arriving at your final stop, bustling Idaho Falls.

## Seismic super-show

Experiencing between 1500 and 2500 earthquakes a year, the national park's Yellowstone Supervolcano is one of the most seismically active in the United States. Most of these quakes are far too weak to be felt by humans, but every hiccup is recorded and analyzed by a sophisticated network of seismographs. One place you might feel the earth move is the Norris Geyser Basin, which sits at the intersection of three faults. Here, molten magma lies close to the Earth's surface, and ground motion is a common indicator of activity in Yellowstone's superheated plumbing system. The most devasting recent earthquake to hit the region was in August 1959 – 28 people were killed when 80 million tons of rock slid off one side of the Madison Valley – burying two campgrounds, setting off a 12-hour series of standing waves on Hebgen Lake, blocking Madison River and giving birth to Quake Lake. At the same time, several hundred of Yellowstone's thermal features simultaneously erupted, cars plunged into holes in the highway and hurricane-force winds ripped through the valley. To learn more about it, stop by West Yellowstone's Earthquake Lake Visitor Center.

**Clockwise from top left:** the Beartooth Mountains near Cooke City; Lone Star, one of Yellowstone's 500-plus geysers; Lamar Valley, Yellowstone National Park

**Below:** Yellowstone's Old Faithful in full flow
**Right:** bison grazing below the Grand Teton peaks

**Distance: 211 miles (340km)**

**Duration: 7 days**

# Mammoth to Jackson via Yellowstone & Grand Teton

**WYOMING**

Geysers, hot springs and bubbling mudpools, canyons, mountains and forests – all await on this star-studded drive by EV through a swathe of American wilderness where nature's grandeur reaches epic proportions.

Whether it's your first visit or your fiftieth, the raw, elemental landscapes, abundant wildlife and spectacular hiking of Yellowstone and Grand Teton never fail to impress. You could spend a lifetime here and still not explore it all, but Yellowstone's Mammoth Hot Springs is a suitably magnificent place to begin. Formed over some 100,000 years, the springs' pale travertine terraces are interlaced with shallow pools and dotted with bulbous outcrops. The hour-long walk around the Upper and Lower Terraces passes many of the 50 hot springs and the weird formations created by cooling limestone and mineral deposits.

Leaving Mammoth, head east to Tower Junction then south along a narrow, winding road that climbs 37 miles (60km) to Dunraven Pass and into Canyon Village, gateway to the Grand Canyon of the Yellowstone, a searing gash in the landscape pitted with thundering falls. Lookout Point on North Rim Dr gives clear views of the plunging Lower Falls; the South Rim's Artist Point overlooks sheer canyon walls lit up in rainbow hues.

## MUDPOTS & GEYSERS

Continuing south, your EV's relative silence emphasizes the majesty of the landscape as dense forest gives way to

## Plan & prepare

### Tips for EV drivers

Calculating battery range is an inexact science at the best of times, but factoring in the strain of steep inclines versus the benefits of regenerative braking combined with high-altitude driving makes it all the harder. Luckily, the parks are well set up for EV drivers and, with a speed limit of 45mph (72km/h) in most places, relatively kind on your battery. Charging is free, but with mostly Level 2 chargers, allow for a little extra time at stop-offs.

### Where to stay

Snag your accommodation well in advance (though some park service campgrounds don't take reservations, so you'll need to arrive early). Book online (via yellowstonenationalpark lodges.com) for Yellowstone's Old Faithful Lodge, with its newly renovated frontier cabins; and the comfortable Mammoth Hot Springs Hotel, with rooms and rustic cabins. Near Hayden Valley, lakeside Signal Mountain Lodge (signalmountainlodge. com) has cozy lodge rooms, cabins, bungalows and scenic camping. All offer EV charging.

### When to go

Most roads, campgrounds and visitor centers close from October to April, making May to September the time to visit. June to August is peak season: prices are at their highest and lodgings book out months in advance. The fall sees incredible color in Yellowstone and Grand Teton courtesy of the changing foliage; only 5% of visitors come to the parks in winter, when the only way to get around is by snow-coaches or on skis, but it's a magical time to visit.

### Further info

If you can, catch one of the free ranger-led activities or walks while in the national parks. They'll give you far greater insight into what it is you're looking at and experiencing, and the broad range of options include Junior Ranger and Young Scientist activities. Alternatively, download the National Park Service app for interactive maps, geyser predictions, self-guided tours and suggestions for things to do. Parking at popular trailheads often fills up by 10am, so plan to arrive early.

## Mighty microbes

With over 10,000 active thermal features, Yellowstone is at the forefront of research into thermophiles (heat-loving microbes). These microorganisms were first discovered in the park's boiling waters, and are responsible for the bright colors seen around Grand Prismatic Spring, Clepsydra Geyser, Firehole Spring and on Mammoth's terraces. The discovery of thermophiles has had a huge impact on scientific history, most notably in the 1966 identification of *Thermus aquaticus*. A unique enzyme later isolated from this thermophile proved crucial to the invention of the Polymerase Chain Reaction (PCR) process for rapidly replicating DNA. Still the most common process used for DNA sequencing, it is crucial to forensic investigations and to the diagnosis and treatment of serious diseases. Another microorganism found in the Hayden Valley is thought to hold key information about the origin and evolution of life on Earth, and NASA is studying cyanobacteria found in Yellowstone in an attempt to match it to similar activity on Mars. Researchers believe they have identified only 1% of the species in the park's most extreme environments – and suggest that those yet to be discovered may hold answers to many of life's biggest questions.

**Clockwise from top left:** Mammoth Hot Springs; en route to Jackson in the shadow of the Tetons; marvelous microbes at Grand Prismatic Spring

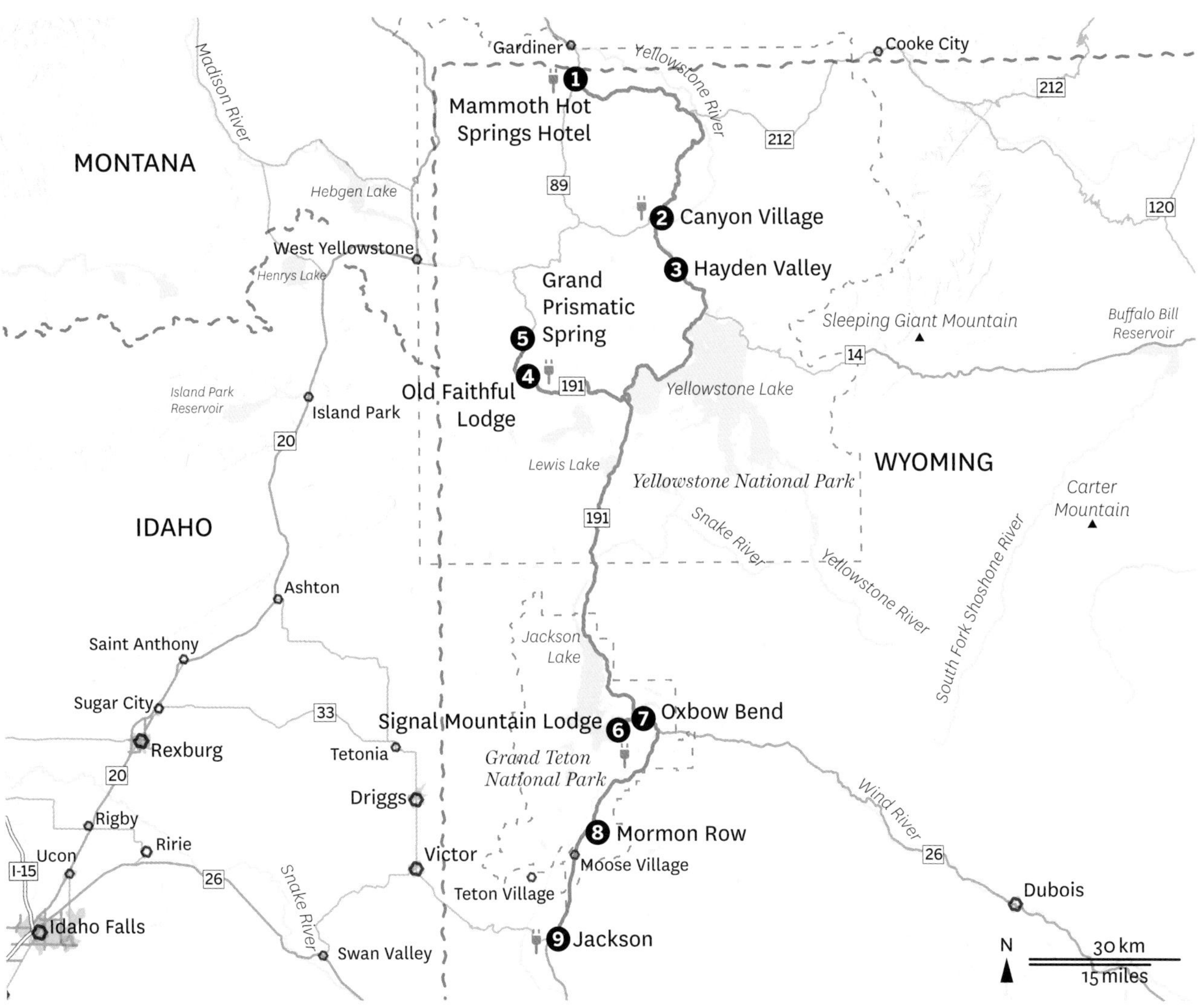


the lush Hayden Valley, where bear, bison and elk roam. Mudpots and sulfur pits line the road at Mud Volcano before you sweep along Yellowstone Lake to the geysers and pools at West Thumb. From here it's 19 miles (30km) to the park's most famous attraction, Old Faithful.

Leave the car to charge and pop into the visitor center to check eruption times. Shooting water up to 180ft (55m) into the air roughly every 90 minutes, Old Faithful may make you wait, but use the time to meander up Observation Hill for an overview of the basin and loop back by Solitary Geyser, which lets rip every four to eight minutes.

It's only 7 miles (11km) further on to Yellowstone's poster child, the Grand Prismatic Spring, where turquoise water is surrounded by rings of yellow, orange and green microbial mats. Walk the Overlook Trail for a bird's-eye view, get up close on the boardwalk then hike the surrounding trails to lose the crowds.

## GRAND TETON PEAKS

Back on the road, double back to Yellowstone Lake and south into Grand Teton National Park. Stop at Oxbow Bend to see snowcapped peaks reflected in the winding Snake River or continue to Mormon Row, 20 miles (32km) south, to see a collection of picturesque old homesteads and barns set against the sculpted peaks of the Tetons.

It's a short drive south to Moose Village, where you can rent canoes and stand-up paddleboards to explore String and Leigh Lakes; get a permit and you can also paddle to a backcountry campsite with spectacular Grand Teton views. If you'd prefer to get out on foot, rugged and rewarding Cascade Canyon Trail promises lakes, falls and frequent wildlife sightings.

From Moose, it's just a 13-mile (21km) drive south to Jackson, an outdoor adventure center and hip hangout with galleries, boutiques and an ever-impressive range of restaurants lining the streets.

**Below:** downtown Vail under a dusting of snow **Right:** driving the Top of the Rockies Byway along Hwy 82 near Independence Pass

**Distance: 115 miles (185km)**

**Duration: 2-3 days**

# Vail to Aspen on the Top of the Rockies Byway

**COLORADO**

Colorado's tallest peaks, a pair of mountain passes and two mining-era ghost towns make for a natural Rocky Mountains high on this EV-accessible route that's bookended by legendary ski towns.

A meandering scenic byway through the high country links two of Colorado's most prestigious Rocky Mountain resort towns, Vail and Aspen. The route cuts ledges into stone cliffs, threads through mountain passes, edges alpine lakes and offers stunning views of some of the highest peaks in the US, known as "fourteeners" for their height over 14,000ft (4267m). EV charging is a risky gambit in most mountain regions, but in a bid to decarbonize its state power grid, Colorado has stationed chargers no more than 50 miles (80km) apart along key routes – including the Top of the Rockies Byway.

## MOUNTAIN PANORAMAS

The history of flower-box-trimmed, pedestrian-friendly Vail is tied to that of the 10th Mountain Division, an elite WWII infantry unit that trained in the peaks near here. After the war, the soldiers came back home and, inspired by the resorts of the European Alps, established ski villages such as Vail in their image.

Just west of Vail, from the laid-back former railroad town of Minturn, the Top of the Rockies Byway heads south into the mountains. Originally built to haul out silver and gold mined in the Rockies during the 19th

## Plan & prepare

### Tips for EV drivers

Mountain driving can play havoc on electric batteries, which lose power quickly on uphills but replenish via regenerative braking on downhills. The Colorado Department of Transportation has helped to ease range anxiety by installing charging stations regularly along the Top of the Rockies Scenic Byway. You'll find fast chargers in Vail and Aspen, with slower ones between designed to encourage motorists to take a break in tourist-friendly towns like Leadville.

### Where to stay

In Vail, park your car at the EV chargers in the public garage – which get primo placement – across the street from Gravity Haus Vail (gravityhaus.com), a modern mountain lodge in walking distance of village attractions. Mid-drive, at Buena Vista, check into the Surf Hotel (surfhotel.com), above the rapids of the Buena Vista Whitewater Park, to watch paddlers or take a dip; there are chargers onsite. In Aspen, recharge overnight at the Hotel Jerome (aubergeresorts.com/hoteljerome), an 1889 landmark turned luxury hotel.

### When to go

Winter driving at these elevations is tough on both EV batteries and drivers, due to wet, snowy and slippery conditions. Many high-altitude roads in Colorado close in winter, including Hwy 82 around Independence Pass, making the full Top of the Rockies route impassable between early November and late May. Summer is a great time to catch wildflowers and rivers gushing with snowmelt. By September, the aspens at high elevations are beginning to turn golden: leaf-peeping tours are popular here throughout October.

### Further info

Reserve an EV at one of the airports at either end of this itinerary, including Eagle County Regional Airport, which services Vail, and Aspen/Pitkin County Airport. Driving in the Rocky Mountain region may be subject to road closures due to excessive snow, avalanches or rock slides. For road conditions and travel alerts, check the transportation department's website COtrip (cotrip.org). Be prepared to share this scenic road with cyclists.

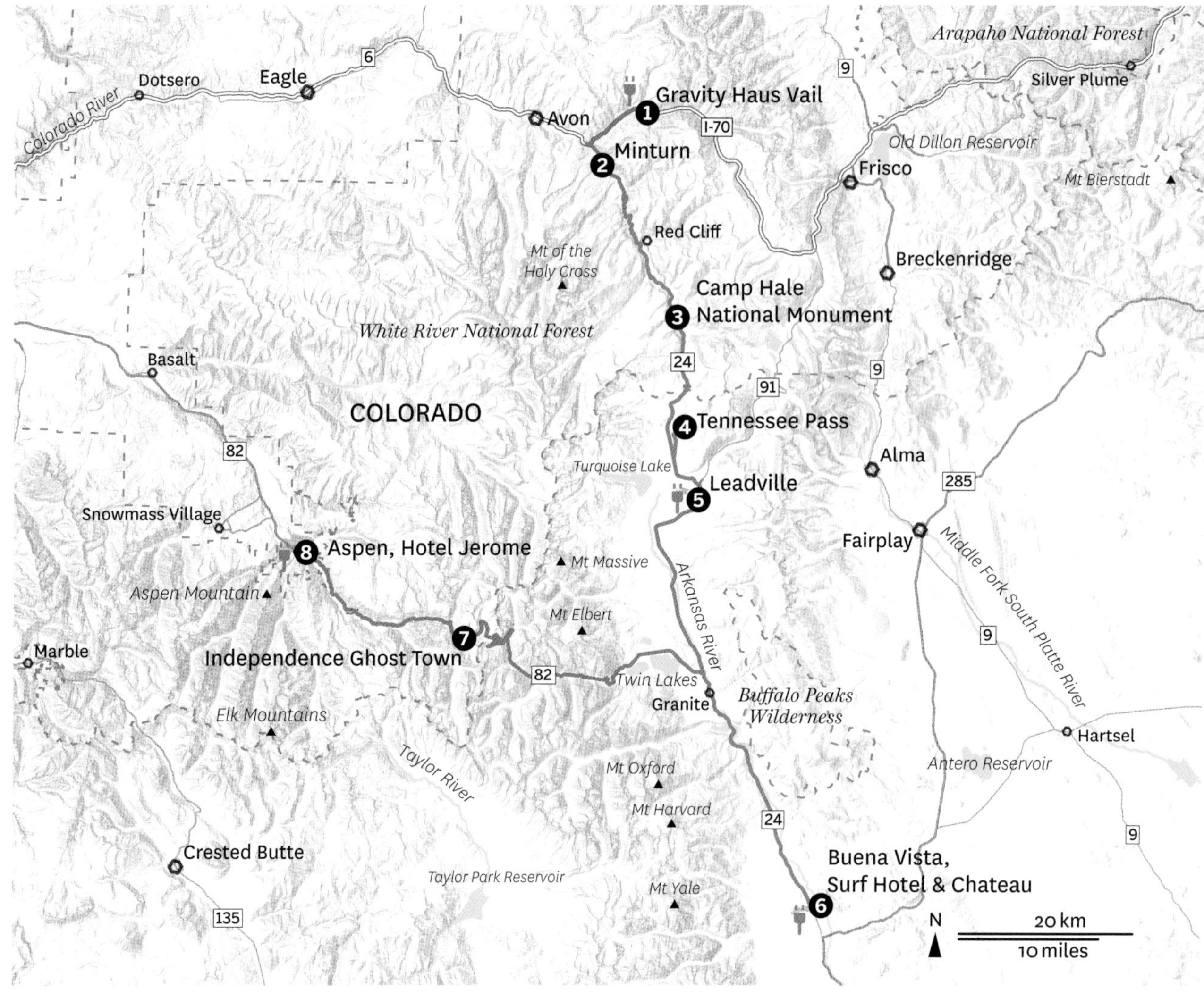


century, this engineering feat of a road weaves toward Red Cliff and its dramatic truss bridge, vaulting the Eagle River far below. A short way south, a roadside turnoff gives access to Camp Hale National Monument, former training ground of the 10th Mountain Division, its ruined barracks now colonized by wildflowers and birds.

Moving on, park at Tennessee Pass to breathe in the rare air at 10,424ft (3177m). Not more than 10 minutes' drive further, you'll reach Leadville, which boomed around 1880 when miners struck silver and the population peaked at 30,000. Today, just 3000 or so residents remain in the spiffed-up Victorian village that includes an opera house, museums and a tourable mine, along with gift shops and roadhouses catering to the many roadtrippers who pass through. Continue another half-hour south to the charming village of Buena Vista, set on the Arkansas River and popular with rafters, to overnight at the waterside Surf Hotel.

## THE SLOW ROAD TO ASPEN

The next morning, backtrack 18 miles (29km) to Granite; just beyond here, the Top of the Rockies turns westbound onto Hwy 82 at Twin Lakes, backdropped by impressive Mt Elbert, the state's tallest peak at 14,440ft (4401m). With a battery fully charged overnight, make the 3000ft (914m) ascent to Independence Pass, sitting at 12,095ft (3686m) on the Continental Divide. Views here are compelling and even in summer you're likely to see some snow or ice on the ponds, amid meadows filled with wildflowers.

From here, the road drops 20 miles (32km) into Aspen, but take it slow – not just for the hairpin turns and distracting views, but to stop for hiking and picnicking in the Lost Man Wilderness, to see the ghost town of Independence and its aging rustic wood cabins, and to cool off in the Grottos, where the Roaring Fork River carves through stone. Decelerate in tony Aspen, where ski bums rub elbows with the ultra-wealthy and EVs abound.

## The Bauhaus in Aspen

Aspen wasn't always Teslas and furs – its prestige also has roots in high culture. Originally the summer hunting grounds of the Indigenous Ute people, Aspen exploded in 1870 with a silver strike that attracted 12,000 miners and their kin and inspired the construction of redbrick Victorian buildings here, including the Hotel Jerome and the Wheeler Opera House. But the mine soon played out and Aspen went bust until the late 1940s, when Chicagoans Walter and Elizabeth Paepcke visited. They envisioned its future as a gathering place for artists, musicians, thinkers and leaders who would be inspired by the mountain-ringed setting, a vision that would become today's Aspen Institute. With this utopian plan, they recruited Herbert Bayer, an Austrian-born artist and graphic designer who taught in the prestigious Bauhaus in Germany. Bayer, a skier, fell in love with Aspen, remodeling the opera house, hotel and crumbling Victorian houses, often accenting them in primary colors associated with the Bauhaus. Visitors today can see his work in the logo of the local ski company, and at the campus of the Aspen Institute and the Resnick Center for Herbert Bayer Studies, which stages exhibitions devoted to his wide-ranging talents.

**Clockwise from top left:** climbing Mt Elbert, Colorado's highest "fourteener"; Wheeler Opera House, Aspen; summer wildflowers in bloom

**Below:** dried red chiles for sale, Santa Fe
**Right:** hiking the gypsum dunes at White Sands National Park

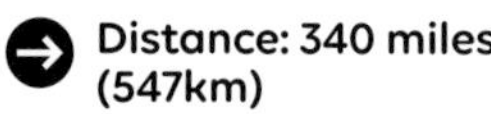
Distance: 340 miles (547km)

Duration: 7 days

# Santa Fe to White Sands on the I-25

**NEW MEXICO**

Bisecting the state from north to south, I-25 lines up New Mexico's greatest hits for easy EV access, from one of the country's oldest cities to a surreal national park.

Prepare to fall under the spell of the "Land of Enchantment." New Mexico is bewitching in every sense, so kick off this journey through time and space in state capital Santa Fe. Established in 1610 as a regional capital of New Spain, Santa Fe was a hub of culture and commerce long before the United States even existed. The city radiates out from the Plaza, end point of the Camino Real from Mexico and the Santa Fe Trail from Missouri. Leave your EV charging at La Fonda hotel's parking garages or near Sandoval St or San Francisco St, then stroll the sociable square, which often has street performers, food vendors and jewelry sellers.

It's a quick walk from here to the Georgia O'Keeffe Museum, dedicated to the works of this 20th-century artist (who lived in nearby Abiquiú), or the many galleries on Canyon Rd. One of the city's hottest arts tickets is Meow Wolf, in an old bowling alley donated by *Game of Thrones* author George RR Martin. This immersive installation is part escape room, part murder mystery, part drug-free psychedelic trip – its 70-plus rooms feel like portals into another realm.

## ON TO ALBUQUERQUE

Unless you're headed to the Bandelier or Fort Union

## Plan & prepare

### Tips for EV drivers

Unlike in some parts of the country, EV chargers in New Mexico pop up in a wide variety of locations, from accommodations and gas stations to grocery stores and restaurants, meaning EV drivers have more freedom and flexibility for a road trip around the state. In rural areas away from the highways, however, RV parks are often the only option, so call ahead of time to find out whether they allow EV charging for non-guests.

### Where to stay

There are ample accommodations along I-25, but a handful of historic digs tell New Mexico's story. In Santa Fe's central plaza, and with onsite chargers, La Fonda (lafondasantafe.com) has a 400-year history and is known as the "Inn at the end of the Santa Fe Trail." Built in 1937, Albuquerque's revamped El Vado (elvadoabq.com) lies on a newer but equally famous trail, Route 66; there are chargers nearby. In Truth or Consequences, the Holiday Inn Express (ihg.com) has Tesla Superchargers.

### When to go

New Mexico shows off its best side in spring and fall, which bring balmy weather and a burst of wildflowers. Summer is the prime time for outdoor activities, but be aware that monsoon storms (June to September) can leave you drenched in the afternoon downpours. To taste the best of the state's traditional flavors, time your visit for August or September to sample freshly harvested green chiles.

### Further info

Like other states, New Mexico is building out its EV charging network, and it's installing only Level 3 chargers, the fastest available, which can fully fill batteries in 30 to 45 minutes. State authorities are aiming to construct 20 stations along New Mexico's three interstates, to meet the National Electric Vehicle Infrastructure goals set out by the federal government, and plan to direct any remaining funding to more rural areas.

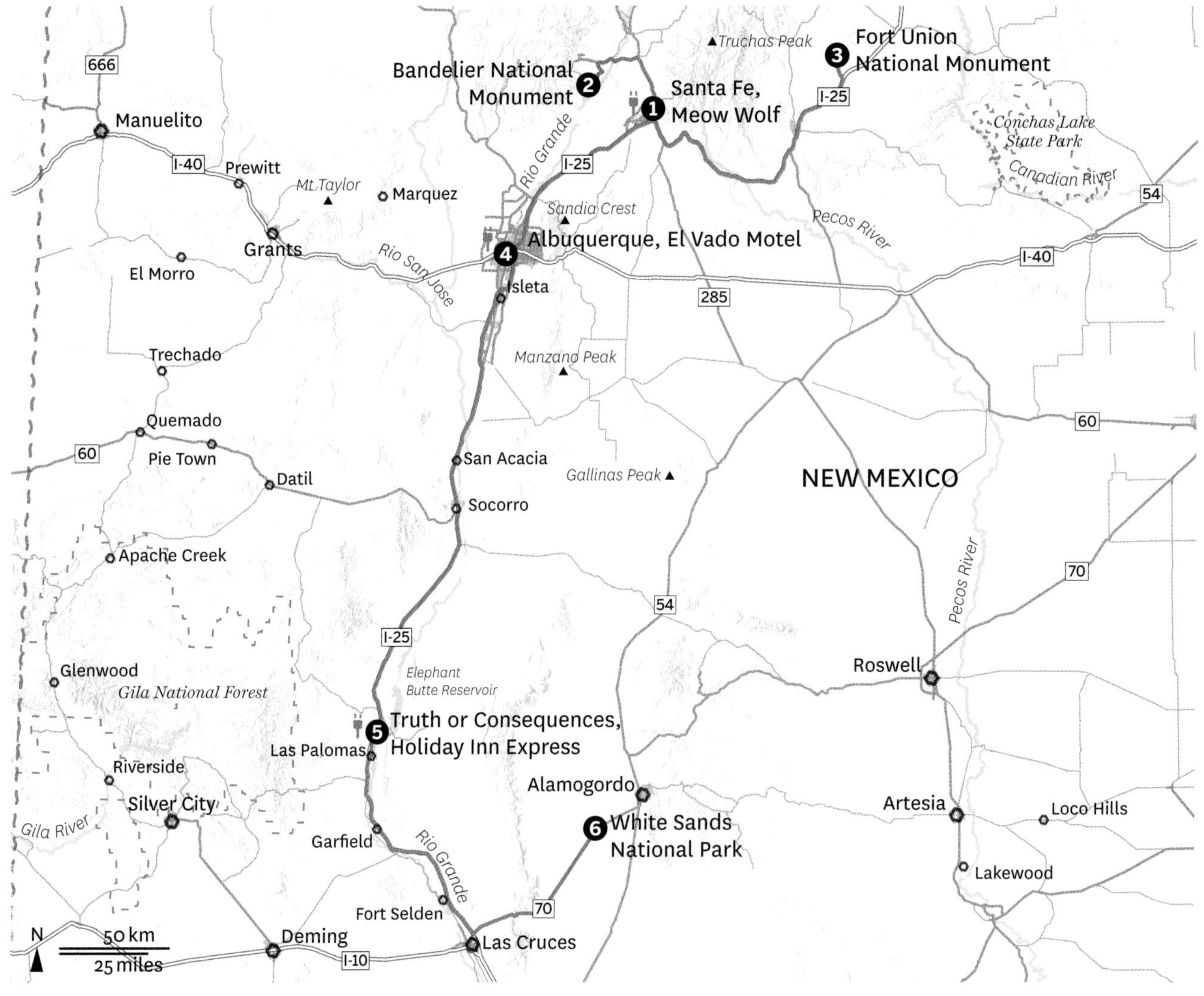


National Monuments (see opposite), depart Santa Fe via the I-25 for the 64-mile (103km) drive to Albuquerque. While it might not have the cultural swagger of the capital, New Mexico's biggest city has plenty to distract, and it's an excellent place to taste-test the state's traditional flavors. Snag a seat at Duran's Pharmacy, which does still dispense medication as it has since 1942, but also hot-buttered fresh tortillas and its famous red or green chile sauce, which comes atop nearly everything on the menu. Bow & Arrow Brewing Co was started by two Native women and pours excellent beers in its industrial space. Chain hotels around downtown ABQ, including Best Western, Econo Lodge and Hilton Garden Inn, have chargers.

## THE TRUTH IS OUT THERE

Fully charged, point your EV south again for the 150-mile (241km) leg to the town of Truth or Consequences, stopping after 76 miles (122km) in Socorro's historic plaza for a top up if needed. Certainly one of the US' most curiously named towns, Truth or Consequences has an enviable location hugged by the Rio Grande, though its former name of Hot Springs provides a better description of its appeal. (It changed its name as part of an NBC radio contest in the 1950s.) Riverbend Hot Springs has supremely relaxing hot tubs at the river's edge, and accommodations decorated by local artists; the Holiday Inn Express is equipped with Tesla Superchargers.

The final out-of-this-world stop is White Sands National Park, 125 miles (201km) from Truth or Consequences. If you need to charge, pull off at Las Cruces, which has options around downtown. New Mexico's newest national park – designated in 2019 – is filled with snow-white sand dunes that roll like waves to the distant Sacramento and San Andres Mountains. Wrapping up this trip by kicking off your shoes and walking through the powdered gypsum crystals at sunrise or sunset is pure magic.

## Two national monuments

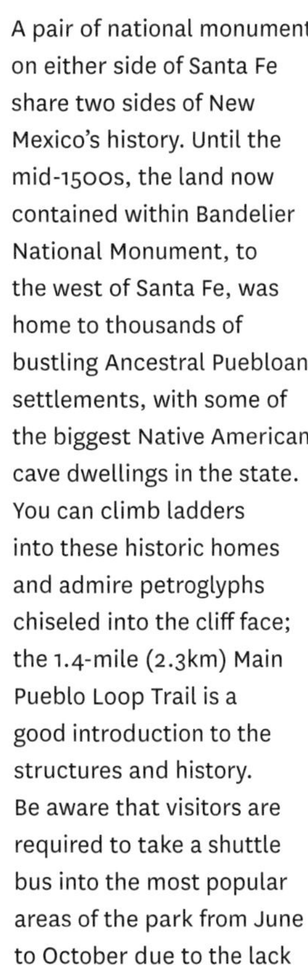

A pair of national monuments on either side of Santa Fe share two sides of New Mexico's history. Until the mid-1500s, the land now contained within Bandelier National Monument, to the west of Santa Fe, was home to thousands of bustling Ancestral Puebloan settlements, with some of the biggest Native American cave dwellings in the state. You can climb ladders into these historic homes and admire petroglyphs chiseled into the cliff face; the 1.4-mile (2.3km) Main Pueblo Loop Trail is a good introduction to the structures and history. Be aware that visitors are required to take a shuttle bus into the most popular areas of the park from June to October due to the lack of parking spaces. On I-25 east of Santa Fe, Fort Union National Monument might seem quiet now, but this dusty, windblown outpost was once the largest military fort between California and Kansas, built in the 1850s to protect the stream of covered wagons on the Santa Fe Trail and to continue the takeover of Native lands and food supplies. A trail circles the remnants of the captain's quarters, the prison and a central grassland strewn with wagon wheels and axles.

**Clockwise from top left:** adobe style at the New Mexico Museum of Art, off Santa Fe's Plaza; Bandelier National Monument; White Sands National Park

**Below:** Rapid City's Firehouse Brewing
**Right:** Spearfish Canyon Scenic Byway

- **Distance: 182 miles (293km)**
- **Duration: 3-4 days**

# The Black Hills: Rapid City to Mt Rushmore

**SOUTH DAKOTA**

The Black Hills' scenic backroads link chiseled canyons and peaks with Gold Rush–era towns, glittering cave systems, bison-grazed grasslands, dramatic rock formations and the monumental carvings at Mt Rushmore.

Sacred to the Lakota Sioux, the Black Hills are named for the darkness of the ponderosa pines that grow between their sun-bleached granite outcrops. They're a stark sight lording over the grassy plains below, and the winding roads to scenic overlooks and wildlife-rich valleys are perfect for exploring by EV.

Regional hub Rapid City is a lively, cosmopolitan place where statues of former presidents adorn many street corners. Pick up a self-guided walking tour at the visitor center and bone up on local landscapes at the Museum of Geology before hitting the road. Head northwest for 28 miles (45km) to Sturgis, for a slice of motorcycle history and a (beef) knuckle sandwich at the Knuckle Saloon and Brewing Company. Filled with biker bars, tattoo parlors and leather stores, Sturgis hosts one of the world's largest annual motorcycle events each August.

At Spearfish, further west, the history of the region's Native Americans and pioneer settlers is explored at the High Plains Western Heritage Center, a good stop before driving south on the glorious Spearfish Canyon Scenic Byway, a meandering route that climbs up into the hills past towering cliffs and gushing waterfalls; get sweeping views of the steep-sided canyon itself by walking the short but challenging 76 Trail.

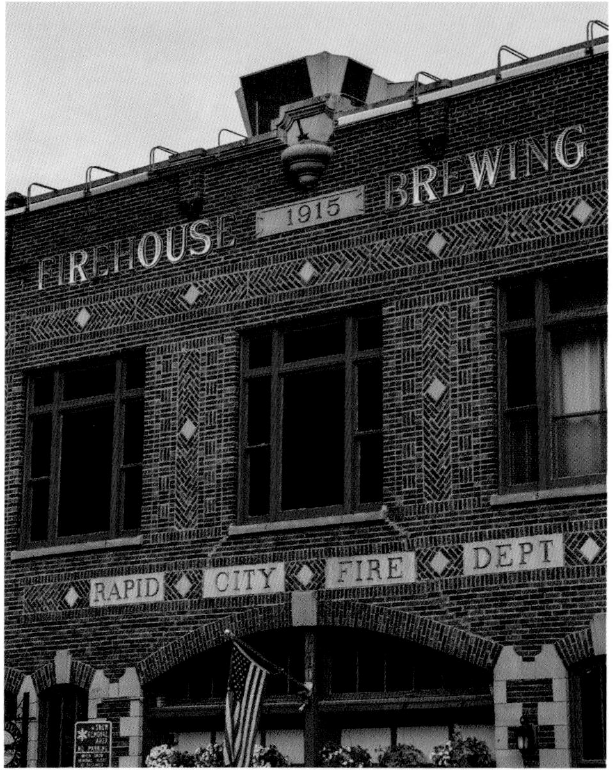

## Plan & prepare

### Tips for EV drivers

Although there are plenty of chargers available along this route, not all are fast chargers and many are at hotels and motels, some of which are reserved for patrons only; check ahead and plan accordingly. Be prepared for journeys to take far longer than you expect as the lure of scenic pull-outs and the speed of ambling RVs can slow you right down. You may also encounter mountain goats or deer crossing the roads, so take your time.

### Where to stay

Stay overnight at the Rushmore Hotel (therushmorehotel.com) in Rapid City, a high-rise offering large, modern rooms with contemporary styling and a nod to green living. In Custer, the Rock Crest Lodge & Cabins (rockcrestlodge.com) is more traditional, with rustic rooms and cozy log cabins with a shared pool, while the Lodge at Deadwood (deadwoodlodge.com) has spacious, comfortable rooms and its own casino. All have onsite chargers.

### When to go

May to September is the best time to visit, but arrive early or late in the season for quieter roads and the most pleasant temperatures. The hugely popular Volksmarch organized hike up to the Crazy Horse Memorial takes place in June and September/October each year, while the roads are packed with bikers during the first week of August for the Sturgis Motorcycle Rally. Late September sees brilliant fall foliage and the Custer State Park Buffalo Roundup and Arts Festival.

### Further info

It's possible to tag on a side-trip to Badlands National Park, with an Electrify America charging station in Wall about 50 miles (80km) east of Rapid City on I-90. From here, take the Badlands Loop State Scenic Byway to drive past the park's most dramatic rock formations, jagged spires and corrugated buttes. Give yourself plenty of time to stop and admire the gorgeous views, and to get out on foot to see the crumbling rocks up close.

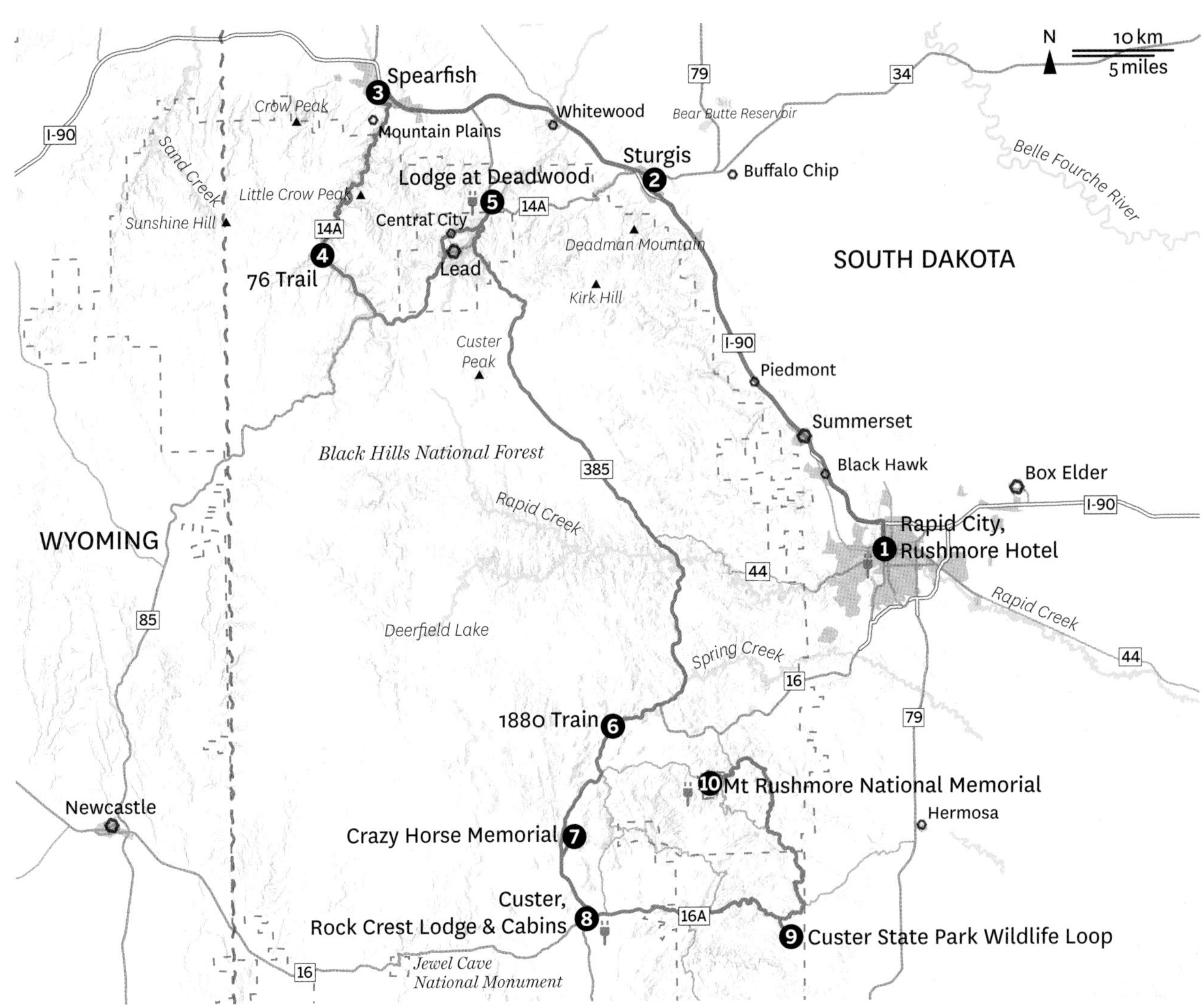


## DEADWOOD TO CRAZY HORSE

Beyond the byway, continue northeast for 17 miles (27km) to Deadwood, location of the eponymous HBO series and the epitome of lawlessness in the 1870s. Leave your EV to charge and wander the restored gambling halls, Gold Rush–era buildings and the Mt Moriah Cemetery, where Calamity Jane was laid to rest.

You'll pass through a patchwork of lakes, rivers and meadows on the 42-mile (68km) drive south to Hill City, from where you can delve into the Black Hills backcountry aboard the 1880 Train, a classic steam loco that once serviced local mines and mills. Then continue south to the Crazy Horse Memorial, a mammoth rock carving of the Sioux leader, under construction since 1948 and set to be one of the tallest sculptures in the world once completed.

## CUSTER TO MT RUSHMORE

From a base in Custer, 7 miles (11km) south, visit the crystal-encrusted walls of Jewel Cave National Monument; and Wind Cave National Park, its cavern adorned with thin blades of honeycomb-like calcite. Above ground, the big draw is Custer State Park. The 18-mile (29km) Wildlife Loop Rd offers good chances of spotting the park's 1400 free-roaming bison, plus deer, elk and big horn sheep, while to the north, strikingly spiky granite formations flank the aptly-named Needles Hwy.

Finish your trip with a thriller of a drive along Iron Mountain Rd, where hairpin bends and corkscrew loops combine with narrow tunnels, teasing glimpses of Mt Rushmore and panoramic views. As the giant heads of George Washington, Thomas Jefferson, Theodore Roosevelt and Abraham Lincoln loom closer you'll begin to understand the sheer scale of Gutzon Borglum's super-sized lifework; the engaging Sculptor's Studio gives the lowdown on their creation. Mt Rushmore is understandably popular: arrive early or visit midweek.

## A broken treaty

For the Lakota Sioux, the Black Hills are sacred. A place of origin, prayer, food and medicine, they are the heart of everything. The Lakota fought fiercely to defend the hills and eventually secured them as a permanent home via the 1868 Treaty of Fort Laramie. Six years later, gold was discovered and the federal government forced the Sioux to surrender the land. Crazy Horse and Sitting Bull retaliated by killing George A Custer and 265 of his men at the Battle of the Little Bighorn in 1876. Since then, the Lakota have fought for the return of the hills, and a long-running legal battle – first started in the 1920s – culminated in a 1980 Supreme Court ruling awarding financial compensation of $105 million for the stolen land. The Lakota refused it and instead advocate for the Black Hills to be returned to their stewardship. With mounting public pressure and the appointment of Deb Haaland – the first Native American to hold a US cabinet position – as Secretary of the Interior in 2021, followed by a meeting with local tribal leaders in January 2022, hopes are high for a new chapter in Black Hills history.

**Clockwise from top left:** ride the historic 1880 Train from Hill City; Spearfish Canyon's Bridal Veil Falls, in the northern Black Hills; Mt Rushmore

**Below:** bull bison, Tallgrass Prairie National Preserve
**Right:** driving west through Kansas on I-70

**Distance: 450 miles (724km)**

**Duration: 2-3 days**

# East on the I-70 from Kansas City

**KANSAS**

Whoosh by amber waves of grain and intriguingly offbeat towns along I-70 through Kansas. Mind-boggling scenery might be lacking, but the Heartland delivers super state parks and quirky, soul-stirring stops.

Kansas might be smack-dab in the middle of the country, but the interstate started here: the I-70 west of state capital Topeka contains the first segment of completed road in the US interstate system. Today, I-70 is essentially a straight shot across Kansas – but not so fast. While your EV charges, you can fuel up on culture, art and live music here, visit near-empty but nationally important historic sites, and get out into the iconic landscapes.

## KANSAS CITY TO LAWRENCE

With world-class museums, a thriving live-music scene and more than 100 barbecue restaurants smoking it up, Kansas City is split between two states (Kansas and Missouri) and makes a perfect starting point for a road trip west – it was once a stop on the historic Oregon, California and Santa Fe wagon trails. Admire the impressive collection of globe-spanning works at Nelson-Atkins Museum of Art (which has EV chargers in its parking garage) and dive into history at the National WWI Museum, the country's congressionally designated memorial to the Great War.

Two miles (3km) northeast is 18th and Vine, a historic Black neighborhood considered one of the birthplaces of jazz. Grab a beer at Vine Street Brewing, which opened

© Arina P. Habich/Shutterstock

## Plan & prepare

### Tips for EV drivers

Though a $4 billion EV battery manufacturing plant is set to open between Kansas City and Lawrence, Kansas' EV infrastructure lags behind other states'. However, the Department of Transportation is pumping nearly $40 million into constructing EV charging corridors, which will bring fast-charging stations to 1600 miles (2575km) of highways, including along I-70. In Kansas City, the only Tesla Superchargers are at suburban grocery stores, but the city council has been piloting a program of curbside chargers that plug into streetlights.

### Where to stay

Chain hotels and motels crop up in towns of all sizes along the interstate, and are often the only options for overnight stays with EV chargers. If you're happy to charge a short distance away, seek out B&Bs with more personality, which are often in ornate homes; good choices include the Truitt in Kansas City (thetruitt.com), Woodward Inns on Fillmore in Topeka (thewoodward.com), and Abilene's Victorian Inn Bed & Breakfast in Abilene (abilenesvictorianinn.com).

### When to go

Spring and fall are the best times to take this road trip, but be weather-aware in spring and summer when huge thunderstorms barrel across the Plains and tornadoes can descend from the sky with little warning; check weather.gov to see what's forecast. The scorching sun and stifling humidity make time outdoors miserable at the height of summer and will leave you scurrying for the air-con, while winter blizzards can close the interstate, sometimes for several days.

### Further info

The section of I-70 between Kansas City and Topeka is tolled. For cheaper tolls and to be able to drive 70mph (113km/h) under electronic readers instead of having to stop at the booths, request a free K-TAG online before your trip (via myktag.com), which will be mailed to you. Payment tags from some other US states, such as Best Pass, Pikepass, EZ-Tag and SunPass, can also be used on the Kansas Turnpike.

## Preserving the prairie

Prairie once covered more than 30% of North America – some 265,625 sq miles (687,966 sq km) – but thanks to agriculture and urban development, only a tiny sliver remains, mostly in Kansas' Flint Hills. Run by the National Park Service (nps.gov), the Tallgrass Prairie National Preserve protects one of the last stands of this ecosystem, a landscape that's symbolic of the USA's center. Walking trails meander along rolling hills – including through a pasture where reintroduced bison roam – as well as to the Lower Fox Creek Schoolhouse, a one-room limestone building that drew in students from 1882 to 1930. Near the visitor center, an impressive 1881 ranch house seems surprisingly sophisticated for its remote location, built in Second Empire style with a mansard roof and grand walnut staircase. The Tallgrass Prairie Preserve is about 65 miles (105km) south of I-70 via Hwy 99. From the town of Council Grove, where the Santa Fe Trail became Main St, follow the Flint Hills National Scenic Byway, where grasses and wildflowers wave you on through the landscape that looks much as it did when the Kaw, Osage, Pawnee and Wichita Native people called it home.

**Clockwise from top left:** Kansas State Capitol, Topeka; Tallgrass Prairie National Preserve; charge up in Kansas City and points all along I-70

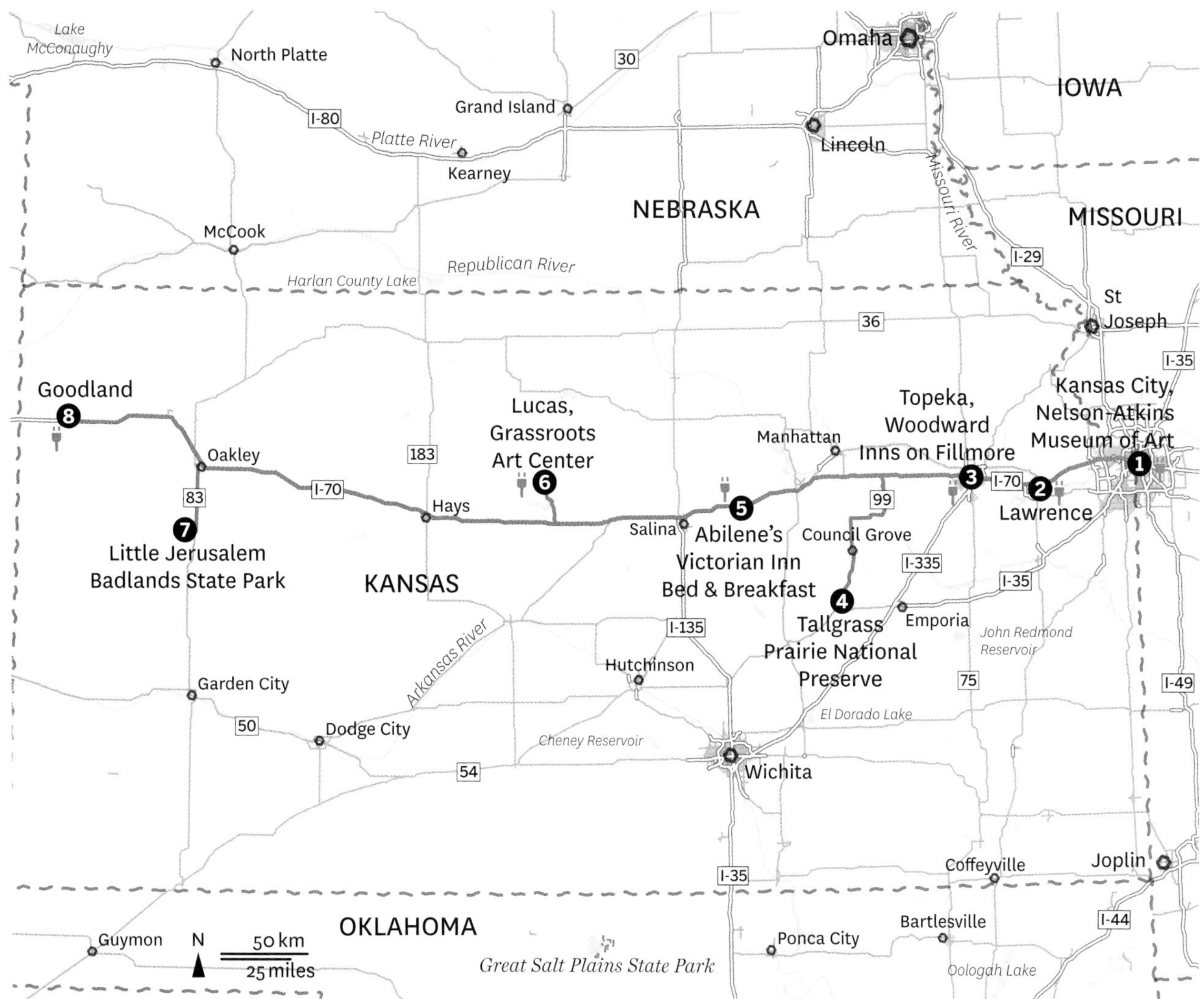


as Missouri's first Black-owned brewery in 2023, and stay up late for live music: try the Blue Room, a performance space at the American Jazz Museum; or the Mutual Musicians Foundation, a former union hall for Black musicians that doesn't even open until midnight or later, when the players finish their gigs elsewhere.

Next morning, hit I-70 and drive your EV 40 miles (64km) west to Lawrence, stopping at the Lawrence Service Area (mile marker 209) charging station if needed. A charming college town with attitude, Lawrence has been an island of progressive ideals since its founding in 1854 by east-coast abolitionists as the Civil War loomed. Park your EV at the lot on New Hampshire St, between 7th and 8th streets, to charge while you stroll Mass (Massachusetts St), lined with historic buildings and boutiques, bars and restaurants that punch well above their weight for a town of this size. College kids attending the University of Kansas or Haskell Indian Nations University make up nearly a third of Lawrence's population, and the strong student scene brings in tons of live shows, best enjoyed at Liberty Hall – a cultural hub for more than a century – and the Bottleneck.

## THE KANSAS CAPITAL

Just 25 miles (40km) of I-70 lie between Lawrence and Topeka, the state capital – you'll find another charging station at the Topeka Service Area (mile marker 188), the last one directly on the interstate for the route's duration. Leave your EV charging at one of the spots near 8th and Kansas Ave while you tour the State Capitol – you can even climb 296 steps into the huge copper dome. Don't miss *Tragic Prelude*, a mural of abolitionist John Brown, who fought to keep Kansas from becoming a slave state: he holds a rifle in one hand and a Bible in the other.

One mile (1.6km) south is the Brown v. Board of Education National Historic Site, set in the old Monroe

## Little Jerusalem Badlands SP

Kansas has the highest percentage of privately owned land in the country, so it's nothing short of a miracle when a new park gets added to the state's roster. Unveiled in 2019, Little Jerusalem Badlands State Park (ksoutdoors.com) might make you think you're not in Kansas anymore – 100ft-high (30m) columns and cliffs of Niobrara Chalk rise from the otherwise horizontal plains like magnificent towers. A vast inland sea once covered much of Kansas and deposited this sediment 80 million years ago; the ocean is far away today, but you can still spot well-preserved fossils of ancient sea critters in the formations. Two short hiking trails give a high-level view into the depths. To reach the park, exit I-70 at the town of Oakley and drive south for about 25 miles (40km) on Hwy 83. The park charges a day-use fee of $5.

**From far left:** chalk columns in Little Jerusalem Badlands State Park; Tallgrass Prairie National Preserve; offbeat art at Lucas' Garden of Eden

Elementary, one of four formerly segregated Black schools. The children of 13 Black families from Topeka were denied enrollment at white schools, and the case reached the Supreme Court, which made a landmark ruling in 1954 that "separate but equal" facilities were unconstitutional.

## OFFBEAT ART & KANSAS PARKS

Hop back on I-70 for a 175-mile (282km) ride west, stopping for a boost in Abilene or Salina, which both have Tesla Superchargers and slower options at stores and gas stations just off the interstate; past Salina, you might also detour north to the Tallgrass Prairie National Preserve (see p102). Back on I-70, exit at Hwy 232, driving the Post Rock Scenic Byway north to Lucas.

Nothing is too weird for this tiny town, population 337, a hub of "outsider" art made by self-taught creators. Even if you only have time for a bathroom break, Bowl Plaza is worth the stop – these public restrooms have a toilet-shaped entrance and are covered in mosaics and trinkets. Also on Main St are the Grassroots Art Center and the World's Largest Collection of the World's Smallest Versions of the World's Largest Things, which is just as intriguing as its name suggests. A few blocks east is the Garden of Eden, the former home of a Civil War veteran who decorated his yard with kooky concrete sculptures of bankers, politicians and religious figures – and even his own mausoleum, where you can see his moth-munched remains under a glass-topped coffin.

Back on I-70, draw your EV road trip through Kansas to a close by heading on west, perhaps detouring south to Little Jerusalem Badlands State Park (see opposite). From Goodland, where charging stations offer a top-up, you'll hit the Colorado border after 205 more miles (330km) on the tarmac.

**Below:** tipis under the stars at Marfa's El Cosmico
**Right:** the landmark Mule Ears, Big Bend National Park

**Distance: 170 miles (274km)**

**Duration: 7 days**

# Marfa loop via Big Bend National Park

**TEXAS**

Welcome to the final frontier. Texas is a land of wide-open spaces, and nowhere is this more apparent than in its eclectic, tumbleweed-strewn far western reaches near the border with Mexico.

The wonders of West Texas are vast and encompass much more than just the landscape. Home to a national park that's the size of an east-coast state but sees only the most intrepid of travelers – especially those in an EV – this region also has surprisingly cultural small towns and maybe even a touch of extraterrestrial activity in the otherworldly desertscape.

## MIRACULOUS MARFA

Pulling in to Marfa, you might well think you're on another planet. This town has a population of just 1750 but is a must-visit destination for culture lovers, and the contrast between the floppy hats and flowy Instagram dresses of coastal artsy types and the genuine 10-gallon hats and muddy boots of West Texas ranchers is stark. Marfa's artistic allure comes from the legacy of Donald Judd, a minimalist artist who moved here and started creating large-scale works in concrete and aluminum. The Chinati Foundation shows more than a dozen of Judd's pieces on a decommissioned military base, as well as work by artists such as Dan Flavin and John Chamberlain. More galleries are scattered around town (see p110 for more on the nearby Prada Marfa installation), as are hip indie boutiques, and food trucks

## Plan & prepare

### Tips for EV drivers

As the largest state in the Lower 48, it's perhaps no surprise that Texas has the most roads in the US, notching up some 685,000 miles (1.1 million km) of roadway. That might give EV drivers range anxiety, but the state is building an extensive EV charging network, with plans to have chargers every 50 miles (80km) along major highways. For now, fill batteries at the charger-equipped accommodations mentioned on this route, where they are mostly reserved for guests' use.

### Where to stay

EV roadtrippers will find charming accommodations on this drive, from Marathon's Gage Hotel (gagehotel.com) and Alpine's Spanish Colonial-style Holland Hotel (thehollandhoteltexas.com), both built in the 1920s, to an artsy stay at Marfa's El Cosmico (elcosmico.com). At Basecamp Terlingua (basecampterlingua.com), you can stargaze from bed in one of the bubble domes or opt for a wood-beamed casita. As well as campgrounds, Big Bend has Chisos Mountains Lodge (chisosmountainslodge.com) in the heart of the park.

### When to go

Thanks to often balmy temperatures and rainbows of blooming wildflowers, spring and fall are great times to take a West Texas EV road trip. If you're looking to keep your heavy coat and snow boots in storage, this region also makes a good place for a winter break – the mercury stays at a moderate level, and the land is dry. Avoid the scorching summer, when daytime temperatures can reach potentially lethal levels for those unprepared, with the high heat setting in well before noon.

### Further info

The winds in West Texas can be seriously strong, especially in spring, kicking up dust that can transform into sandstorms called haboobs that change the landscape from full color to sepia. Two of the state's windiest cities – Amarillo and Lubbock – are in this region. Headwinds can be a drag on EV efficiency, so be sure to include plenty of battery buffer between destinations.

## The River Road

Extend your EV trip in the Big Bend region with a drive along the River Road, officially called Farm to Market 170. This roller-coaster road – which includes a section with a 15% grade, the steepest paved street in Texas – travels through wonderful scenery and rock formations along the Rio Grande. Just west of Terlingua, Big Bend Ranch State Park has hiking trails that lead to slot canyons and weave among hoodoos, thin eroded-rock spires that are sometimes also called fairy chimneys or tent rocks. From Terlingua, the River Road runs for 62 miles (100km) to Presidio, which has a couple of RV parks where overnight guests can charge. If you're up for the adventure and have the battery range, you could press on to Ruidosa, a town of 40 or so souls with an early 1900s church. Half a mile north is the turnoff for Chinati Hot Springs, an off-grid respite with adobe cabins, a hilltop pool with mountain views, a creekside hot tub – and zero wi-fi or cell service. Go old school and consult Chinati Hot Springs' website (chinatihotsprings.net) for directions here instead of relying on GPS or Google Maps, which might well lead you astray.

**Above:** driving the River Road along the Rio Grande
**Opposite, from left:** a big Texas welcome in Alpine; hiking Big Bend National Park

and restaurants that punch well above their weight for a place of this size and remoteness.

Stay overnight in a tipi, trailer or safari-style tent at El Cosmico, which has a couple of EV chargers. When darkness falls, head east on Hwy 90 to the Marfa Mystery Lights Viewing Area. Keep an eye out for blinking signals beneath the Chinati Mountains – they might seem no more mysterious than car headlights, but the first reports of the phenomenon were in 1883, long before automobiles. No one knows for sure what causes them – or whether you'll even see them.

### ALPINE TO MARATHON

Back on the road, drive east on Hwy 90 for 25 miles (40km) to Alpine, a small spot curled up at the foot of the Davis Mountains. This laid-back railroad and ranching town has a good selection of hotels and restaurants that are far less pretentious than those in Marfa. Plug in at 10th St and Holland Ave and stretch your legs by going for a stroll downtown, which has cute cafes, shops, a bookstore and a historic movie theater.

When you've had your fill, pick up Hwy 90 and drive 30 miles (48km) on to Marathon. Book a room at the historic Gage Hotel, built in 1927 and one of the only places in town with EV chargers. The stylish low-rise yellow-brick hotel is decked out in taxidermy, leather accents and Native American printed blankets, and has a phenomenal restaurant that fuses seasonal Texas fare with European and North African flavors.

### DESERT MEETS MOUNTAINS IN BIG BEND

Everything is bigger in Texas, and that statement absolutely includes the state's largest national park, Big Bend. At 1252 sq miles (3243 sq km), it covers a larger land area than Rhode Island state, packing in hiking trails that loop through the majestic Chisos Mountains, across the otherworldly Chihuahuan Desert and into impressive river canyons. The Rio Grande marks the border with Mexico and Big Bend's southern boundary – the national park even has a border crossing, so bring your passport if you want to take a day trip to another country. You can raft or wade into the water in scenic Santa Elena Canyon, whose sheer walls – up to 1500ft (457m) high – provide much-needed shade. The canyon is at the end of the winding Ross Maxwell Scenic Drive, which climbs around gorgeous overlooks, trailheads and historic ranchers' cabins and military barracks.

Prada Marfa 2
Valentine
Davis Mountains State Park
Fort Davis
Rio Grande
17
90
118
385
Marfa, El Cosmico 1
3 Alpine
90
Marathon, Gage Hotel 4
Haymond
Candelaria
Chinati Hot Springs 7
67
169
USA
Elephant Mountain
Rudiosa
Chinati Peak
Fort Pena Colorado Park
Las Conchas
Plata
170
TEXAS
MEXICO
118
385
Indio
Casa Piedra
Nine Point Mesa
El Paradero
Ojinaga
Presidio
Rosillo Peak
16
Rio Conchos
Tabaloapa
El Mangle
Redford
Panther Mountain
River Road
CHIHUAHUA
La Paz de Mexico
67
El Mulato
Basecamp Terlingua 6
170
Panther Junction
Rio Grande
Lajitas
5 Big Bend National Park
N
20 km
10 miles
Potrero del Llano

## Prada Marfa

No, your eyes aren't deceiving you. Appearing like a mirage out of the desert haze on the side of the heat-shimmering highway, Prada Marfa has all the labels of the luxe store, and is even stocked with the 2005 collection. But put your credit card away: this boutique is a fake, and the front door doesn't open. Created by Elmgreen & Dragset, an artistic duo from Scandinavia, this installation is a tongue-in-cheek dig at consumerism. In a modern take on the oddball attractions on US highways, Prada Marfa has become an essential road-trip stop on this lonely stretch of pavement northwest of Marfa – even Beyonce has posted a photo of herself in front of the store on Instagram. The artists' original idea was that the building would naturally deteriorate, but despite the odd bit of graffiti, it's still holding its own after two decades.

**Clockwise from top left:** critiquing consumerism at Prada Marfa; the Rio Grande at Santa Elena Canyon, Big Bend National Park; the Starlight Theater, Terlingua's cultural hub



Amenities within the bounds of Big Bend are quite limited, and for the moment there are no EV charging stations. Make sure you're ready for the drive by staying in Terlingua, 8 miles (13km) from the park's western entrance station, where a handful of accommodations – such as Basecamp Terlingua – have EV chargers for guests. Terlingua itself is a delightfully weird place. Once a mercury-mining boomtown, it shriveled up and nearly blew away like a tumbleweed when the mines closed in the 1940s. Buildings were abandoned and fell into ruins, but this ghost town has been brought back to life by a small population of artists, retirees, river guides and loners. The must-do activity is sitting on the front porch of Terlingua Trading Company with a beer, chatting with your neighbors and watching the sunset. Next door is the Starlight Theatre, a 1930s cinema turned cultural hub, restaurant and bar.

Complete your EV road trip loop by heading north on Hwy 118 to Alpine, some 84 miles (135km) away; or driving the River Road along the Rio Grande (see p108) before turning north on Hwy 67, reaching Marfa after 60 miles (97km). Expect to be stopped at US Border Control checkpoints; if you're not a US citizen, you will need to show your passport at these.

**Below:** outside the first store owned by Walmart founder Sam Walton, Bentonville
**Right:** the route winds through the Ozarks

- **Distance: 316 miles (508km)**
- **Duration: 3-5 days**

# Eureka Springs to Little Rock

**ARKANSAS**

A remote but gorgeously scenic backwater of lakes, rivers and peaks, dramatic karst formations and historic hill towns, the Ozark Mountains have always made a great escape from the everyday.

Once the stomping ground of fur trappers, farmers and fleeing fugitives, the Ozarks later attracted hippies eschewing the rat race and outdoors lovers bent on adventure. The region's relative isolation bestowed a sense of mystery on its limestone bluffs, cascading falls and thick forests. All that combined with a warm welcome, it now makes a glorious place for some leisurely EV exploration.

## EUREKA SPRINGS TO FORT SMITH

Start in the once fashionable spa town of Eureka Springs, the steep streets flanked by Victorian homes with ornate turrets and wrought-iron balconies. A thriving artists' community where biker bars sit side by side with New Age crystal shops, offbeat art galleries and gay bars, the town is a quirky hub for hiking, biking and horseback riding, a soak and a steam at the Palace Bath House, or a visit to the Thorncrown Chapel, a majestic wood-and-glass structure that rises elegantly into the forest.

Stop off to see underground streams and waterfalls at War Eagle Cavern on the 46-mile (74km) drive along a twisting ribbon of road to Bentonville, home to the first store owned by Walmart's founder and now the company HQ. Sculptures, murals and neon installations sit all over

## Plan & prepare

### Tips for EV drivers

By their nature, the Ozarks are rather wild and remote, so you'll need to plan a trip with regular stops in the larger towns and cities to stay charged. Bear your battery range in mind if you get sidetracked down some gorgeous mountain road, as chargers are few and far between in the more isolated parts of the Ozark National Forest. And if you're visiting the wine region, bring a designated driver so you can enjoy the delights on offer.

### Where to stay

Combining boutique hotel, contemporary art museum and art center, Bentonville's slick 21C Museum Hotel (21cmuseumhotels.com) has sleek, understated rooms with designer style, the fabulous chef-led Hive restaurant, and onsite chargers. The Fairfield Inn & Suites (marriott.com) in Russellville has spacious guest rooms, a pool and a gym, and is close to plenty of chargers on the nearby university campus. Little Rock's Capital Hotel (capitalhotel.com), in the heart of town, has stately, Southern-style rooms and onsite charging.

### When to go

With waterfalls at their gushing best, wildflowers in full bloom and the forests a deep, intense green, spring is a wonderful time of year in the Ozarks. Summers are hot and humid, and fall a glorious patchwork of ochre, scarlet and burnt sienna, while winters can be cold and snowy but also quite magical. The Ozark Mountain Music Festival takes place in Eureka Springs in January, and the Arkansas State Fair thrills Little Rock over 10 days in October.

### Further info

A great side-trip from Little Rock, Hot Springs is the state's only national park. Just 50 miles (80km) southwest of the capital, the park has 47 thermal springs, miles of hiking trails and is home to the historic Bathhouse Row, where eight bathhouses from the 19th and early 20th century survive intact. You can still take the waters in two of them, while Hot Springs' Gangster Museum of America tells the tale of the city's gambling, bootlegging and mob activity.

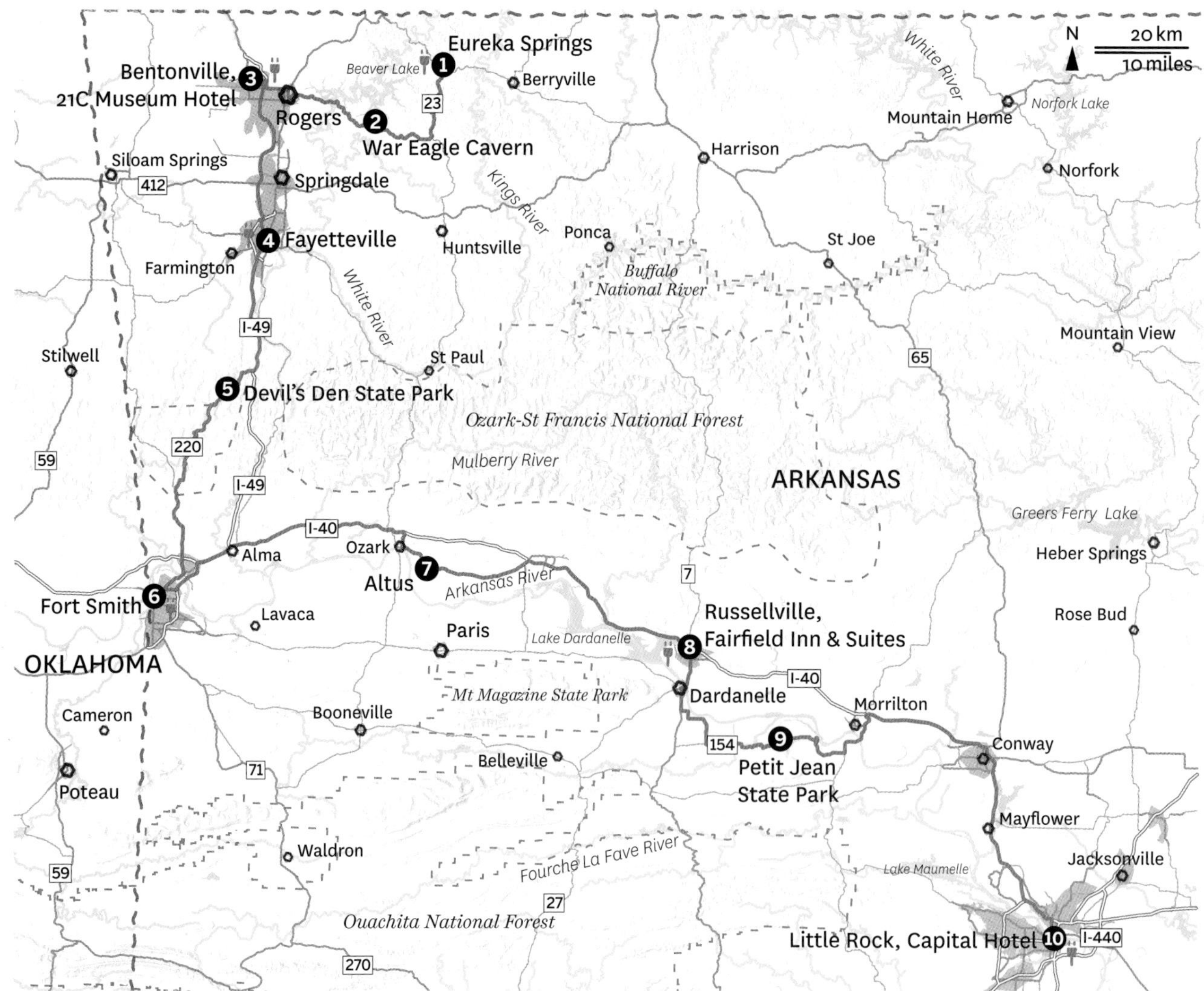


town alongside museums and galleries like the Crystal Bridges Museum, with a collection of American art.

Lively Fayetteville, 27 miles (43km) south, hosts the University of Arkansas and a bumper crop of cafes and galleries, craft brewers and bars. South of town you can get out into the wilderness at Devil's Den State Park to see exposed fossil beds and dramatic rock formations, while at Fort Smith, 58 miles (93km) further south, a military post grew into a rowdy Wild West town at the confluence of the Arkansas and Poteau Rivers. Visit the Fort Smith National Historic Site to learn about its history; Miss Laura's – a former bordello – for some social insights; or the glittering new US Marshals Museum, which chronicles the life of America's marshals from colonial days to the present.

## SOUTHEAST TO LITTLE ROCK

Downstream, the Arkansas River wine region centers around Altus, 45 miles (72km) east. It's a short drive in your EV between estates such as the historic Mount Bethel Winery, Chateau aux Arc (known for its Chardonnay and Zinfandel), or Post Winery (renowned for its Muscadine, a Southern specialty). Nearby Petit Jean State Park is on the historic Trail of Tears, the walking route west taken by Southeastern Native American tribes after their forced removal from their ancestral lands. Head to the overlook at Stout's Point for sweeping views, Rock House Cave to see 500-year-old pictographs, or the Seven Hollows Trail to pass through small canyons and a rock arch beneath a canopy of forest.

From here, it's 68 miles (109km) into state capital Little Rock, where the Little Rock Nine tested the Supreme Court's ruling on desegregation of schools in 1957. Hear their story at the Little Rock Central High School National Historic Site, and sample the state's best street food at River Market, then head for Pinnacle Mountain State Park for panoramic river views to mark the end of your trip.

## Buffalo River adventures

America's first National River, the Buffalo weaves its way through 135 miles (217km) of the Ozarks' finest territory. It's one of the few undammed rivers in the Lower 48 and passes through a series of deep valleys flanked by sheer limestone cliffs and dramatic bluffs, pouring over rapids, by sandy banks and into languid pools. Paddling your way down a section of the river offers the chance to get into the Ozarks' backcountry, where the beautiful landscape can be appreciated in utter tranquility. Ponca, 50 miles (80km) south of Eureka Springs, is a good place to start a trip; the Buffalo Outdoor Center here (buffaloriver.com) has a Tesla charger onsite and offers river trips as well as mountain-bike rental, cabins and camping. If you would prefer to hike, it's also a great base for a series of local trails: the Glory Hole route leads to a waterfall cascading through a hole in a bluff; Pedestal Rocks delights with sculpted limestone formations; Whitaker Point is a theatrical overlook; and the tough Big Bluff to Goat Trail walk rewards those willing to take on a challenge with panoramic views.

**Clockwise from top left:** Arkansas River views from Stout's Point; kayaking the Buffalo National River; Seven Hollows Trail rock arch, Petit Jean State Park

**Below:** Stone Arch Bridge, Minneapolis
**Right:** Mississippi River views at Effigy Mounds National Monument

Distance: 1470 miles (2366km)

Duration: 5-7 days

# The Great River Road, Minneapolis to New Orleans

**MINNESOTA TO LOUISIANA**

Get a taste of multiple states on an EV drive through the heart of America along the course of the Mississippi River, taking in big cities, quiet towns, historic sights and epic landscapes.

There's a clue in the name of the Great River Road, a ten-state-traversing drive of a lifetime – all accessible by EV – that follows the USA's greatest waterway, the Mississippi, from its northern reaches near the Canadian border to where it joins the sea in the Gulf of Mexico.

## TWIN CITIES & ANCIENT CIVILIZATIONS

Though the Mississippi's primary source is in northern Minnesota's Lake Itasca, this drive begins in state capital, St Paul, and largest city, Minneapolis – the "Twin Cities", which sit on the east and west banks of the river respectively and are a more accessible starting point. Spend a night or two enjoying some "Minnesota nice" time, visiting one of the many art collections during the day and one of the many music venues in the evening.

Moving on, pause at Water Power Park, right in the middle of the Mississippi, for skyline views and to see the river's only natural waterfall, then head south on West River Parkway where, surprisingly quickly, city sights are replaced by the gorgeous, tree-lined Mississippi Gorge. Cross into Wisconsin and after 80 miles (129km) take a look at the replica "Little House" where Laura Ingalls Wilder was born. It inspired the first

## Plan & prepare

### Tips for EV drivers

The Great River Road (experiencemississippiriver.com) mostly follows Rte 61 (and the Mississippi), but in terms of EV chargers you'll have to veer off regularly, or use alternative roads, to keep your car topped up. All the towns and cities covered in this trip have several charging options available, but distances between them are sometimes long (and, especially in the South, battery-drainingly hot), so check where your next charging station is before you set off each day.

### Where to stay

A hilltop position and cute rooms make Dubuque's Front Porch (staylongerbnb.com) a great first-night option. St Louis' Missouri Athletic Club (mac-stl.org) is a historic hotel (and sports club) near the Gateway Arch; Memphis' Victorian-era James Lee House (jamesleehouse.com) has charm and luxury in equal measures. Natchez has a wealth of characterful options, but for some antebellum grandeur you can't beat Monmouth Historic Inn (monmouthhistoricinn.com). All the above have chargers onsite or nearby.

### When to go

Minnesota winters are long, so start your trip when the cold has abated – ideally May onwards. Many cities and sights on this route are on the beaten path so avoid school vacations if possible. An alternative to heading "down" the Mississippi over a week or so is to travel "up" it over a longer period of time. Start in balmy New Orleans around March and drive at a sedate pace, following spring as it progresses up the country.

### Further info

The Great River Road has distinctive road markers to help you know you're on the right route as you wend your way down the country – look for a green paddleboat and a pilot's wheel on a white background. There are 100 or so interpretive centers along the road, offering insights into local history and geography, all connected to the Mississippi and its important role in all the states it visits.

## Sweet sounds of the Mississippi

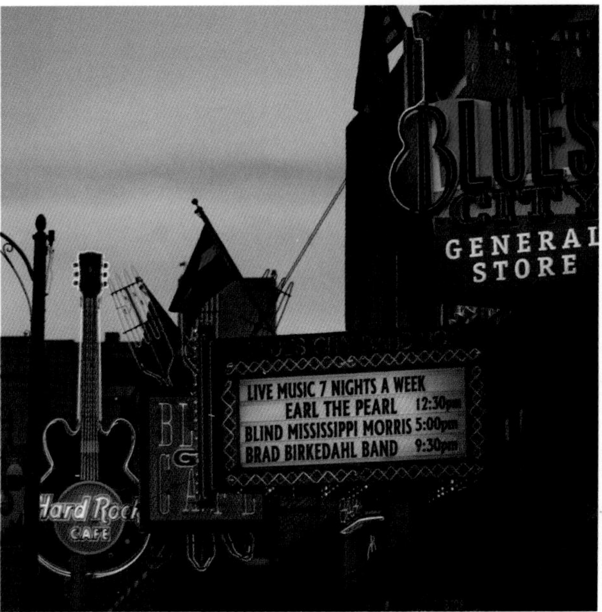


Music and the Mississippi don't just alliterate, they're historically intertwined. All along the river's course people have created genres that define their regions and then reach out around the world to draw fans from far and wide. Minneapolis has a storied musical heritage, focused on its landmark venue, First Avenue. Pay your respects to the city's most famous singer-songwriter with a visit to Prince's Paisley Park. In Memphis, Beale St has become something of a victim of its own success but authentic blues, the city's signature style, can still be enjoyed at old favorites like BB King's, where late evenings slide effortlessly into early mornings. For more blues, a stop 90 minutes south of Memphis in Clarksdale allows for an exploration of the Delta Blues Museum – the highlight of the small but engrossing collection is the cabin in which Muddy Waters grew up. End-of-the-road New Orleans is the start of more musical magic. Jazz is king here, and while you can hear top-notch performers at clubs along Frenchmen St, you're just as likely to catch memorable, impromptu moments on street corners and in parks all around the Big Easy.

**Above:** Memphis' Beale St, the "Home of the Blues" **Opposite, from left:** prehistoric burial mounds of Cahokia, Illinois; Elvis' grand Graceland, Memphis

of her *Little House on the Prairie* books. It's close to cute riverside Pepin village, as is the Nelson Cheese Factory, a purveyor of the state's celebrated cheeses.

Continuing south, take your pick of river-related highlights. On the western side, Effigy Mounds National Monument has pre-Columbian earth mounds; just beyond, Pike's Peak State Park delivers one of the best views of the drive. East, across the river, Villa Louis was the imposing, waterfront home of a 19th-century fur trader. Finish the day in attractive Dubuque.

### INTO THE SOUTH

Day two begins with the Quad Cities (Davenport, Bettendorf, Rock Island and Moline) which straddle the river, as well as Iowa and Illinois, and offer craft breweries and hiking trails to while away a few hours. Back on the road it's around 220 miles (354km) to your next stop, so stretch your legs and charge your EV along the way at any park, town or historic location that draws your attention. At Collinsville, cap the day with one of the country's most awe-inspiring pre-European sights, Cahokia, where huge mounds overlook the Mississippi. Cross the river into state five, Missouri, and stay the night in St Louis.

Having ascended the Gateway Arch (more awesome vistas) and been left wide-eyed at the shoe-factory-turned-bonkers-but-brilliant City Museum, it's back in your EV and back on the road. Crossing the river again, the South starts in earnest: Kentucky – where the Ohio River joins the Mississippi and Columbus-Belmont State Park delivers more ancient mounds and views – is followed quickly by Tennessee, where the river forms the state's western border. Landscapes that change from bluffs to woodlands to floodplains ensure the drive doesn't lack scenic variety, so pull over for a walk or just to revel in nature's beauty whenever the mood takes you. Around 260 miles (418km) from St Louis, a major Civil War site will tempt anyone with an interest in history. Fort Pillow saw a brutal massacre of its Union defenders, mostly Black soldiers, by Confederate attackers under the notorious Nathan Bedford Forrest in April 1864.

It's easy – and highly recommended – to park your EV and spend a few days exploring the Mississippi's next great city, Memphis, 63 miles (101km) south of Fort Pillow. Elvis' Graceland home, the National Civil Rights Museum and Sun Studio all repay your time, as do sunset strolls along the River Walk and nights out on legendary Beale St.

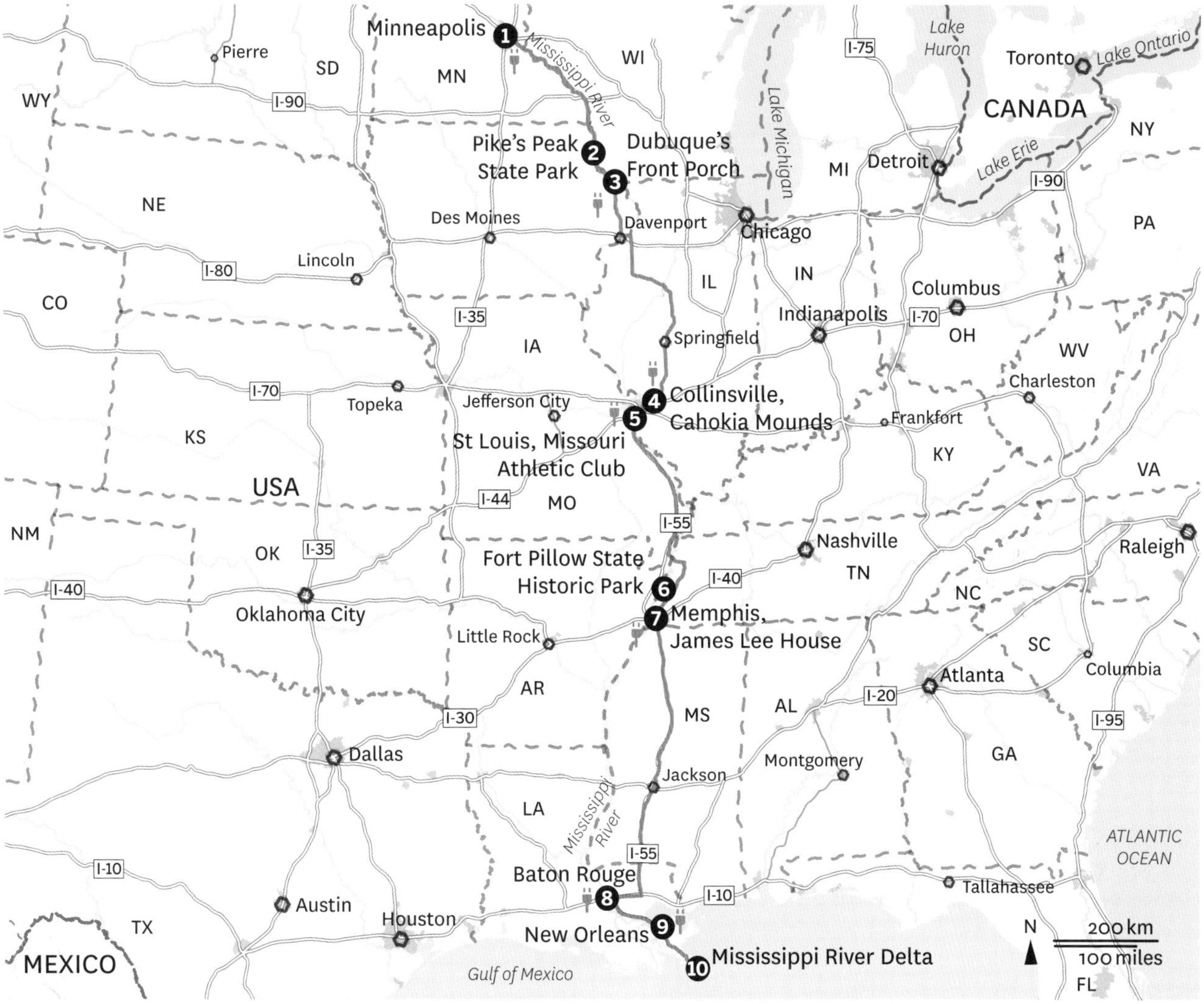

## Central USA

Minneapolis 1
Pike's Peak State Park 2
Dubuque's Front Porch 3
Collinsville, Cahokia Mounds 4
St Louis, Missouri Athletic Club 5
Fort Pillow State Historic Park 6
Memphis, James Lee House 7
Baton Rouge 8
New Orleans 9
Mississippi River Delta 10

Mississippi River
Lake Huron
Lake Ontario
Lake Michigan
Lake Erie
Toronto
CANADA
Detroit
Chicago
Des Moines
Davenport
Lincoln
Pierre
Columbus
Indianapolis
Springfield
Jefferson City
Topeka
Frankfort
Charleston
USA
Nashville
Raleigh
Oklahoma City
Little Rock
Atlanta
Columbia
Dallas
Jackson
Montgomery
Austin
Houston
Tallahassee
MEXICO
Gulf of Mexico
ATLANTIC OCEAN
WY SD MN WI NE CO IA IL IN OH MI NY PA KS MO KY WV VA NM OK TN NC AR SC MS AL GA LA TX FL
I-90 I-75 I-80 I-35 I-70 I-44 I-55 I-40 I-30 I-20 I-95 I-10
N
200 km
100 miles

## Making his Mark

One man synonymous with the Mississippi is Samuel Clemens – better known as Mark Twain. In his two most famous works, *The Adventures of Tom Sawyer* (1876) and its sequel *The Adventures of Huckleberry Finn* (1884), Twain not only gained an enduring name for himself and his two characters in the literary world, but also created an image of the third primary character in the novels, the "mighty Mississippi" (as he described it), that informs people's ideas today – a brown, sluggish, beautiful, lawless body of water that represents freedom, for Tom and Huck and also for Twain himself. The writer spent most of his childhood in Hannibal, Missouri, in a house right by the river that proved such a strong influence on him. Today that home is a museum covering his life and works, and is an easy stop on this road trip.

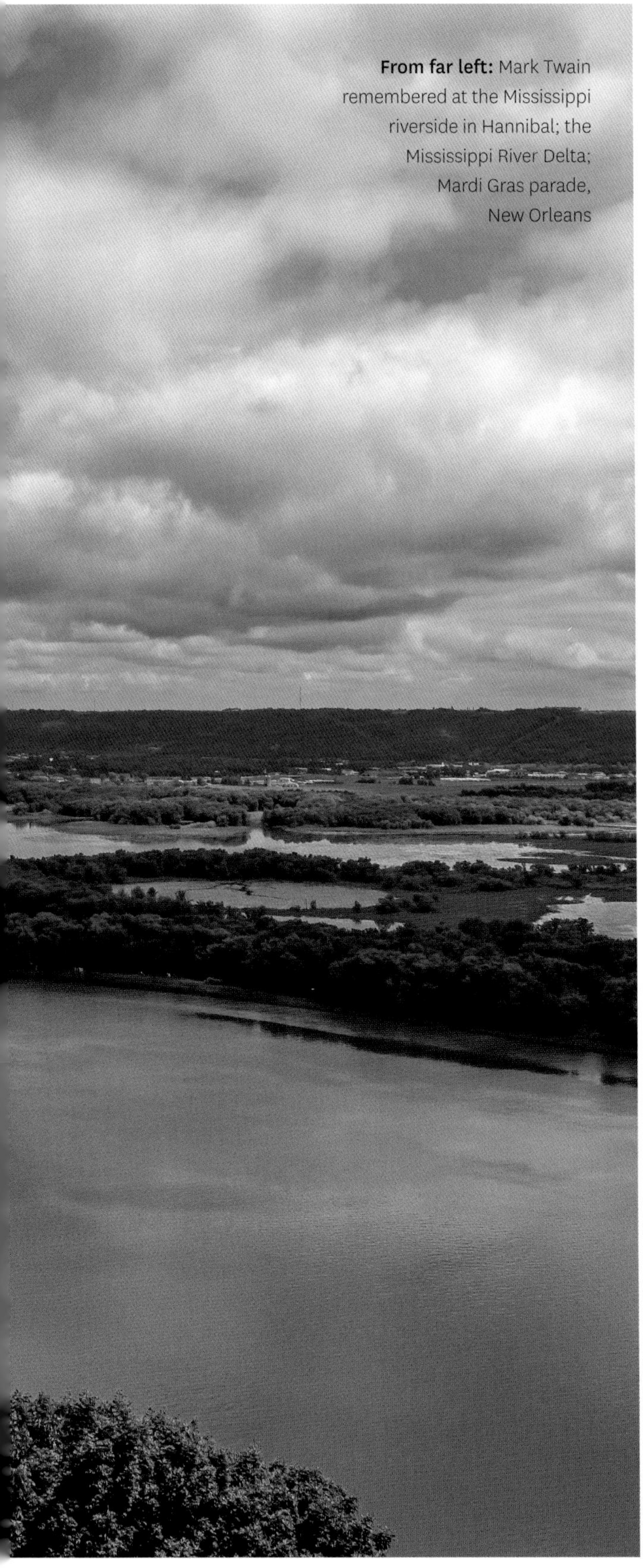

**From far left:** Mark Twain remembered at the Mississippi riverside in Hannibal; the Mississippi River Delta; Mardi Gras parade, New Orleans

© Rush Jagoe/Lonely Planet; EyeTravel/Shutterstock; Photoservice/Getty Images

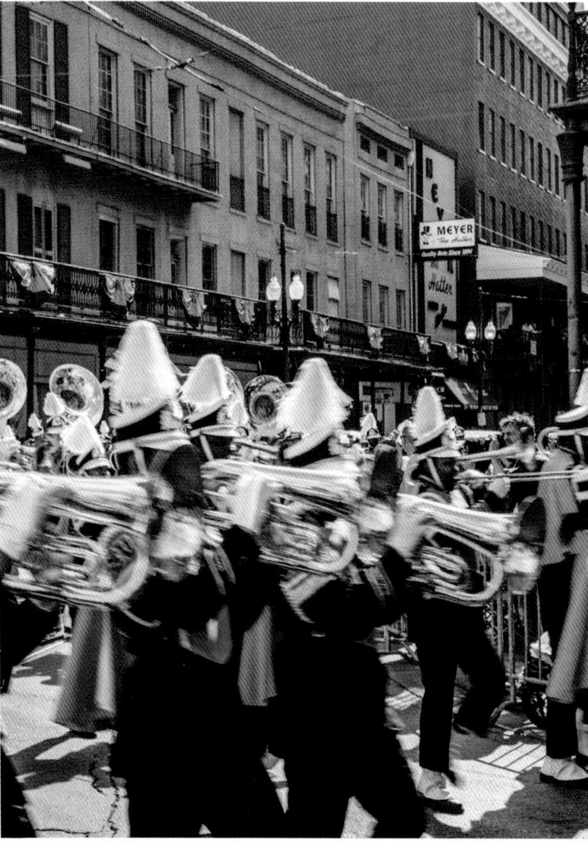

## SO LONG MISSISSIPPI

A short drive into state eight, Arkansas, brings you to Marion's Sultana Disaster Museum, where the tragic story of the US' worst maritime disaster is told: in 1865 boilers on the steamboat *Sultana* exploded and somewhere from 1200 to 1800 people died. Cross the river east again and you're soon in the namesake state of Mississippi, where a long drive is rewarded with time in Natchez. One of the handsomest towns on the river, Natchez has a postcard-pretty downtown made for wandering and historic homes for perusing. Overnight to make the most of the city's charms before continuing south, with the finish line in sight, into Louisiana. Break up the journey in Baton Rouge, where riverside trails, the Old State Capitol Museum and the Rural Life Museum are reason enough to stop, charge the EV and explore Louisiana's capital.

It's 81 miles (130km) to the state's – and arguably the Mississippi River's – most famous city, New Orleans. There's plenty to fill a few days, from the French Quarter's bars and restaurants to the Garden District's envy-inducing mansions, but if it's Old Man River's last shout you're after, then leave NOLA and follow Rte 23 to literally the end of the road in the Mississippi River Delta, to bid your aquatic road-trip companion farewell.

**Below:** Dell Rhea's Chicken Basket in Willowbrook, essential first stop on the road from Chicago
**Right:** driving Route 66 through California's Mojave Desert

**Distance: 2448 miles (3940km)**

**Duration: 7 days**

# Route 66

**ILLINOIS TO CALIFORNIA**

Inhale the sweep and grandeur of the American west on this long-distance EV drive, plunging from Chicago into the Great Plains and through the desert to the golden land of California.

In the 1946 song – you know the one – that rocketed the setting for this road trip to icon status, Nat King Cole told us to motor west on the highway that's best, and get our kicks on Route 66. Apologies to him, but we're here to tell you: it's not all kicks. Route 66, the historic highway running from Chicago to Santa Monica, is 2448 miles (3940km) of asphalt. There are endless stretches with nothing to see but corn to the left and soybeans to the right. There are storms that come from nowhere, and the occasional cloud of locusts hitting your windshield like hail with legs (and guts). There are places with nowhere to stay but a motel last updated during the Reagan administration.

But, see, the hard parts – the boring, the empty, the sad – are what make Route 66 a genuine journey. Driving it takes commitment. It takes planning, particularly when you're in an EV. But do it – the whole thing – and you'll come out the other end transformed.

## ILLINOIS & MISSOURI

Start, of course, in Chicago, where you'll find the "Begin Route 66" sign at Adams and Michigan Ave. Rolling southwest out of the city, your first stop (just off the I-55 in Willowbrook) should be a fried-chicken lunch at Dell

## Plan & prepare

### Tips for EV drivers

Route 66 by EV is doable, but takes planning. All major and medium-sized cities along the way have fast chargers, and so do many smaller towns and pit stops where Route 66 follows major highways like I-40. Things get dicier in places like the rural Great Plains, where drivers with shorter-range vehicles may need to settle for a slow overnight charge.

### Where to stay

Chicago, St Louis, Tulsa, Oklahoma City, Albuquerque and LA have a wide variety of choices, including hotels with charging stations. Original midcentury motels include the Wagon Wheel (wagonwheel66cuba.com) in Cuba, Missouri; Tucumcari's Blue Swallow (blueswallowmotel.com) and Motel Safari (themotelsafari.com), and Albuquerque's El Vado (elvadoabq.com) in New Mexico; and Deluxe Inn (deluxeinnaz.com) in Seligman, Arizona. Many national chains along the I-40 section have chargers.

### When to go

Route 66 traverses a variety of climate zones. Southern California is always mild, but the Mojave is deathly in the summer, and Chicago and much of the Great Plains frigid in winter. Getting stuck in a blizzard in Illinois = no fun. Both heat and cold will affect your range, so plan ahead. In general, spring or early fall tend to be the best bets for good weather across the route.

### Further info

Route 66 will celebrate its centennial in 2026, and some states – like Illinois – are boosting their EV infrastructure ahead of time, so expect more chargers. Other places are revitalizing roadside landmarks for the celebration. Oh, and though we didn't mention it before, Route 66 cuts across 13 miles (21km) of Kansas, so you can cross the state off your "places I've visited" list.

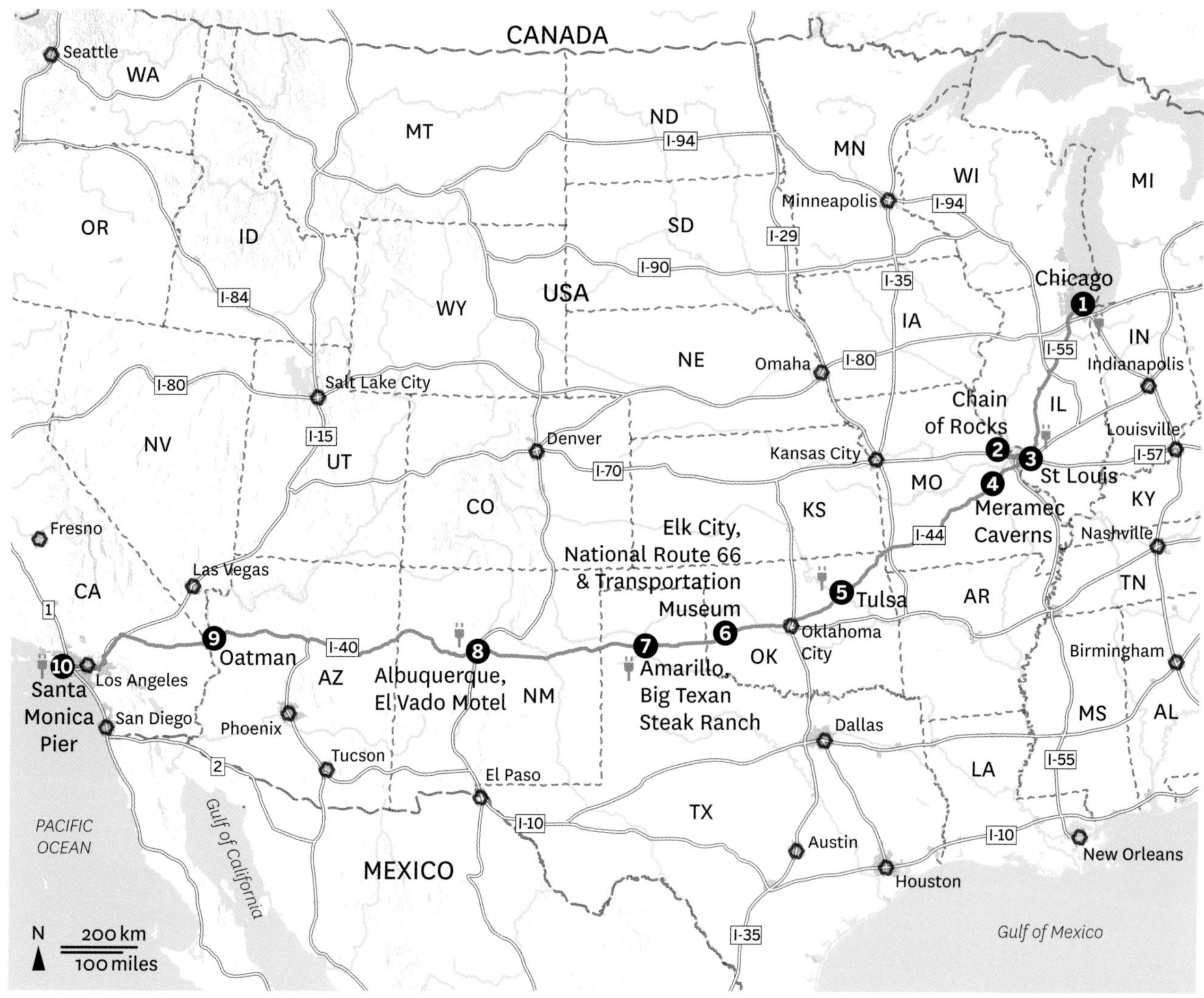


Rhea's Chicken Basket, with its classic midcentury neon sign. Wipe your greasy fingers and keep on southwest into the farmland of central Illinois. There's a Tesla Supercharger at Dwight, near photogenic Ambler's Texaco Gas Station, but other options are slow until Bloomington, 144 miles (232km) from Chicago. This college town has numerous fast chargers, and makes a good pit stop ahead of an overnight (and a corn dog from Cozy Dog drive-in) at Springfield, another 64 miles (103km) on.

In the morning, it's 96 miles (155km) south to St Louis, Missouri. But before you cross the muddy Mississippi, stop at the old Chain of Rocks Bridge, which carried Route 66 until 1970. Today the dramatically angled span is bike- and pedestrian-only; the new bridge is just to the north. Charge up in the city, ogle the 1965 Gateway Arch and keep your eyes open for classic art deco signage, then continue southwest. Roll your EV through hills, valleys and flatlands, going underground at Meramec Caverns and giggling at the signage in Uranus; stop for a charge in Rolla, if necessary. Spend the night in the border town of Joplin, which has good charger availability.

## OKLAHOMA & TEXAS

Oklahoma is on the horizon now, with the longest unbroken stretch of Route 66. The Ozarks give way to the Great Plains, so flat you can see a storm rolling in a hundred miles away. You'll hit Tulsa (look out for the kitschy whale statue in the suburb of Catoosa) and Oklahoma City, both good places to charge. Just outside OKC, you can't miss the 66ft-high (20m) LED-lit soda bottle outside the Pops service station.

Route 66 joins I-40 at Oklahoma City and heads straight west, the landscape turning drier and redder towards the Texas border. Before you cross, overnight at Elk City, 112 miles (180km) on, home to the National Route 66 & Transportation Museum, stuffed with fun memorabilia.

## The Mother Road

Established in 1926, Route 66 was one of the first roadways in the American highway system. Paved in parts, dirt or gravel in others, the route quickly became a crucial path for Dust Bowl migrants heading west during the Great Depression. It was the Dust Bowl's great chronicler, John Steinbeck, who dubbed it the "Mother Road," a nod to the route's place in birthing a new American Dream. During and after WWII, Route 66 was busy with truckers, military workers at route-adjacent bases and vacationers exploring a new concept known as a "road trip." Motels, filling stations and restaurants, many with striking midcentury architecture, sprang up to fulfill travelers' needs. But by the 1960s the route was already being replaced by larger multi-lane highways. Stretches were abandoned, once-thriving roadside attractions became ghost towns, quirky local motels were replaced by national chains. Today, Historic Route 66 is designated a National Scenic Byway. Most – though not all – of the original road is still connected and drivable, though the journey is now a patchwork of various state roads and highways. Many original buildings remain, though some are long-shuttered monuments to a bygone era.

**Clockwise from top left:** Ambler's Texaco Gas Station in Dwight, Illinois; retro 66 chic at a routeside diner, Albuquerque; Amarillo's Cadillac Ranch, Texas

## Architecture of Route 66

There are many sorts of architectural styles on display on Route 66, from the International-style skyscrapers of Chicago to the art deco offices of Tulsa to the adobe homes of New Mexico. But the style most associated with Route 66 goes by the rather goofy name of Googie. Popular from the 1940s through the 1960s, Googie was all about midcentury ideas of modernity, with geometric shapes inspired by cars and rocket ships, atomic diagrams and flight parabolas. Googie was often used for buildings associated with travel and speed – motels, gas stations, fast-food restaurants. You'll spot it mostly in the southwest and west portions of Route 66: Motel Safari in Tucumcari, New Mexico; Kap's Coffee Shop in Albuquerque; Roy's Motel & Cafe in Amboy, California; and Mel's Drive-In in Santa Monica (with a penguin atop its famed neon sign).

**From far left:** Roy's Motel & Cafe in Amboy, California; the Gateway Arch in St Louis, Missouri; Santa Monica Pier, California

The Texas stretch of the route cuts through the top of the Panhandle. The highlight here is Amarillo, where you can park your EV along the highway at Cadillac Ranch, a 50-year-old public art installation consisting of 10 Cadillacs planted nose-down in a pasture. Pick up a can of spray paint and leave your mark on a car – it's encouraged. Then it's on to the famed Big Texan Steak Ranch, where those who can consume a 72oz (2kg) steak in an hour get it free. Charge up in Amarillo, though there are also chargers dotting highway-side towns en route to Albuquerque, 288 miles (464km) west.

## NEW MEXICO, ARIZONA & CALIFORNIA

You're now in southwestern Route 66 territory. The route cuts through New Mexico's largest city, Albuquerque, on Central Ave, still lined with neon signs and vintage motels. Overnight here at El Vado, a Pueblo Revival–style motel open since 1937. Then on through the silvery desert, mesas rising and disappearing as your EV glides west towards Arizona. Gallup and Winslow make good charging stops, as does Flagstaff, as you climb the Kaibab Plateau into cool spruce forest. At the California border, Oatman is a Wild West village with a "haunted" hotel and roaming donkeys (though nearby Kingman has more – and less haunted – hotels, as well as chargers).

Now you're on the homestretch! You're heading into California's Mojave Desert, its vast sandiness studded with cacti. I-40 ends at Barstow and you'll plunge south through the valleys of the Inland Empire region before making a sharp westward turn. Route 66 ends at Santa Monica Pier, where the sun sinks low over the Pacific. You're here. You've done it.

**Below:** Indianapolis' leafy University of Indiana campus
**Right:** George Rogers Clark Memorial Bridge, spanning the Ohio River in Louisville

**Distance: 165 miles (266km)**

**Duration: 3-4 days**

# Indianapolis to Louisville

**INDIANA & KENTUCKY**

Glide your EV through the US Midwest, from the Hoosier State's capital of Indianapolis to the lively university town of Bloomington, and through Civil War heritage to Louisville, Kentucky's bourbon hub.

Kick off your trip perusing Indianapolis museums such as Newfields, with contemporary art galleries set in a garden campus. Along White River State Park's canals (with charging stations a few blocks away), Eiteljorg Museum explores the culture of the American West and its Indigenous peoples. Then follow restaurant-lined Massachusetts Ave to the Bottleworks District, to snack at the Garage Food Hall before hitting the road.

## CAMPUS CALLINGS

Navigate out of downtown Indianapolis, heading west on I-70, south on I-465 and exiting almost immediately onto Hwy 67, which leads south to the town of Mooresville and a roadtrippers' icon: Gray Brothers Cafeteria, sustaining travelers with fried chicken, Jell-O salads and strawberry pie since the 1940s. It's only 35 miles (56km) further south to Bloomington, via Hwy 67 and I-69. After checking into your hotel, stroll the wooded campus of Indiana University, following the walking paths linking its limestone buildings to the excellent Eskenazi Museum of Art. You'll find EV chargers in Bloomington's downtown parking garages, at College Mall just east of campus, and at Switchyard Park, where you can enjoy the sunshine in this former railroad hub turned urban green space.

## Plan & prepare

### Tips for EV drivers

You'll find EV chargers throughout Indiana and Kentucky, although you may have to hunt a little harder for them, particularly outside the major cities. Look for charging stations in city parking garages, shopping centers and local parks. Indianapolis' attractions are quite spread out, so it's easiest to explore by car, but in Bloomington, Columbus and Louisville, you can park your EV at a charger while you wander on foot.

### Where to stay

In a former Coca-Cola bottling plant, Indianapolis' Bottleworks District includes a food hall, entertainment venues and the Bottleworks Hotel (bottleworkshotel.com); the city's boutique Alexander (wyndhamhotels.com) has onsite chargers. Hyatt Place Bloomington (hyatt.com) and the Graduate (graduatehotels.com) are on student hub Kirkwood Ave, with EV chargers nearby. In downtown Louisville, there's the eclectic 21c Museum Hotel (21cmuseumhotels.com) and the stylish Grady (thegradyhotel.com).

### When to go

Southern Indiana's rural roads are most beautiful in September and October, when the trees turn brilliant red, yellow and gold. April and May bring spring flowers, before the summer turns hot and humid. While this region doesn't normally receive heavy snowfalls, winter travelers should check forecasts before setting out. Try to avoid Indiana University's special-event weekends, such as homecoming and graduation, when hotel availability in Bloomington can be scarce; see the IU events calendar (events.iu.edu) for specifics.

### Further info

State tourism site Visit Indiana (visitindiana.com) provides general info on travel through the region. Kentucky Tourism (kentuckytourism.com) has similar travel services for that state. Useful local and regional planning resources include Visit Indy (visitindy.com), covering Indianapolis; Visit Bloomington (visitbloomington.com); Columbus Area Visitors Center (columbus.in.us); Clark-Floyd Counties Convention-Tourism Bureau in Southern Indiana (gosoin.com); and Louisville Tourism (gotolouisville.com).

## Louisville's food artisans

This Kentucky city on the Ohio River is best-known for its bourbon, with distillery tasting rooms lining its downtown streets. But Louisville has become a culinary hub as well, with diverse entrepreneurs devising new, locally focused food products and creative dining destinations. Foodie hotspots include Logan Street Market, where the two-dozen vendors serve up everything from third-wave coffee to Cold Smoke bagels; and Paristown, with a food hall and a regular schedule of concerts and other events. In the hip Nulu (New Louisville) district, the Mayan Café crafts Mexican fare highlighting foods of the Yucatán; Biscuit Belly specializes in, yes, Southern-style biscuits; and Louisville Cream creates ice cream in fabulous flavors like banana pudding and bourbon-smoked pecan. For chicken and waffles, fried green tomatoes and other upscale soul food, head for Dasha Barbours; Georgia's Sweet Potato Pie Company not only sells personal-sized versions of this classic Southern sweet, but also donates books to Louisville children. The city even has a soy-sauce microbrewery, Bourbon Barrel Foods, where you can sample its umami-rich concoctions. Prefer something sweeter? Art Eatables specializes in bourbon-filled truffles and other distinctive chocolates.

**Clockwise from top left:** Eero Saarinen's North Christian Church, Columbus; bourbon-based sundowner in Louisville; the city's signature Hot Brown

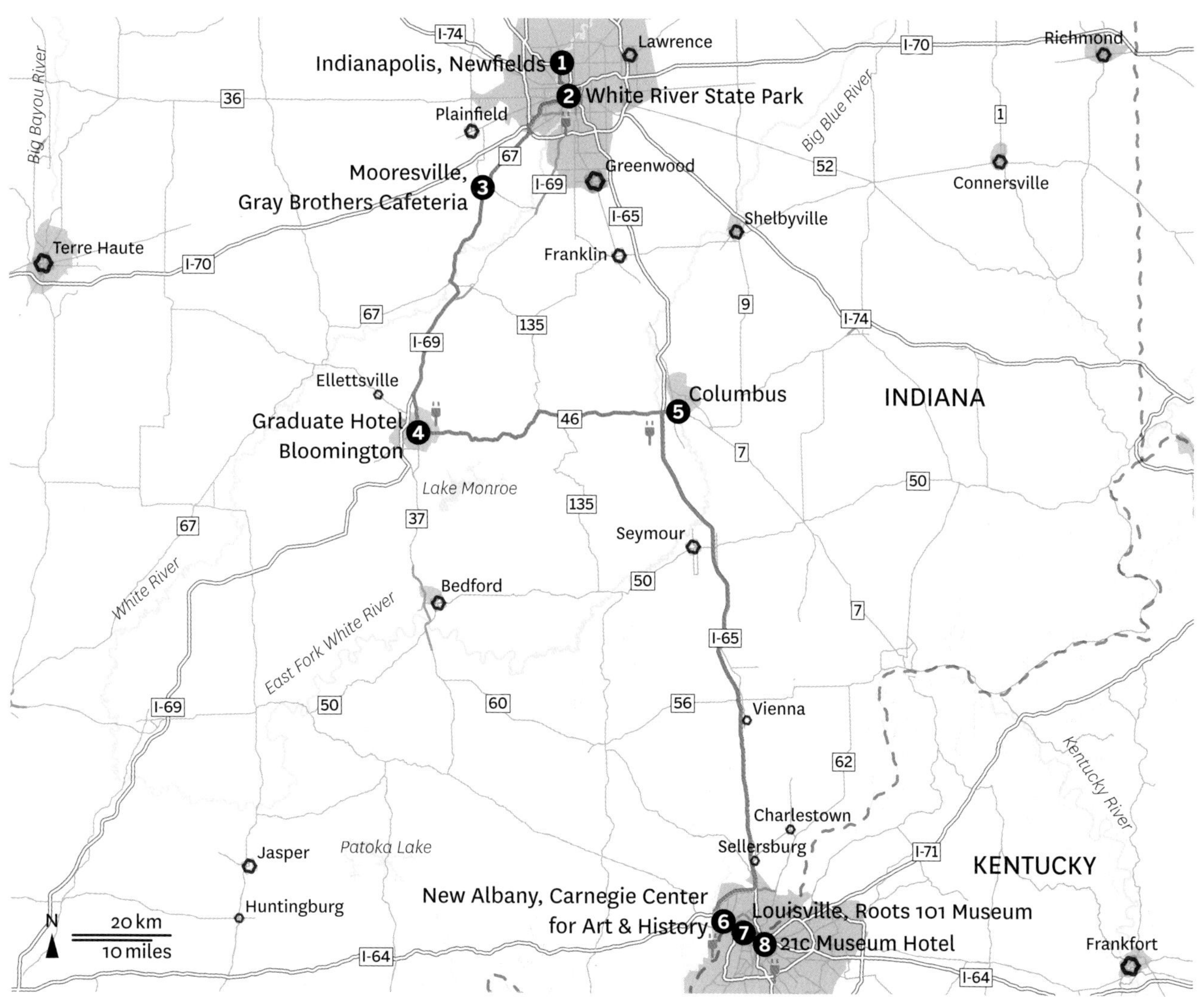


Wander the buzzing West 4th district off Kirkwood to eat at international restaurants such as Burma Garden, Anyetsang's Little Tibet or Longfei Chinese. Check the calendar for the regular concerts staged by Indiana University's highly regarded music school, from student recitals to chamber groups to opera. Many local bars host music, too, including the Bluebird and the Back Door.

## MODERN ARCHITECTURE, BLACK HISTORY

After brunch at the Hive on Bloomington's east side or the vegan/vegetarian Owlery in the Square district, head east on Hwy 46, driving 36 miles (58km) to Columbus, a city of 50,000 souls that has become an unlikely hub for modern architecture. IM Pei, Robert Venturi and Eliel and Eero Saarinen are among the big-name architects who've designed buildings here. At the Visitor Center, pick up a guide to the notable structures or join an architectural walking tour.

Then buzz south along I-65 for 70 miles (113km) toward Louisville, stopping before you cross the Ohio River in New Albany. Visit the city's Carnegie Center for Art & History for its exhibits on the Civil War–era Underground Railroad and Southern Indiana's complex heritage as a nominal "free state." Down the street, tour the Town Clock Church, which sheltered formerly enslaved people on their journey north. Stay in New Albany for an inventive multicourse feast at Mesa, a collaborative kitchen space that hosts chefs from around the region.

In downtown Louisville, park at a charger and head to the museums around West Main St. Roots 101 traces African American history from centuries ago to the present day, while the well-designed Frazier History Museum illuminates everything from the bourbon industry to the region's diverse residents. Wrap up your road trip with a Hot Brown, Louisville's famed open-faced sandwich: turkey and bacon slathered in Mornay sauce.

**Below:** barrels by the route near Bardstown
**Right:** Kentucky Bluegrass Region horse ranch

Distance: 100 miles (161km)

# Louisville to Lexington

**KENTUCKY**

Make a Bourbon Trail triangle between Louisville, Bardstown and Lexington, sipping Kentucky's golden nectar at source, sampling hearty local fare and relishing the breeze through the bluegrass on rural highways.

First, a definition. Bourbon: a whiskey distilled in the US from at least 51% corn, and aged in charred oak barrels. Technically it can be made anywhere in the country, but its roots are deep in Kentucky's limestone-rich soil. Bourbon's been distilled here for more than 200 years, the tradition brought to the region by Scottish and Scots-Irish settlers and since refined into a high art. Today, Kentucky's official Bourbon Trail includes dozens of tourable artisan distilleries, as well as bourbon-centric museums, restaurants and inns. Seeing it all could easily take a week, so think of this trip as a sip, rather than the whole bottle – and bring along a designated driver, or take turns (see "Further info" opposite for more advice).

## THE BOURBON TRAIL FROM LOUISVILLE

Start in Kentucky's biggest city, Louisville, where you can rent an EV or top up your own at numerous charging stations. At downtown's Frazier History Museum, the Kentucky Bourbon Trail Welcome Center is the trail's official start point, its Spirit of Kentucky exhibition offering an excellent intro to bourbon lore: check out the bourbon-baron portraits, and sniff the barrel-woods used for aging. Don't miss must-prebook programing like tours on the history of Black Americans in bourbon-making.

© Irina Mos/Shutterstock

## Plan & prepare

### Tips for EV drivers

The territory here is slightly hilly, and most of the driving is on rural highways. This is a year-round trip, but winters can be freezing and therefore will lower an EV's range. Be sure to top up your battery in cities – charging points are few and far between in rural Kentucky. In Lexington, the University of Kentucky campus has a number of public charging points.

### Where to stay

As well as the usual chains in the outer rings, downtown Louisville has a wealth of historic hotels and B&Bs – notable bourbon-friendly ones include the Brown (brownhotel.com) and the Seelbach (seelbachhilton.com); 21c Museum Hotel (21cmuseumhotels.com) is a boutique hotel/art gallery with its own chargers. In Lexington, its sister hotel will charge guests' EVs for a valet fee, while hotels near KU campus, like the Campbell House (thecampbellhouse.com), are also a good choice for charger proximity.

### When to go

Kentucky's prettiest seasons are early spring (April and May) and early fall (September and October). But be aware: the first Saturday in May is the Kentucky Derby, preceded by a two-week Derby Festival: Louisville becomes massively crowded and prices skyrocket. September brings Bardstown's Kentucky Bourbon Festival, which is fun but packed. Summer can be unpleasantly hot and humid – though a mint julep will help – and winter ranges from mild to snowy.

### Further info

In Kentucky, like all US states, the legal BAC (blood alcohol concentration) limit is 0.08% for adult drivers. Nominate a designated driver or consider other options: the Louisville bars and distilleries mentioned can be visited on foot. Louisville and Lexington have a service called Dryver (dryver.com) to pick up drivers and their cars, and ride services like Uber and Lyft are ubiquitous in both cities, along with Bardstown.

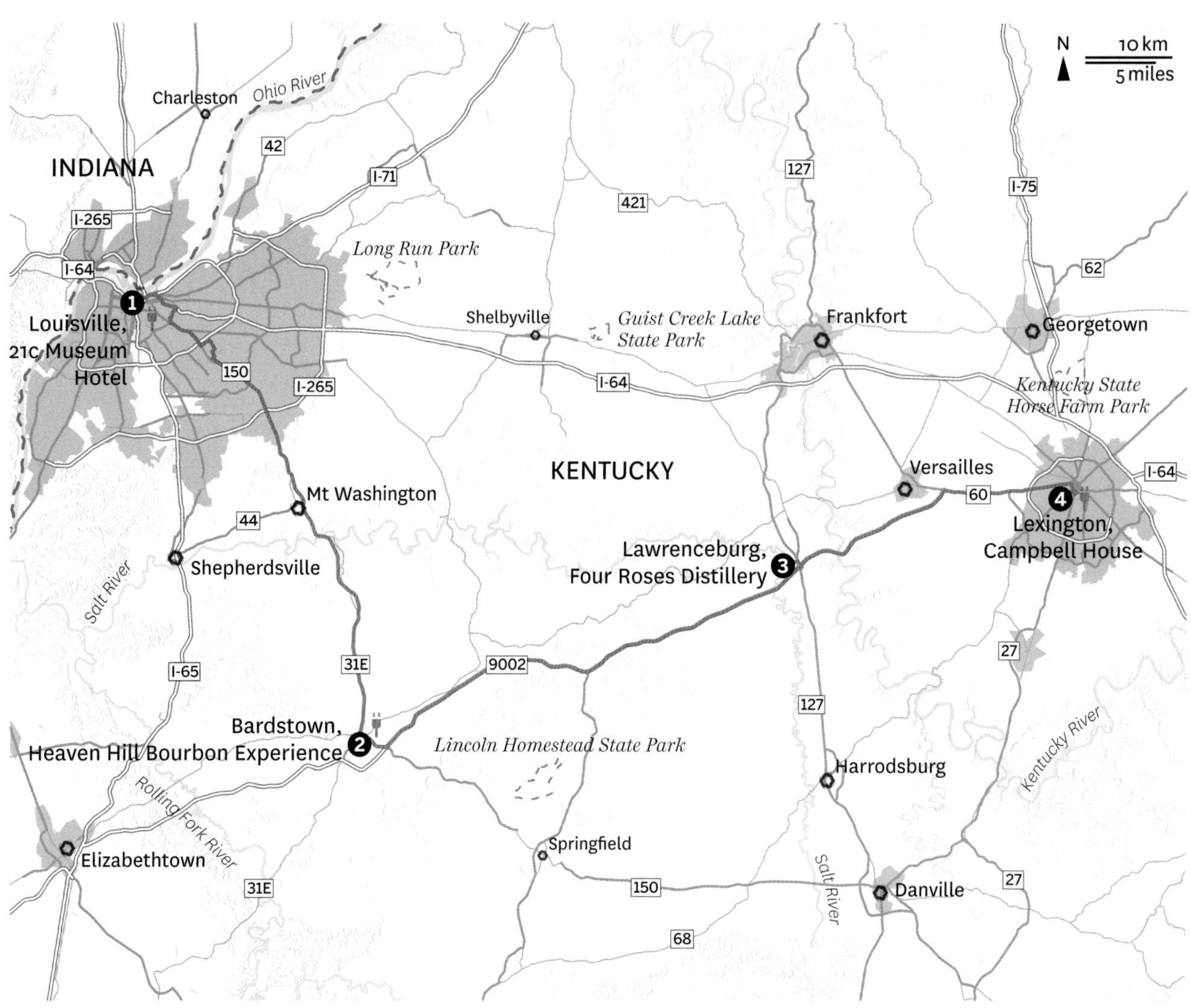


Turn left from the museum exit and you'll find four Bourbon Trail distilleries in walking distance. Hit Michter's Fort Nelson Distillery, Evan Williams Bourbon Experience, Old Forester Distillery and Angel's Envy Distillery. At Michter's, the second-floor bar features cocktails created by a cocktail historian (job envy?); try a Fort Nelson Crusta – bourbon, yellow chartreuse, lemon, demerara sugar, honey and Creole bitters. Have a nightcap before bed at the EV-friendly 21c Museum Hotel.

## BARDSTOWN TO LEXINGTON

In the morning, it's southeast towards Bardstown on the scenic route – Bardstown Rd, aka Hwy 150. It's a 40-mile (64km) drive through luscious green hills dotted with farmhouses and old country stores, so take your time. Bardstown itself is the spiritual heart of bourbon country, and home to Heaven Hill, the state's largest distillery. Explore the freshly renovated museum-like space on a Bourbon Experience tour, sample a flight of whiskeys, and create your very own label. For lunch, hit the historic Old Talbott Tavern, built in 1779 as a stagecoach stop, to fortify yourself with a country-fried steak and a slab of bourbon-caramel bread pudding. Hit the free city charging station at the farmers market parking lot if you need to top up.

The 60-mile (97km) drive east to Lexington takes you through the Bluegrass Region, where million-dollar racehorses graze behind artful stone fences. On a sunny day, it's hard to think of a landscape more delightfully serene. Just west of Lexington, near Lawrenceburg, stop at Spanish Mission–style Four Roses Distillery, its grounds blooming with – yes – roses. There are a half-dozen other distilleries in the area, if you're feeling energetic. Or save them for tomorrow and glide east into town for dinner at OBC (Old Bourbon County) Kitchen – cola-braised short ribs with a flight of rare bourbons – and a night at the Campbell House hotel. Cheers!

## Horse country

In Kentucky, horses that cost more than your car live in barns than cost more than your house. You'll no doubt see them grazing in enclosed meadows on the side of rural highways, practicing jumps at training academies, and galloping at blinding speeds. The state has a long equine history: settlers from the eastern seaboard noticed that the climate seemed especially horse-healthy, and that the limestone-rich terrain grew especially nutritious grass. Today, Kentucky horseracing is a multi-billion-dollar industry. Top racing venues include Louisville's Churchill Downs, home to May's Kentucky Derby; and Lexington's Keeneland, with race meets in April and October. Also in Lexington, the Red Mile is a clay track that hosts harness racing, with riders pulled in carts called sulkies; the city's Kentucky Horse Park has a fantastic equine museum, and presents a seasonal twice-daily Parade of Breeds, with everything from high-stepping Tennessee Walking Horses to clompy Clydesdales. Annual breeding earnings for a top stud horse can be as high as US$250,000; no wonder the security systems on some Bluegrass Region barns seem more fit for a bank.

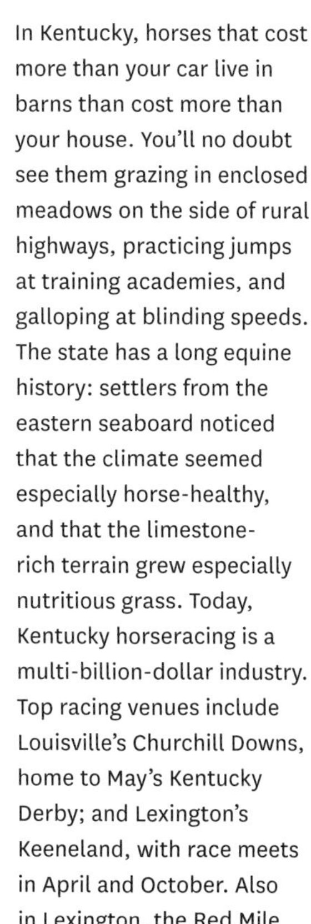

**Clockwise from top left:** driving through the paddock-studded outskirts of Lexington; race day at Louisville's Churchill Downs track; tasting flight at Michter's Fort Nelson Distillery, Louisville

**Below:** at the "Gateway to the Blues," Tunica
**Right:** live blues at Red's, Clarksdale

**Distance: 439 miles (707km)**

**Duration: 3 days**

# Memphis to New Orleans

**TENNESSEE, MISSISSIPPI & LOUISIANA**

Discover the sound of America in the neon-lit clubs of Memphis' Beale St through the tiny Mississippi Delta towns that birthed the blues to the all-night-jazz of NOLA's Bourbon St.

Memphis' Beale St doesn't play it cool. Every shop, every restaurant, every club blinks neon orange or pink or blue. Touts stand outside bars, enticing you with drink offers, with half-price wings. Bachelorette partiers spill into the street, clutching day-glo plastic yard glasses. A see-it-from-Mars sign overhanging the street reads "Home of the Blues."

And it's true. This neon-and-rum wonderland is the latest iteration of a street that's played an outsized role in US musical history. This makes Beale the right first stop on a musical trip from Memphis to New Orleans. So c'mon – order a drink, stay for the rest of the set.

It's late now, so crash at the nearby Peabody Hotel. Tomorrow will be a big day.

## INTO THE DELTA

Breakfast is at Sunrise Memphis, a cheeky modern Southern diner. Try the Dirty South biscuit, with fried green tomatoes and pimento cheese – it'll fuel you right over the state line and into the next portion of your road trip, the Mississippi Delta.

The Delta is technically the land between the Mississippi and Yazoo Rivers. But culturally it's much more. The floodplain's rich soil was perfect

## Plan & prepare

### Tips for EV drivers

The scenic drive through the Mississippi Delta is not the easiest route, charge-wise. You may need to detour onto I-55, which has more options. But if you plan carefully – so, plan to charge overnight at least once – you can make it. As for the cities bookending the route, Memphis' fast chargers are mostly in the wealthier suburbs; New Orleans recently launched a free public charging pilot program. The route is flat, but hot in summer, which affects range.

### Where to stay

Memphis has the usual gamut of cheap to expensive chains and a few renowned local choices like the Peabody (peabodymemphis.com). New Orleans has everything from hostels to ultra-chic boutique hotels and luxury chains. In both cities you can find hotels with chargers either onsite or nearby, such as Hotel le Marais, New Orleans (hotellemarais.com). The Delta has a burgeoning number of boutique hotels – such as the Alluvian in Greenwood (thealluvian.com) – as well as plenty of chains along I-55.

### When to go

Memphis in May is a huge festival and makes for a fun, though more crowded and more expensive, visit. Mardi Gras, 47 days before Easter (so usually February, sometimes March), turns New Orleans into an absolute madhouse. Unless that's your thing, don't attempt. New Orleans Jazz & Heritage Festival in April/May is also wildly crowded. Weather-wise, anytime but ghastly-hot midsummer is fine.

### Further info

The Delta portion of this trip largely follows Hwy 61, sometimes called the "Blues Highway." It's a rural route through cotton fields and small towns. Bigger, faster I-55 is slightly to the east. You can always look there for better charger options and more national chain hotels. New Orleans has famously bad road conditions – potholes, sinkholes – so drive cautiously to avoid a flat or worse.

## Beale Street Blues

Memphis' most famous street was established in 1841, but its fortunes were written in the 1870s by a formerly enslaved man named Robert Reed Church, who acquired the land and built Robert Church Park at the corner of 4th and Beale. The park became a hotspot for blues musicians, and its amphitheater attracted speakers from Booker T Washington to Teddy Roosevelt. Black business lined Beale – Ida B Wells' anti-segregationist newspaper had its office there – and a unique "Beale Street sound" developed in its nightclubs. WC Handy wrote *Beale Street Blues* in 1916, which quickly became a blues standard. A few decades later, musicians like Louis Armstrong, Muddy Waters and BB King played Beale, and a young Elvis was inspired by what he heard. But by the 1970s Beale, like much of downtown Memphis, had fallen victim to industrial decline and poor urban planning. People stayed away, storefronts were abandoned or boarded up, once vibrant clubs fell silent. But recent decades have seen a major revival, and now Beale throbs with life again. It's especially dynamic in May, when the Beale Street Music Festival kicks off the month-long Memphis in May celebrations.

**Above, from left:** neon nights along Beale St; a blues legend remembered in Clarksdale **Opposite:** French Quarter street musicians, New Orleans

for growing cotton, which in antebellum Mississippi meant plantation owners grew rich on the backs of enslaved people. The region still contends with deep poverty and disenfranchisement, but it's also been a wellspring of music and cuisine. Just across the border, in a Tunica cotton field off Hwy 61, the Gateway to the Blues Museum and Visitor Center displays memorabilia from famed blues musicians – see WC Handy's first cornet – and interactive exhibits (learn how to play a lap steel guitar!).

### SOUTH TO NEW ORLEANS

Then it's time to head south in your EV through the fields for 37 miles (60km) towards Clarksdale, where clubs like Red's and Ground Zero (the latter co-owned by the actor Morgan Freeman) demonstrate that this city remains central to the blues. The guitar sculpture you'll spot at the intersection of highways 61 and 49 marks the location where legendary Delta bluesman Robert Johnson was said to have sold his soul to the devil for his musical success.

Greenwood is another 57 miles (92km) south. Spend the night at the boutique-y Alluvian and dine at the Crystal Grill, with delights like lemon icebox pie and hot tamales (a Delta specialty, a twist on the Latin American version). Presently the only chargers here are slow; you'll have better access in Vicksburg, some 100 miles (160km) south – and check out the crayon-colored downtown of Yazoo City on the way.

Get onto I-55 and drive south for 200 miles (322km), stopping at McComb or Hammond for a charge if needed. Enter New Orleans as the sun is dropping below the wrought-iron terraces and live oaks of the French Quarter. Hear that throb? It's Bourbon St, and it is to jazz what Beale St is to blues. So park your EV, step out into the hot sticky night, and head through the worn wooden doors of Preservation Hall. People come from all across the globe to hear jazz in this hallowed venue. Tonight you're among them.

**Below:** Cumberland River waterfront, downtown Nashville
**Right:** Natchez Trace Parkway Bridge

➔ **Distance: 518 miles (834km)**

➔ **Duration: 3-5 days**

# Natchez Trace Parkway

**TENNESSEE & MISSISSIPPI**

Following a scenic byway from glitzy Nashville, past ancient burial mounds and historic trading posts to Civil War and Civil Rights sites, this leisurely EV drive meanders through Southern history.

Loosely following the Old Trace trail, once an important route across the southwest, this leafy drive through forests, farmland and hills has sights aplenty, from vestiges of Chickasaw, Natchez and Choctaw culture to antebellum grandeur, historic battlefields and the birthplaces of everyone from Elvis to Oprah.

## ONTO THE PARKWAY FROM NASHVILLE

Singers, songwriters and music fans have been flocking to Nashville for over a century, building its reputation as country music's global HQ. Today, its booming music scene and great nightlife give it a perennial party atmosphere. Join the masses and catch a performance at the iconic Grand Ole Opry, see Elvis' gold Cadillac at the Country Music Hall of Fame, pay homage to the "Man in Black" at the Johnny Cash Museum, or tour Historic RCA Studio B where Dolly Parton, Elvis and a whole host of others recorded classic hits.

Leaving Nashville, head south over the delicate Natchez Trace Parkway Bridge, 26 miles (42km) southwest, detouring to nearby Leiper's Fork with its collection of heritage buildings, antiques stores, artisan boutiques and art galleries. Consider continuing on to Victorian-era Franklin, with its historic downtown and Civil War

## Plan & prepare

### Tips for EV drivers

The bad news is there are presently no chargers along this route except in the major towns it passes close to. The good news, however, is that you won't have to detour far to recharge, but it pays to plan ahead and plot your route even more carefully than usual. The only stretch of this drive with fewer options for recharging is between Starkville and Jackson, so make sure you're fully charged before setting out from either destination.

### Where to stay

For period styling and old-world elegance, the Blythewood Inn (blythewoodinnbb.com) in Columbia is an antebellum home built in French Colonial style. The boutique Stricklin Hotel (thestricklin.com) in downtown Florence has bright, modern rooms featuring exposed brick, large windows and contemporary styling, while the Hampton Inn (hilton.com) in Starkville has spacious modern rooms. All have chargers onsite or within a short walk.

### When to go

March to June or September to November are the best times to travel, avoiding the oppressive heat and humidity of high summer. In Nashville, the CMA Music Festival, a foot-stomping celebration of all things country, takes place in June; the Tennessee State Fair gives the city a harvest focus in September; and the beers and bratwurst come out for Oktoberfest in the fall. Over in Natchez, July's Natchez Food and Wine Festival offers the pick of Southern-style food.

### Further info

Part of the Parkway's scenic charm stems from its ban on trucks, billboards, hotels or gas stations, but this does mean you'll have to detour off the route for food, lodgings (unless you plan to camp) and to recharge. The speed limit is also worth noting, just 50mph (80km/h) unless otherwise stated. It's a green route that's very popular with cyclists, so expect to find slow-moving traffic in places.

## Southern soul food

Food plays a huge part in big-hearted Southern hospitality, and a trip along the Natchez Trace takes you past old-school diners, soda fountains and bars bursting with local character. On the western edge of Nashville, make your way to the Loveless Cafe, well known for its biscuits, barbecued pulled pork and fried chicken; or sample the city's signature "hot chicken" at one of its myriad fried-chicken joints. To the south, Grays on Main in Franklin is set in an atmospheric Victorian building where you can fill up on pimento cheeseballs and shrimp with grits. In nearby Leiper's Fork, the historic Fox & Locke grocery serves fried catfish, smoked meatloaf and chicken tenders to adoring regulars, and has live music and a legendary open mic night on Thursdays. In Florence, don't miss the orange-pineapple ice cream at Trowbridge's Ice Cream and Sandwich Bar, which opened in 1918; while in Jackson, make a beeline for Brent's Drugs, a traditional soda fountain in the hip Fondren District that appeared in 2011 movie *The Help*. To the rear is the Apothecary, a hidden speakeasy-style cocktail bar in the original pharmacy storeroom. Finish up in Natchez at Biscuits & Blues to sample delights such as crawfish nachos, gumbo and catfish po'boys.

**Clockwise from top left:** take a break from the Trace to hike boardwalk paths into Mississippi's Cypress Swamp; "hot chicken" in Nashville; EV-charging signage at Nashville's Loveless Cafe

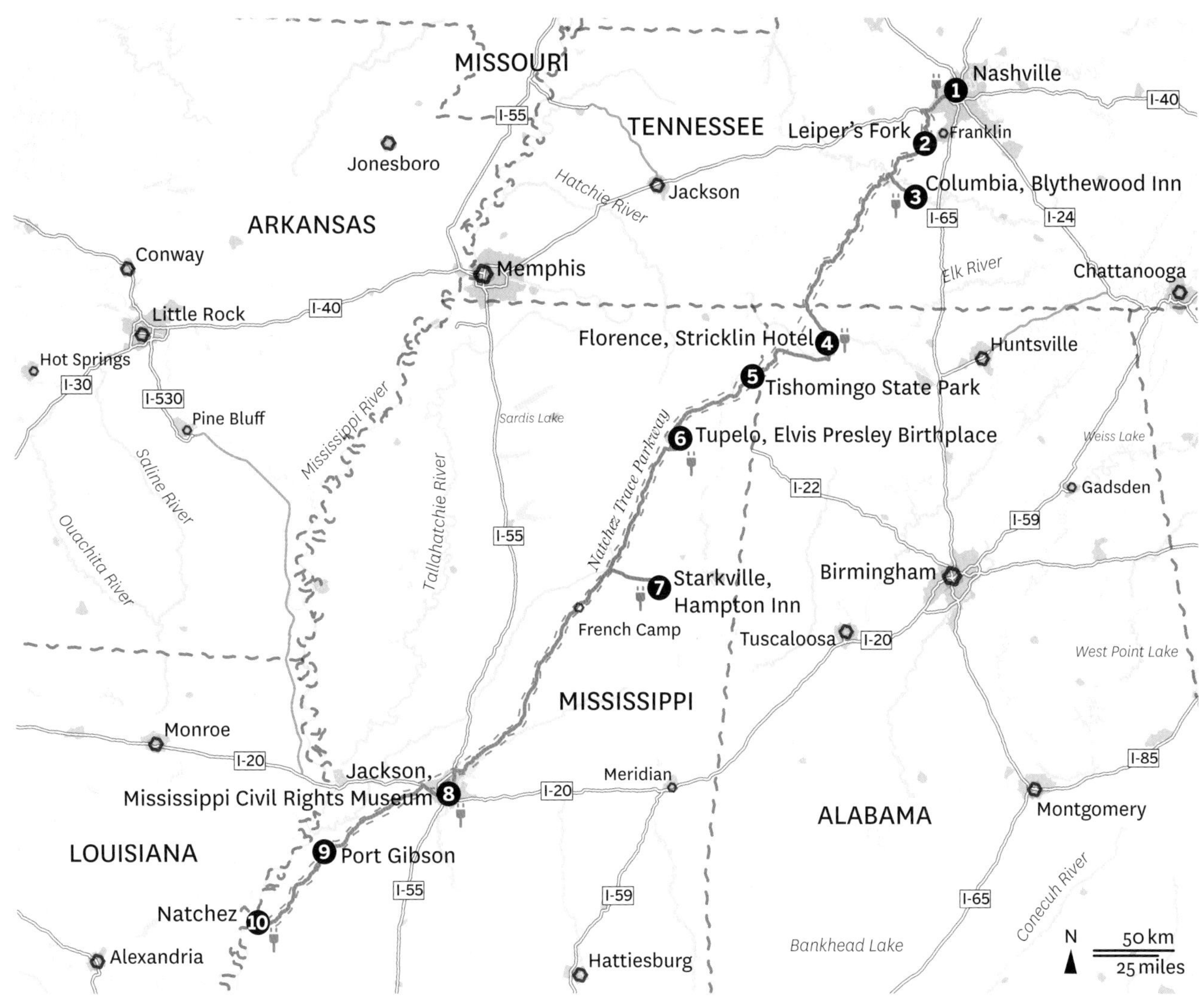


battlefield – the Battle of Franklin proved a pivotal moment in US history and you can visit the Carter House, which bears the scars of more than a thousand bullets. At Old Trace, 29 miles (47km) southwest, you can walk a section of the original trace, hike to nearby Jackson Falls, or visit the Meriwether Lewis Site a few miles on, which marks the burial place of the famed explorer.

From here, the road winds through dense forests to Bear Creek Mound, an ancient Indigenous burial site built between 1100 and 1300 CE, which may have once been topped by a temple or chief's house. Detour to nearby Tuscumbia to recharge as you tour Ivy Green, the home of Helen Keller, to learn about her remarkable life writing and campaigning for the rights and education of the deaf and blind.

## SOUTH TO JACKSON

Tishomingo State Park, 40 miles (64km) away in the foothills of the Appalachian Mountains, is a wonder of sandstone cliffs and waterfalls, massive moss-covered boulders and fern-flushed gullies. Walk the trails or canoe down Bear Creek before continuing past the 2000-year-old Pharr Mounds to the lively commercial hub of Tupelo. Here, you can visit the Elvis Presley Birthplace, the King's modest childhood home, and the chapel where he took his first steps towards stardom.

Nearby, drop into Chickasaw Village to learn about life in the fur-trading days of the early 19th century before heading south through the Tombigbee National Forest to the ancient Bynum Mounds and Jeff Busby Park. Set at the route's highest point, the park offers sweeping views over the forests and hills that lead to the historic trading post at French Camp, where the log cabins, bakery and smithy sit next to an ornate stagecoach that took the last Choctaw chief to Washington to negotiate with then-president Andrew Jackson.

## Tracing Natchez's history

A wildlife corridor along a ridge in the thick Southern forests, the "trace" later became a walking route for Native Americans before settlers, traders and explorers added another layer of history to this well-trodden path. Walkers took about 35 days to make the 444-mile (715km) journey – on horseback it was closer to 25 – and over time, the trail sank until it ran between steep-sided banks where bandits often lurked to pounce on unsuspecting travelers. The trace became a postal road in 1801 and was widened for wagons in 1809, but fell quiet with the advent of steamboat transport in the 1820s. In the early 20th century, the Daughters of the American Revolution campaigned for signage to commemorate the route's importance in the region's history and in 1938 the National Park Service took over, completing the Natchez Trace Parkway in 2005.

**Clockwise from top left:** Corinthian columns of Windsor Ruins, Mississippi; Natchez–Vidalia Bridge over the Mississippi; the Sunken Trace, a portion of the eroded Old Trace near Port Gibson

Further on, turtles and gators lurk in the dark waters of scenic Cypress Swamp, where tupelo and bald cypress line boardwalk trails that lead through the sculptural roots of these giant trees. From here, it's 30 miles (48km) to the Mississippi state capital, Jackson, where you can recharge as you tour the compelling Mississippi Civil Rights Museum. Throwing light on the long fight for racial equality, it explores the brutality of the past and the bravery of the Freedom Riders. For more local history, the Museum of Mississippi History reaches back to 13,000 BCE to tell the story of the state from prehistoric civilizations through Choctaw and Chickasaw culture to the cotton industry, the Civil War and modern times.

## PORT GIBSON TO NATCHEZ

Back on the road, handsome Port Gibson lies 63 miles (101km) to the southwest. Wander the historic streets, with their ornate heritage buildings, before detouring to the Windsor Ruins, where 23 slender Corinthian columns are all that remain of what was Mississippi's largest Greek Revival antebellum mansion. At Mt Locust you'll find the only surviving inn on the route, while ceremonial Emerald Mound is the most impressive of the Indigenous mound sites in the region and the second-largest in the US.

The final 22 miles (35km) of the Parkway lead through moss-draped oaks to Natchez, a city with a glut of stately homes – including the unfinished, six-story octagonal Longwood Mansion, and the William Johnson House, built by a prosperous free Black man who was also the owner of enslaved people. Natchez's wealth was built on the back of enslavement and it became a significant center for the Civil Rights movement, a period of history explored at the Museum of African American History and Culture. Finish your trip at the 200-year-old Under the Hill Saloon, to sip a drink overlooking the Mississippi and think of all those who made it here before you.

**Below:** guitars for sale in Nashville
**Right:** neon-lit Lower Broadway, Nashville's live-music hotspot

➔ **Distance: 210 miles (338km)**

➔ **Duration: 3 days**

# Nashville to Memphis on the Music Highway

**TENNESSEE**

Drive your EV from Nashville's honky-tonks to the blues bars of Memphis, from the hilly highlands to the sultry shores of the muddy Mississippi, with music in your ears all the way.

Technically, the "Music Highway" is the stretch of I-40 between Nashville and Memphis. Spiritually, it's a journey into America's stomping, fiddling, guitar-picking, wailing, hallelujah-shouting soul. What musical genre *doesn't* have a claim on Tennessee? Blues, country, gospel, bluegrass, soul, rock 'n' roll – they all have roots in the state's loamy soil.

## NASHVILLE & MIDDLE TENNESSEE

Begin in Nashville, long home to the country music industry but lately swollen into a gleaming metropolis of Michelin-starred restaurants and starchitect-designed towers. It's easy to rent an EV here, and easy to charge up too. But much of the action requires no driving: downtown's Broadway has multiple days' worth of attractions, from the unmissable Country Music Hall of Fame and the Ryman Auditorium – winter home to the Grand Ole Opry live country show – to honky-tonks like Tootsie's Orchid Lounge, which throb into the wee hours, seven days a week. Get in the spirit at Robert's Western World, a beloved boot shop/honky-tonk where you can eat a Recession Special – fried bologna sandwich, bag of chips, a MoonPie and a beer – while tapping your toes to up-and-coming country stars. After dancing yourself

## Plan & prepare

### Tips for EV drivers

Tennessee is one of the biggest EV producers in the US, but electric cars haven't yet caught on quite as much with the general population. Charging can be tricky between major cities, so stay flexible. Infrastructure stands to improve in coming years, with more funding coming down the pike. Drive Electric Tennessee (driveelectrictn.org) has a website full of useful info and charger maps.

### Where to stay

Memphis and Nashville both have the full gamut of accommodations, from hostels to exurban motels to storied luxury hotels, for instance the Peabody in Memphis (peabodymemphis.com). Nashville has several hotels with a commitment to sustainability, including the 1 Hotel (1hotels.com) and the Kimpton Aertson (aertsonhotel.com). Many hotels offer charging, though not necessarily fast. Between the two cities, options are mostly limited to basic and midrange national chains and campgrounds.

### When to go

This is the South (the "Midsouth," locals may tell you), and it gets hot, hot, hot. EV range declines with high temperatures, so keep an eye on levels if driving the route between May and September. Fall and spring are generally pleasant, and winter often fairly mild. Among the many big annual events, early June sees the CMA Fest in Nashville, which means crowds of country music fans. Memphis hosts the popular Memphis in May festival of music, BBQ and culture, and mid-August is Elvis Week.

### Further info

Parking's not cheap in downtown Nashville, but EV owners can apply for a Green Parking Permit. It costs $10 and will allow you to park in any designed Green Parking spot downtown. If you're staying a while, get one at the county clerk's office. Note that both Memphis and Nashville airports have chargers, useful if you need to top up your battery level before returning a rental car.

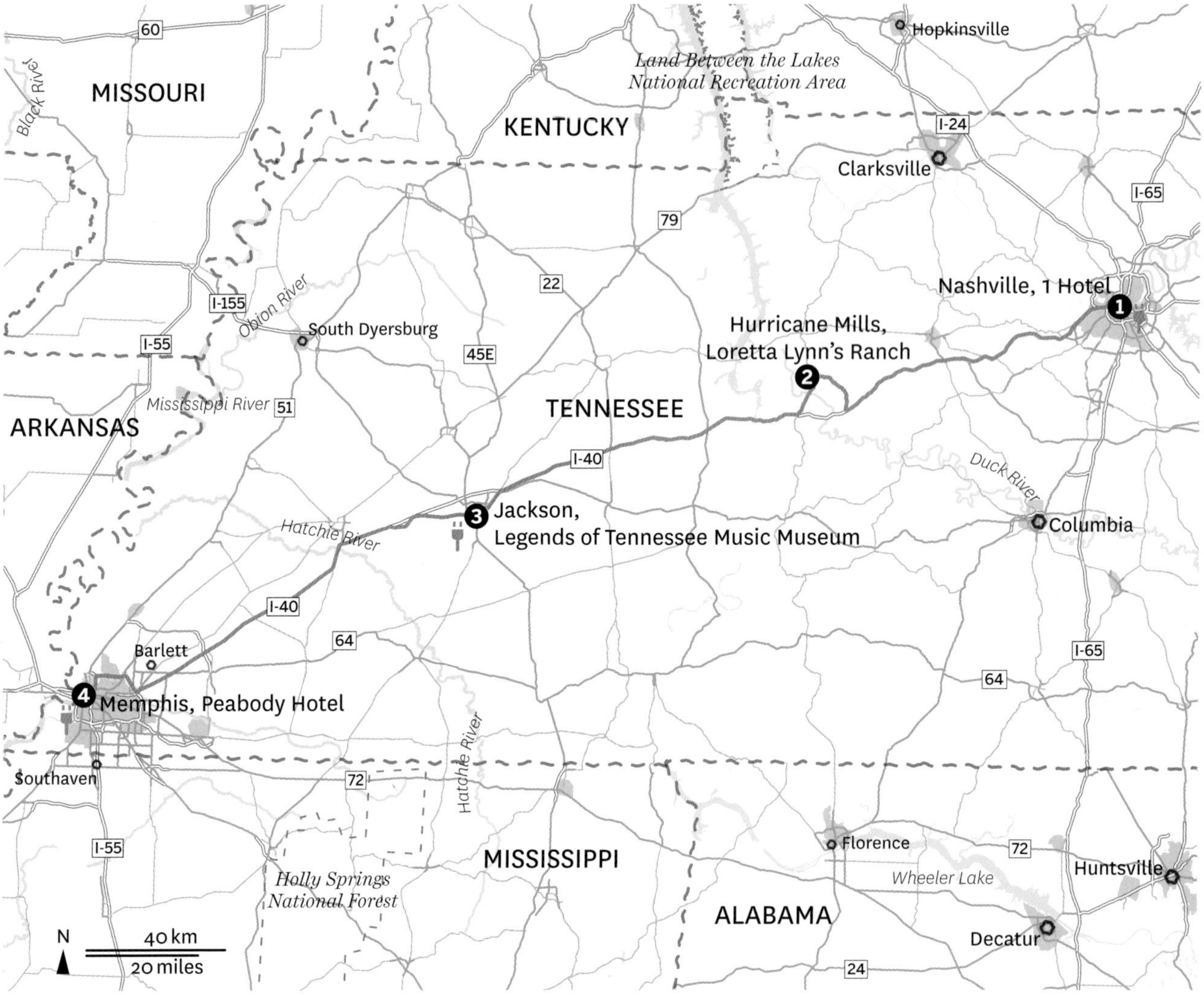

sweaty, upgrade for the night at charger-equipped 1 Hotel, a downtown luxury property with muted, California-crunchy vibes. In the morning, point your EV southwest and drive about 70 miles (112km) to the town of Hurricane Mills, just north off I-40. Here you'll find Loretta Lynn's Ranch, a sprawling campground, event space and replica of the late country star's humble Kentucky hometown. Tour the Coal Miner's Daughter Museum, browse the giftshop and – if you time it right – check out one of the country-fried special events, from rodeos to jamborees. Cabins for overnight guests have 50-amp outlets outside.

Another 70 miles (112km) of descending southwest through the gentle hills of Middle Tennessee take you to Jackson, where the Legends of Tennessee Music Museum is housed in a charmingly old-fashioned former library. The museum's glass cases hold memorabilia from Tennessee legends like Carl Perkins, Tina Turner and Big Maybelle. You'll find varied charger options close by.

## MEMPHIS

From Jackson it's 86 miles (138km) southwest to Memphis, sprawling in the heat on the banks of the Mississippi. Memphis is to blues what Nashville is to country, and Beale St is its Lower Broadway. But before music, food. If you've only got one meal in Memphis, make it BBQ, which here means succulent pork ribs or long-smoked pork shoulder in a sweet-tangy tomato sauce. Cozy Corner does them both. Then hit Beale for a night of foot-stomping blues in garishly neon-lit clubs where the drinks are cheap and the floors are sticky. A short way north – but a whole different world – the opulent Peabody Hotel has a grand marble lobby with a fountain full of live ducks. Wait… what? Yes, a century-old hunting-party joke has become a Memphis institution, with ducks marching between the fountain and their penthouse suite every morning and evening. The valet will whisk your EV to a charger while you retreat to bed, music still ringing in your ears.

## Elvis has left the building

While Elvis Presley was born in Tupelo, Mississippi, Memphis was his true home. It was here that a young Elvis cut his teeth on Beale St blues, pored over vinyl in local music shops, and was inspired by radio stations playing Black music. He recorded his first records at the Sun Studio, which now calls itself the "birthplace of rock 'n' roll" – visit for a tour. Memphis disc jockey Dewey Phillips launched him to fame in 1954 by playing *That's All Right* on his *Red, Hot & Blue* radio show; the rest is history. Elvis used his early earnings to buy a white columned mansion south of downtown, naming it Graceland after its builder's daughter. Today, it's a pilgrimage site – visitors flock from all over the world to tour the tiki-themed jungle room, gawk at memorabilia like rhinestone-studded jumpsuits, admire the car and airplane collections, and weep by Elvis' poolside grave. Follow up your tour with an Elvis-approved lunch: the fried peanut butter and banana sandwich at the Arcade, Memphis' oldest diner. Cap the experience with a selfie next to the guitar-strumming Elvis statue on Beale St.

**Clockwise from top left:** learn about a country-music icon at Loretta Lynn's Ranch near Hurricane Mills; Elvis memorabilia, Graceland; catch live blues performances on Beale St in Memphis

# EASTERN USA

**Below:** the Lake Superior shoreline at Whitefish Point
**Right:** Eagle Harbor Lighthouse near Copper Harbor, Keweenaw Peninsula

**Distance: 751 miles (1209km)**

**Duration: 5 days**

# Upper Peninsula loop, Sault Ste Marie to St Ignace

**MICHIGAN**

Tracing the shores of Great Lakes Superior and Michigan, this rugged and remote EV route promises mile upon mile of hushed hardwood forest plus waterfalls, a shipwreck museum and sweet, unpretentious villages.

You're headed out of Sault Ste Marie (the Soo to locals), bound for Paradise. Literally. Some 61 miles (98km) northwest along Lake Superior's Whitefish Bay, Paradise is a quintessential Upper Peninsula (UP) village, with fried-fish restaurants and rental cabins lining the water. It's the jumping-off point for Tahquamenon Falls, 200ft (61m) wide and amber-colored thanks to the presence of tannins from decaying leaves. Another 11 miles (18km) north takes you to Whitefish Point, where the wide, windy beaches are beloved by birders and beachcombers. The waters here are known as the "graveyard of the Great Lakes," with some 200 shipwrecks resting on the lakebed. Learn about them – the most famous being the *Edmund Fitzgerald* – at the Great Lakes Shipwreck Museum.

## PICTURED ROCKS TO COPPER HARBOR

Heading on, drive 114 miles (184km) west to Munising, then hit Pictured Rocks National Lakeshore, probably the UP's top sight. Multicolored sandstone cliffs, sandy dunes and forests shot through with silvery streams make it a northern fairyland. The best way to see the cliffs is via cruises leaving Munising's waterfront; charge your EV while you're on the water.

## Plan & prepare

### Tips for EV drivers

Charging infrastructure is improving in the UP, but slowly. For now, many of the towns are limited to Level 2 chargers, so you'll need to charge up at your accommodation overnight, or plug in for a few hours while you're doing a non-driving activity like cruising the cliffs of Pictured Rocks. The towns near the border with Wisconsin generally have better charging options.

### Where to stay

Cabin rentals – such as at Keweenaw Mountain Lodge near Copper Harbor (keweenawmountainlodge.com) – are a popular option in much of the UP; check in advance to see if it's fine to bring a plug for slow overnight charging. There are seasonal inns and motels along the lakes, and even hotels resembling beach resorts, with chairs and umbrellas on sandy shores. National chains are few and far between. Camping is ubiquitous in the state parks (see midnrreservations.com); bring bug spray.

### When to go

Summer is high season in the UP, which hardly makes it Disneyworld, but you'll still need to book ahead for popular accommodations. It's the only time of year you can reasonably swim in the Great Lakes without courting hypothermia. Fall is gorgeous, though temperatures are dropping quickly. Winter is fabulous for cross-country skiers, snowmobilers, ice fishers and dog sledders, but many things are closed.

### Further info

Michigan's Upper Peninsula sits like a crooked hat on top of Wisconsin. It's not connected at all by land to Lower Michigan, though the spectacular Mackinac Bridge links St Ignace to Mackinaw, spanning the Straits of Mackinac, the waterway between Lake Michigan and Lake Huron. Sault Ste Marie has a bridge over to its larger Canadian sister-city of the same name.

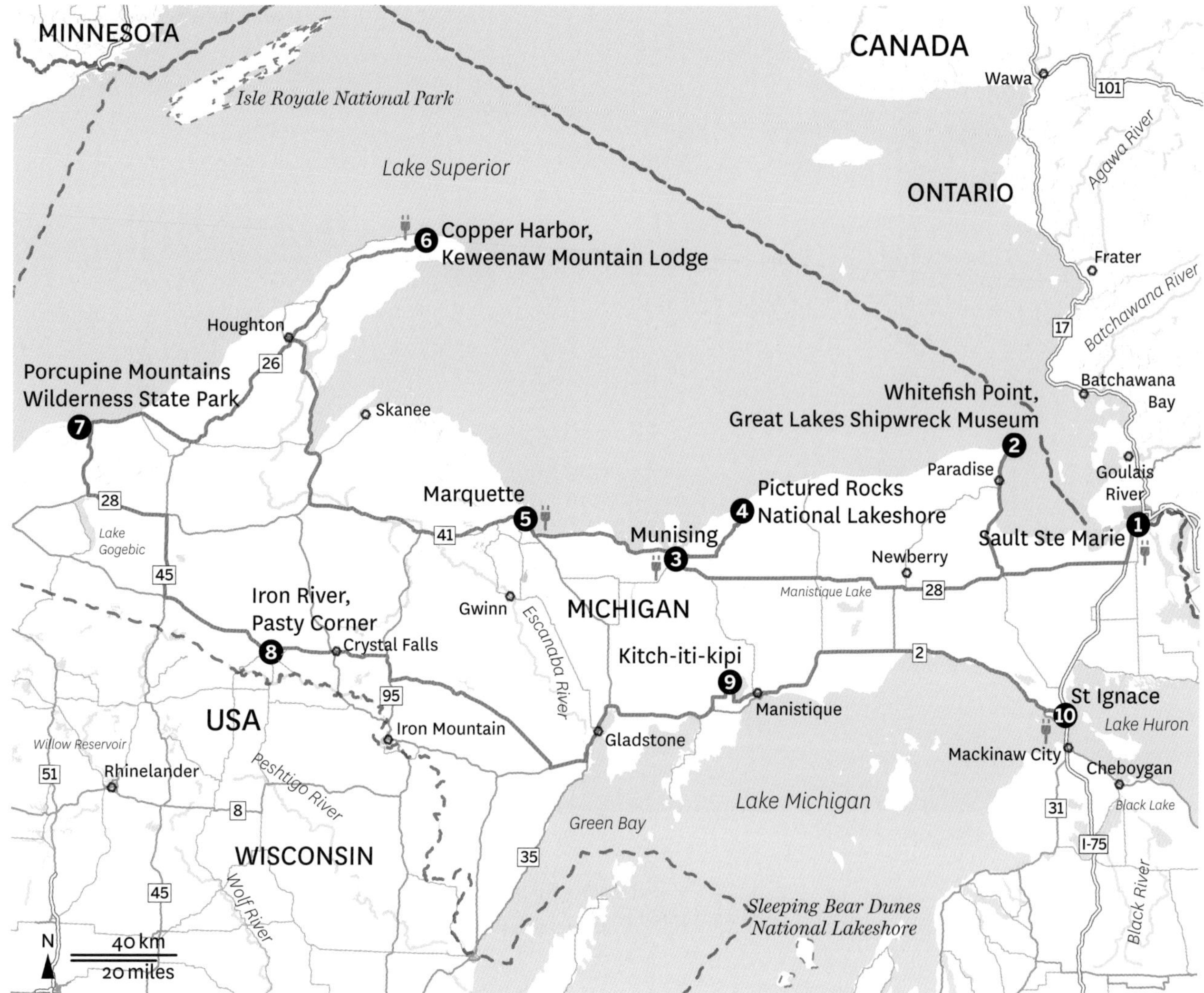


The next day, make the 43-mile (70km) hop to Marquette, the UP's biggest city, population a cool 21,000, a former ore-mining port turned college town. Grab a bite in the cute waterfront downtown and head to Presque Isle Park, on a sandstone peninsula jutting into the lake. Drive your EV in a loop around it, stopping at Black Rocks Beach and taking in the sunset from the western shore.

In the morning, it's 146 miles (235km) up the Keweenaw Peninsula to Copper Harbor, with a stop for charging at Houghton if necessary. As the name suggests, this was the center of Michigan's copper boom back in the mid-1800s. Today it's an outdoor hotspot: walk the boardwalks through rare old-growth white pines at Estivant Pines Wilderness Nature Sanctuary, birdwatch on the pebbly beach at Hunter's Point, hike to several waterfalls or kayak the craggy coastline. Overnight at 1930s-era Keweenaw Mountain Lodge, with log cabins (and fast chargers) tucked in the forest.

## PORKIES, PASTIES & A PIC-PERFECT POOL

Another 110 miles (177km) west, the Porcupine Mountains Wilderness (aka the "Porkies") encompasses 55 sq miles (142 sq km) of old-growth northern hardwood forest, cut through with nearly 100 miles (160km) of trails. The most spectacular spot is probably Lake of the Clouds, its vivid blue waters reflecting the sky. But you be the judge.

Now it's back east in your EV for around 100 miles (160km). At Iron River's Pasty Corner, fill up on fresh, hot "Yooper pasties": flaky hand-pies traditionally filled with meat and root veggies. Charge up here or in Crystal Falls (home to a massive honey mushroom called the "humongous fungus," possibly the world's largest living organism), then it's on east to Kitch-iti-kipi. Some 200ft (61m) wide, this photogenic spring is a shockingly clear emerald green. It's another 96 miles (154km) to St Ignace, last stop before crossing the bridge into Lower Michigan. Beware the trolls! (If that makes no sense, see opposite...)

## So what is a Yooper?

Residents of Michigan's Upper Peninsula are lovingly referred to as Yoopers. Being totally separated from the rest of the state, it's no wonder Yoopers have developed their own culture – there's even a distinct Yooper accent, influenced by the region's Scandinavian, French Canadian and Finnish heritage. You'll see Finnish influence in local culture, from the love of saunas to the concept of *sisu*, which translates to something like "stoicism and tenacity, with a dash of bravery" – which makes sense for a place with such geographic isolation and such snowy, unforgiving winters (200in/508cm snowfalls are not uncommon). The frigid winters mean sports like snowmobiling, ice fishing, ice climbing, snowshoeing and cross-country skiing are popular; note that hunting is also a big pastime in rural areas. As for cuisine, there's the Yooper pasty, a version of the Cornish pasty brought to the UP by Cornish miners during the mineral rush of the 1840s. Finnish-influenced dishes include sweet, cardamom-spiced breads and *pannukakku* (a baked pancake). Then there's local bounty like maple syrup, chokecherry jam and lake trout. As for residents of Lower Michigan, Yoopers refer to them as "trolls" – because they live under the (Mackinac) bridge!

**Clockwise from top left:** fall color en route to Copper Harbor, Keweenaw Peninsula; Yooper pasty; Porcupine Mountains Wilderness

**Below:** South Haven's 1872 lighthouse
**Right:** steep shores at Sleeping Bear Dunes National Lakeshore

**Distance: 337 miles (542km)**

**Duration: 3-5 days**

# Along Lake Michigan, New Buffalo to Traverse City

**MICHIGAN**

Follow the "Sunset Coast" of mighty Lake Michigan for a relaxing freshwater-beach vacation, visiting the sand dunes, state parks, buzzy resort towns, orchards and wineries that line up along the lakeshore.

Popular summer destinations, the resort towns along Lake Michigan's east shore largely began as shipping ports in the 19th century, when the Great Lakes were the highways to the Midwest. Lumber from Michigan's abundant forests was a primary product and while light industry and agriculture still support the region, tourism is its biggest driver today. The impetus to preserve the trees rather than cut them has resulted in a series of parks and preserves, and the network of slow two-lane highways that connect them are perfect for exploration by EV.

## LIGHTHOUSES & DUNES

Only an hour from Chicago, on the border with Indiana, New Buffalo marks the start of a 30-mile (48km) stretch through what's known as Harbor Country, home to small towns filled with vacation cottages along the Red Arrow Hwy. Just a few minutes down the road, stop in Sawyer to climb the 260ft-high (79m) sand dunes at Warren Dunes State Park – the payoff for the scorching climb is running back down into chilly Lake Michigan. Another 44 miles (71km) north, snap a shot of the big red lighthouse in South Haven, dating back to 1872 and still guiding freight traffic that plies the lakes. Then press on 20 miles (32km) in your EV to Saugatuck, long a destination for artists.

## Plan & prepare

### Tips for EV drivers

For a state that prospered producing combustion engines, Michigan has a robust network of EV charging stations clustered in cities, but also sprinkled throughout resort towns like Northport and South Haven on this drive, where you can plug and play for part of a day. The closest convenient airport to the route – about an hour from New Buffalo – lies in Chicago, where EV rentals are not hard to find.

### Where to stay

Near Saugatuck, enjoy a dose of retro Americana, including plastic decorative flamingoes, at the Pines Motor Lodge (thepinesmotorlodge.com), a stylishly updated 1950s-era motel. Stay like a local at Parkview Cottages (parkviewcottages.com), a block from the beach in Ludington, with knotty pine interiors and fieldstone fireplaces. Bay-view rooms at Delamar Traverse City (delamar.com) come with free EV parking and s'mores kits for fireside treats; there are EV chargers onsite.

### When to go

Lake Michigan's east coast is a year-round playground, though winter brings frigid temperatures and windy conditions. The lake's size and depth mean its waters remain chilly most of the year, though summers are popular for swimming and dune climbing. In July, Traverse City's annual Cherry Festival draws peak crowds to celebrate the local harvest. Fall attracts roadtrippers seeking the changing foliage, and harvest-your-own pumpkin farms and apple orchards.

### Further info

Along the roads hugging Lake Michigan, you'll see signs for the Lake Michigan Circle Tour, a 1100-mile (1770km) route that rings the lake, traveling through Michigan, Wisconsin, Illinois and Indiana. Its website (lakemichigancircletour.com) is a good source for local intel. Some motorists expedite the tour with a four-hour ferry crossing aboard the SS *Badger* between Sheboygan in Wisconsin and Ludington in Michigan. There are no EV chargers on the ferry, but you can top up at either end.

## Petoskey stones

Michigan's official state stone, the Petoskey is a Lake Michigan beachcomber's treasure. Fossilized prehistoric rugose coral (*Hexagonaria percarinata*), Petoskey stones have distinctive patterns of six-sided corallites, which are the skeletons of coral polyps deposited during the Devonian period, roughly 350 million years ago. The hexagons are tightly packed together and each has a dark center or eye. Rockhounds will want to get the stones wet to reveal their distinctive pattern; when dry they can look like any other on the beach. They can be as small as a pebble, though a 93lb (42kg) Petoskey stone holds the record as the largest ever found. Unique to the Great Lakes, where glaciers ground the stones from the bedrock, they are most often found along Lake Michigan and the northern inland lakes of Michigan's Lower Peninsula. Note that while you can pick up a few Petoskey stones on state lands, collection from federal lands – including Sleeping Bear Dunes – is prohibited. Search for them in the Leelanau Peninsula outside of Traverse City or near the Point Betsie Lighthouse in Frankfort; they're also sold in Northern Michigan's gift and souvenir shops, made into jewelry, paperweights and even Christmas ornaments.

**Clockwise from top left:** Petoskey stones; Traverse City cherries; Warren Dunes State Park; cherry blossom and vines on the Leelanau Peninsula

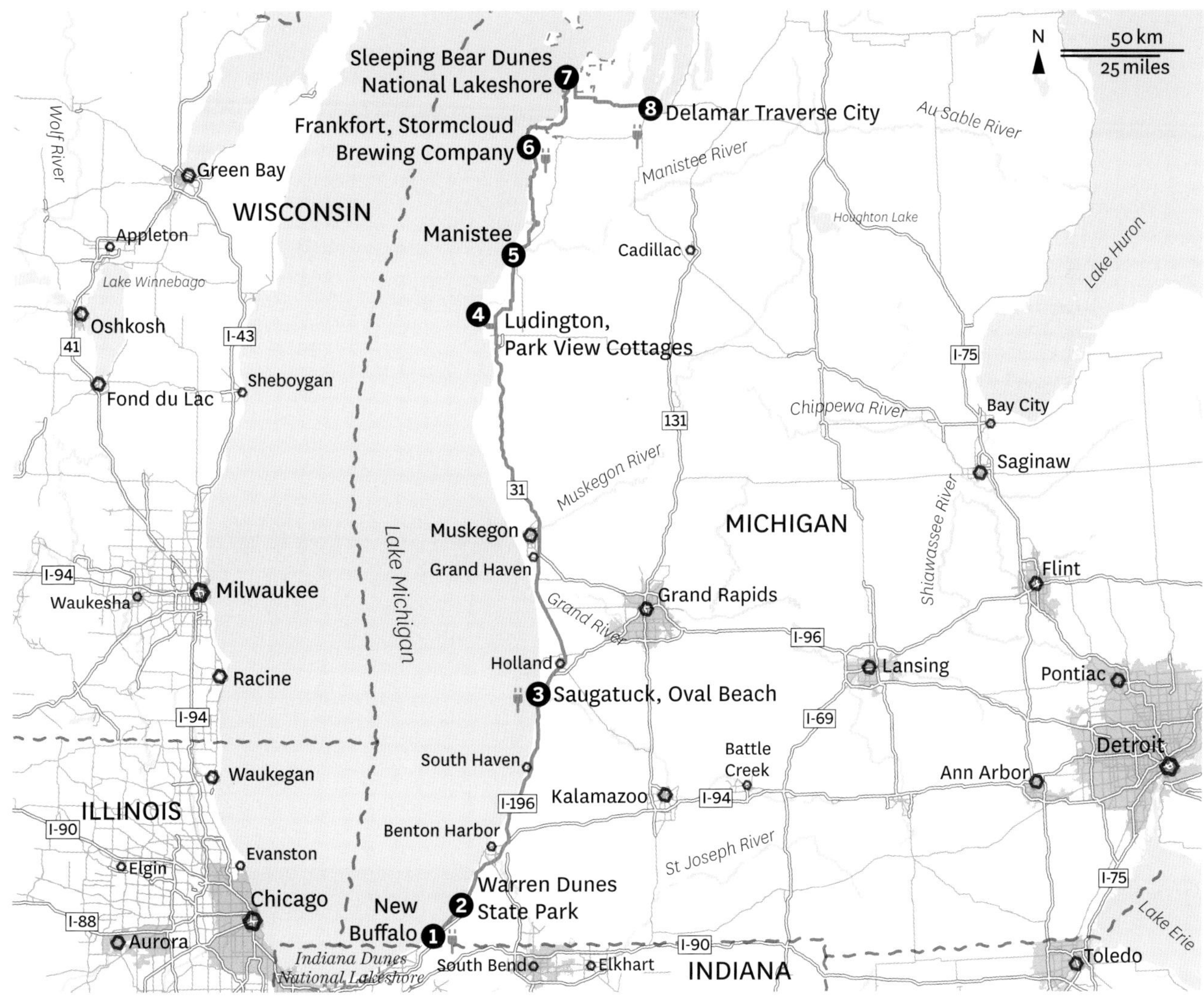


Park at a public charging station downtown to peruse the galleries and shops. It's work to climb the 303 steps to the top of Mt Baldhead, but you're rewarded by panoramic views and an undulating dune trail to popular Oval Beach.

## SUNSETS & CHERRIES

Just north of Saugatuck, Holland celebrates its Dutch roots with a tulip festival each May, while the working windmill at Windmill Island Gardens still grinds flour. North in nearby Grand Haven, a few blocks from public EV chargers, a 2.5-mile (4km) boardwalk along the harbor offers views of its 1839 lighthouse. Refuel with Great Lakes fish and chips at the Paisley Pig Gastropub before pressing north. In the warmer months, stay in Ludington, which has good charging availability, to swim, hike and catch one of Lake Michigan's epic sunsets at Ludington State Park.

Start the next day with a thrilling dune-buggy ride over the sands at Silver Lake State Park, just north of Ludington, with Mac Wood's Dune Rides. Near Manistee, pick up scenic Rte 22 northbound to quaint Frankfort, with a lively Victorian downtown and ample chargers. Hook up and share some honey-and-sriracha popcorn and a BLT pizza at Stormcloud Brewing Company.

With dunes on one side and cherry orchards or vineyards on the other, Rte 22 continues north along the increasingly rolling coast through the scenic agricultural lands of Leelanau Peninsula. Its chief attraction, Sleeping Bear Dunes National Lakeshore, preserves Michigan's highest sand dunes along 65 miles (105km) of coast. Traverse City, the state's self-declared "Cherry Capital" of the state, is less than an hour away and a great base for spending a few days dune-climbing, beachcombing or tasting along the wine trail that links over 20 vineyards throughout Leelanau Peninsula. Don't leave without trying the array of cherry-based foods in Traverse City, from ice cream and pie to salsa and cherry-chicken salad.

**Below:** the Catskills' Diamond Notch Falls, near Phoenicia
**Right:** Binghamton's stately Broome County Courthouse

**Distance: 405 miles (652km)**

**Duration: 3-5 days**

# Poughkeepsie to Niagara

**NEW YORK STATE**

With its gorgeous mountain scenery, Gilded Age homes, serene lakes and Ivy League colleges, this EV-friendly route wanders through the Catskills and Finger Lakes to the world's most famous falls.

Is Poughkeepsie upstate? No one can ever decide, but it's a good place to start the trip via a stroll across the Walkway Over the Hudson, the world's longest pedestrian bridge. Known for its Victorian cottages, handsome farms and stately mansions, the wider Hudson Valley was a retreat for the New York elite: north of Poughkeepsie you can visit Staatsburgh State Historic Site, a Beaux-Arts beauty once home to financier Ogden Mills. Filled with Flemish tapestries, gilded plasterwork and Asian art, it sits just south of affluent Rhinebeck, with its elegant boutiques and fine-dining restaurants.

## THE CATSKILLS TO ITHACA

Cross the Hudson in your EV and drive the 17 miles (27km) to artsy Woodstock, a free-spirited, music-loving town, although not the venue for the eponymous 1969 festival. Drop into the Center for Photography to see a changing program of exhibitions before heading on to Phoenicia, a great place to organize hiking, biking or float trips in the Catskills. Nearby, Peekamoose is a rustic local hotspot famed for its divine farm-to-table food; stop for a bite or head on along winding roads through mountain villages, keeping an eye out for bald eagles and ospreys along the way.

## Plan & prepare

### Tips for EV drivers

Upstate New York is well set up for EV drivers: you'll have no problem finding chargers, except perhaps in the more remote areas of the Catskills. Some chargers at accommodations are for patrons only, however, so check ahead. Winter temperatures drop to between −2°F and 4°F (−18°C to −15°C), which will affect your battery range; bear this in mind when planning charging stops.

### Where to stay

In the heart of the Catskills, the 15 rooms at 1920s Shandaken Inn (shandakeninn.com) promise refined yet rustic decor. Expect half-tester beds, traditional styling and a spa at Ithaca's La Tourelle Hotel (latourelle.com), set in attractive grounds and in walking distance of Buttermilk Falls. Buffalo's characterful Richardson Hotel (therichardsonhotelbuffalo.com) is located in a former asylum, though its wide corridors, high ceilings and contemporary styling give few clues to its past. The latter two options have chargers.

### When to go

Summer in the region brings long, hot, lazy days, open-air swimming and lots of concerts, but also throngs of visitors to Niagara Falls. If you're planning on doing some walking, more manageable temperatures make hiking easier in May or September. Expect gorgeous fall foliage in late September and October; in winter, although temperatures can be bitter, the falls look magical partially frozen, and you'll find cross-country and downhill skiing in the Catskills and around the Finger Lakes.

### Further info

This is a popular region so book accommodations well in advance, especially between June and September. Most roads are well maintained in winter, but when on higher ground (such as in the Catskills), be prepared for patches of black ice or snow. If you plan to cross into Canada to see Niagara Falls from both sides, you'll need a passport or enhanced driver's license to do so.

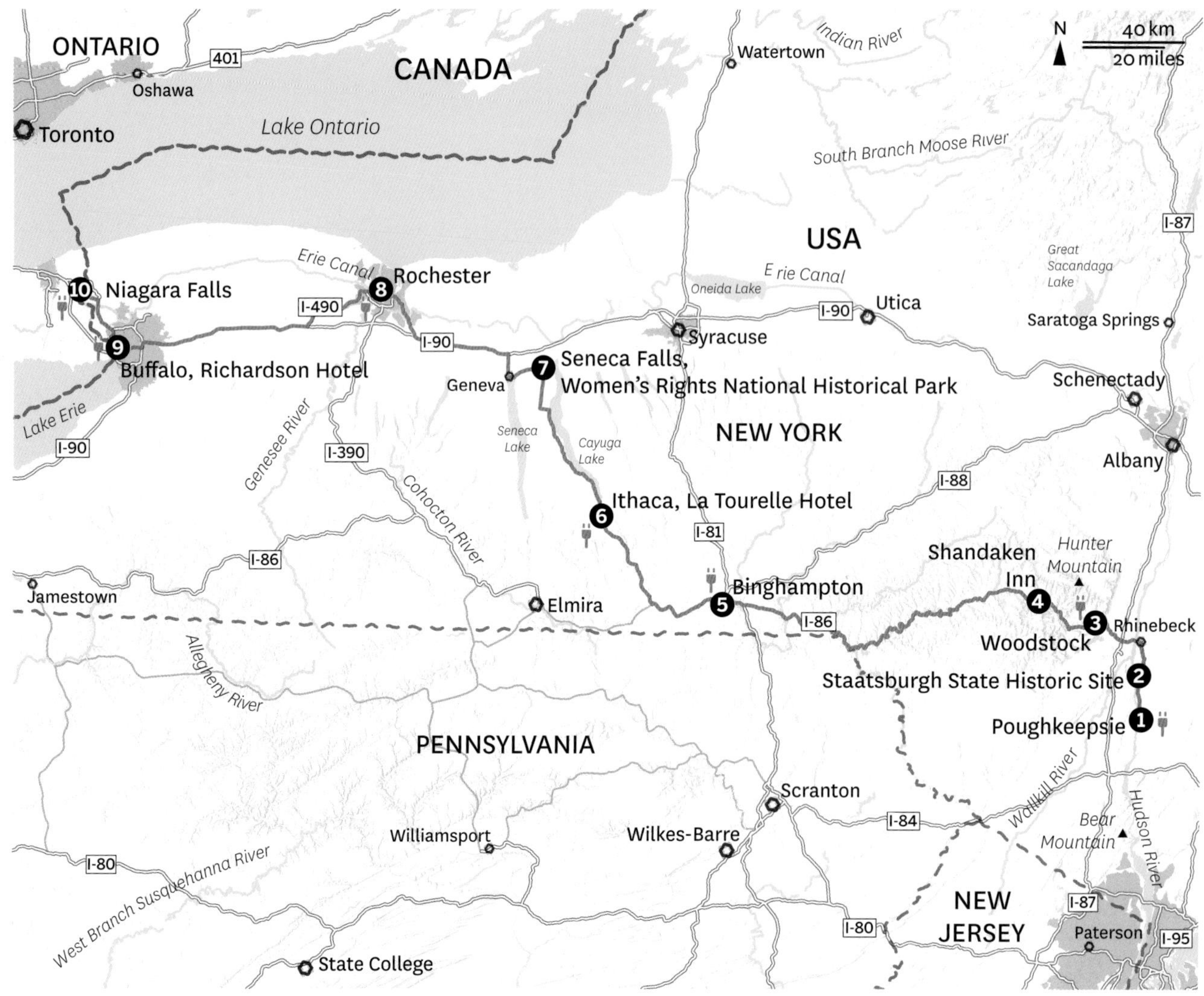


The next big stop en route west is Binghampton, where you can join a walking tour to learn about the city's heritage architecture. Explore life in the Gilded Age at the Phelps Mansion Museum or the Bundy Museum (Bundy Manufacturing was the precursor to IBM), then stroll down "Artists Row" on State St for galleries, restaurants, cafes and boutiques before driving on to cover the 49 miles (79km) northwest to Ithaca.

## THE FINGER LAKES

Set on the shore of Cayuga Lake, Ithaca is most famous as the home of Cornell University. Lush quads, bright young students, Victorian homes and a glut of restaurants, bars and boutiques give the town a firmly collegiate vibe. Cornell was founded in 1865 and the campus is well worth a wander. Architecture buffs shouldn't miss the Herbert F Johnson Museum of Art, set in a brutalist building by IM Pei and housing a major collection of pre-Columbian, Asian, American and European art. Around Ithaca, you'll find some of New York's most impressive gorges and waterfalls. Walking trails lead through the Buttermilk Falls and Robert H Treman state parks to scenic views and natural pools pummeled by gushing cascades.

From Ithaca, it's about 40 miles (64km) to sleepy Seneca Falls, a town with strong links to the women's rights movement. It was here, in 1848, that Elizabeth Cady Stanton and her friends drafted a declaration stating all men and women were created equal. Follow the story at the Women's Rights National Historical Park or visit the National Women's Hall of Fame, which honors inspiring American women.

Turn-of-the-century living was good in nearby Geneva, where period Italianate, Federal and Greek Revival homes survive in perfect shape. Stroll around the sights or catch a show at the historic Smith Opera House, one of the oldest still-operating performing arts theaters in the US.

## End of the line

It's just over 1000ft (400m) across the Niagara River to Canada at Buffalo's Broderick Park, and for many people escaping enslavement via the perilous Underground Railroad journey north, this was the end of the line. New York was the first state to abolish slavery, in 1827, but while some African Americans who made the journey here managed to live freely in Buffalo, many still feared the bounty hunters who rarely cared who they captured. Escape to Canada, where enslavement had effectively ended early in the 19th century, seemed the only safe option. A steady flow of African Americans took the Black Rock Ferry from what is now Broderick Park on Unity Island across the Niagara River right up until the American Civil War. Their story is explained in more detail on the interpretative signs in the park and along the 1.5-mile-long (2.4km) Bird Island Pier, which forges a trail right into the mighty Niagara. It's also worth visiting the Niagara Falls Underground Railroad Heritage Center (niagarafallsunderground railroad.org), which tells the story of those fighting for freedom and of the network of abolitionists and anti-slavery activists in western New York at the time.

**Clockwise from top left:** spring sunshine at Cornell University, Ithaca; signage on Broderick Park's Bird Island Pier; pastel perfection in Geneva

## The Cayuga Wine Trail

Although it's thought that European settlers were the first to plant vines in the Finger Lakes region, the winemaking industry only really took off here in the 1970s. Today, there are about 130 wineries in the area, most of them small-scale. A large number are clustered around Cayuga Lake, which gave rise to the US' very first wine trail over 40 years ago. Best known for their fine Riesling and Gewürztraminer, the wineries also produce excellent Chardonnay, Merlot, Pinot Noir, Cabernet Franc and Pinot Gris. Designated driver permitting, you could easily spend your whole weekend flitting between wineries, sipping and sampling New York's finest vintages and attending the regular free summer concerts hosted by the vineyards. If you fancy immersing yourself with an overnight stay, head to the Belhurst Castle in Geneva (belhurst.com), the region's finest wine hotel. Visit cayugawinetrail.com to find out more.

**From far left:** Finger Lakes winery; Niagara Falls; Buffalo's art deco City Hall, fronted by the McKinley Monument

Hop back in your EV and make your way to Rochester on the shores of Lake Ontario, a 45-minute drive away, to visit the George Eastman Museum, the world's oldest photography collection. A pioneering advocate for popular photography, Eastman built the imposing mansion which now holds several million photographic and cinematic artifacts. Wander the always-excellent exhibitions, take in one of the frequent talks or simply explore the gorgeous grounds.

## BUFFALO TO NIAGARA

From Rochester, it's 73 miles (117km) to historic Buffalo, New York State's second-largest city, set at the eastern end of Lake Erie. The downtown core is awash with heritage buildings dating to Buffalo's heyday at the turn of the 19th century. For culture, tour Frank Lloyd Wright's Martin House, six interconnected buildings completed in 1909; or the superb collection at the neoclassical Buffalo AKG Art Museum. You'll find political history writ large at the Theodore Roosevelt Inaugural Site, where you can join a guided tour to hear the dramatic tale of Roosevelt's emergency swearing-in here in 1901. Then stroll along the riverfront, take to the water in a kayak, relax in the cafes, bars and restaurants in Victorian Elmwood Village, or seek out some of the city's many craft breweries.

From Buffalo, it's just 20 miles (32km) in your EV to the thundering Niagara Falls. Here, the Niagara River plunges over three sets of cascades, the most monumental being Horseshoe Falls, which surge over an arch of rock in a crescendo of mist. You'll get some of the best views from Table Rock on the Canadian side, but for a sense of nature's sheer power head to Terrapin Point on Goat Island. Alternatively, take the classic *Maid of the Mist* boat cruise to the base of the falls for the full Niagara experience.

**Below:** Polestar 2 EV in Manhattan
**Right:** Bear Mountain State Park

**Distance: 170 miles (274km)**

**Duration: 2-3 days**

# Hudson Valley, Manhattan to Albany

**NEW YORK STATE**

Leave the NYC skyline behind and follow the Hudson River north on a drive past historic mansions, art galleries, quaint towns and the country's oldest vineyards to state capital Albany.

From Fort Tryon Park, at Manhattan's northern tip, the glimpses of the Hudson River – your watery companion on this trip – give a taste of what's to come. Heading north in your EV along Broadway (less poetically, Rte 9), you pass through commuter towns like Yonkers, where you can divert west to Warburton Ave, a quieter route that parallels the river.

## HISTORIC HOUSES & SPOOKY TALES

After 16 miles (26km), you'll approach Tarrytown – look for "Lyndhurst Mansion" signs and follow them. At the end of a long driveway stands a Gothic Revival masterpiece built by architect Alexander Jackson Davis. Hudson Valley's many grand houses mostly date to the late 19th century's Gilded Age, but Lyndhurst is much older, having been built in 1838. A few miles north is Sleepy Hollow, famous for its eponymous story, penned by Washington Irving in 1820, involving a headless horseman and spooky goings-on. Find Irving's grave (and those of other famous locals including Andrew Carnegie, William Rockefeller and Walter Chrysler) in the town's cemetery, before exploring another historic house, Philipsburg Manor, a short walk away. Constructed by a Dutch immigrant in the late 17th century, it offers an

## Plan & prepare

### Tips for EV drivers

Distances between stops on this drive are short and you're never far from a charger. There are plenty of places to plug in around New York City and Albany, though in the latter the chargers tend to be slower. Elsewhere they are easily found at or close to each destination, and are a mix of Tesla Superchargers and slower ones. As well as having lovely river views, Long Dock Park in Beacon has free chargers; it's just a few minutes' walk from the Dia gallery.

### Where to stay

This trip can easily be done with just one overnight stay, at the Roundhouse (roundhousebeacon.com) in Beacon, but to spread things out and follow a more leisurely pace there are good options elsewhere – from Bear Mountain Inn (visitbearmountain.com) in the state park of the same name to one of the country's longest operating inns, the Beekman Arms in Rhinebeck (beekmandelamaterinn.com); ask for a room in the original building. All options have chargers nearby.

### When to go

Spring and summer are when the valley is at its lushest and the weather warmest, but it gets oppressively humid and very busy in July and August. Almost as busy is fall, when the woods covering much of the valley put on a magnificent autumn display and Halloween is a big deal. Winter snow gives the cute towns and beautiful countryside a magical feel – and you can even skate at Bear Mountain Ice Rink.

### Further info

Bridges across the Hudson River have tolls for eastbound drivers (so on this trip that's just one payment, when heading for Beacon). The payment system is complicated. Cash payments on the spot are not accepted, so sign up for an E-ZPass (e-zpassiag.com) for discounts if bringing your own car (electric vehicle drivers get an additional 10% off) or, if renting, check with the rental company about toll payments being included in the cost.

## Grand homes

Hudson Valley's rural appeal and proximity to New York have long made it a favorite second-home location for the wealthy – so if Lyndhurst Mansion (lyndhurst.org) piques your interest, you'll find there are plenty more grand houses to visit. Kykuit (savingplaces.org/places/kykuit), close to Sleepy Hollow, gets its name from the Dutch for "lookout" and was home to four generations of Rockefellers. Guided tours of varying lengths start from Philipsburg Manor and give access to the interior of Kykuit, its art galleries and its gardens created by Olmsted (of Central Park fame). The Beaux-Arts beauty that is Vanderbilt Mansion (nps.gov/vama), in Hyde Park, still holds most of the furniture its owner, railroad tycoon Frederick Vanderbilt, had shipped over from Europe in the late 19th century to fill the 54 rooms of his summer residence. Further north, Olana (olana.org), on the outskirts of Hudson, is one of the valley's finest houses. Sitting on a hill with panoramic views, it was designed by landscape painter Frederic Church, who took inspiration from his travels in the Middle East. The park is free; the house itself can be visited on paid tours.

**Clockwise from top left:** Italian Gardens at the Vanderbilt Mansion, Hyde Park; Hudson Valley vineyard; the 17th-century Philipsburg Manor, Sleepy Hollow; New York State Museum, Albany

illuminating look at colonial life, including how enslaved people kept the farm running.

Back in the car, the river and railroad track accompany you until just past Peekskill, where you leave Rte 9 and follow a single-lane road, cut into the cliffs, that leads over the Hudson to its west bank and Bear Mountain State Park. Drive to the summit of the park's namesake peak and you'll be rewarded with views over the wooded surroundings and along the Hudson to, on a clear day, the skyscrapers of New York City. Set off on other hiking trails around Bear Mountain while charging your car in the main parking lot.

Legs stretched and EV charged, it's time for a scenic 19-mile (31km) detour into Hudson Valley Wine Country. This area has the USA's oldest vineyards, none older than Brotherhood Winery, established in 1839. Take a tour of the cellars then enjoy a tasting (they produce mead as well as wine) and maybe a plate of charcuterie before letting the designated driver get back behind the wheel. Your next destination is the Roundhouse, only 17 miles (27km) away, on the east bank of the river in Beacon. Dine in the restaurant – your meal comes with a waterfall backdrop – then sleep in one of its hotel rooms.

### ART, ANTIQUES & ALBANY

Start the day with some monumental art at Dia Beacon, marveling at works by Louise Bourgeois and Gerhard Richter – and river views from the gallery's terraces – before beginning today's 93-mile (150km) drive. Break the trip up by crossing the pedestrian-only Walkway Over The Hudson bridge just north of Poughkeepsie. Then it's on to Hudson, a former whaling port full of old-town charm; it's well worth a stop for a wander down lively Warren St and a browse in the many antique shops and art galleries.

For the home stretch, follow tranquil Rte 9J until you cross the Hudson one final time and enter the state capital, Albany. Expand your knowledge in the New York State Museum, smell the flowers in Washington Park, then shop and eat on Lark St.

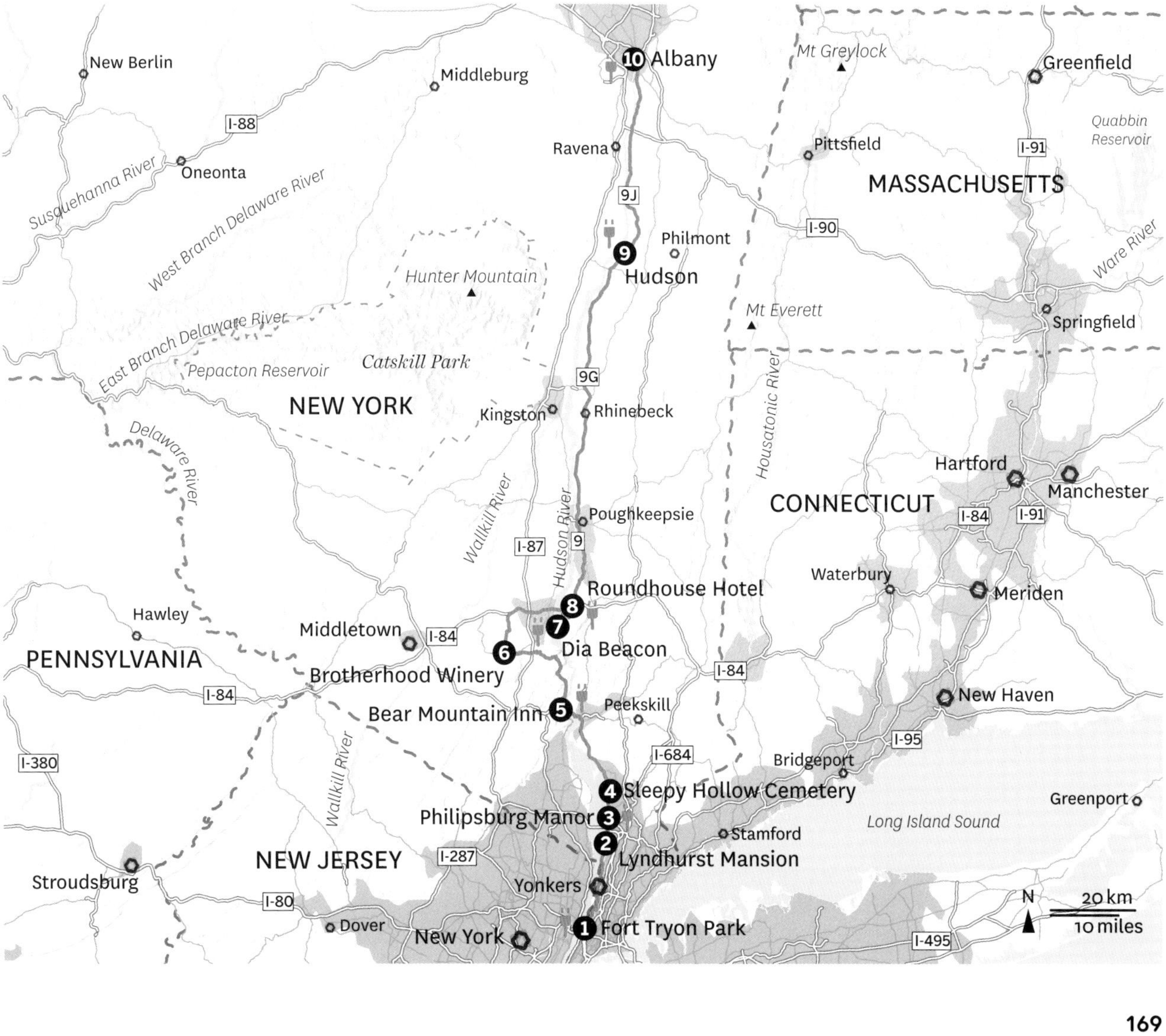

1 Fort Tryon Park
2 Lyndhurst Mansion
3 Philipsburg Manor
4 Sleepy Hollow Cemetery
5 Bear Mountain Inn
6 Brotherhood Winery
7 Dia Beacon
8 Roundhouse Hotel
9 Hudson
10 Albany
New Berlin
Middleburg
Mt Greylock
Greenfield
Quabbin Reservoir
I-88
Ravena
Pittsfield
I-91
Oneonta
Susquehanna River
West Branch Delaware River
MASSACHUSETTS
9J
I-90
Philmont
Ware River
Hunter Mountain
Mt Everett
Springfield
East Branch Delaware River
Pepacton Reservoir
Catskill Park
9G
NEW YORK
Kingston
Rhinebeck
Housatonic River
Delaware River
Hartford
Manchester
Wallkill River
Poughkeepsie
CONNECTICUT
I-84
I-91
I-87
Hudson River
9
Waterbury
Meriden
Hawley
Middletown
I-84
PENNSYLVANIA
I-84
I-84
Peekskill
New Haven
I-95
I-380
I-684
Bridgeport
Wallkill River
Greenport
Long Island Sound
Stamford
NEW JERSEY
I-287
Stroudsburg
Yonkers
I-80
N
20 km
10 miles
Dover
New York
I-495

**Below:** digging in to a seafood feast, Baltimore
**Right:** the LV116 *Chesapeake* museum ship at Baltimore's Inner Harbor

**Distance: 460 miles (740km)**

**Duration: 7 days**

# Baltimore to NYC

**MARYLAND TO NEW YORK STATE**

Take a Mid-Atlantic foodie tour by EV, stopping at every fried-chicken joint, pizzeria and backroad crab shack along the way, breathing in Chesapeake Bay breezes and New Jersey turnpike smog alike.

Baltimore – "Charm City" – sometimes gets left in the dust on the dash from DC to NYC. Big mistake. That's why this tour starts here, in this down-to-earth harborside city, where immigrants from all over the world have long made the local bounty – crabs, oysters, fresh produce – into some of the nation's best food.

On Downtown's Eutaw St, Lexington Market was established in 1782. Today it's what some might call a tourist trap, but it's still charming, and also an easy place to sample several "Bawlmer" classics – try the fudge-covered cake rounds known as Berger cookies, or the "chicken box" – wings in a cardboard take-out box with wedge fries. Walk along the museum-filled Inner Harbor, then mosey over to Fell's Point, where boutiques and bistros take up the brick-built former shipbuilding warehouses along the Patapsco River. Spend the night at one of the city's EV-friendly hotels, like the splashy Sagamore Pendry, in a 1914 Beaux Arts cargo warehouse.

## ANNAPOLIS & THE EASTERN SHORE

In the morning, head southeast towards Maryland's state capital, Annapolis, 33 miles (53km) away. If you get an early start, you can make it for breakfast at Chick & Ruth's Delly (just kidding – breakfast is served all day),

## Plan & prepare

### Tips for EV drivers

With the exception of Maryland's Eastern Shore and the Delaware coast, this is a drive through some of the USA's most populated terrain, with plenty of charger stops – though they may be busy. All the major cities mentioned have both municipal and private charging stations. You'll be doing a lot of urban driving on this trip, which isn't taxing on range.

### Where to stay

You'll have your pick of places to stay in the major cities, with many hotels offering chargers, such as the Sagamore Pendry in Baltimore (pendry.com). Maryland's Eastern Shore has high-end tourist towns with plenty of inns and B&Bs, as well as rural agricultural villages with few options. The distances aren't far, though, so you're unlikely to get caught out. On the Delaware coast some motels may close for the winter.

### When to go

Ideal times would be late spring (May to June) or early fall (September). The weather will still be warm, but crowds and traffic won't be at their summer peak. Some shops and restaurants on the Delaware coast will shutter for off-season in late fall/winter. Any warm-weather holiday – Memorial Day, Fourth of July, Labor Day – is best avoided because of wild traffic on the interstates.

### Further info

EVs are authorized to drive in the High Occupancy Vehicle (HOV) lanes of the New Jersey Turnpike, regardless of passenger numbers. In addition, NYC and New Jersey also offer tollway, bridge and tunnel discounts for registered EVs – you apply through E-ZPass (e-zpassiag.com). There are similar incentives in Maryland, but they don't apply to the roads you'll be traveling for this trip.

## Chesapeake Bay

Lying between Maryland and Virginia and the Delmarva Peninsula, the Chesapeake Bay is the largest estuary in the US. While it only borders Maryland and Virginia, its watershed covers Delaware, New York, Pennsylvania, West Virginia and Washington, DC. Running north to south from the mouth of the Susquehanna River some 200 miles (320km) to the Atlantic, it's only 30 miles (48km) at its widest. The land around the Chesapeake has been inhabited for more than 10,000 years, first by multiple Native American tribes, then by European colonists in the early 1600s. Some 3600 species of plant and animal life exist in the bay, many of them commercially important. For centuries the people of the area have made their living from blue crabs, oysters and menhaden fish. In the late 19th century, the Chesapeake supplied half the world's oysters, an industry so valuable it spawned piracy during the so-called Oyster Wars. The industry is still worth billions, though climate change and pollution have caused massive declines in fish and shellfish populations. Other animals that call the bay home – or use it as a stop on migration journeys – include ospreys, peregrine falcons, sea turtles, bottlenose dolphins and hammerhead sharks.

**Above:** harvesting Chesapeake Bay oysters
**Opposite, from left:** around Philly – cheesesteak heaven at Geno's; the Liberty Bell

where classic greasy-spoon dishes are named after the politicians who've flocked here for nearly 60 years. You'll find several Level 3 chargers within a few blocks. Stroll the historic waterfront downtown and watch yachts parade along the narrow urban waterway known appropriately as Ego Alley. Then head 3 miles (5km) west to the Pennsylvania Dutch Market, where Amish vendors sell fresh produce and traditional comfort food – soft pretzels, smoked meat, homemade jam – in a perpetually crowded hangar-sized space.

Now it's east across the splendid, 4.3-mile (7km) Memorial Bay Bridge, crossing Chesapeake Bay to Maryland's rural Eastern Shore and driving 50 miles (80km) south through low-lying marshlands cut through with silvery streams, shorebirds wheeling overhead. This is a watery landscape and a watery way of life: fishing, oystering and shipbuilding have long been the main industries. On a curling finger of land between the Chesapeake and the Miles River, St Michaels is as lovely as an oil painting, with 18th-century architecture and water views in every direction. Here you'll find the Crab Claw, a much-loved seafood shack slinging steamed blue crabs by the dozen. The nearby Chesapeake Bay Maritime Museum has chargers – as do several of the B&Bs, where you can sleep to the sound of wind on water.

### DELAWARE TO PENNSYLVANIA

Your next stop is Rehoboth Beach, Delaware, 70 miles (113km) east on the Atlantic side of the Delmarva Peninsula. It's a sweet little vacation town with shingled cottages and a lengthy boardwalk. Get some vinegar-soaked fries at Thrasher's, a century-old boardwalk institution, then head just north to Lewes for buttery-sweet Delaware Bay oysters in the historic downtown.

In the morning, it's north up the Coastal Hwy (Rte 1) to Philadelphia, 120 miles (193km) on – you can charge in Dover or Wilmington en route. On the banks of the Schuylkill River, historic, diverse Philadelphia is one of the USA's greatest eating cities. Spend at least a day just eating and walking around: cannoli or roast pork sandwiches in South Philly's historic Italian neighborhoods, which also host some of the country's best taquerias (head to the Italian Market area for all the above); cheesesteaks at Pat's or Geno's (they're rivals, directly across from one another); soft pretzels, jerk chicken and Amish specialties at the Reading Terminal Market. EV chargers are clustered around Center City, home to some of the most famous attractions – the Liberty Bell, Independence Hall, the Franklin Institute science museum – as well as many historic hotels.

Hazleton
Lake Hopatcong
I-80
Palisades Park, Broad Ave 7
I-95
Hudson River
Lehigh River
New York 8
Hempstead
PENNSYLVANIA
Easton
I-81
I-78
Allentown
Raritan River
Reading
Doylestown
Princeton
Harrisburg
Schuylkill River
I-95
Long Branch
Trenton 6
I-76
NEW JERSEY
York
I-76
5 Philadelphia
Beachwood
I-83
I-95
Newark
Wilmington
9
MARYLAND
I-95
Middletown
Atlantic City
I-70
Ellicott City
1 Baltimore, Sagamore Pendry
ATLANTIC OCEAN
1
I-95
Dover
Chesapeake Bay
Rockville
I-97
Delaware Bay
2 Annapolis
50
Milford
Washington, DC
Easton
3 St Michaels, Crab Claw
VIRGINIA
4 Rehoboth Beach
DELAWARE
N
30 km
15 miles

## You say hotdog, I say Texas Tommy

You'll find hotdogs in every corner of the US, but nowhere but the Mid-Atlantic are there so many regional varieties in such a condensed space. New York means kosher-style beef dogs with sauerkraut and mustard, or dirty-water dogs fished out of a ketchup- and cumin-scented broth and slapped on a bun by street vendors. In New Jersey, Italian-style dogs are deep-fried and served in an Italian bread roll with onions and peppers, while local Koreatowns serve up the gamja-hotdog, fried in a sweet batter studded with French fries. Philadelphia has the Texas Tommy: split down the middle, stuffed with Cheez Whiz and wrapped in bacon. Baltimore's Jewish delis offer the bologna dog, a beef hotdog sharing the bun with griddled slices of bologna (why? Why not). DC is all about half-smokes, coarsely ground hotdogs with chili and chopped raw onions.

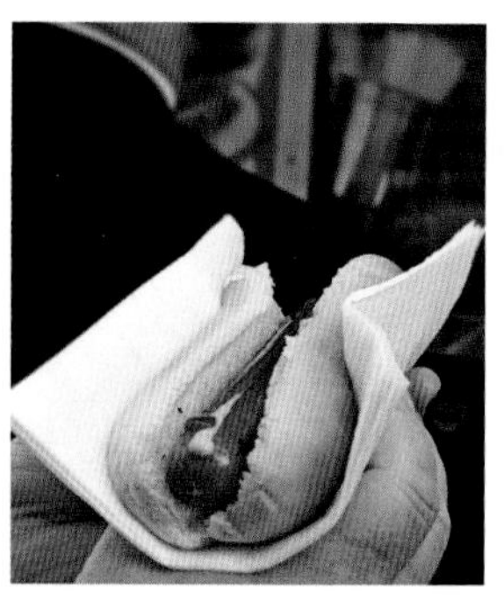

**From far left:** hotdog to go, New York; the George Washington Bridge between Jersey and NYC; dim sum in Manhattan



## NEW JERSEY TO NEW YORK CITY

It's 35 miles (56km) up I-95 to Trenton – stop for a tomato pie (a thin-crust, sauce-on-top pizza) – and then on to Bergen County, New Jersey, a stone's throw across the Hudson from Manhattan. Here, the town of Palisades Park is home to one of the biggest Koreatowns in the US. Broad Ave is packed end-to-end with Korean BBQ restaurants, where you grill your own meat at small in-table braziers; plus dessert cafes specializing in *bingsu* (shaved ice with toppings like red bean and condensed milk), and tempting markets selling dozens of kinds of kimchee.

And now, it's east over the George Washington Bridge to the finale, New York City. Epics have been written about the city's food – the Jewish delis with sky-high pastrami on rye, the red-sauce Italian joints, the park vendors hawking dirty-water hotdogs, the burn-your-tongue soup dumplings, the sour-cream-topped *pelmeni* dumplings in the Russian enclave at Brighton Beach, the three-star restaurants full of movie stars, the molecular-gastronomy hotspots, the ice cream trucks, the dim sum palaces of Flushing, the soul food of Harlem, the pizza. All we can say is give yourself time – and a pair of stretchy pants.

**Below:** candy-colored storefronts, Bar Harbor
**Right:** on the road in Acadia National Park

➔ **Distance: 65 miles (105km)**

➔ **Duration: 2-3 days**

# Acadia loop, Mt Desert Island

**MAINE**

Loop Mt Desert Island for a classic Maine weekend, complete with rugged hiking, frigid swimming, spellbinding coastal scenery and unlimited lobster stops – plus a chance to meet your EV's ancestors.

Gateway to Mt Desert Island, Bar Harbor is a sweet but touristy town, its Main St lined with art galleries and souvenir shops, ice-cream stands and seafood shacks. Book a room at a historic seaside inn to rest up and charge up before your island tour.

## PARK LOOP ROAD

Motor south out of town and hook up with Park Loop Rd, a scenic drive around the eastern part of the island. This route gets congested in July and August, so start early to beat the crowds. Your first stop is Sieur de Monts Nature Center, with exhibits on the natural and cultural history of Acadia National Park. The onsite Wild Garden of Acadia replicates the park's various habitats and displays hundreds of plant species found therein.

Head 3.5 miles (5.6km) south on Park Loop Rd to reach Sand Beach, an unexpectedly long and luscious strand tucked in between coastal mountains. The water here – 55°F (13°C) even in summer – makes for chilly swimming. Hike out to Great Head, with craggy coast and crashing surf all around; or test your scrambling skills on the Beehive Loop, a rung-and-ladder trail over granite cliffs.

Continuing south, your EV hugs the coast for about 5 miles (8km), with scenic spots on the way. Admire

## Plan & prepare

### Tips for EV drivers

Acadia GEM (acadiagem.com) in Bar Harbor has EVs for rent. Most of their fleet are street-legal carts or micro-cars, but they also offer regular electric cars for longer distances and higher speeds. EV charging stations are sparse outside of Bar Harbor, but there are several at Acadia National Park Headquarters on Eagle Lake Rd, with more planned installations at Acadia campgrounds. See Efficiency Maine (efficiencymaine.com/ev) for information about driving and owning an EV in Maine, including a charging-station locator.

### Where to stay

You're spoiled for choice in Bar Harbor, where cozy cottages and historic inns line the residential streets. Bar Harbor Inn & Spa (barharborinn.com) is an elegant lodging near the Town Beach, while Atlantic Oceanside (barharbormainehotel.com) is a sprawling hotel and event center north of town. In Southwest Harbor, the Seawall Motel (seawallmotel.com) is a classic oceanfront motor lodge with rather dated decor but an unbeatable location. All three have chargers onsite.

### When to go

Acadia National Park is technically open year-round, but note that all paved roads are closed from December 1 to April 15. Visitor centers, Jordan Pond House and other attractions generally open in the last week of May and close in the last week of October, although specific dates vary. Unsurprisingly, July and August are extremely busy in Acadia, and October attracts leaf-peepers. Beat the crowds by taking this drive in June or September.

### Further info

All visitors to Acadia National Park must purchase a pass (US$35 per vehicle) and display it on their vehicle's dashboard. From late May to late October, your EV also needs a reservation for Cadillac Mountain Summit Rd (US$6). Both passes are available at the National Park Service website (nps.gov). For maps and more, stop at Hulls Cove Visitor Center, located 3 miles (5km) north of Bar Harbor.

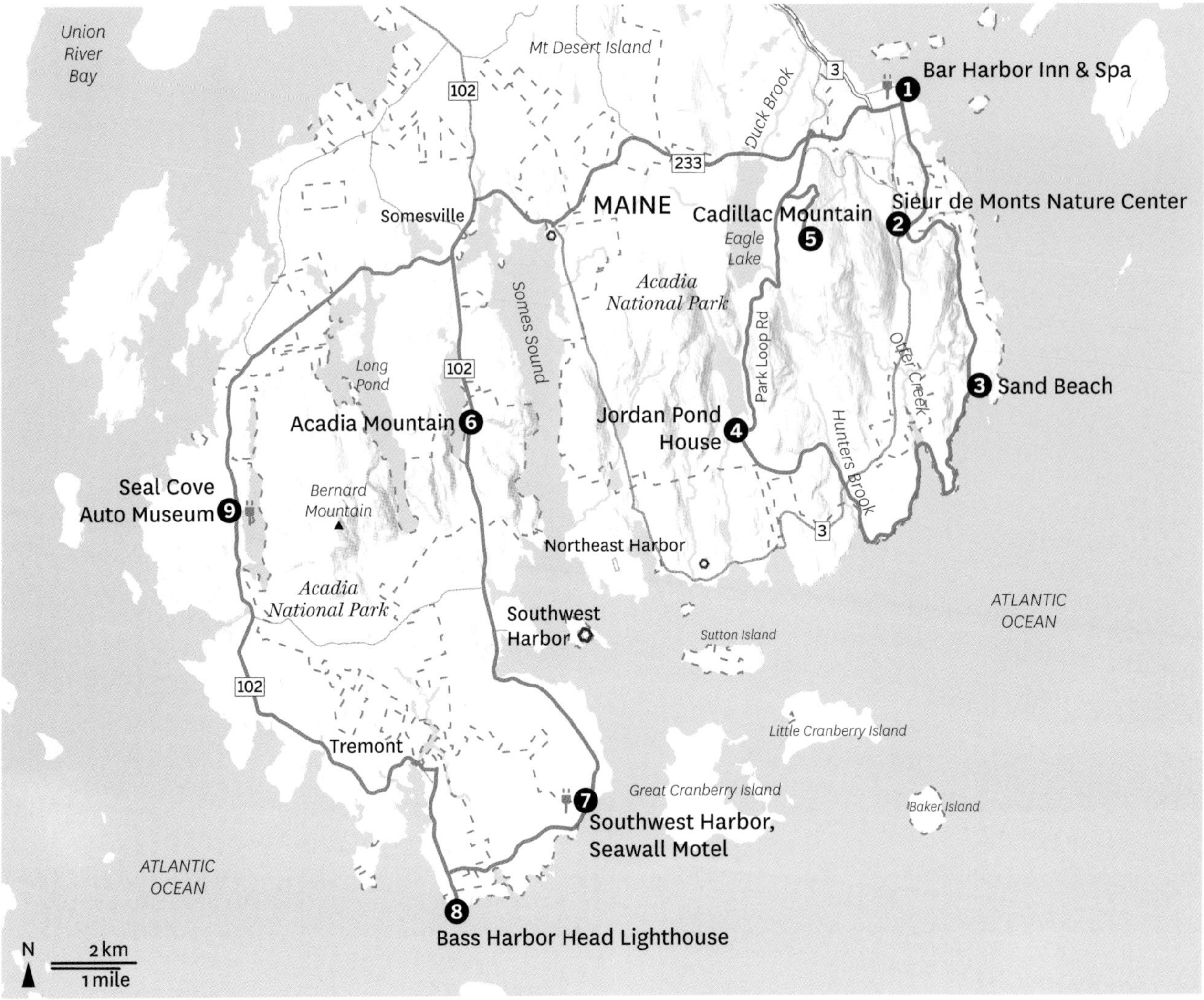

ocean-sculpted cliffs at Thunder Hole and Otter Cliff, then stay on Park Loop Rd as it turns inland. If you're feeling peckish, stop for a spot of tea at Jordan Pond House, an Acadia tradition since 1893; the wide lawn overlooks Jordan Pond, with its mirror-like reflection of Mt Penobscot. Enjoy the view while you fill up on fresh popovers or heartier fare like lobster stew. The last Park Loop Rd stop is the 1530ft (466m) summit of Cadillac Mountain. Hike the strenuous North Ridge Trail, or just drive your EV up Summit Rd. A short walk at the top yields glorious views of Frenchman Bay and beyond.

## THE QUIET SIDE

When you've had enough of the crowds, head over to the western part of Mt Desert Island, fondly called the "quiet side." After skirting Somes Sound, the only fjord on the eastern seaboard, turn south on Rte 102 and continue another 5 miles (8km) to the Acadia Mountain Trailhead. The hike to the summit rewards with views of Somes Sound and Cadillac Mountain in the distance.

Further south, the tranquil fishing village of Southwest Harbor is a welcome pit stop. You can't go wrong with a lobster roll and a slice of blueberry pie from Beal's Lobster Pier, followed by a peaceful afternoon sniffing flowers and spying butterflies at Charlotte Rhoades Park. Then it's on to the Bass Harbor Lighthouse, perched on pink cliffs at the island's southern tip. This is a picture-perfect sunset spot – which also means it's often busy with spectators as the sun drops into the sea.

Stay on Rte 102 as it circles north to Seal Cove. You'll see how far your EV has come, both literally and figuratively, at the Seal Cove Auto Museum. This is an impressive collection of late 19th- and early 20th-century vehicles – some of your EV's distant ancestors – and an appropriate cap to your Mt Desert Island driving tour.

## Ride the carriage roads

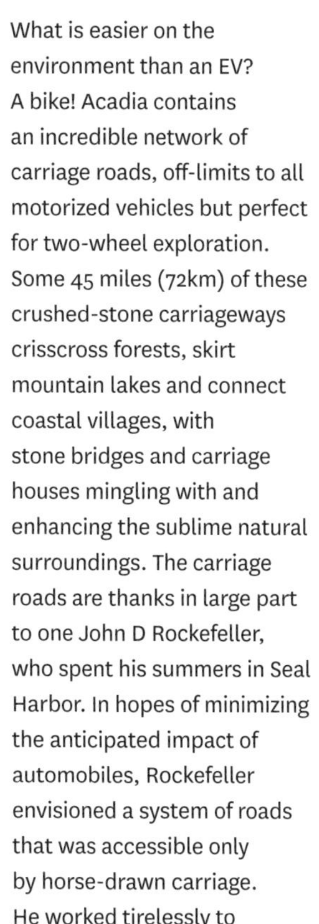

What is easier on the environment than an EV? A bike! Acadia contains an incredible network of carriage roads, off-limits to all motorized vehicles but perfect for two-wheel exploration. Some 45 miles (72km) of these crushed-stone carriageways crisscross forests, skirt mountain lakes and connect coastal villages, with stone bridges and carriage houses mingling with and enhancing the sublime natural surroundings. The carriage roads are thanks in large part to one John D Rockefeller, who spent his summers in Seal Harbor. In hopes of minimizing the anticipated impact of automobiles, Rockefeller envisioned a system of roads that was accessible only by horse-drawn carriage. He worked tirelessly to design and finance this infrastructure, which exists today as a unique feature of Acadia National Park. You probably don't have access to a horse-drawn carriage, but you can rent a bike from the Bar Harbor Bicycle Shop (barharborbike.com) or Acadia Bike (acadiabike.com). The Bicycle Express Shuttle (exploreacadia.com) takes cyclists from downtown Bar Harbor to Eagle Lake. Access the carriage roads from Jordan's Pond House or Eagle Lake; the NPS website (nps.gov) also has a downloadable Carriage Road Users' Map.

**Clockwise from top left:** sunrise from Cadillac Mountain; cycling Acadia National Park; coastal hiking from Bar Harbor

**Below:** Vermont's green and serene dairy country
**Right:** leaf-peeping perfection near state capital Montpelier

**Distance: 77 miles (124km)**

**Duration: 1-3 days**

# Burlington to Montpelier

**VERMONT**

A spin along the Green Mountain Byway introduces quintessential Vermont, an EV-friendly state of dairy farms, cheddar shops, hiking trails, intriguing towns and a verdant landscape.

Vermont is one of the smallest US states by both land area and population, and you could easily zip through it in the blink of an eye. But the "Green Mountain State," famous for its fiery-hued maples in the fall, warrants slowing down and savoring a scenery that's unmarred by billboards, which are banned throughout Vermont. A concentration of attractions – from cheese shops to covered bridges, historic towns and highland hiking trails – calls for frequent stops.

## BURLINGTON TO STOWE

Vermont's largest city, proudly progressive Burlington is a logical place to spend a day or two before embarking on your EV road trip, and is easily explored on foot or by bicycle. Rent e-bikes at Local Motion to ride the 14-mile (23km) Island Line Trail along Lake Champlain and across it on a causeway. In town, drive to the Ethan Allen Homestead Museum to see where Revolutionary War hero and Vermont founding father Ethan Allen settled in the 18th century, on the banks of the Winooski River.

Within 20 minutes of leaving Burlington, you're deep in dairy country, passing milking barns and fields of Holstein cows, and several covered bridges. In Jeffersonville, some 36 miles (58km) northeast of

© Dave and Les Jacobs/Getty Images

## Plan & prepare

### Tips for EV drivers

The Green Mountain State is renowned for its progressive environmental policies, and by one estimate just over half the vehicles on the roads here are electric. Fast chargers cluster in cities like Burlington and Montpelier, with slower chargers sprinkled throughout smaller towns. Mind your charge levels: mountain driving and cold temperatures can sap batteries more quickly than normal conditions.

### Where to stay

In Burlington, park at one of the complimentary chargers at Hotel Vermont (hotelvt.com), and make use of the hotel bikes to ride the lakeside Island Line Trail. EVs get preferred parking and onsite chargers at Stowe's Topnotch Resort (topnotchresort.com), which offers indoor and outdoor tennis courts, a 20-treatment-room spa and views of Vermont's tallest peak. In the capital, the Inn at Montpelier (innatmontpelier.com) occupies two former homes built in the early 1800s, within walking distance of chargers and local attractions.

### When to go

With dozens of resorts offering downhill and cross-country skiing, Vermont is the eastern US' favorite winter playground. All that snow in the White Mountains closes Rte 108 through Smugglers' Notch between November and early May. Spring may be muddy along the trails but lets you catch flower blooms; summer attracts hikers and climbers to the mountains; and fall is high season in the state, when leaf-peepers flock to rural areas to see the sugar maples in full autumn blaze.

### Further info

From Vermont, it's very easy to reach New York's Adirondack Mountains on the west side of Lake Champlain, or the neighboring mountain state of New Hampshire. Drivers in Vermont commonly cross the border to Canada; Burlington is only about 43 miles (70km) from Montréal. To get information on road conditions across the northeast, check the website New England 511 (newengland511.org).

## Vermont's Long Trail

The 2190-mile (3524km) Appalachian Trail, or AT, running from Maine to Georgia, is the USA's most famous long-distance hiking trail. But it wasn't the first. Vermont's Long Trail, running north to south through the state along the spine of the Green Mountains, was the inspiration for the AT; in fact, the pair share 100 miles (161km) of trail in southern Vermont. The Green Mountain Club (greenmountainclub.org) formed as a volunteer organization in 1910 to build a wilderness trail that would span the length of Vermont's mountains. It took 20 years to create the footpath, which stretches 272 miles (438km) and usually takes three to four weeks to complete, camping en route. Though most people who use the Long Trail do so for only a day, anyone who's done the whole thing, either in one go or in pieces, is known as an "End-to-Ender" and is eligible to be entered in the club's official records. Today, the Green Mountain Club stations guides in the high country to help hikers find water and campsites, and operates two visitor centers – the Waterbury Center and the Barnes Camp in Stowe – where they offer hiking advice and outdoor-skills workshops.

**Above, from left:** Long Trail highlights – climbing Mt Mansfield; Brandon Gap
**Opposite, from left:** Stowe's gondola; Ben & Jerry's factory

Burlington, turn south on Rte 108. This seasonal two-lane road snakes through Smugglers' Notch, a mountain pass historically used by dealers of contraband, including bootleg liquor, during Prohibition. Turnouts along the road offer short walks to Smugglers' Cave – where the banned goods were often cached – and longer hikes to mountain sites including Sterling Pond, where the mile-long (1.6km) climb gives rewarding panoramic views. Veering from the main route, the seasonal Stowe Scenic Auto Rd climbs 4.5 miles (7km) to dead-end at the 4393ft (1339m) summit of Mt Mansfield, Vermont's highest peak, for peerless views of the surrounding range. Returning downhill, you'll soon hit Stowe, a legendary ski town where the tidy collection of shops and restaurants warrants a stroll. Overnight at the Topnotch Resort, where EVs get curb-front parking.

### WATERBURY TO MONTPELIER

Grab a latte to go at Black Cap Coffee & Bakery in Stowe before heading 10 minutes down the road to Waterbury, known for its architecture. Take a walk around downtown to see examples of Victorian, Gothic Revival and Queen Anne mansions, churches and inns. Waterbury's best-known resident lies on the edge of town in the form of the Ben & Jerry's ice-cream factory, drawing 1000-plus people a day in summer's high season for a tour of the production floor, scoops of renowned flavors like Chunky Monkey and Cherry Garcia, and rock-star EV parking. Its neighbor, Cabot Farmers' Store, offers tastes of Vermont's celebrated cheddar cheese, produced by a co-op of more than 500 family farms in New England and New York State.

From Waterbury, it's a quick spin southeast to Montpelier, the nation's smallest state capital, where visitors are free to wander around the impressive Greek Revival–style Vermont State House to see its art collections. At the intersection of two rivers, and with walking and cycling trails, arty and outdoorsy Montpelier is a good place to stop, recharge (look for EV chargers beside the capitol building) and overnight to dine at locavore restaurants like the Three Penny Taproom, or take in a music performance.

Lake Eden
Grand Isle
Georgia
108
Waterville
100
Fairfax
7
15
Cambridge
104
Jeffersonville
Johnson
Lamoille River
Milton
Westford
89
Whiteface Mountain
108
Hyde Park
Lake Champlain
Lamoille River
Morristown
3 Smugglers' Notch
Mt Mansfield
Ethan Allen Homestead Museum
Colchester
Jericho
4 Stowe Scenic Auto Road
5 Topnotch Resort
2
Essex Junction
NEW YORK
1 Burlington, Hotel Vermont
Mt Clark
6 Stowe
NEW HAMPSHIRE
100
Mt Putnam
Shelburne Bay
2A
I-89
Waterbury Reservoir
Winooski River
Bolton
7 Waterbury, Cabot Farmers' Store
Lake Iroquois
Worcester
8 Ben & Jerry's
7
Hinesburg
Huntington
14
Charlotte
Camel's Hump State Park
Middlesex
116
I-89
Inn At Montpelier
9
100
12
N
10 km
5 miles

**Below:** look for moose in the Whites' Presidential Range
**Right:** above the clouds on the Mt Washington summit drive

**Distance: 150 miles (241km)**

**Duration: 3-5 days**

# White Mountains loop

**NEW HAMPSHIRE**

Spend a few days exploring New England's highest mountains by EV, taking in rural villages, expansive vistas, and – in the right season – the region's most magnificent fall foliage.

It's a challenge to keep your eyes on the road as you weave your EV through the glorious White Mountains, where every turn shows off remarkable views of picture-perfect peaks and tree-clad valleys, rushing brooks and placid lakes. Your journey starts in the side-by-side tourist hubs of Lincoln and North Woodstock, where you can stock up and charge up for the coming days' adventures. Hike into the hills – or take the Loon Mountain Resort gondola – to get an overview of where you're headed: the spectacular northern peaks.

## NORTH THROUGH THE NOTCH

Heading north, it's less than 10 miles (16km) to Franconia Notch, the scenic mountain pass between Cannon Mountain and Mt Lafayette. The surrounding wilderness of Franconia Notch State Park offers waterfalls, glacial lakes and hiking trails to suit every ability (including the paved, wheelchair-accessible 9-mile/14.5km Franconia Notch Path). An aerial tramway flies to the 4080ft (1240m) summit of Cannon Mountain for more heady views.

On the north side of the Notch, time slows down in the tiny village of Sugar Hill, population approximately 600. It's named for its large grove of sugar maples, which makes it the perfect place to indulge in a plate of pancakes

© Mihai_Andritoiu/Shutterstock

## Plan & prepare

### Tips for EV drivers

EV rentals are scarce close to the route, but if you're flying into Boston Logan, head to Ufodrive (ufodrive.com) in Cambridge. New Hampshire cities and towns have a decent amount of public charging stations, many free to use. However, chargers in rural areas are sparse. For now, most stations have Level 2 chargers, with fewer fast chargers and Tesla Superchargers. Drive Electric NH (driveelectricnh.org) has a map of chargers and other resources for EV drivers in New Hampshire.

### Where to stay

Lincoln's Indian Head Resort (indianheadresort.com) is a classic mountain lodge on lovely Shadow Lake. Woodstock Inn (woodstockinnbrewery.com) offers rustic style and an onsite brewery. Romantic Sugar Hill Inn (sugarhillinn.com) occupies a welcoming farmhouse on the Sugar Hill outskirts; Gorham's Top Notch Inn (topnotchinn.com) is functional and affordable. North Conway Grand Hotel (northconwaygrand.com) has a convenient location and every amenity. All have onsite chargers.

### When to go

Early to mid-October is usually the best time for leaf-peeping, and you can track fall foliage on the Visit New Hampshire website (visitnh.gov) to try to see the "peak" colors. Keep in mind that this is an extremely busy time in the White Mountains. Hiking is best from May to October. Of course, where there's hiking in summer there's often skiing in winter, usually from December to March.

### Further info

Stop at the White Mountains Visitor Center, off I-93 in North Woodstock (near your starting point), to pick up maps and information about what to do in the area. Keep in mind that throughout the White Mountains region, there is a notable lack of amenities between towns, especially going through Franconia Notch (between North Woodstock/Lincoln and Sugar Hill), and along the Kancamagus Hwy (between North Conway and Lincoln).

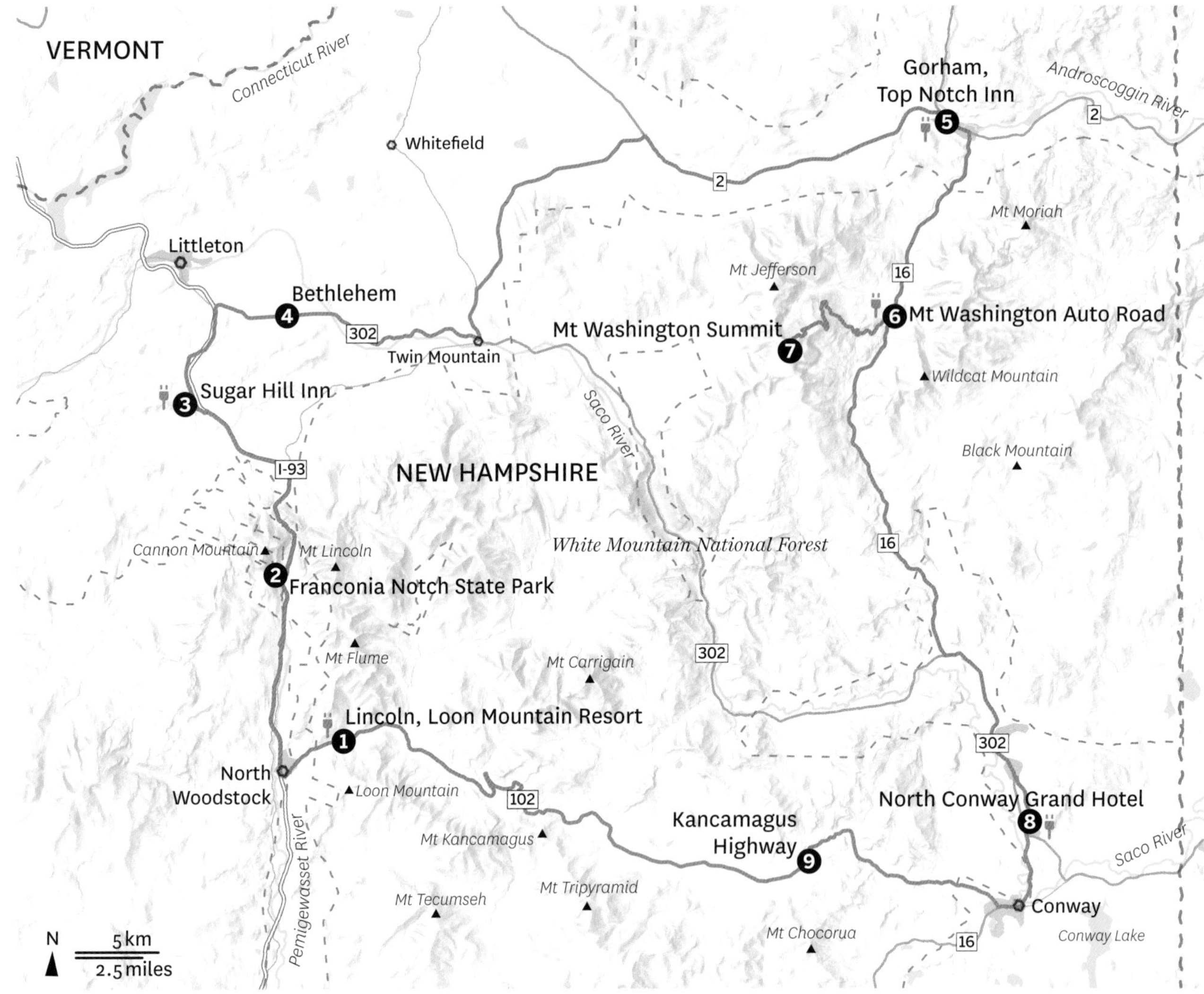


doused in maple syrup – and Polly's Pancake Parlor is here for you, just as it has been since 1938. The Sugar Hill Inn makes for an atmospheric overnight stop.

Moving on, head 7 miles (12km) northeast to the little town of Bethlehem, another New England charmer. The historic Colonial Theater sets the tone for this artistic hub, hosting live-music performances and indie films, while WREN's Local Works Marketplace features arts and crafts by local makers. From Bethlehem, head east across the top of the Presidential Range, marveling at the scenery all around. Keep eyes peeled for moose; to increase your chances of spotting these elusive creatures, take a ride with Gorham Moose Tours while your EV is charging.

## MT WASHINGTON TO THE KANCAMAGUS

Buzz 10 miles (16km) south from Gorham to drive the Mt Washington Auto Rd, which traverses 7.6 miles (12km) of narrow, unguarded roadway and hairpin turns, gaining more than 4000ft (1220m) in elevation to reach the bald peak of Mt Washington. Climbing will consume extra battery power, so charge up before your ascent. This is sure to be the highpoint of your trip, in every sense – celebrate by snagging a bumper sticker ('This car climbed Mt Washington") for your hardworking EV.

Continue south to North Conway, adventure capital of the Whites. Five ski-area resorts offer tons of fun in any season, from ziplines and mountain-coaster rides to mountain-bike trails. Drive, hike or climb to the top of the famed 700ft (213m) Cathedral Ledge; kids might enjoy Story Land amusement park.

Then it's time to complete the loop, traveling west on the 35-mile-long (56km) Kancamagus Hwy. Unmarred by buildings or billboards, this scenic byway cuts through the White Mountain National Forest, offering access to a wonderland of hiking trails, swimming holes, waterfalls and marvelous mountain scenery.

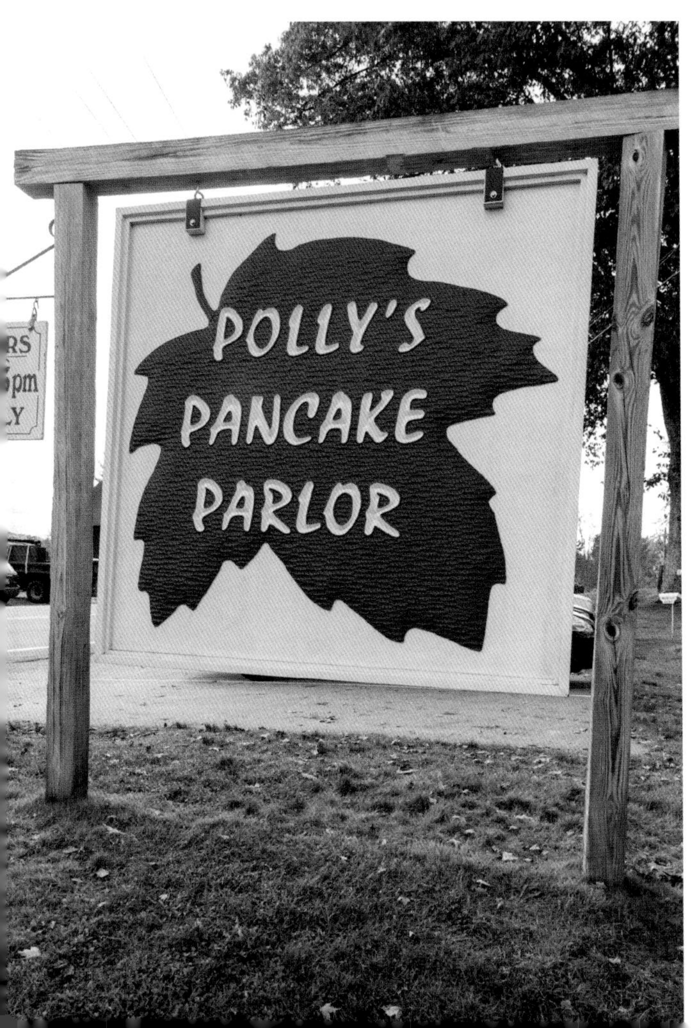

## The Old Man of the Mountain

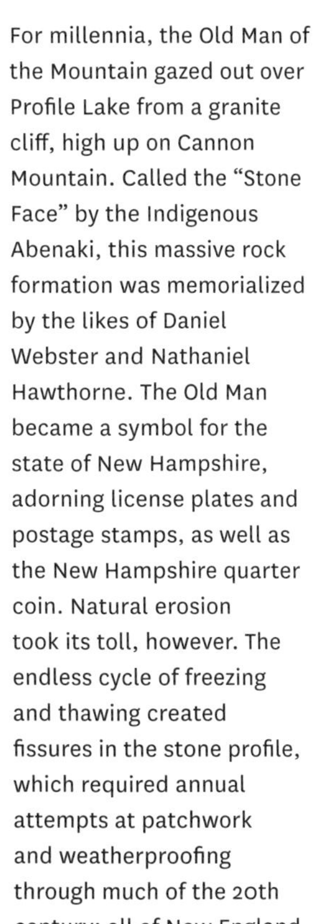

For millennia, the Old Man of the Mountain gazed out over Profile Lake from a granite cliff, high up on Cannon Mountain. Called the "Stone Face" by the Indigenous Abenaki, this massive rock formation was memorialized by the likes of Daniel Webster and Nathaniel Hawthorne. The Old Man became a symbol for the state of New Hampshire, adorning license plates and postage stamps, as well as the New Hampshire quarter coin. Natural erosion took its toll, however. The endless cycle of freezing and thawing created fissures in the stone profile, which required annual attempts at patchwork and weatherproofing through much of the 20th century; all of New England mourned when he finally collapsed in 2003. The face of Cannon Mountain is now conspicuously plain, but the Old Man of the Mountain Profile Plaza in Franconia Notch State Park gives visitors a sense of its former appearance. Around the memorial plaza, sculpted steel "profiler rods" point toward the cliff and fill in the details of the facade for the viewer. Surrounded by the knockout mountain scenery, it is a spectacular spot and a fitting tribute to the beloved New Hampshire icon.

**Clockwise from top left:** North Conway, the "Adventure Capital of the Whites"; the Old Man of the Mountain pictured on a vintage postcard; Polly's Pancake Parlor, Sugar Hill

**Below:** a classic Maine lobster roll
**Right:** follow Boston's Freedom Trail to Bunker Hill Monument and the USS *Constitution* at Charlestown Navy Yard

**Distance: 200 miles (322km)**

**Duration: 2 days**

# New England coast, Providence to Portland

**RHODE ISLAND, MASSACHUSETTS & MAINE**

Cruise the rocky New England coast from one great foodie city to another, stopping for lobster rolls and lighthouse vistas along the way – the Yankee summer dream.

For a glorious few months, the churning gray Atlantic becomes smooth and calm, the bitter winds turn balmy, and New Englanders' thoughts turn to sand and seafood. The road trip from Providence, Rhode Island to Portland, Maine is chock full of both. It's ideal for EVs, with short distances between sights and chargers aplenty.

## PROVIDENCE TO BOSTON

Your launchpad, Providence, is an underrated charmer of hilly streets, 18th-century architecture and indie bars and coffee shops. Since your aim is seafood, set your GPS straight for Dune Bros Rhode Island Seafood, an urban fish shack with a walk-up window and rows of picnic tables. The sustainably sourced "dock-to-dish" menu is ultra-simple: fish and chips, fish sandwiches, clam cakes and chowder. Go for the crispy-fried cape shark (aka spiny dogfish) with a side of beef-tallow fries. Belly full, cross the Providence River and wander around College Hill, the (yes, hilly) neighborhood surrounding Brown University's campus, where architecture ranges from early 1700s colonial to turreted Victorian mansions.

When you've walked your fill, pull your EV onto I-95 heading northeast and cross into Massachusetts. Skim past the Boston exurbs into the great metropolis itself,

## Plan & prepare

### Tips for EV drivers

This route is a breeze for EVs, with short distances between stops and ample public charging stations – though if you stay in Gloucester, charge up before you head too far from the I-95 (Boston and Gloucester are only 40 miles/64km apart, so you can just charge before you leave the city, too). It's a warm-weather journey, and largely flat, so ranges should be longer than in winter. The trip also includes lots of urban driving, which is especially efficient for EVs.

### Where to stay

Boston has a wealth of hostels and hotels – try the charger-equipped Lenox (lenoxhotel.com) – though prices tend to be high. You're never far from a charging station, even if your accommodation doesn't have its own. In Cape Ann, Gloucester's Vista Motel (vistamotel.com) is on the beachfront, and in Portland, the comfortable Hyatt Place (hyatt.com) in Old Port has free chargers for guests in its garage.

### When to go

New England summer goes into full swing in mid-June and lasts through Labor Day, the first Monday in September. It's the most pleasant time to be near the North Atlantic coast, but also the most crowded, so book ahead. Expect traffic, especially heading into weekends, when city folk will be making for the shore. The shoulder seasons of May and September can be lovely, but some restaurants and shops will be closed.

### Further info

Some seafood sustainability guides rescinded Maine lobster's sustainability label in 2022, amid concerns that the industry doesn't do enough to protect endangered right whales from becoming entangled in fishing gear. Lobstermen vehemently deny this, and research is ongoing. Nevertheless, there's plenty of other local seafood, should you prefer to avoid lobster. Shellfish like oysters are considered especially sustainable, and have the benefit of helping filter seawater.

## Lights with longevity

Between Rhode Island, Massachusetts and Maine, there are nearly 150 lighthouses, many still working. Not only are these structures picturesque, they're a fascinating part of the region's history. Lighthouse keepers lived in seclusion for months on end, often alone, maintaining the lenses that kept ships from sailing into rocks or shallow waters. When ships did founder, keepers were responsible for rescuing victims from the icy Atlantic. The keeper of Maine's Cape Elizabeth Light Station, Marcus Hanna, was awarded a medal of valor after saving two sailors when their schooner ran aground in an 1885 blizzard. Think of him while you eat your lobster in the lighthouse's shadow.

In 1866, the Lighthouse Board began sending library books to lonely keepers, eventually maintaining 420 lighthouse libraries. The last manned lighthouse, in Boston Harbor, was automated in 1988. Today, some New England lighthouses are open for climbing during the summer. Massachusetts' Cape Ann has five lovely lighthouses, including the Eastern Point, once home to the artist Winslow Homer. In York, Maine, the Nubble Light is so famed its image was included in the Voyager Golden Record, carried to outer space in 1977.

**Clockwise from top left:** Portland Head Light, Cape Elizabeth; Boston's "lobster tail" pastry; the Freedom Trail's Granary Burying Ground

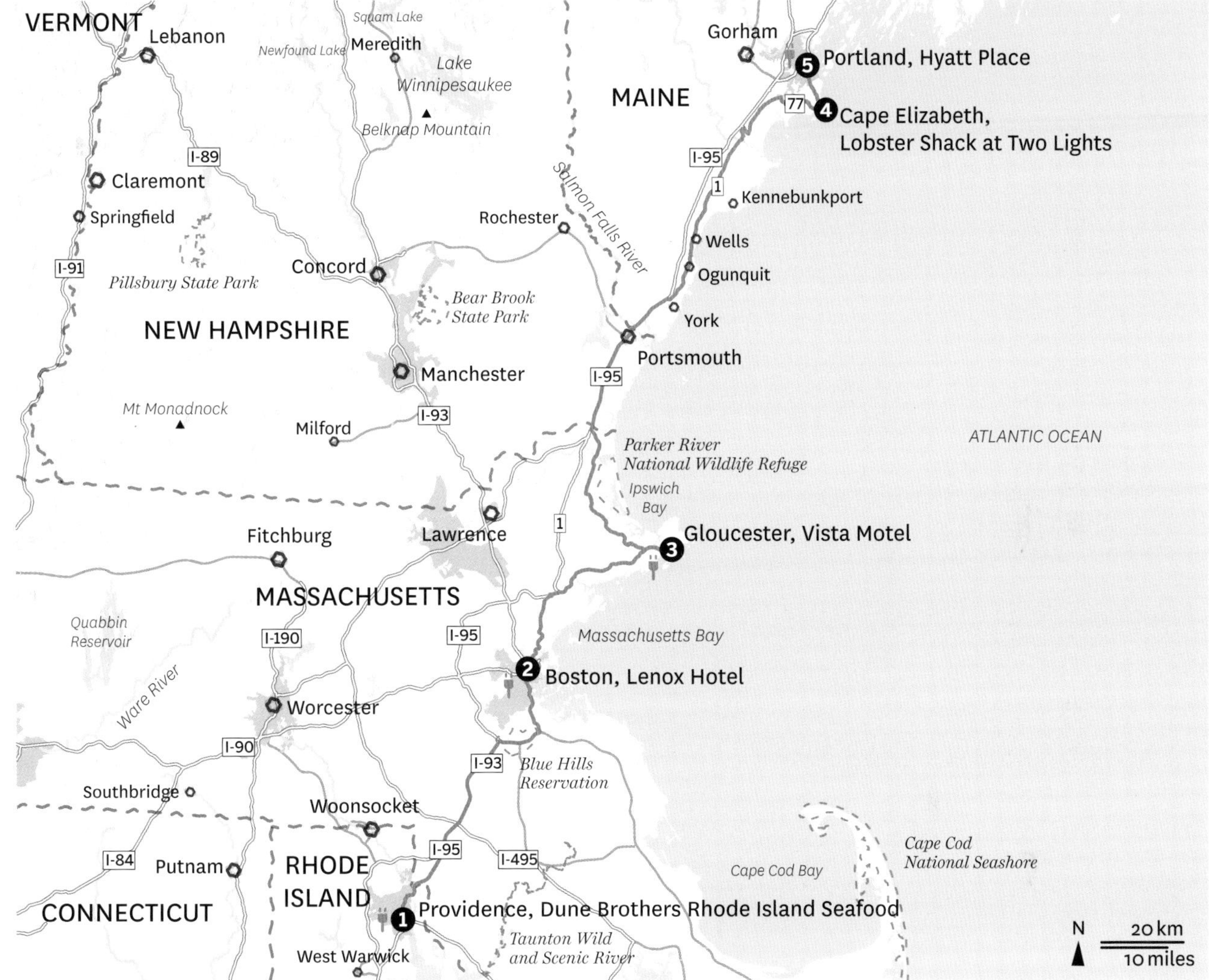


50 miles (80km) away. There are plenty of chargers in the city – a good choice is the Copley Place fast-charger station in Back Bay. Charge your own battery sleeping in Beaux Arts luxury at the nearby Lenox Hotel, favorite of politicians and movie stars for more than 120 years.

After breakfast, head directly to Boston Common, the USA's first public park and the city's spiritual heart. Summer here means sunbathers on the grass, kids running through the "frog pond" splash-pads, free yoga near the carousel, and classic swan-boat rides in the adjacent Public Garden. Afterwards, have a wander along the Freedom Trail, a self-guided walking tour of Boston's Revolutionary War historic sites, including several atmospheric cemeteries, the Benjamin Franklin statue and Paul Revere's house. Wind up along the harbor, where you can have a drink and watch the tall ships sail past. Oh, and if you need an afternoon pick-me-up, pop into one of the bakeries in the North End, Boston's historic Little Italy, for a "lobster tail": it's not seafood, but rather a crunchy pastry shell filled with sweet ricotta cream.

## CAPE ANN & INTO SOUTHERN MAINE

You could spend days enjoying Boston, but this is a road trip. So hop back in your EV and head north on Rte 1, then cut east. Your destination is Gloucester, on the tip of Cape Ann, long a center of the fishing industry and home to a sizeable Portuguese American community. Here, the Azorean Restaurant & Bar is a firm favorite for Portuguese flavors: cold octopus salad, littleneck clams with chouriço sausage, or pan-fried haddock with garlicky Molho de Vilão sauce. After dinner, walk beneath the late-setting summer sun on Good Harbor Beach. This dune-fringed stretch is good for swimming, or just sitting and wiggling your toes in the white sand. Before bedding down at the retro-chic Vista Motel, grab a nightcap at the Crow's Nest. This local haunt was featured in *The Perfect Storm*, the

## New England sweets

This trip focuses on seafood, but we'd be remiss not to include the finale of any proper New England meal: dessert. Common offerings on lobster-shack menus include Maine blueberry pie, Indian pudding (a cornmeal and molasses confection), and local ice cream: favorite only-in-New-England flavors include Grape-Nuts cereal, maple-walnut and even lobster – better than it sounds. In Massachusetts you'll find Boston cream pie, which is actually a yellow cake filled with pastry cream and topped with chocolate. Maine loves its whoopie pies, an Amish-origin treat of two small frosting-filled cake rounds. Rhode Island has a sweet official state drink – coffee milk, which is like chocolate milk but made using coffee syrup. A "coffee cabinet" adds coffee ice cream to the mix for a milkshake-like treat. In the rest of New England, "frappe" is the term of art for such concoctions.

**From far left:** Maine's blueberry pie; Cape Elizabeth coastline; New England lobster and clams

dramatization of the last voyage of the *Andrea Gail*, a Gloucester vessel lost at sea in 1991.

In the morning, it's just over 100 miles (160km) north to Portland. Rte 1 is far more charming than I-95, passing through classic seaside towns like Kittery, Ogunquit and Wells. Drive slowly and stop at any fudge shop, ice-cream stand or antiques store that catches your eye, or park for a walk along one of Southern Maine's plentiful pebbly beaches. Hit Cape Elizabeth by lunchtime, even after stopping to charge up at York or Kennebunkport. The Lobster Shack at Two Lights here – named for the cape's twin lighthouses – is famous for its location, perched on the shoreside rocks. But its food is worthy too: go for the classic lobster dinner, a ruby-red crustacean served with a veritable swimming pool of drawn butter. Afterwards, visit the lighthouses before hopping back in your EV for the quick drive into Portland proper.

## PORTLAND

On a peninsula extending like a beckoning finger into Casco Bay, Portland is small but mighty. In recent years, its postcard-pretty brick downtown has become a foodie destination. Near the waterfront, Eventide Oyster Co has won plaudits for its internationally-inflected seafood menu and Maine-centric oyster offerings. Slurp a plate of firm, lemony Pemaquids or sweet, briny Winter Points, all washed down with a creative cocktail (a celery gimlet, perhaps?). Should you feel the need to share your seafood bounty with friends or family, several fish markets in the cobblestoned Old Port area will ship live lobster on ice to anywhere in the country. Cap off your trip with a sunset cruise, zigzagging among the tree-capped islands of Casco Bay as the water turns golden. It's hard to imagine a more perfect end to a journey along the Atlantic than this.

**Below:** Tesla Superchargers in the Boston exurbs
**Right:** Massachusetts fall foliage in the Berkshires

**Distance: 226 miles (364km)**

**Duration: 2 days**

# The Mass Pike, Boston to North Adams

**MASSACHUSETTS**

From tree-tastic Mt Auburn Cemetery to the peaks and waterfalls of the Taconic Mountains, this is a leaf-peeping fall trip to savor – with a cup of hot apple cider, of course.

This trip starts in a cemetery. But please, wipe all images of creepy, crooked gravestones from your mind. In Cambridge, across the Charles River from central Boston, Mt Auburn is the USA's first "garden cemetery," dedicated in 1831 and with 175 acres (71 hectares) of woods and meadows, duck-filled ponds and Victorian-style gardens. And yes, it's the final resting place of some 100,000 people, including luminaries like poet Henry Wadsworth Longfellow and author and abolitionist Julia Ward Howe. In autumn, the cemetery's 5500-plus trees – including white oak, beech, gingko and maple – glow in sublime shades of saffron and russet. You can drive your EV on the cemetery's roads, but do get out and explore by foot, climbing the Washington Tower to behold leafy Boston and beyond in its fall finery.

## PEEPING ALONG THE PIKE

Heading west of Boston, hit the Mass Pike – the Massachusetts portion of I-90. After about 38 miles (61km), detour north to the 171-acre (69-hectare) New England Botanic Garden at Tower Hill. Dozens of themed areas include oak-lined Pliny's Allée, specially designed for fall color with an understory of purply-bronze oakleaf hydrangeas and flaming Virginia sweetspire.

## Plan & prepare

### Tips for EV drivers

Massachusetts is an exceptionally EV friendly state. Boston has a wide network of charging stations and chargers are a common amenity at the city's hotels. EV chargers on the Mass Pike's service plazas have had problems, with replacements needed, but you'll find options at gas stations and shopping centers along the route. In some of the smaller Taconic towns, overnight charging at an inn or B&B is your best bet.

### Where to stay

Boston has the gamut of options, while Western Mass is all about the charming inns and B&Bs. The Inn at Stockbridge (stockbridgeinn.com) and the Porches Inn at MASS MoCA (porches.com) both have EV chargers, which is pretty common at more upscale places. If range isn't a great issue, consider trying to snag a reservation at rustic Bascom Lodge (bascomlodge.net), a 1930s Civilian Conservation Corps–built stone inn on the summit of Mt Greylock.

### When to go

This is a fall foliage trip: high season starts in mid-September and peaks around Columbus Day, the second Monday in October. However, climate change is altering foliage-change patterns, keeping leaves green for longer or causing droughts that make leaves go straight from green to brown – so peak leaf color varies depending on annual conditions. Check forecasts online: accuweather.com and smokymountains.com are useful sites. Always book accommodations ahead in high season.

### Further info

The road up Mt Greylock is only open through October. The Mass Pike is a toll road, with all payment by E-ZPass (e-zpassiag.com) or the more expensive Pay by Plate (paybyplatema.one); for the latter, gantries take pictures of your license plate, and you're mailed a bill. The Pike has seven service plazas with food and (at some) E-ZPass offices selling passes.

## Fall in Western Mass

Western Massachusetts goes all-in for fall. Apple picking is a much-loved day trip for urban dwellers. A short drive northwest of Stockbridge in the foothills of the Berkshires, Hilltop Orchards makes artisanal hard cider; come to hike the apple orchards and surrounding forest, eat fresh cider donuts, lounge in an Adirondack chair or warm yourself by the fireplace; apple picking is by reservation. Just north of Stockbridge, Bartlett's Orchard has pick-your-own for 13 varieties of apples, including harder-to-find cultivars like crisp, berry-scented macoun and tart-honey mutsu. Their bakery sells cider donuts, apple turnovers and apple muffins, and the farm stand is open year-round. Eight miles (13km) from the New England Botanic Garden, Schartner Farm does apples, but also has a corn maze, hayrides, goats to pet, and a loop trail around the fields. Another fall classic: the Big E, formerly known as the Eastern States Exposition, New England's annual fair. Staged just off the Mass Pike in West Springfield every September, it's two weeks of funfair games, rides, agricultural expos, music, car shows and, of course, food – the signature dish is a cream puff the size of your head.

**Above, from left:** Massachusetts' autumn bounty; Mt Auburn Cemetery **Opposite:** Mass MoCA's historic North Adams home

From the garden, drive southwest back to I-90, passing through Worcester, a good place for a recharge if needed. Then it's another 100 miles (161km) on to Stockbridge, where Stockbridge Bowl, aka Lake Mahkeenac, is nestled amidst the Taconic Range and the Berkshires. The lake is ringed by Gilded Age cottages; stroll the Bullard Woods to the grounds of Tanglewood, summer home to the Boston Symphony Orchestra. On sunny days the lake's waters mirror the fiery foliage of the surrounding hills. Stockbridge itself is practically a caricature of a charming New England village – its downtown Main St was made iconic by the 1967 painting *Home for Christmas*, by resident Norman Rockwell. Here, the Inn at Stockbridge, a white Georgian mansion with free chargers, makes an idyllic overnight.

### MOUNTAINS AND MASS MOCA

From Stockbridge, drive south 20 miles (32km) to Bash Bish Falls, where Bash Bish Brook cascades gracefully into a jade-colored pool. In autumn, the contrast between the green water and the orange trees is the stuff of landscape paintings. Getting to the falls means a short but steep hike; take the side trail for panoramic views of the Hudson Valley and Catskills.

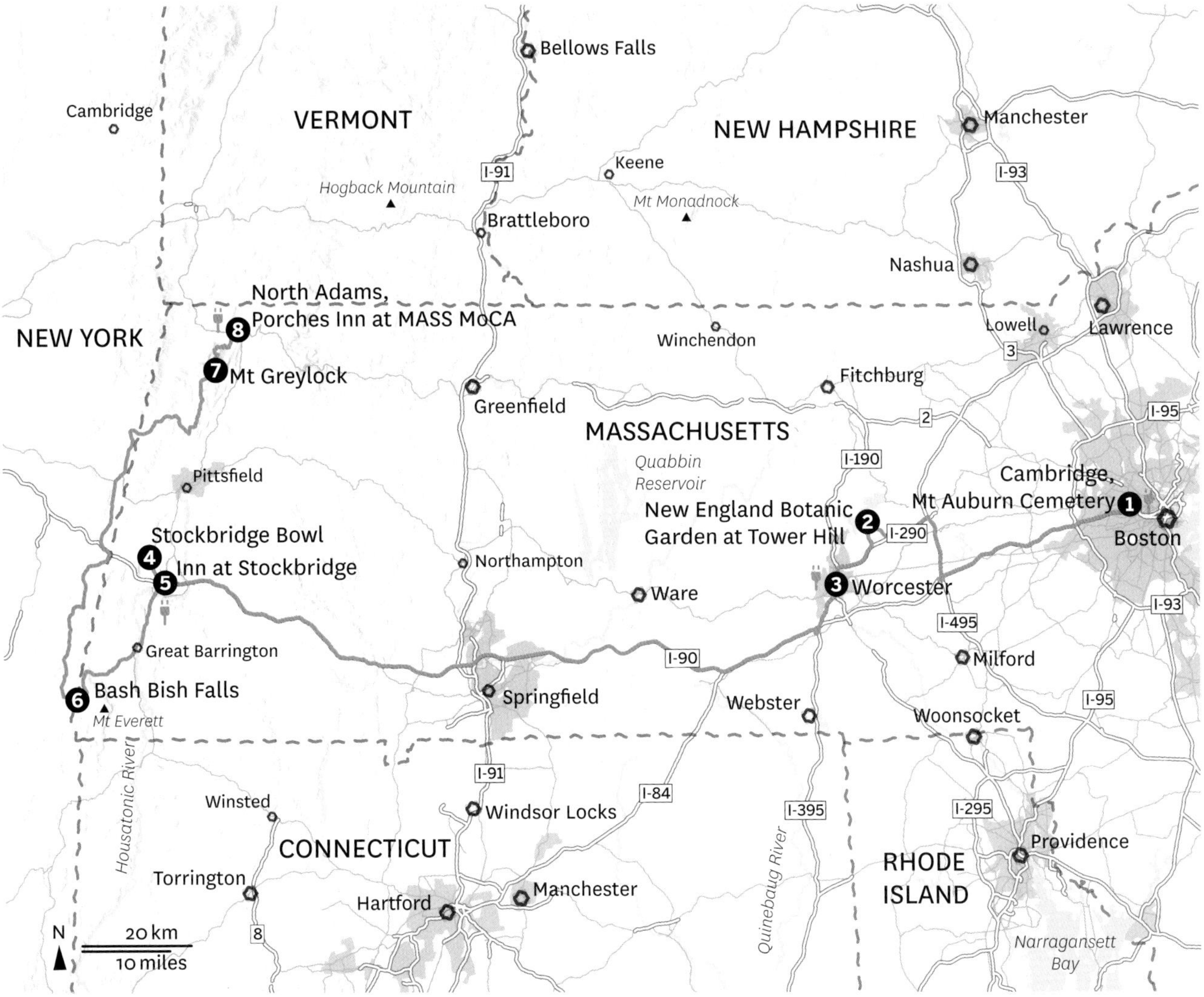

Next, you'll skirt north along the New York side of the border for some 55 miles (89km), through a rolling landscape of warm-toned maple, beech and birch. Your destination is Mt Greylock, which at 3491ft (1064m) is Massachusetts' highest peak, with clear-day views of five different states. You can drive to the top or make a day-hike out of it. Afterwards, descend into the town of North Adams for a visit to the Massachusetts Museum of Contemporary Art (MASS MoCA), its world-class collection housed in an old textile-printing factory along the Hoosic River. Plug in at the museum's ChargePoint while you peruse, then stroll over for a bite at Jack's Hot Dog Stand, serving chili-cheese dogs in a postage stamp-sized space since 1917. Spend the night at MASS MoCA's Porches Inn, capping your trip off with a cocktail by the bonfire pit while the autumn sun sinks low.

**Below:** peeking through brick-built Annapolis to Maryland State House
**Right:** the elegant Chesapeake Bay Bridge

**Distance: 170 miles (274km)**

**Duration: 3 days**

# Chesapeake Bay, Annapolis to Baltimore

**MARYLAND**

Circle round rural upper Chesapeake Bay, skipping between tiny fishing villages, watching herons glide through the salt-smelling air and eating a full bushel (at least) of sweet, succulent blue crabs.

Expert advice: wear the bib. Yes, it seems ridiculous; you're not a baby. But you'll thank us when you get up from the table in an hour or two and your shirt is not covered in crab guts and butter. Crab cracking: it's a messy process. They know that here at Cantler's Riverside Inn in Annapolis, where former waterman Jimmy Cantler has been serving freshly steamed blue crabs by the dozen since 1974. A crab feast at Cantler's, on the deck overlooking Mill Creek, is an Annapolis ritual, and the perfect way to start a drive around the northern Chesapeake Bay.

Bordered by Maryland and Virginia, the 200-mile-long (322km) Chesapeake Bay holds an outsized importance for Mid-Atlantic culture. For centuries inhabitants of the area have relied on the bay's bounty for their livelihood: entire towns were built on crabbing or oyster farming or shipbuilding. Those days have waned, but the landscape, the charm and the seafood remain.

## OUT AROUND THE BAY

Annapolis, Maryland's underrated state capital, is all about the water. Its downtown defines the word "quaint," with Georgian-style brick mansions, crayon-colored 18th-century shophouses and a cobblestoned

## Plan & prepare

### Tips for EV drivers

Maryland's Eastern Shore is very rural, and you'll tend to only find chargers in the larger towns and the ones that cater to tourists. But since distances between stops are short on this drive, it should be easy to charge when needed. Annapolis and Baltimore both have good EV infrastructure. You can rent an EV at the airport in Baltimore or in nearby Washington, DC.

### Where to stay

The towns highlighted on this route all cater to visitors, and all have multiple historic inns and B&Bs – such as the Old Brick Inn, St Michaels (oldbrickinn.com), and Chestertown's Brampton Inn (bramptoninn.com). There are plenty of national chains, from budget to high-end, around Annapolis and Baltimore. On the Eastern Shore, budget and midrange options are mostly limited to bigger towns like Salisbury, which have less in the way of traditional sights but are not far from the quaint coastal villages.

### When to go

Any time between April and October is likely to offer pleasant weather along the bay. Peak season for blue crabs is April through November – September through November means bigger, heavier crabs (and less work for you). Summer is crab-molting season, which means softshell-crab sandwiches. Chestertown reenacts its tea party in May, with Patriots and Redcoats in full costume.

### Further info

Driving a full loop around the Chesapeake Bay is possible. It means heading south into Virginia's Eastern Shore, then crossing the Chesapeake Bay Bridge-Tunnel, a 17.6-mile (28.3km) engineering marvel of connected bridges and underwater tunnels spanning the mouth of the Chesapeake. You'll come out at Hampton Roads, Virginia, and can then return north along the western side of the bay.

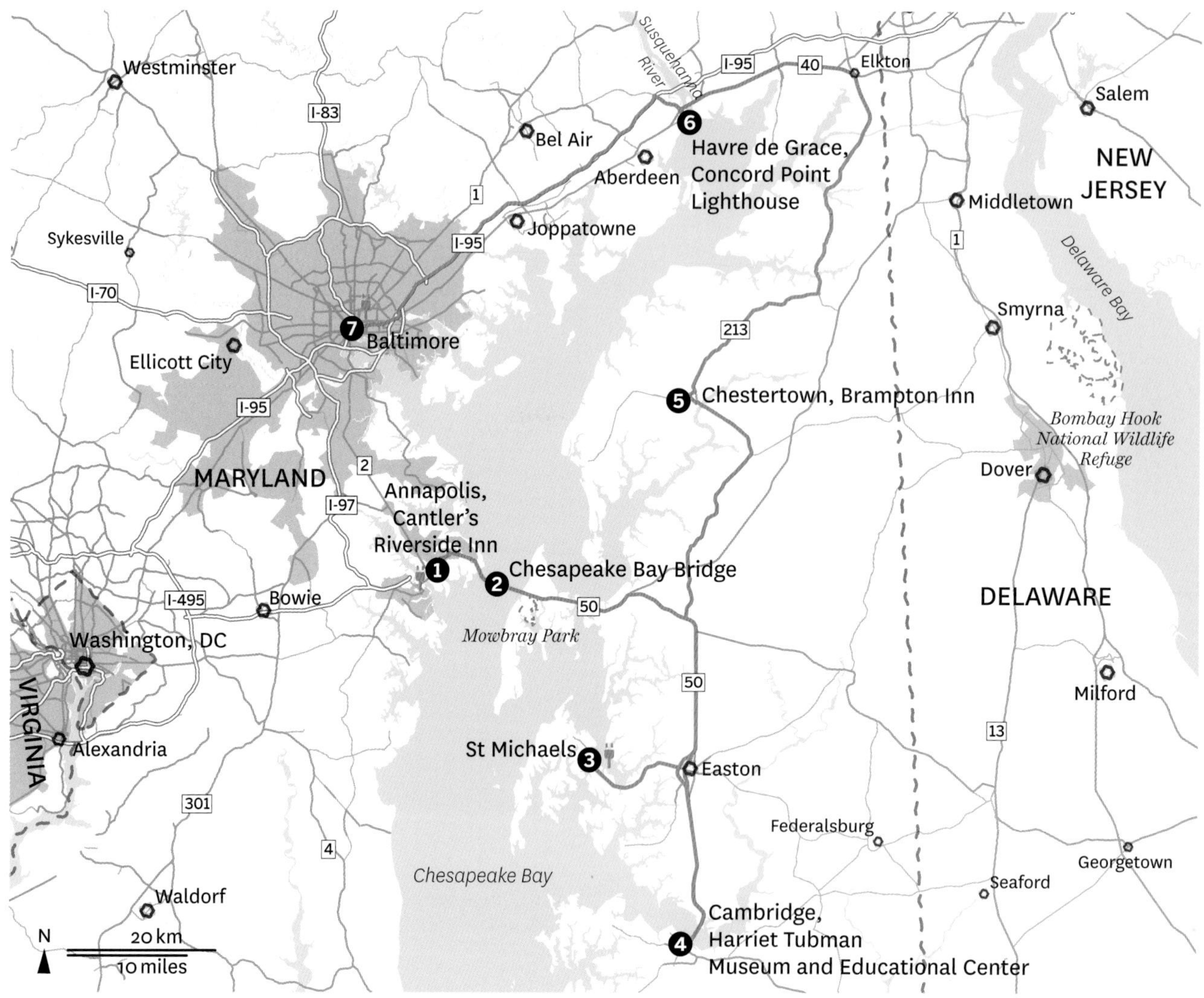


waterfront lined with sailboats. The town has excellent EV infrastructure, with fast chargers at downtown parking garages, the library and more, so you can head east fully charged.

The elegant steel span of the Chesapeake Bay Bridge is about 10 miles (16km) east of Annapolis. Glide your EV high over the navy waters en route to Maryland's Eastern Shore, then cross the marshlands of Kent Island – the bay's largest island – and amble south along the coast until you hit charm-packed St Michaels, an overnight stop of historic inns and crab houses along a narrow finger of land jutting into the bay.

In the morning it's another 50 miles (80km) east and then south to Cambridge. Harriet Tubman was born near this 17th-century town, which became a stop on the Underground Railroad – learn more at the Harriet Tubman Museum and Educational Center downtown. Then suck down some steamed clams and a crab-cake sandwich at Portside Seafood, along Cambridge Creek, before hopping back in your EV.

## CIRCLING BACK TO BALTIMORE

Head back northwards another 52 miles (84km) to Chestertown, a Revolutionary-era village along the Chester River that held its own tea party, in 1774, to protest British taxes. On summer Saturdays you can sail on the reproduction 18th-century schooner *Sultana*; if that doesn't align with your schedule there are daily cruises aboard a 1920s-era pleasure boat as well. The Civil War–era Brampton Inn has EV chargers and breakfasts of eggs with homegrown asparagus.

In the morning, you'll drive back to the mainland through the marshes and farm fields. Havre de Grace is at the mouth of the Susquehanna River, about 51 miles (82km) on. Stop here to stroll the waterfront promenade between the yacht basin and the photogenic 1827

Concord Point Lighthouse. Cap your trip off with a mess of crabs and a dozen local Tilghman Island oysters for lunch at the colorful picnic tables at Water Street Seafood. Then back in the EV to Baltimore where, if you haven't had enough, there are plenty more crabs to be had.

## How to eat a blue crab

While blue crabs can be found as far south as Argentina and as far north as Canada, they're most associated with Maryland, where they breed in abundance in the Chesapeake Bay. Locals have invented an impossible number of ways to eat them – from crab cakes, crab soup and fried softshell-crab sandwiches to crab omelets and crab tacos – but the classic option is a plate of steamed crabs, sold by the pound. They're seasoned with either Old Bay or JO Seasoning, rival spice mixes based on celery salt and paprika (chefs often give the edge to JO, for its finer texture). Dump them on your butcher-paper-covered table and go to work: pry off the apron (the bit of shell that looks like a triangle, or perhaps the Eiffel Tower), scoop out the gills, break the crab in half, then use a picker to pull out the leg meat and a mallet to crack the claws. Skip the "mustard," which is actually the crab's hepatopancreas, an organ that filters out toxins (and thus is full of them). Cracking completed, dip the pearlescent meat in drawn butter and revel at the fresh, sweet taste. Oh, and like we said: always wear the bib.

**Clockwise from top left:** hit Chestertown on a Saturday to sail the schooner *Sultana*; a feast of freshly steamed Maryland blue crabs; hauling in oysters from Chesapeake Bay

**Below:** rural roadway near Frederick, Maryland
**Right:** DC's Tidal Basin and the Washington Monument

**Distance: 97 miles (156km)**

**Duration: 2 days**

# DC to Harpers Ferry

**WASHINGTON, DC, MARYLAND & WEST VIRGINIA**

Zip backwards in time by EV, from the bustle of the capital to the sleepy Civil War town of Harpers Ferry, stopping en route for mountain vistas, quirky museums and more.

You've spent the day at the Smithsonian or touring the National Mall monuments, and now you're ready to get out of town? Ignore your GPS and point your EV northwest up Massachusetts Ave. It may not be the most direct route to the highway, but it's by far the most fascinating. Known as Embassy Row, the avenue is lined with Gilded Age townhouses, midcentury estates and Modernist mansions, home to many of the world's embassies to the US – like the splendiferous neo-baroque Indonesian embassy at 2020, fronted by a statue of the Hindu goddess Saraswati; Estonia's columned and turreted pile at 2131; Brazil's mirrored cube at 3006; and the elegantly minimalist Finnish embassy at 3301.

## INTO MARYLAND

Embassies give way to upscale private homes as Massachusetts Ave passes into Maryland. Keep northwest and find your way to I-270 N. You'll drive 30-some miles (48km) as suburbs become small towns and small towns dissolve into farmland. Take a detour southeast on Rte 109 to the trailhead for Sugarloaf Mountain. Stretch your legs on the Green Trail, a short uphill climb to a summit with panoramic views over the patchwork farm fields of Maryland's Monocacy Valley.

Jon Bilous/Shutterstock

## Plan & prepare

### Tips for EV drivers

EV rentals are easily available in DC, but be sure to book your car early. The route gets hillier the closer you get to West Virginia, so that will affect your range, as will very hot or cold conditions. The drive is short enough that you may not need to charge up, but if you do, Frederick is a good place to replenish your battery.

### Where to stay

Frederick has plenty of chain hotels, many of which offer EV charging, and a handful of smaller inns and B&Bs that do as well, such as Hollerstown Hill B&B (hollerstownhill.com). If you want to stay in Harpers Ferry proper, there are scads of charming historic B&Bs, though most do not offer chargers – you'll need to go slightly further afield if you want to charge overnight at a chain hotel, or continue on to Antietam Overlook Farm (antietamoverlook.net), which has free Tesla and non-Tesla chargers for guests.

### When to go

Fall – especially September and early in October – is definitely the most picturesque time to visit, as the Appalachians turn gold and orange. Spring is a close second. Fourth of July is a big weekend for Harpers Ferry. Summer (June through August) can be scorching, and winter (November through March) brings snow and frigid temperatures.

### Further info

Getting into and out of DC at rush hour (7am to 9am and 4pm to 7pm) can be a nightmare, so plan accordingly – leaving the city is especially bad on Friday afternoons. EV drivers who pay $5 at the Maryland Department of Transportation (mva.maryland.gov) are eligible to travel in High Occupancy Vehicle (HOV) lanes; this may be worth it if you're planning on spending a lot of time in the state.

## Harpers Ferry history

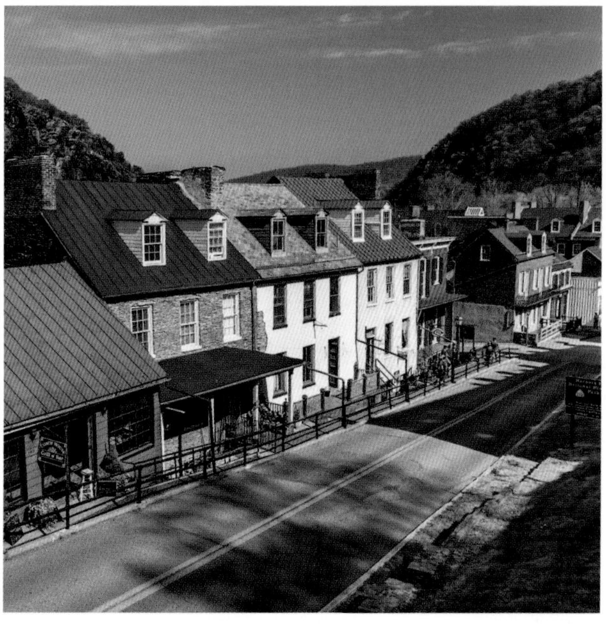

Harpers Ferry has been a crossroads for centuries. The town was once a manufacturing hub, with goods transported via the Potomac River and, later, by railroad, which arrived in the 1830s. The population exploded once the trains arrived, and by the mid-19th century Lower Town was full of hotels, saloons and brothels catering to some 3000 citizens and numerous visitors. In 1859, Harpers Ferry made national and international headlines when the abolitionist John Brown raided the federal armory with a group of Black and white soldiers, intending to use the weapons to arm enslaved people throughout the South and spark a wider rebellion. But the raid failed – all his men fled, or were captured or killed – and Brown himself was tried and hung for treason. A year later, the South seceded from the Union. In September of 1862, the Battle of Harpers Ferry saw some 12,000 Union troops surrender to the Confederacy; it would be the largest surrender of US troops until WWII. Following the war, the town became a hub for education and tourism for Black Americans. Today, Harpers Ferry is a National Historic Park with a population of less than 300.

**Clockwise from top left:** High St, Harpers Ferry; Civil War cannon at Bolivar Heights battlefield, Harpers Ferry; Maryland's Monocacy Valley from Sugarloaf Mountain

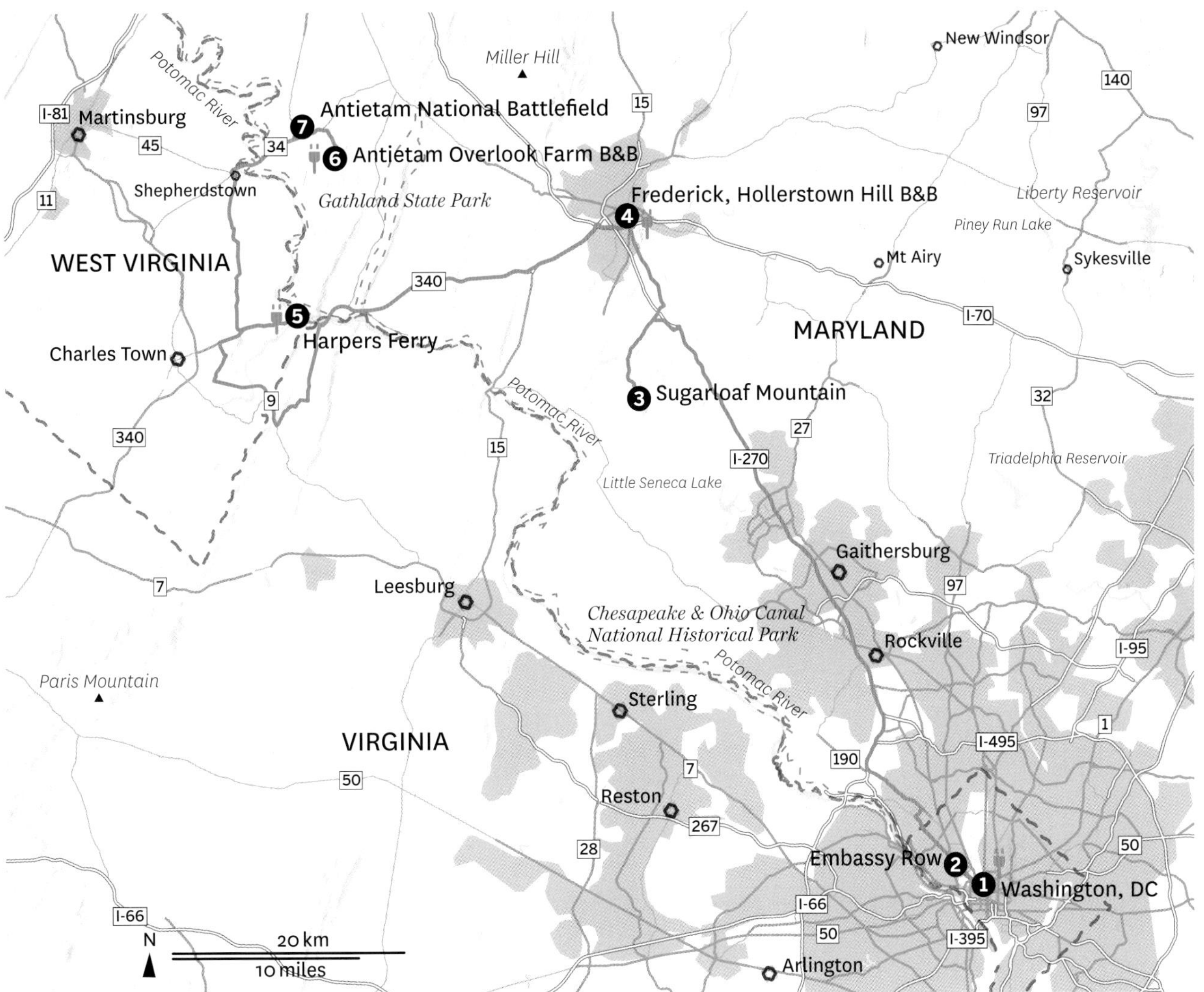


Afterwards, head back onto the highway and continue another 10 miles (16km) north to the well-preserved colonial town of Frederick, with a postcard-pretty downtown of brick buildings and soaring church spires set against a backdrop of the Appalachians. Stroll the boutiques and microbreweries, and amble across the stone bridges over Carroll Creek. Then check out the National Museum of Civil War Medicine, a quirky and sometimes gory collection of artifacts and dioramas dramatizing battlefield amputations and public embalmings, all set in a 19th-century former undertaker's office.

If your stomach's not too turned, walk over to Thacher & Rye for cheffy mid-Atlantic cuisine – Chesapeake oysters, shrimp with Old Bay seasoning and charred lemon. If your battery's low, head for the variety of chargers near the Walmart southeast of downtown. Or make use of the Level 2 charger at Hollerstown Hill B&B, a sweet Victorian done up in florals and frills.

## HARPERS FERRY

In the morning, it's a 21-mile (34km) hop across to West Virginia, where Harpers Ferry is tucked into the Blue Ridge Mountains at the confluence of the Shenandoah and Chesapeake Rivers. The entire Lower Town is a Historic District; squint and it's 1865 again. Park your EV and take in the sights – the John Brown Museum, telling the story of the abolitionist's doomed raid on the town's armory; and the lovely trail along the Chesapeake and Ohio Canal (C&O) Canal. Pop into True Treats, a historic candy store where you can taste Civil War–era confectionary like molasses pulls and sassafras sticks.

A 20-minute drive north of town, EV-friendly Antietam Overlook Farm is a 19th-century farmhouse B&B. Check in and take a late afternoon stroll through Antietam National Battlefield, where a bloody day of fighting on September 17, 1862 began to turn the war in the Union's favor. Tomorrow it's back to DC – and back to the 21st century.

**Below:** sunrise over the Blue Ridge Mountains
**Right:** driving the Parkway's sinuous Linn Cove Viaduct

➔ **Distance: 469 miles (755km)**

➔ **Duration: 5 days**

# The Blue Ridge Parkway

**NORTH CAROLINA & VIRGINIA**

With its endless, perfectly composed vistas, this celebrated scenic highway is like an open-air art museum. Break up the drive with waterfall hikes and dips into charming mountain towns.

Parked at the first viewpoint on the Blue Ridge Parkway, just outside Great Smoky Mountains National Park, you can see why the Cherokee called this land Shaconage, "place of the blue smoke." Wave upon wave of blue-gray mountains recede towards the horizon, their peaks shrouded in haze – but this haze is not actually smoke: it's caused by organic gases released by trees and plants, which scatter the light at the blue end of the color spectrum. The result is one of the loveliest and most beloved parts of the Appalachian Mountain range, a place of story and song, of scenic vistas and foggy hollows, of silent deer and silvery waterfalls. And for the next few hundred miles, it's all yours.

## CHEROKEE TO ASHEVILLE

Though the Parkway can be traveled in either direction, you're starting in the south, near the town of Cherokee. Fill your battery at the welcome center's chargers, then hit the Parkway going north. You'll wind past panoramic viewpoints, grassy balds (Appalachian mountain crests) and ancient rock formations – at mile marker 417, check out Looking Glass Rock, like the hump of an enormous sleeping buffalo. At mile marker 382, the Folk Art Center makes an excellent afternoon stop, with three sleek

## Plan & prepare

### Tips for EV drivers

Expect plenty of climbs and descents, with the highest point being 6053ft (1845m) at Richland Balsam in North Carolina. Weather varies from warm summers to freezing winters, when snow sometimes closes sections of the Parkway. You'll be traversing rural areas with few amenities, so be sure to charge and stock up at every opportunity. Speeds are inconsistent – it's common to be slowed behind a group of cyclists.

### Where to stay

Small cities (Asheville, Roanoke) and mountain towns along the route are well-equipped with public and hotel chargers. Options range from luxurious national chains in Asheville to historic B&Bs, rustic guesthouses and cabins. Characterful options include the 1899 Wright Inn & Carriage House, Asheville (wrightinn.com) and Peaks of Otter Lodge, Bedford (peaksofotter.com). Camping is also an option, with numerous campsites along the Parkway, though this means giving up the option of overnight charging.

### When to go

Spring and fall are the most scenic (and yes, crowded) seasons along the Parkway. Spring means blooming rhododendron and dogwood, carpets of wildflowers and waterfalls swollen with spring thaw. Fall brings endless vistas of russet and gold, and the smell of campfire smoke in the air; mid-October is typically peak season for leaf-peeping. Winter snows can disrupt travel; always check ahead.

### Further info

The Blue Ridge Parkway Association website (blueridgeparkway.org) maintains an incredibly useful list of EV charging stations along the route (search "gas availability" and scroll down). The North Carolina side, especially around Asheville and the environmentally-conscious mountain towns of Boone and Blowing Rock, is better equipped compared to the Virginia side of the border. If you want to rent an EV near the Parkway, Asheville is your best bet.

## Parkway history

The Blue Ridge Parkway is one of the most extraordinary things to come out of Franklin Delano Roosevelt's New Deal during the Great Depression. Construction began in 1935, with much of the work carried out courtesy of federal work relief programs like the Civilian Conservation Corps, which gave jobs to unemployed Americans – the first batch of whom worked 6 days a week for 30 cents an hour. The project was overseen by Stanley Abbott, a New York landscape architect who envisioned a natural-seeming – but highly intentional – series of vistas, almost like an outdoor museum. It would ultimately take more than half a century to finish. Work was completed by 1966, except for a 7-mile (11km) section around Grandfather Mountain. That small stretch, which includes the Linn Cove Viaduct, wasn't done until 1987. The viaduct was a major feat of engineering – some 1200ft (366m) of concrete clinging to the side of Grandfather Mountain without damaging it; the only trees cut were the ones directly beneath the bridge. Today the Parkway is the most-visited part of the National Park system, attracting nearly 16 million visitors a year.

**Above, from left:** Parkway signage; Asheville storefronts **Opposite, from left:** Looking Glass Falls, near its namesake rock; hiking rhododendron-rich heights at Craggy Gardens

modern galleries exhibiting traditional Appalachian crafts like quilting and basket-weaving. By now you're just outside the art deco downtown of Asheville, long a retreat for the wealthy and well-connected. Today it's a progressive hotspot chockablock with inventive restaurants, quirky boutiques and, yes, plenty of EV chargers in the downtown parking garages. Sleep in a restored Queen Anne mansion at 1899 Wright Inn & Carriage House, providing fresh-baked cookies, nightly wine-and-charcuterie social hours and onsite charging.

### PARKWAY PERFECTION

In the morning, it's back to the Parkway. Stop almost immediately at Craggy Gardens, a jagged summit that explodes with pink and purple rhododendron blossoms each June. From here on the views come thick and fast – rain-fed Glassmine Falls at mile marker 361 and glimpses of Grandfather Mountain at mile marker 349 among them. At mile marker 304 you'll glide over the Linn Cove Viaduct, one of the Parkway's greatest engineering feats, winding sinuously around the side of Grandfather Mountain – driving it feels like flying through the trees. Should you stop to climb the mountain's famous swinging bridge, you can charge up at a free public station.

After the Boone's Trace Overlook at mile marker 285, exit for the night to the groovy little mountain town of Boone, with public chargers aplenty. Sample down-home Southern cuisine at Dan'l Boone Inn, where fried chicken, ham biscuits and stewed apples have been served family-style for over 60 years.

The next two days will serve up miles of yawning gorges and gentle valleys, photogenic gristmills and decaying mountain churches. You'll find a number of chargepoints just off the Parkway, including Floyd and Roanoke, Virginia. At mile marker 84, the three mountains known as the Peaks of Otter attract scores of hikers. Nearby, the Peaks of Otter Lodge has chargers and a restaurant overlooking Abbott Lake.

The Parkway ends at Rockfish Gap, where it blends seamlessly into Shenandoah National Park's Skyline Drive, another 105 miles (169km) of desperately scenic mountain road. Tempted?

Charleston
WEST VIRGINIA
I-64
Cave Run Lake
Big Sandy River
Guyandotte River
I-77
Greenbrier River
Cowpasture River
Shenandoah National Park
Rockfish Gap 9
I-64
Beckley
I-64
White Sulphur Springs
James River
KENTUCKY
8 Peaks of Otter Lodge
7 Roanoke
I-81
Balsam Beartown Mountain
Roanoke River
Floyd
VIRGINIA
Cumberland River
Clinch River
Mt Rogers
New River
Bristol
Kingsport
I-81
Norris Lake
Blue Ridge Parkway
Dan River
Johnson City
I-77
Haw River
TENNESSEE
Boone
6
Blowing Rock
5 Grandfather Mountain
Winston-Salem
Greensboro
I-40
I-26
Durham
Great Smoky Mountains National Park
Asheville, 1899 Wright Inn & Carriage House
NORTH CAROLINA
Lake James
Hickory
I-85
Raleigh
4 Craggy Gardens
I-40
Salisbury
Deep River
B Everett Jordan Lake
3
2 Folk Art Center
1 Cherokee
19
Lake Norman
Broad River
I-73
N
40 km
20 miles
Charlotte

© makasana/Getty Images; Margaret.Wiktor/Shutterstock

**Below:** charge up in Wilmington at the start of this epic drive
**Right:** sunset over the Mojave Desert, near the end of your I-40 odyssey

**Distance: 2554 miles (4110km)**

**Duration: 10 days**

# I-40 end-to-end

**NORTH CAROLINA TO CALIFORNIA**

From Atlantic shores to the glitter of Nashville, past the Oklahoma stockyards, New Mexico's mesas and on to the California deserts, this is the ultimate cross-country drive by EV.

It's not an auspicious looking start. An exurban highway fringed by scrubby pines, a subdivision just off the shoulder, a gas station up ahead. It might have more of a sense of occasion, had the sign not been stolen so many times the DOT stopped replacing it: "Barstow, Calif. 2,554." That's where you're headed. But right now you're in Wilmington, a riverside city on North Carolina's Atlantic coast. You've got another six states between here and the California. Are you charged up? Good.

## NORTH CAROLINA, TENNESSEE & MEMPHIS

The first stretch of I-40 goes north through the Sandhills and into the Piedmont. There's not much to see, just pines and the occasional whiff of hog farm. Top up your battery and grab lunch in Raleigh, 125 miles (201km) in, then head eastward another 100 miles (161km) to Winston-Salem, where the photogenic 18th-century Moravian village of Old Salem promises a pleasant afternoon. Asheville, an EV-friendly hippie-chic mountain town, is your overnight stop – if your budget can swing it, the Grand Bohemian, in a 19th-century Bavarian-style lodge, is a charmer with chargers.

The highway grows sinuous as you cross the Blue Ridge, their ancient peaks shrouded in haze. Pull off

© Halfpoint Images/Getty Images

## Plan & prepare

### Tips for EV drivers

All the major and medium-sized cities along the route have good fast-charger availability. In between, there will be long stretches where you'll want to fully charge at every available fast-charger stop, lest the next one be busy or offline. Desert weather, especially in the Mojave, can be meltingly hot, which will affect range. Your levels will also take a hit during the mountain crossing from North Carolina to Tennessee.

### Where to stay

All the big cities on the route have hotels offering overnight charging – including Asheville's Grand Bohemian (marriott.com) and Oklahoma City's Skirvin (skirvinhilton.com) – as do many of the national chains along the highway throughout the route. Always call ahead to be sure that a hotel's chargers are indeed existent and working, especially when it's the only stop in the area. The Route 66 portion of I-40 has some fun classic midcentury motels, especially in New Mexico.

### When to go

This trip can be done year-round; few of the locations, with the exception of the Flagstaff area, get regular heavy snows. Summer is more of a concern, with average summer temperatures in the Mojave at 110°F (43°C) or more, and hot and humid conditions across much of the rest. Asheville gets crowded during fall leaf-peeping season, Memphis has festivals all May, and Albuquerque has a major hot-air balloon festival in October.

### Further info

If the Wilmington suburbs and the Mojave don't seem like choice spots to begin and end a trip, just stretch a bit. In Wilmington, it's a 10-minute drive west from the start of I-40 to the restaurant-filled riverfront downtown, surrounded by walkable neighborhoods of azalea-fronted mansions. From Barstow, it's another 125 miles (201km) to Los Angeles, if you'd rather end your journey at the Pacific.

## Fast highway, fast food

Of course you want to try unique locally owned restaurants. But sometimes you're only stopping briefly and you need something quick and highway-adjacent while your EV charges or your companion takes a bathroom break. So here's a rundown of regionally specific fast-food chains for just such occasions: North Carolina, Bojangles: "Cajun-style" but born in NC, Bojangles is beloved for its fried chicken-filet biscuits and seasoned fries. Tennessee, Krystal: Chattanooga-founded Krystal's signature item is the hamburger slider on a steamed, square-shaped bun. Arkansas, Slim Chickens: chicken-finger baskets and desserts served in Mason jars are the order of the day here. Oklahoma, Sonic Drive-In: retro spot for chili dogs and slushies, eaten in your car. Texas, Whataburger: customizable burgers sold from signature white-and-orange buildings. New Mexico, Blake's Lotaburger: classic stop for New Mexican-style green-chile cheeseburgers and breakfast burritos. Arizona, Cold Stone Creamery: now-national ice-cream chain with choose-your-own mix-ins – cake batter flavor is the fave. California, Del Taco: sure, In-N-Out gets all the love, but this Mojave-born joint serves up inexpensive, filling American-style Mexican like hard tacos and chili nachos.

**Clockwise from top left:** Bojangles, NC's beloved chicken chain; Cummins Falls State Park; BBQ and the blues on Memphis' Beale St

at Exit 7 for the spectacular Buzzard's Roost Overlook, then drive on to Tennessee. It's just over 100 miles (161km) to Knoxville, with the gold disco-ball of the 1982 World's Fair Sunsphere crowning the skyline. Find fast chargers in the western suburbs. Break up the journey on to Nashville with a jaunt to the north at Cummins Falls State Park, where a mile-long (1.6km) trail takes you to a deep green swimming hole at the base of a waterfall (snag an access permit online). Then it's 83 miles (134km) to Music City. Spend the night honky-tonk hopping on neon-lit Lower Broadway, gorge on the city's signature spicy "hot chicken" and, in the morning, hit the Country Music Hall of Fame.

Now it's a straight shot southwest for 212 miles (341km) to Memphis. Charge up midway in Jackson if you need, and roll into Memphis for an evening of BBQ and blues on Beale St. After a morning trip to Graceland, cross the shimmering brown Mississippi and you're in Arkansas.

## ARKANSAS, OKLAHOMA & TEXAS

Your EV will glide through the flat plains for 137 miles (221km) to Little Rock (along the way, you'll find fast chargers at Forrest City and Tesla versions at Brinkley). If you've only got time for one sight, make it the Little Rock Central High School National Historic Site. The Gothic Revival building grabbed global attention in 1957, when nine Black students faced a jeering mob when attempting to enter after integration orders. Still a working public school, the building now houses a museum on the Civil Rights era and desegregation.

The following day, it's 339 miles (546km) to the next state capital, Oklahoma City, with a midway pause at Fort Smith. Once a major stop for Cherokee people forcibly marched along the Trail of Tears, it's now a National Historic Site. By the time you hit OKC, as it's known by locals, you'll be ready for dinner at Cattlemen's Steakhouse in historic Stockyards City.

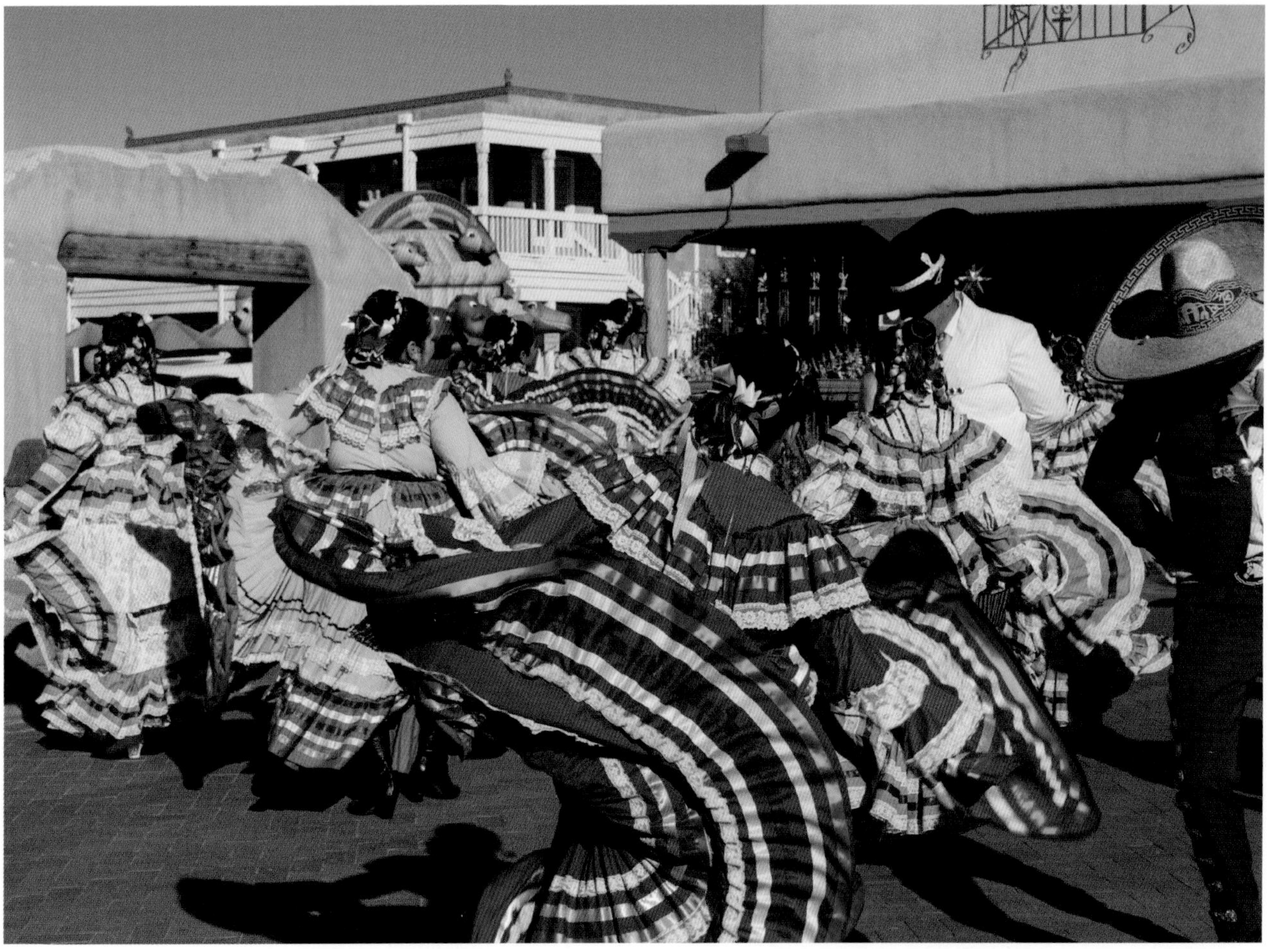

## The Continental Divide

In Western New Mexico, a half-hour outside Gallup, you'll come to an unincorporated community called Continental Divide. This is marked by a vintage gas station and a Navajo souvenir shop, and it stands on a site of geographic importance: the actual Continental Divide. This ridgeline, which runs from the Arctic Circle all the way down to South America, divides two drainage basins. On the west side, water flows into rivers leading to the Pacific. On the east side, it flows towards the Atlantic. At this particular location, the altitude is 7245ft (2208m). In the late 1800s the Atchison, Topeka and Santa Fe Railway chose the spot, also known as Campbell Pass, to route their railroad. Today the community is marked by a Continental Divide sign on the access road, which makes for a good photo op.

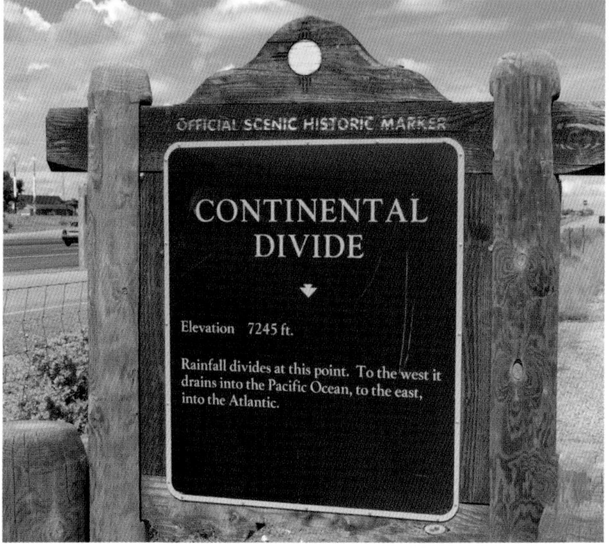


**Clockwise from top left:** Ballet Folklórico dancers, Albuquerque; vintage Route 66 digs at Tucumcari's Blue Swallow Motel; roadside Continental Divide marker, New Mexico

Less than 10 minutes away, the Skirvin Hilton has free chargers and historic ambience.

The sky goes wider as you roll through western Oklahoma and into the Texas Panhandle. You're following the old Route 66 now – snap a photo of the iconic art deco–style Conoco gas station in Shamrock, then pass the cattle yards of Amarillo and cross the state line into New Mexico.

## NEW MEXICO, ARIZONA & CALIFORNIA

Amarillo and Albuquerque are 289 miles (465km) apart through the silvery New Mexico desert. En route, Tucumcari is a classic, quirky Route 66 town with several photogenic vintage motels and restaurants (try Del's, with the cow atop its neon sign), and the small-but-wonderful Mesalands Dinosaur Museum.

In Albuquerque, the Indian Pueblo Cultural Center is a fascinating museum dedicated to the state's Indigenous Pueblo peoples. It's just off the highway north of Old Town, where the narrow adobe-lined streets are filled with restaurants serving sopapillas and green-chile enchiladas. On your way out in the morning, stop at Petroglyph National Monument, where trails loop past volcanic rocks carved with more than 23,000 designs, etched into being some 700 years ago.

Heading west afterwards, the landscape gets redder, the sky a deeper and more luminous blue. You're bound for Flagstaff – good charging stops are Grants, Gallup, Holbrook and Winslow. Flagstaff, amid the ponderosa pine forest at the edge of the Colorado Plateau, is the gateway to the Grand Canyon, 90 minutes north.

More classic Route 66 towns – Seligman, Kingman, Needles – fly past your EV's windows as you leave Arizona and enter the final stretch: California. From the border, it's 140 miles (225km) through the Mojave to Barstow. Here, your journey ends like it began – on a stretch of highway that doesn't look anything, yet means so much.

**Below:** Spanish moss-draped live oak trees near Savannah, Georgia
**Right:** Bonaventure Cemetery, just east of Savannah's Historic District

**Distance: 233 miles (375km)**

**Duration: 3-5 days**

# Savannah to Charleston

**GEORGIA & SOUTH CAROLINA**

Bookended by two richly historic cities and replete with sandy beaches and coastal wildlife refuges, this easily covered route offers big rewards as well as ever-present reminders of a troubled past.

Built on the back of enormous wealth, the grand and opulent homes that litter the Southern coast are matched by the natural splendor of moss-draped oaks, shimmering lagoons and wide expanses of white sand buffeted by Atlantic rollers. It makes a glorious area for a leisurely EV road trip, but a challenging one too as each piece of heritage architecture brings an uncomfortable reckoning with the past.

## SAVANNAH & THE LOWCOUNTRY

Leafy streets shaded by giant live oaks are flanked by heritage houses of the grandest style in affluent Savannah, a city oozing Southern charm. You may recognize the imposing Mercer-Williams House from the 1997 movie *Midnight in the Garden of Good and Evil*, but it is the Owens-Thomas House & Slave Quarters which sheds light on the unequal distribution of power and wealth in Savannah during the early 19th century. The city's park-like cemeteries with their elaborate tombs and statues are equally evocative, though here too history's injustices are laid bare.

Heading northeast, you'll quickly cross into South Carolina's Lowcountry region. Stop off at the Savannah National Wildlife Refuge, 10 miles (16km) from the city,

## Plan & prepare

### Tips for EV drivers

The short distances involved on this route mean there should be no problem maintaining your EV's battery levels. You'll find chargers clustered in the larger cities and towns or at the most popular oceanfront resorts – just check ahead to see if non-residents can access hotel chargers. In Georgia, EVs with an alternative-fuel license plate can use HOV (high occupancy vehicle) and HOT (high occupancy toll) lanes regardless of the number of passengers.

### Where to stay

In Savannah, the Kimpton Brice Hotel (bricehotel.com) is a sleek, design-conscious den with large modern rooms and a private-club vibe. For period style, Beaufort's 19th-century Rhett House Inn (rhetthouseinn.com) carries all the elegance and tradition of its time, and a stay includes free bike hire. Over on Edisto Island, you'll get spacious suites with private balconies and access to a championship golf course at the Club Wyndham Ocean Ridge (wyndhamhotels.com), near Edisto Beach. All have chargers onsite or nearby.

### When to go

Avoid the oppressive summer heat and visit between March and mid-June or in late September and October. The Charleston Jazz Festival in mid-April is a big draw, as is the Spoleto Festival USA, for performing arts, in late May or early June. For traditional storytelling, dancing, drumming, arts and food, Beaufort is the place to be in late May for the Gullah Festival. Late August to early September is hurricane season; winters are pleasant and mild, and hotel prices are often reduced from December to February.

### Further info

Although this is a short road trip, there's lots to see and digest. Plan to spend at least a full day each in Savannah and Charleston, and as much time as you can to meander in between. For a proper insight into Gullah culture, language and customs, the role of enslavement in the region and the rich traditions of the area, take a tour with a Gullah guide in Charleston; visit gullahtours.com or gullahgeecheetours.com for more information.

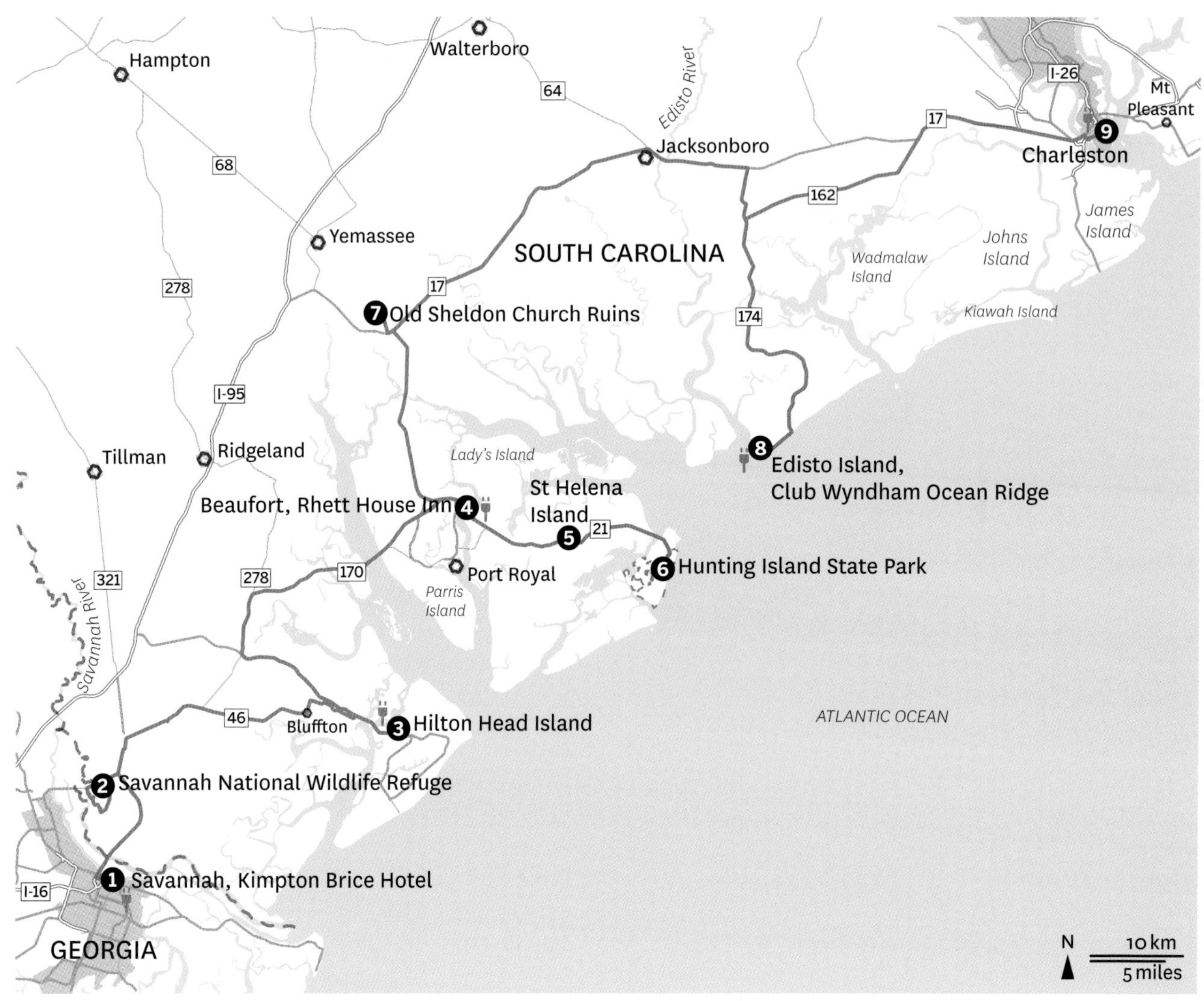


to hike, bike or paddle around hardwood forests and freshwater marshes to the chirps and croaks of tree frogs. From here, it's a 24-mile (39km) drive through salt marshes to Hilton Head Island, a beloved destination for summer holidaymakers who kayak along creeks, lagoons and rivers, golf at the 26 courses, laze on white-sand beaches and take boat trips to see bottlenose dolphins.

Beaufort (byoo-furt), 35 miles (56km) away, is another stunner of a town with restored mansions and live oaks lining the winding, narrow streets. The whole downtown area is a designated Historic District and regularly used as a movie location. Take a stroll before continuing 7 miles (11km) to St Helena Island, where descendants of West African enslaved peoples known as the Gullah protect a rich cultural heritage. The Penn Center offers a unique insight into Gullah culture, language and history, while Beaufort's art galleries display vibrant local works, and cafes and restaurants proudly serve dishes that combine Southern mainstays with a strong African influence. For relaxation, nearby Hunting Island State Park sees lush maritime forest give way to saltwater lagoons and powdery beaches.

## EAST TO CHARLESTON

Backtracking inland in your EV, stop at the Old Sheldon Church, 34 miles (55km) away. Built in the 18th century in the style of a Greek temple, the roofless church with its high arches and many brick columns has a haunting

beauty. Return to the coast at Edisto Beach for long stretches of quiet sands and low-key watersports, or head east into Charleston, where a languid, antique charm radiates from brightly colored Georgian houses and antebellum homes with leafy gardens and ornate balconies. Charleston's social history is explored at the 1820 Aiken-Rhett House, while the McLeod Plantation traces the emergence of Gullah culture. Walking the streets, the weight of a complex history lingers in the air – from the Old Slave Mart Museum to the remains of Fort Sumter, where the first shots of the Civil War rang out. Take time to digest it all and mark the end of your journey with a sunset drink on a breezy rooftop bar.

## South Carolina's sea turtles

Every year South Carolina's barrier islands play host to large numbers of sea turtles, which come ashore to nest here. The endangered loggerhead is the most common visitor, but you'll also see Kemp's ridley, green and leatherback turtles. Loggerheads come ashore between May and mid-August, digging a nest and laying about 120 eggs each. Roughly two months later, the eggs hatch at night and the tiny turtles make their way to the ocean. Although at times perilous, this first journey from nest to sea imprints the beach's location on the hatchlings so they can remember it; females return to nest as adults. You can learn more about the turtles on a ranger-guided nighttime beach walk at Edisto State Park, through the educational program at Hunting Island State Park, or volunteer conservation projects on Hilton Head Island. If you come across nesting turtles or hatchlings, observe them from a distance, never shine lights on them and never pick up a hatchling, even if it appears to be lost. The South Carolina Marine Turtle Conservation Program (dnr.sc.gov/seaturtle) is a good place for further reading as well as real-time nesting information.

**Clockwise from top left:** sunset over Hunting Island State Park, South Carolina; loggerhead turtle hatchling; Beaufort's beautiful Historic District

**Below:** look for manatees along Florida's Intracoastal Waterway **Right:** bridges spanning the Halifax River at Daytona Beach, Florida

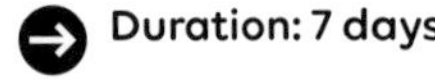

**Distance: 1924 miles (3096km)**

**Duration: 7 days**

# East-coast USA on the I-95

**FLORIDA TO MAINE**

Drive the entire length of the East Coast by EV, from sultry South Florida to the peach orchards of Georgia to the Mid-Atlantic megalopolises and into tranquil seaside New England.

It's autumn in Miami, but you wouldn't know it. The air is balmy and scented with jasmine, and swimmers are paddling blithely into the Atlantic. The ocean will be your companion for much of the journey ahead, changing colors from turquoise to jade to brown to icy gray as you move north.

It's 75-some miles (121km) north to the palm-lined byways of arty West Palm Beach, which has fast chargers in town parking garages. Stretch your legs with a stroll along the Intracoastal Waterway; from November through March you might spot manatees lounging like aquatic housecats. Then hop along coastal towns such as Jupiter, Vero Beach, Melbourne and Daytona Beach, all with good charging options, and overnight in Jacksonville, where the funky Riverside Arts Market is held right under the I-95 overpass on Saturdays.

## INTO GEORGIA & THE CAROLINAS

Heading north again, cross the state line into Georgia. You'll cut through the longleaf pine forests of the humid coastal plain, crossing rivers as many-branched as trees. If you need a charge, Brunswick is a good choice before hitting Savannah, 139 miles (224km) north. With its 19th-century architecture and Spanish moss–dripping

## Plan & prepare

### Tips for EV drivers

Traffic jams are common on the crowded mid-Atlantic stretches of I-95, so don't get caught out. Parts of rural Georgia, North and South Carolina and southern Virginia can have long distances between towns, as does Maine once you leave the coast. Do your best to fully charge overnight in such places. Oftentimes the nearest chargers will be a short drive from the highway, near Walmarts or shopping malls.

### Where to stay

Outside of cities, midrange national chains catering to interstate travelers are your best bet for overnight charging. In larger cities you'll have a wider variety of choices, such as the Eaton Workshop in DC (eatonworkshop.com) and the Seaport Hotel in Boston (seaportboston.com). Indeed in Boston, for example, nearly every luxury hotel has chargers (or valets to ferry your car there). Historic cities like Charleston, Boston and Portland have all sorts of adorable B&Bs and inns to choose from.

### When to go

Fall is an excellent time for this trip, since the south will be cooler but the north not yet frigid – plus fall color in New England is a huge draw. Ditto for spring, though sub golden leaves for blooming trees and meadows. Any holiday or long weekend – Memorial Day, the Fourth of July, Labor Day etc – means extra crowds on highways and the possibility of jams.

### Further info

I-95 contains stretches of toll roads, all of which use E-ZPass (e-zpassiag.com). These include Maryland's Fort McHenry Tunnel and the John F Kennedy Memorial Hwy, the Delaware, Pennsylvania and New Jersey Turnpikes, New York's George Washington Bridge, the New England Thruway, and the New Hampshire and Maine Turnpikes. Always check ahead for construction that could impact your time and range: state Department of Transportation websites are a good resource.

## State-by-state specialties

I-95 passes through 15 states, plus the District of Columbia, each with its own food culture, so try this highly subjective list of food and drink along your drive. Florida: key lime pie, fresh-squeezed orange juice, Cuban sandwiches, fried conch. Georgia: peaches, caramel-covered pecan logs, pimento cheese, biscuits and gravy. South Carolina: boiled peanuts, Lowcountry boil, shrimp and grits, Gullah red rice. North Carolina: pulled pork BBQ, collard greens, Cheerwine soda. Virginia: country ham, oysters, Brunswick stew. DC: half-smoke hotdogs, *doro wat* and *injera*, wings with Mumbo sauce. Maryland: blue crabs, pit beef, Berger cookies. Delaware: scrapple, fried chicken, fries with vinegar. Pennsylvania: Philly cheesesteak, Tastykakes, soft pretzels. New Jersey: pork rolls, salt water taffy, tomato pie, gyros. New York: cream cheese bagels, halal chicken over rice, dirty-water dogs, *mofongo*, dim sum. Connecticut: white-clam pizza, Foxon Park white birch soda, steamed cheeseburgers. Rhode Island: coffee milk, *caldo verde*, stuffed clams. Massachusetts: clam chowder, fried cod, Portuguese egg tarts, baked beans. New Hampshire: cider donuts, steamed clams, maple syrup. Maine: lobster rolls, whoopie pies, oysters, Moxie soda.

**Above, from left:** NC's pulled pork BBQ; Savannah's Forsyth Park Fountain, Georgia
**Opposite:** antique Elfreth's Alley in Philadelphia

live oaks, Savannah is one of the most photogenic cities in the US. Park your EV at one of the charging stations in the Historic District's parking decks, and see the sights: the fountain at Forsyth Park, the waterfront cobblestones of River St.

In the morning you're off into South Carolina's Lowcountry, flying past small towns with gas stations advertising boiled peanuts. Find charging options at Walterboro, Manning and Florence, respectively 70 miles (113km), 131 miles (211km) and 179 miles (288km) from Savannah. Before you cross into North Carolina you'll be subjected to the strange sight of South of the Border, a crassly Mexican-themed fireworks stand/roadside attraction marked by a sombrero tower. The Sunoco station here does have a good fast charger.

In North Carolina, skirt Fayetteville and pass through miles of the wiregrass and pine that define the Sandhills region. Stop in Wilson for local-style BBQ (pulled pork with vinegar sauce) at Parker's before crashing at an EV-friendly hotel in nearby Rocky Mount.

### VIRGINIA & WASHINGTON, DC

Things remain mostly rural into Virginia. The historic town of Petersburg lies 103 miles (166km) north, at the confluence of the James and Appomattox Rivers. Mosey around the Old Towne, where 19th-century brick buildings now hold antiques shops and boutiques. Pass the state capital of Richmond (or stop for spine tingles at the Edgar Allan Poe Museum) on your way to the nation's capital. Washington, DC is about 109 miles (175km) from Richmond, though getting in can be super-slow during rush hour/construction/holiday weekends.

You're spoiled for choice when it comes to EV-friendly DC hotels, but we like the Eaton, with its of-the-moment

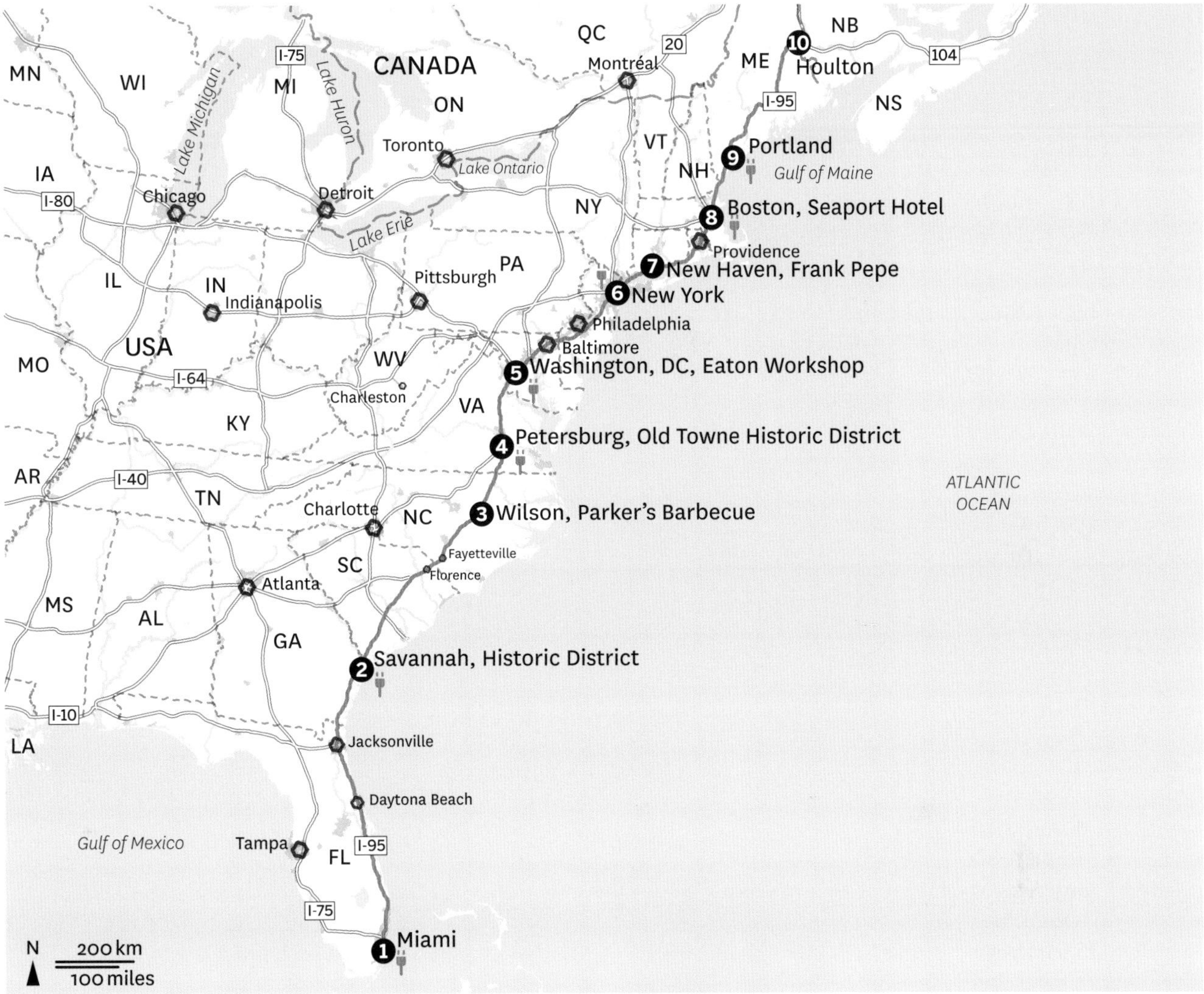

CANADA
QC
ON
NB
NS
ME
VT
NH
NY
PA
MN
WI
MI
IA
IL
IN
MO
KY
WV
VA
AR
TN
NC
SC
MS
AL
GA
LA
FL
USA
Lake Michigan
Lake Huron
Lake Ontario
Lake Erie
Gulf of Maine
Gulf of Mexico
ATLANTIC OCEAN
I-75
I-80
I-64
I-40
I-10
I-95
20
104
Montréal
Toronto
Chicago
Detroit
Pittsburgh
Indianapolis
Charleston
Charlotte
Atlanta
Fayetteville
Florence
Jacksonville
Daytona Beach
Tampa
Providence
Philadelphia
Baltimore
1 Miami
2 Savannah, Historic District
3 Wilson, Parker's Barbecue
4 Petersburg, Old Towne Historic District
5 Washington, DC, Eaton Workshop
6 New York
7 New Haven, Frank Pepe
8 Boston, Seaport Hotel
9 Portland
10 Houlton
N
200 km
100 miles

amenities (record players, infrared saunas in the spa). It's walking distance to the National Mall; give yourself at least a full day for museums and monuments.

## MARYLAND TO MAINE

DC to New York is a 225-mile (362km) run through some of the most densely populated parts of the US. Just past DC, Baltimore is exceptionally EV-friendly for a midsized city. So, if you're tempted to stop for a mess of crabs slathered in Old Bay seasoning, indulge. Up next is Philadelphia, with the Liberty Bell and other classic Revolutionary-era sites. Both are worth an overnight stop.

In New Jersey, I-95 carries the New Jersey Turnpike, so getting on and off means tolls. Detour east through the Holland Tunnel to hit the storied sights of Manhattan, or roll along the Cross Bronx Expressway and through the suburbs to Connecticut, where I-95

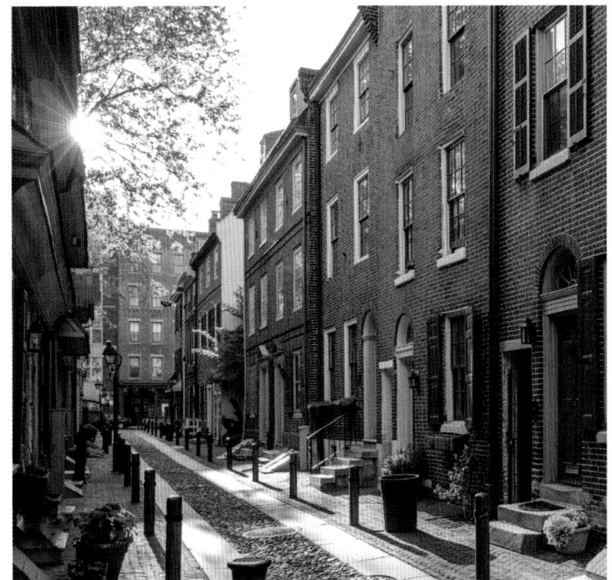

## I-95 history

One of the oldest roads in the US' federal highway system, I-95 was established in 1956, part of President Dwight Eisenhower's vision of a system of linked superhighways. It was built over existing roads, which in turn were built over paths trod by Revolutionary War soldiers. Today it serves some 40% of the USA's population, making it the country's most used highway. (Fun fact: the highway had a "gap" at the New Jersey–Pennsylvania border until 2018, thanks to local opposition in the early days of development.) Recently, archaeologists investigating around the site of an I-95 repair project in Philadelphia discovered a huge span of artifacts, with pieces from 6000-year-old Native American cultures as well as 18th-century privies, Industrial Revolution glassware and WWI-era toys. The website diggingi95.com has interactive photo galleries; see the artifacts in real life on Wednesday afternoons at Philadelphia's I-95 Archaeology Center.

**Clockwise, from above:** Portland's Breakwater Light; white-clam pizza; I-95 signage, Connecticut; history reenacted at Boston's Old State House

connects tony towns like Greenwich and Darien along the Long Island Sound – stop in Yale's hometown of New Haven for a white-clam pizza at Frank Pepe.

It's another 103 miles (166km) northeast to the charmingly scruffy Rhode Island capital of Providence. Find plenty of Level 2 chargers in the city, or faster ones in the suburbs. Spend the night and check out the Victorian manses around Brown University before moving on to Boston, another 58 miles (93km) north and a short detour off the highway. Spend a day or so basking in Beantown's history, walking the Freedom Trail and getting the college vibes in Harvard Square. The Seaport Hotel has EV chargers, plus views across the harbor.

The autumn breezes grow sharper as you skirt along the eastern edge of New Hampshire and into Maine. I-95 connects the holiday towns along the state's southern coast, though Rte 1, slightly to the east, is more scenic. After Portland, and a night of sucking down lobsters and exploring the cobblestoned Old Port, the highway moves inland. End your journey here or – if you're a completist – follow the route through northern forests dotted with old lumber towns until you get to Houlton, 247 miles (398km) on, which is the end of the road. Any further and you'll need your passport.

**Below:** the geodesic-domed home of St Pete's Salvador Dalí Museum
**Right:** crossing Florida's Everglades on the Tamiami Trail

**Distance: 280 miles (451km)**

**Duration: 5 days**

# St Petersburg to Miami

**FLORIDA**

Cruise quietly by EV along the Gulf Coast and across the Everglades to discover Florida's richest cultural hubs and most fascinating natural habitats, with a few beach stops along the way.

Downtown St Petersburg is a surprising center of art and architecture tucked into a quaint seaside enclave. You might not think you came to Florida for its culture, but this town's museums are eclectic and wonderful, showcasing everything from surreal paintings to contemporary glass sculpture and art of the Western US. The excellent new Museum of the American Arts & Crafts Movement is a highlight. Charge your EV at St Pete Pier while you explore.

## THE GULF COAST

Leaving town, cruise south over the incredible, 4-mile-long (6.4km) Sunshine Skyway Bridge, enjoying views over Tampa Bay and out to the Gulf of Mexico, then continue about 40 miles (64km) to Sarasota. The main draw to this fair city is the dazzling beach at Siesta Key, famous for white-quartz sand and turquoise-blue water. But for culture, explore the varied attractions at the Ringling Museum, with 21 galleries of European art and unique exhibits on the history of the circus.

It's another 75 miles (121km) south to Fort Myers, its historic downtown and River District packed with 19th-century buildings. Don't miss the side-by-side Edison and Ford Winter Estates, where these two scions of

## Plan & prepare

### Tips for EV drivers

Florida ranks second among US states in terms of the number of EV registrations, and it has the infrastructure to support them. Note that most EV charging stations here are located at shopping centers and parking garages – presently less so at hotels or other tourist facilities. See Drive Electric Florida (driveelectricflorida.org) for information about owning and driving electric vehicles in this state.

### Where to stay

Less than a mile (1.6km) from the chargers at St Pete Pier, Hollander Hotel (hollanderhotel.com) is a classy choice with an "Old Florida" atmosphere. Sarasota has many functional chain hotels near the University Station Tesla Superchargers. The beautiful Spanish-style Bellasera Hotel (bellaseranaples.com) is a short walk from the Bayfront charging station in Naples. Of the dozens of hotels in South Beach, the exquisite boutique Casa Tua (casatualife.com) has several charging stations in the vicinity.

### When to go

The best time to go to Florida is between November and March, when weather is pleasant, warm and dry; this dry season in the Everglades is also better for hiking and wildlife-watching. From June to November, temperatures soar and hurricanes threaten (peaking in September). Wet season in the Everglades extends from April to November, when hiking trails may become flooded and wildlife is more dispersed and difficult to see.

### Further info

Once you cross the Sunshine Skyway Bridge heading out of St Petersburg, you can choose to drive on the interstate (I-75) or the old Tamiami Trail (Hwy 41). Though it's usually slower and not necessarily more scenic, the Tamiami does provide an alternative to interstate driving, and offers opportunities to stop at attractions en route when crossing the Everglades. Note that all visitors must pay an entrance fee for Everglades National Park (see nps.gov).

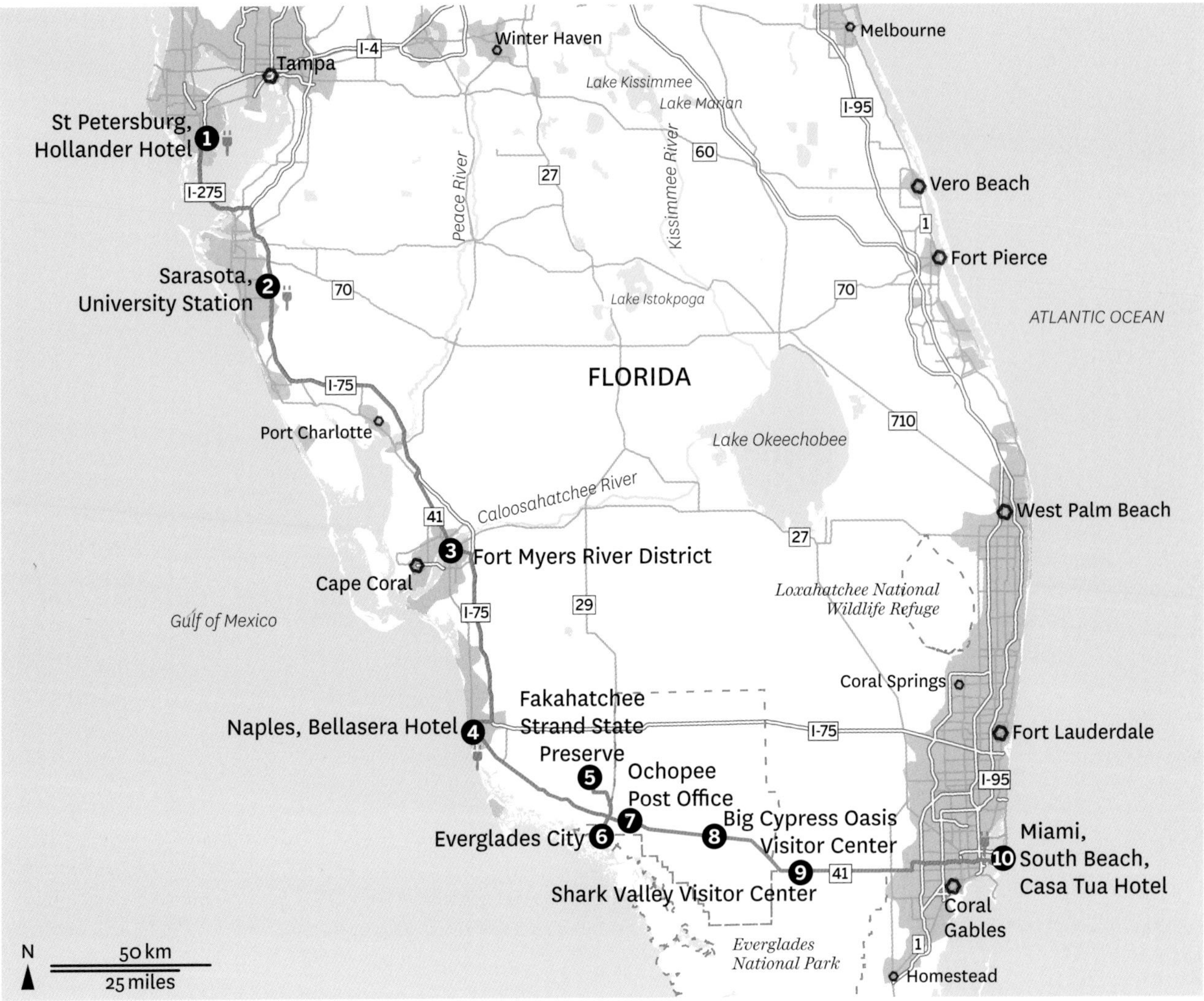

the industrial age lived and socialized, and invented and innovated. For close encounters with local nature, walk the boardwalk trail at Six Mile Cypress Slough Preserve or kayak in Manatee Park (best December through February).

## THROUGH THE EVERGLADES TO MIAMI

Continue 36 miles (58km) to Naples, then turn west to cross the Everglades. Take the Tamiami Trail on this next stretch (as opposed to I-75, aka Alligator Alley), as the smaller road allows you to move slower and see more, with interesting stops along the way; gentle coasting and braking has benefits for battery range, too. Note that there are no charging stations on the 110 miles (177km) between Naples and Miami, so start out with a full battery.

There is much to do and see in the Everglades. You might hike among cypress trees and wild orchids in Fakahatchee Strand State Preserve, then stop in Everglades City to feast on fresh stone crabs and rent a kayak, which you can launch from the Gulf Coast Visitor Center. Mail a postcard from the postage-stamp-sized Ochopee Post Office (the smallest in the country), then stretch your legs on the Kirby Storter Boardwalk or the Gator Hook Trail. Pause at the Big Cypress Oasis Visitor Center to check out the wildlife observation deck (with plenty of gators during the dry season). Your final stop is Shark Valley Visitor Center, where you can rent a bike or take a tram tour along a 15-mile (24km) paved loop, spotting otters, turtles, wading birds and (of course) alligators along the way – although perhaps not sharks!

It's another 40 miles (64km) to your final destination in Miami, where you can park up your EV and immerse yourself in the culture of Florida's most cosmopolitan city. Ogle the street art in Wynwood, browse the galleries in the Design District, go salsa dancing in Little Havana. Or... just ease yourself down on the South Beach sand to soak up the sun and positive vibes.

## Keeping things flowing in the Everglades

Though the Everglades might look like a giant swamp, it is actually a shallow, slow-moving river, stretching 40 miles (64km) across – 60 miles (97km) during the wet season – and flowing from Lake Okeechobee out to Florida Bay. It is truly a "River of Grass" (saw grass, that is), per its nickname. Alligators nest in the thick grass, while turtles, snakes and fish thrive in the sloughs that flow between the marshes. West Indian manatee swim among the mangroves, and the endangered Florida panther inhabits the hardwood hammocks and pine groves on the high ground. The Tamiami Trail cuts right through this natural wonder – it was considered a feat of engineering when it was completed in 1928, but the road blocked the natural flow of the "river," with disastrous consequences for the fragile ecosystem. Nearly 100 years later, engineers and environmental scientists have implemented a solution, which involves a series of raised bridges and under-road culverts to allow for maximum water flow. With these in place, water levels in the Everglades have increased, and park officials are hopeful that resident species – flora and fauna alike – will flourish in turn.

**Clockwise from top left:** Calle Ocho snack shop in Miami's Little Havana; Everglades alligator; flamingos in Everglades National Park

**Below:** Lucid Air EV at Miami Beach
**Right:** South Beach art deco meets neon on Ocean Drive, Miami

**Distance: 200 miles (322km)**

**Duration: 4 days**

# Miami to Key West

**FLORIDA**

This island-hopping EV odyssey takes in art deco Miami, snorkeling and sea turtles, beachside daiquiris in Key West and as many slices of key lime pie as you desire.

Miami, the glittering metropolis on the edge of Biscayne Bay, is a car town. Vintage Cadillacs cruising down Calle Ocho, Jeep Wranglers with surfboards peeking out the back, Porsche owners tossing their keys to the valet outside see-and-be-seen restaurants. So it's no surprise that the city has eagerly adopted electric cars as well. Renting one is a cinch, and charging it within city limits a breeze. So take your EV for a spin up South Beach, gawking at the retro-modern 1920s buildings and the constant parade of the bold and beautiful.

## FRUIT SHAKES & BIG SNAKES

After an ocean dip, head south about 70 miles (113km) along inland roads. After negotiating your way through the Miami traffic, the second half of the drive runs through the Southern Glades Wildlife and Environmental Area, some 47 sq miles (122 sq km) of sawgrass marsh and marl prairie dotted with darker-green tree islands. It's flat, hot and wild, full of snakes, alligators and deer – watch out for the latter in the road, especially at dusk. But before you hit the Glades, make a pit stop at the famed Robert is Here in Homestead. Begun by the eponymous Robert when he was six years

© Felix Mizioznikov

## Plan & prepare

### Tips for EV drivers

This drive is completely flat, though it can be extremely hot, and air-con drains batteries faster than in more moderate temperatures. There are plenty of Tesla chargers, but otherwise plan on slow overnight charging at some places outside Miami. You can rent EVs at a number of agencies in Miami, though you'll pay a drop-off fee if you leave the car in Key West.

### Where to stay

With the exception of Key West, most of the Keys have a good choice of moderately priced hotels, motels and B&Bs. If you think you'll need a charge between Miami and Key West, plan to stay at a hotel with a charger, such as Islamorada's Postcard Inn (islamoradaresortcollection.com) and Marathon's Faro Blanco Resort & Yacht Club (faroblancoresort.com). Key West runs expensive, so book well ahead. Options are from B&Bs – try the historic Conch House (conchhouse.com) – to luxurious beachfront resorts.

### When to go

Weather-wise, the best time to visit is November through April, the dry season. The rains blow in after April, and June through November means hurricane season. That said, if you can deal with the occasional soaking and choppy seas, March to May can be the sweet spot in terms of the price-crowds-weather balance. Busy Christmas and Spring Break (the latter is mid-March, typically) bring larger crowds and higher prices.

### Further info

The Overseas Hwy is the only way to travel the Keys, which means the road is for everyone: motorcycles, semi-trucks, distracted visitors in rental cars. An accident (or a turtle-crossing) can slow down traffic for miles, so keep that in mind when planning your pit stops. The Monroe County Sheriff's Office has live traffic updates online (keysso.net/calls), also available via their extremely handy app.

## Key history

The Keys have been inhabited for thousands of years, first by the Calusa and Tequesta Native Americans, who hunted and fished here before the arrival of the Spanish. Explorer Juan Ponce de León mapped the Keys in 1513, naming them Los Martires (the martyrs) because he thought they looked like men suffering. The Keys (pronounced like what you use to unlock the door) comes from the Spanish word *cayo* (little island). After the arrival of Europeans, the Keys quickly became a trading post, as well as a site of deadly shipwrecks. The wrecks attracted salvagers and raiders, giving the islands a pirate-y flavor. Key West grew fat on the salvage trade, and for a while became the largest city in Florida. Until the early 20th century, the Keys were only accessible by boat. Then, developer Henry Flagler built the Overseas Railroad via a series of trestles, a project so complex and expensive it was sometimes called "Flagler's Folly." The railway was finally destroyed by a hurricane in 1935, and the government subsequently transformed it into the Overseas Hwy – the reason we're able to road-trip to Key West today.

**Above:** *Christ of the Abyss*, at Key Largo's John Pennekamp Coral Reef State Park
**Opposite, from left:** mangrove kayaking, Islamorada; Captain Tony's, Key West Old Town

old, this bountiful stand is the spot to try tropical fruits like mamey, carambola, lychee, soursop and sapodilla, and pick up a fruit-based milkshake (key lime is a fan favorite) or a frosty cup of fresh sugarcane juice.

### OUT TO THE KEYS

Leaving the mainland and crossing over Manatee Bay and Blackwater Sound, your first stop is Key Largo, the northernmost of the chain of islands stretching from the Atlantic Ocean to the Gulf of Mexico. This is known as a diving and snorkeling hotspot, and for good reason. Just off the coast, the John Pennekamp Coral Reef State Park is the country's first underwater park. Book a charter to one of the park's reefs to float above or among crayon-colored tropical fish, waving coral fans and neon-bright anemones. *Christ of the Abyss*, a larger-than-life-sized statue of Jesus sunk in 25ft (7.6m) of water, is the top photo spot. After drying off, continue southwest about 19 miles (31km) to the village of Islamorada. Here, the charger-equipped Postcard Inn offers beachy rooms overlooking the ocean or marina, with pools and a popular tiki bar.

Your next stop is Marathon, 32 miles (51km) southwest. The drive – like all inter-island drives in the Keys – is via the Overseas Hwy, a combo of roads and bridges connecting the islands like a spine. This is truly one of the most stunning roadways in the US, if not the world: two lanes of asphalt perched above limpid turquoise water, so close you could almost touch it.

Activity-rich Marathon promises a sea-turtle hospital, a history museum and lagoons ripe for paddleboarding and kayaking. Park your EV to stroll or cycle over the old Seven Mile Bridge, which once connected the Middle and Lower Keys. Gawp at the shimmering waters of the Atlantic and the Gulf, especially wonderful in the early morning or at sunset. Immediately adjacent is the new Seven Mile Bridge, with the same jaw-dropping views. Spend the night here at the Faro Blanco Resort & Yacht Club, with free charging for guests. There's also a charger at the public library.

### KEY WEST

In the morning, it's 45 miles (72km) of sun-soaked Overseas Hwy to Key West, the boozy bohemian jewel at the archipelago's tip. Being the southernmost city in the continental US, and at such a distance from the mainland, it's attracted free spirits and wanderers

Everglades City
Big Cypress National Preserve
41
I-95
836
1 Miami, South Beach
997
FLORIDA
Goulds
Biscayne National Park
Homestead, Robert Is Here 2
Everglades National Park
905A
Gulf of Mexico
Whitewater Bay
1
West Lake
John Pennekamp Coral Reef State Park
Lake Ingraham
Gator Lake
Flamingo
3 Key Largo
Florida Keys
4 Islamorada, Postcard Inn
ATLANTIC OCEAN
Great White Heron National Wildlife Refuge
Overseas Hwy
6 5 Marathon, Faro Blanco Resort & Yacht Club
1
Seven Mile Bridge
Perky
Big Pine
7 Key West
N
20 km
10 miles

## Key limes

You can't miss the signs: "Best Key Lime Pie in Florida!" or "Fresh Key Limeade!" Along with fried conch and rum, the key lime is one of the islands' signature flavors. The lime itself is a cultivar from Southeast Asia, more delicate and floral than the standard Persian lime. It is at its most renowned in the key lime pie, a tart-sweet custard made with lime-laced condensed milk and egg yolks, topped with whipped cream or meringue and typically on a graham-cracker crust. Everyone in Key West has their favorite version: Kermit's, Blue Heaven, Old Time Bakery – the list goes on. The town holds an annual Key Lime Festival on the Fourth of July weekend, with music, cooking classes, multi-course key lime dinners and a "pie drop": see if you can drop a pie from the top of the lighthouse... without breaking it.

**Above, from top:** Key West's ever-photogenic Southernmost Point marker; the Florida favorite – key lime pie
**Opposite:** through the blue on the Overseas Hwy, Islamorada

for generations. Gingerbread-trimmed houses in a riot of pastel colors are fronted with thickets of wildly blooming hibiscus, bougainvillea and frangipani, the tropical scent trailing into the bars of Duval St where it mingles with the spice of rum in sloshing, bowl-sized cocktails. Many visitors are perfectly content to simply drink and absorb the Old Town atmosphere. But spend a day or two taking in the sights as well: Ernest Hemingway's old Spanish-style home; a psychedelically splendiferous butterfly conservatory; the selfie circus at the Southernmost Point marker (it's not, technically, but never mind) at the corner of South St and Whitehead.

To eat, slurp up oysters bar-side or go for a cracked (fried) conch sandwich at BO's Fish Wagon, a driftwood shack that turns into a jam session on Friday nights. When it comes to hotels you're spoiled for choice, and you don't have to worry about charging either – there's a fast-charging station by Electrify America in the Bank of America Plaza on Flagler Ave.

Now, it's your choice: fly out of Key West International Airport to Miami or to a handful of East Coast and Midwestern cities; or point your EV east and do the whole trip in reverse. With a drive as stunning as this, another 160 miles (257km) will feel like a vacation of its own.

# CANADA

**Below:** the First Nation murals of Carcross Commons
**Right:** Emerald Lake, also known as Rainbow Lake, Carcross

**Distance: 440 miles (708km)**

**Duration: 3 days**

# The Klondike Highway

**ALASKA, BRITISH COLUMBIA & YUKON**

The ghosts of the Klondike Gold Rush are ever-present on this EV extravaganza that climbs over White Pass from Skagway, Alaska, and heads north to the Yukon's erstwhile boomtown of Dawson City.

You're set to embark on the Yukon's most historic road, heading south to north to follow the route taken by late 19th-century prospectors on their way to the Klondike gold fields. Begin in the historic Alaskan Gold Rush–era town of Skagway. The 110-mile (177km) South Klondike Hwy harbors the road's most spectacular scenery, cresting the Boundary Range at 2865ft (873m) White Pass and paralleling the course of the White Pass & Yukon Route, a still-operational railway line opened in 1900 and now used primarily by vacation visitors.

## BEYOND THE BORDER TO LAKES & DESERTS

The first Alaskan section of the Klondike is steep and demanding on your EV's battery, climbing from sea level to the US–Canadian border at White Pass in just 14 miles (22km). Here, amid rocky alpine terrain, you'll enter British Columbia.

The only community of any scale in the area is the border service-center of Fraser, little more than a train station and a dozen houses used for customs officials. There's a pull-over nearby where you can admire Bernard Lake and imagine the scene as thousands of inexperienced prospectors dragged tons of gear and supplies through here during the 1897-98 gold rush.

## Plan & prepare

### Tips for EV drivers

From Bellingham in Washington State, you can take your EV on the ferry up the Inside Passage on a glorious three-day journey to Skagway. Make sure the car is fully charged before embarking. There are several Level 2 charging stations in Skagway, and additional fast chargers in Carcross, Whitehorse, Carmacks, Pelly Crossing, Stewart Crossing and Dawson City, all free to use. Most of the Yukon's chargers are operated by Flo (flo.com) and allow drivers guest access with a credit card.

### Where to stay

It's not quite elite standard, but Whitehorse's central Elite Hotel (elitehotel.ca) has reasonable prices, large rooms and a hearty Italian restaurant next door. Hotel Carmacks on the North Klondike Hwy (facebook.com/hotelcarmacks) is one of the few bricks-and-mortar accommodations between Whitehorse and Dawson City. The Westmark Inn (westmarkhotels.com) is Dawson City's most comfortable abode, with retro rooms and a reliable bar and restaurant. All have chargers nearby.

### When to go

Despite cold winter temperatures and regular dustings of snow, the Klondike Highway is open year-round – if you're driving in winter, factor in higher energy usage. The best time to hit the tarmac is between June and September when the weather is relatively warm, roadside attractions are open and the highway is lined with colorful wildflowers. Discovery Days in mid-August, with their numerous parades and picnics, are a good time to visit Dawson City.

### Further info

The Yukon is still new ground for EVs. The best way to access the territory is via the Bellingham–Skagway ferry. Driving up through northern BC is tricky, with only slow campground EV chargers available north of Prince George. The longest distance between chargers on the Klondike Highway is 111 miles (179km) between Stewart Crossing and Dawson City; the latter is well worth a two-day stopover before you retrace your steps.

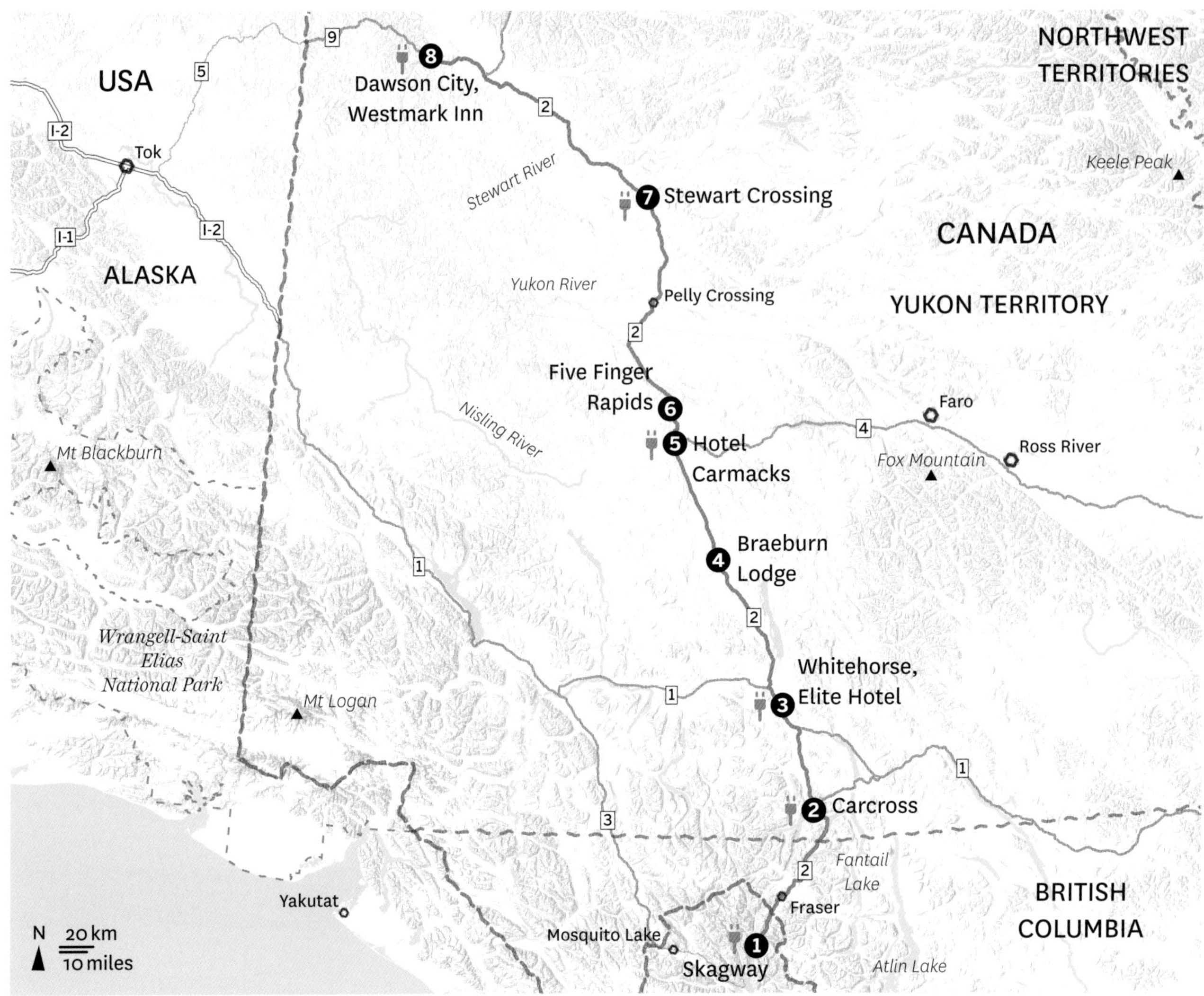


The road soon embraces a more vibrant landscape of turquoise-blue lakes and verdant mountains, as it parallels the shores of the Tutshi and Tagish Lakes before entering the Yukon 49 miles (78km) from Skagway.

Carcross, just across the boundary, is a small settlement that's worthy of an elongated stopover, and there's a fast charger available. Sitting at the head of Nares and Bennett Lakes, it's a historic railroad hub turned tourist village, with a strong Tagish First Nation identity. The local Carcross Commons, made up of a cluster of wooden buildings decorated with Indigenous motifs and totem poles, is home to a carving shed and excellent bakery/cafe. The adjacent Montana Mountain, once crisscrossed with mining roads, has been refashioned with mountain-biking trails. Bike rentals are available at Icycle Sports.

Just beyond the village, the road kisses the edge of the Carcross Desert, a parcel of pale-yellow sand dunes as diminutive as it is incongruous. It is sometimes called the world's smallest desert, its dunes the result of a unique microclimate created by the surrounding mountains. Locals use them for sandboarding.

Just under 32 miles (51km) beyond Carcross, the Klondike merges with the epic Alaska Hwy (Hwy 1). The two run concurrently for 19 miles (30km) through the territorial capital of Whitehorse (see p242), a good place to stay overnight, enjoy a meal and recharge your EV.

## THE NORTH KLONDIKE HIGHWAY

Eight miles (13km) out of Whitehorse, the North Klondike Hwy branches off the Alaska Hwy and heads north-northwest, tracking the path of a former wagon trail to Dawson City. A road of sorts was first built in 1902, with roadhouses every few miles, but paddle-steamers on the Yukon River continued as the main mode of transportation until the 1950s. Now paved – but still a little uneven in places – the long, lightly populated

## The Klondike Gold Rush

Often billed as the 19th century's "last great adventure," the Klondike Gold Rush was first ignited in a remote corner of northwest Canada in 1896, when three mining prospectors discovered large nuggets of placer gold in Rabbit Creek, a tributary of the Klondike River. When the news finally filtered through to an America still in the throes of a severe economic recession, the response was earth-shattering. Over the following two years, some 100,000 prospectors set out for the Klondike to seek their fortune. Many were ill-prepared and didn't make it. Of those who did, only a small fraction found gold. Ultimately the glittering treasure wasn't so important – it was the adventurous journeys that captured the zeitgeist. The mass exodus has gone down in history for its cinematic scale and rugged frontier spirit, from Eric Hegg's famous photo of stampeders tramping over Chilkoot Pass to Jack London's seminal novel, *The Call of the Wild*. The ghosts are still very much alive in Dawson City, Western Canada's historical highlight, where warped wooden sidewalks defy the permafrost and misshapen false-fronted buildings tell the Klondike's rags-to-riches story with refreshing authenticity. Visit the city museum, Dredge No 4, and Jack London's old cabin.

**Clockwise from top left:** well-preserved historic buildings in Dawson City; gold on a wash pan; the epic Klondike Hwy

## Whitehorse

Whitehorse gets its name from a set of foaming rapids on the Yukon River that posed a serious obstacle for Klondike-bound stampeders during the 1890s gold rush. The rapids were later drowned beneath an artificial lake, and the name was transferred to a growing settlement on the banks of the river that expanded during the building of the Alaska Hwy during WWII. When Dawson City's star began to fade in the 1950s, Whitehorse stepped up to become territorial capital, as well as a crossroads on the Alaska and Klondike highways and a terminus for the White Pass & Yukon Railway. Today's modern city guards several historical attractions, including a restored 20th-century paddle-steamer (the SS *Klondike*) and a comprehensive museum. Trails with informative signboards loop around the adjacent Yukon River, offering alluring insights into the wilderness that presses up against the city limits.

**From left:** the SS *Klondike* in Whitehorse; the Klondike and Yukon rivers blend at Dawson City; Five Fingers Rapids

highway passes the windy expanses of Lake Laberge (a widening in the Yukon River) and the community of Braeburn, where the quirky wooden Braeburn Lodge is feted for its football-sized cinnamon buns. The adjacent "airport" is colloquially known as Cinnamon Bun Airstrip.

The scenery along the North Klondike is more subtle than dramatic, a conveyor belt of handsome truss bridges over the river, slender spruce and larch trees and, in summer, ribbons of wildflowers lining the verges. Comprehensive services aren't abundant. The best places to recharge your EV and bolster your energy with gas-station coffee are tiny communities like Carmacks, guarding a crossing over the Yukon. With a basic hotel and campground, Carmacks is a potential overnighter, and a walking tour here directs visitors around a small ensemble of historic log cabins.

## THE LURE OF GOLD

Schedule a stop at Five Fingers Rapids, 15 miles (24km) north of Carmacks, where four river islets mark what was once a tricky spot for rafters heading to the goldfields (many were upended in the whitewater). A stairway leads down to a viewpoint.

Thirty-one miles (50km) north, the Yukon River bends northwest, veering away from the road and following a more backcountry route to Dawson City. Hwy 2 funnels northeast, crossing the Pelly and Stewart Rivers at two more tiny service centers, Pelly Crossing and Stewart Crossing, both with charging stations. The last big road junction, 25 miles (40km) east of Dawson, connects with the Dempster Hwy, one of only two roads in North America to cross the Arctic Circle, heading 458 miles (737km) north to Inuvik in the Northwest Territories.

The Klondike River returns to run parallel with the final section of the road, which is prone to seasonal flooding and landslides. As Dawson approaches, you'll see piles of tailings left over from placer mining, the legacy of huge dredges that scoured the rivers for gold in the early 20th century. Fear not, the town itself, designated a national historic site, is a lot prettier (see p241).

**Below:** the route has plentiful charging options
**Right:** Hwy 99's scenic splendour

**Distance: 76 miles (122km)**

**Duration: 2 days**

# The Sea to Sky Highway

**BRITISH COLUMBIA**

The main transportation link between British Columbia's two most sought-after destinations, Vancouver and Whistler, is an easy drive by EV and one of the most beautiful roads in the province.

The Sea to Sky Highway is the name given to a section of Hwy 99 that runs between the Horseshoe Bay ferry terminal and the world-renowned ski resort of Whistler. Most will begin this EV-welcoming drive in Vancouver, cutting through Stanley Park and crossing Lion's Gate Bridge to enter the wealthy suburb of West Vancouver.

Horseshoe Bay lies slightly to the west, at the mouth of Howe Sound, an attractive waterside community with a small-town vibe that's hemmed in by steep crags and a thick canopy of forest. Grab a coffee from one of the waterfront cafes and stroll over to the Spirit Gallery, stuffed with Coastal Northwest art. The Sea to Sky corridor sits on the land of the Squamish and Lil'wat First Nations, and this is a good place to become culturally acquainted. Leaving town, rejoin Hwy 99 as it weaves north along the dramatic shores of a steep-sided fjord, wedged between high mountain escarpments and island-flecked Howe Sound.

## GOING UNDERGROUND

Britannia Beach, 32.5 miles (52km) north of Horseshoe Bay, is the site of a copper mine that operated between 1903 and 1974. The huge mine buildings that concertina

## Plan & prepare

### Tips for EV drivers

EV rental is available at several places in the Vancouver area, including Zerocar (zerocar.ca) and Hertz (hertz.ca). Vancouver is one of the best cities in the world for charger access, while fast chargers are also available en route at Horseshoe Bay, Squamish and Whistler. Charge up well in advance to deal with the impact on your battery's reserves from tackling the inclines after Squamish, or if you're traveling in cold winter temperatures during the ski season.

### Where to stay

For a splurge in Vancouver, try the downtown Exchange Hotel (exchangehotelvan.com), which transformed the city's former Stock Exchange into a swanky, stylish piece of real estate. Squamish's Howe Sound Inn (howesound.com) has cozy rooms above the town's original microbrewery, with a good restaurant next door. Whistler's Pangea Pod Hotel (pangeapod.com) was Canada's first Japanese-style capsule hotel and offers bed-sized "pods" equipped with double futons and individual air-con units. All have chargers onsite or nearby.

### When to go

These days, Whistler is a veritable year-round destination, although you may want to avoid the shoulder months of April and October when many facilities make a seasonal transition. The Sea to Sky Highway is always well maintained and just as busy in the winter as the summer. The main ski season runs from early December to late April. For ease of driving and optimal battery performance, the warmer months (May to September) are ideal.

### Further info

Squamish Adventure Centre (hellobc.com), next to the highway, dispatches tourist information and also charts local history, sells gifts, rents bikes and has an alfresco rope-climbing playground. The town itself is a good place to overnight, with an abundance of hiking, biking and climbing opportunities; it's known as the capital of BC's rock-climbing community. Horseshoe Bay is one of Vancouver's main ferry terminals, with connections to Nanaimo and the Sunshine Coast.

## Wonders of Whistler

The site of many of the outdoor events at the 2010 Winter Olympics, Whistler Village is a relatively modern creation. It was first laid out as a ski resort in the early 1980s, with attractive alpine-style buildings joined by a lattice of pedestrian paths, and a car-free town center called the Village Stroll. The famous ski area is draped over two adjacent mountains, Whistler and Blackcomb, and is the largest in North America, knitted together by a substantial network of lifts that incorporate the world's longest unsupported span gondola, the Peak 2 Peak. In the last two decades, the village has raised its summer profile with a lift-accessible bike park, a music concert series and the fearsome Sasquatch zipline, Canada's longest at over 7000ft (2150m). Whistler also harbors a robust artistic community. The handsome wood-beamed Squamish Lil'wat Cultural Centre, built in 2008 to resemble a traditional longhouse, celebrates the Indigenous art and heritage of the region. The Audain Art Museum is one of the best galleries in the province, home to a priceless collection of Indigenous masks along with paintings from BC luminaries such as Emily Carr and EJ Hughes.

**Above from left:** the Peak 2 Peak gondola between Whistler and Blackcomb; Shannon Falls **Opposite:** a view of Howe Sound and the Stawamus Chief from Squamish

down a steep hill have since been preserved as a museum: don a hard hat and jump on a bone-rattling train that trundles through a floodlit mine tunnel.

Shannon Falls, 4 miles (7km) north, provides a more salubrious distraction. Here lies the most wondrous water feature on the highway and the third-largest flume in BC, barreling tempestuously 1100ft (335m) down a mountainside. A short trail through woods leads to a viewing platform, from where you can veer north and pick up longer trails to the Stawamus Chief, Squamish's legendary climbing rock (3.6-mile/5.8km loop), or the top station of the Sea to Sky Gondola (4.7 miles/7.5km one-way). Alternatively, let the gondola zip you up to the summit lodge, where an elegant suspension bridge provides access to shorter above-the-treeline trails.

### SQUAMISH & UP TO WHISTLER

Just north of the Chief sits Squamish, a small sports-orientated town with numerous charging points, accommodations and craft breweries. If you're passing in winter, divert west to Brackendale, home to one of the largest populations of wintering bald eagles in North America. A path alongside the Squamish River unveils plenty of eagle-spotting opportunities.

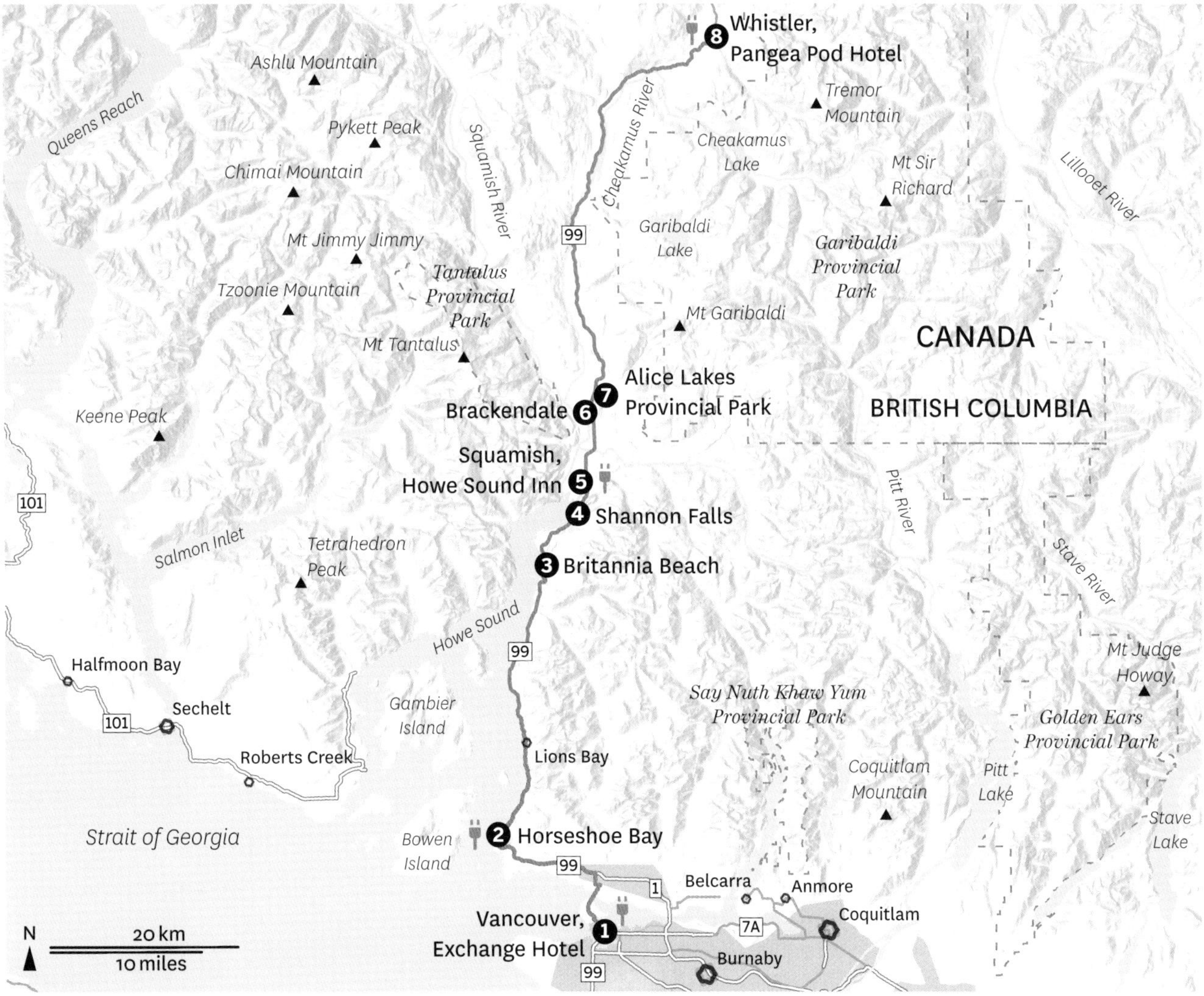

Whistler, Pangea Pod Hotel 8
Ashlu Mountain
Queens Reach
Pykett Peak
Squamish River
Cheakamus River
Tremor Mountain
Cheakamus Lake
Chimai Mountain
Mt Sir Richard
Lillooet River
Mt Jimmy Jimmy
Garibaldi Lake
Garibaldi Provincial Park
Tantalus Provincial Park
Tzoonie Mountain
Mt Garibaldi
Mt Tantalus
CANADA
7 Alice Lakes Provincial Park
Brackendale 6
BRITISH COLUMBIA
Keene Peak
Squamish, Howe Sound Inn 5
101
4 Shannon Falls
Pitt River
Salmon Inlet
Tetrahedron Peak
3 Britannia Beach
Stave River
Howe Sound
99
Halfmoon Bay
Mt Judge Howay
Say Nuth Khaw Yum Provincial Park
Sechelt
Gambier Island
Golden Ears Provincial Park
Roberts Creek
Lions Bay
Coquitlam Mountain
Pitt Lake
Strait of Georgia
Bowen Island
2 Horseshoe Bay
Stave Lake
Belcarra
Anmore
Coquitlam
Vancouver, Exchange Hotel 1
Burnaby
N
20 km
10 miles

Heading on in your EV, consider stopping at Alice Lakes Provincial Park, where the four adjacent lakes fringed by dense old-growth hemlock forest are ideal for summer hiking, biking and waterside picnicking. The road climbs gradually between Squamish and Whistler, gaining 2200ft (670m) in 37 miles (60km) and tugging a little harder on your battery's reserves. Five miles (8km) south of Whistler, it's obligatory to stop at Function Junction to buy a delectable pastry at the Purebread bakery and follow a short trail to Train Wreck, a collection of abandoned carriages that derailed in the 1950s and have since been covered in vivid graffiti.

After passing through the satellite community of Whistler Creekside, turn right off the main highway and into Whistler Village. Set in the shadows of the formidable Whistler and Blackcomb Mountains, BC's golden child is an activity center extraordinaire in which to round off your road trip – ideally for several days.

**Below:** Okanagon Lake, near Penticton
**Right:** a valley-side vineyard, Penticton

**Distance: 142 miles (228km)**

**Duration: 3-4 days**

# Okanagan Valley, Vernon to Osoyoos

**BRITISH COLUMBIA**

The Okanagan Valley has long been celebrated for its excellent wines and abundant fruit orchards, but more recently its farm-to-table food ethic has sealed its reputation as a gourmand's paradise.

The high mountains, steep bluffs, shimmering lakes and desert shrub of the sun-soaked Okanagan Valley have lured in scores of independent vintners, farmers, chefs and craftspeople over the past few decades. Consequently, you'll find breweries, bakeries, vineyards, artisan cheesemakers and farmers markets everywhere, making it a place that rewards those who linger longer to savor leisurely lunches, follow up on recommendations – everyone has their favorite local vineyard – and discover glorious new flavors during this trip by EV.

## VERNON TO PENTICTON

Gateway to the valley, Vernon sits at its northern end between three lakes. It's long been an important fruit-growing region, and you can trace some of that history on a guided tour at Davison Orchards, or head to nearby Planet Bee for an introduction to their wide variety of raw honeys and meads.

Driving south along the shores of Kalamalka and Wood Lakes, it's about 20 miles (32km) in your EV to Gray Monk Estate Winery, one of the region's longest established vineyards. Learn about its signature Pinot Gris on a tour, then enjoy a tasting or a feast of seasonal, local food at the Lookout Restaurant.

## Plan & prepare

### Tips for EV drivers

The Okanagan Valley is well set up for EV driving; all Level 2 public charging stations (so other than Tesla stations) use a standard plug and many are free to use. The PlugShare app lists details of the charging stations in the area. If visiting in winter, be aware that the cold valley temperatures will affect your battery reserves.

### Where to stay

A 12-room heritage hotel close to the lakefront in sleepy Naramata, just north of Oliver, the Naramata Inn (naramatainn.com) has period-style rooms and an exceptional restaurant focused on hyper-local produce. Further south, in Osoyoos, Spirit Ridge at Nk'Mip Resort (hyatt.com) offers golf, horse riding, watersports and an onsite winery, plus fine dining championing Indigenous ingredients. Book well in advance for July or August. Both have EV chargers onsite or within a five-minute walk.

### When to go

With wine festivals in spring, fall and winter, the Okanagan Valley offers year-round interest. July to August is hot, dry and busy, so a visit in May or June is preferable, but September has to be best of all with the grape harvest in full swing, quieter roads and the pick of wines to choose from. Although there's plenty of winter appeal and a host of ski resorts to choose from, many wineries close between November and April.

### Further info

Download the free Wines of BC Explorer app for up-to-date information on vineyards, wines and events. It also gives suggestions for food and wine pairings, allows you to build a digital wine cellar, and has a "taste test" to match you with BC wines that suit your preferences. Another useful feature is the trip planner which allows you to choose an itinerary based on your interests. It's recommended to bring a designated driver.

## Okanagan Valley wines

As wine regions go, the Okanagan is unusually diverse considering its small geographic area. Formed by the vestiges of age-old volcanic activity followed by two ice ages, it has proved ideal for viticulture, although the industry only really got established in the last few decades as increasing production attracted winegrowers from across the globe. Today, there are more than 170 wineries here, ranging from family-run boutique vineyards to world-class producers. The complexity of conditions means the valley is further divided into 11 sub-regions, each with its own distinct soil and climate that affect the grape varieties grown and the wines produced. With more than 60 varietals weaving their way across the sunny slopes of the valley, the region offers a great range of wine to choose from. However, the signature trait is natural acidity caused by the cool nights that follow the hot, dry days of the valley's short but intense growing season. The climate is cooler in the north, best-known for its crisp, delicate whites and aromatic Rieslings, but as you venture south, you'll find full-bodied, sun-ripened reds and Rhône-style whites.

**Clockwise from above:** wine-tasting in Osoyoos; kitesurfing on Skaha Lake; shopping for seasonal produce **Opposite:** Nk'Mip Cellars, a winery owned and operated by Indigenous winemakers

Further south in Kelowna, the valley's major hub, there's a lively arts and food scene. The Okanagan Wine & Orchard Museum throws light on the area's development as a wine region; and if you happen to be here on a Wednesday or Saturday, you can cruise Kelowna Farmers Market for sourdough, crepes and cashew cheese. Save space for dinner, though: the menu at award-winning RauDZ Regional Table celebrates seasonal Okanagan produce. On the outskirts of Kelowna, over on the west side of Okanagan Lake, Mission Hill Family Estate is Canada's five-time winner of Winery of the Year. Known as much for its innovative architecture and Terrace Restaurant as it is for its exemplary wines, it also stages summer concerts in its outdoor amphitheater.

As you weave your EV through the dry hills, the lakes become increasingly attractive on the 40-mile (64km) drive south to Penticton, a great place to take a swim or try some watersports on Skaha Lake Beach. Just north of town, the Lock & Worth Winery is a small-scale vineyard operated on sustainable principles. It shares a tasting room with Poplar Grove Cheese, so you can savor small-batch, handmade cheeses paired with single-vineyard wines – don't miss the rich, white-truffle-tinged double-cream camembert.

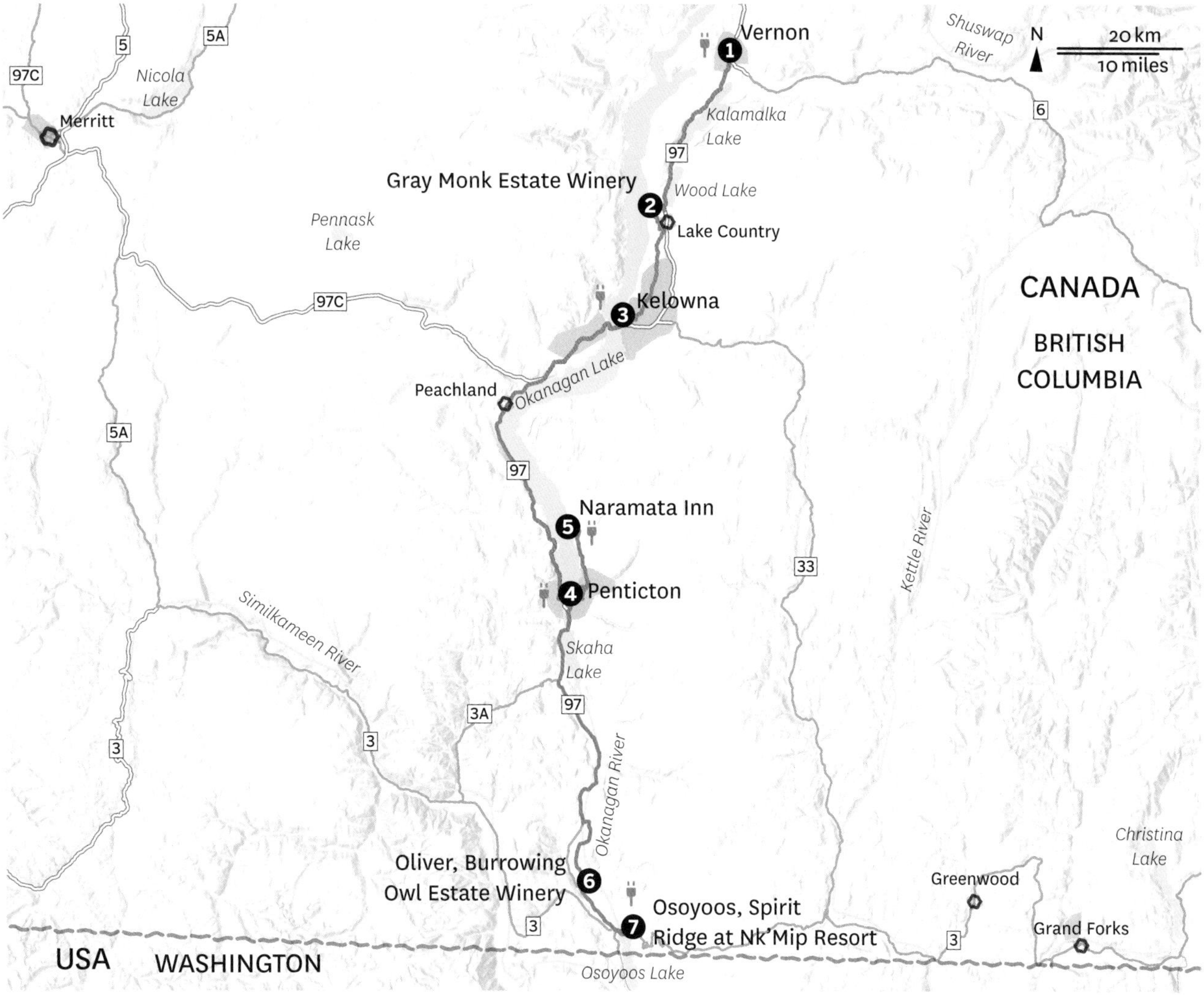

Vernon
Shuswap River
N
20 km
10 miles
97C
5
5A
Nicola Lake
Merritt
Kalamalka Lake
97
6
Gray Monk Estate Winery
Wood Lake
Pennask Lake
Lake Country
CANADA
97C
Kelowna
BRITISH COLUMBIA
Okanagan Lake
Peachland
5A
97
Naramata Inn
33
Kettle River
Penticton
Similkameen River
Skaha Lake
97
3A
3
3
Okanagan River
Christina Lake
Oliver, Burrowing Owl Estate Winery
Greenwood
Osoyoos, Spirit Ridge at Nk'Mip Resort
3
3
Grand Forks
USA
WASHINGTON
Osoyoos Lake

## SOUTH TO OSOYOOS

Forested slopes give way to dry, scrub-covered hills as you head south towards Osoyoos. Around Oliver, you'll find some of the country's most interesting wineries and restaurants. Known as the "Wine Capital of Canada," Oliver also hosts the Festival of the Grape each fall. Drop into the organic Covert Farms Family Estate to learn about their regenerative farming practices and pick your own fruit; or immerse yourself in estate life with a tour, dinner and overnight stay at the highly regarded Burrowing Owl Estate Winery.

If you're craving something different at the end of your drive, head for the Nk'Mip Desert Cultural Centre near Osoyoos. Here you can learn about the land, legends and people of the Okanagan First Nations and walk along trails flanked with sage and antelope brush to the magnificent Chief's Lookout.

**Below:** hiking near Mount Sir Donald, Glacier National Park
**Right:** heading into Glacier National Park

Distance: 1230 miles (1980km)

Duration: 6-10 days

# The Kootenay Rockies

**BRITISH COLUMBIA**

Explore four mountainous national parks, western Canada's largest wine region and numerous funky communities as you travel by EV from Vancouver to the Canadian Rockies and back to the coast.

From Vancouver, your BC road trip starts in earnest with the six-hour drive toward Revelstoke. After the first stretch on Hwy 1, stop to recharge in Hope, which has more EV chargers than communities many times its size (plus tasty pastries at the Blue Moose Coffee House).

Moving on, continue northeast on Hwy 5 (the Coquihalla), climbing over the Coast Mountains into the Okanagan Valley, BC's major wine-producing region, then turn east onto Hwy 97C toward Kelowna. After stopping to eat, buy wine or top up your car's charge at Mission Hill Family Estate, CedarCreek Estate Winery or other Kelowna-area wineries, head north on Hwy 97/97A, then rejoin Hwy 1 into Revelstoke.

## MT REVELSTOKE TO YOHO

After overnighting in Revelstoke, kickstart your day with a coffee-tasting flight at Dose Coffee or farm-to-table breakfast from Terra Firma's Kitchen. Ensure your battery is full for today's adventure: driving the steep Meadows in the Sky Parkway, which winds 16 miles (26km) uphill to Balsam Lake in Mt Revelstoke National Park, from where hiking trails offer expansive views across the mountains.

## Plan & prepare

### Tips for EV drivers

EV charging stations are plentiful along Hwy 1, the main east–west route across BC. Hope, Kelowna, Revelstoke, Golden, Cranbrook and Nelson all have chargers, as do many Okanagan communities. Even in smaller towns, you'll find somewhere to plug in, often at the visitor center, community center or at government offices. Accelerate Kootenays (acceleratekootenays.ca) has useful info on regional EV travel. BC Hydro (electricvehicles.bchydro.com) supplies many of the faster charging stations here.

### Where to stay

Best Western Plus Revelstoke (bestwestern.com) has an EV charger; characterful Stoke Hotel (stokehotel.ca) is nearby. In Golden, sleep at friendly, log-walled Moberly Lodge (moberlylodge.com) or continue to Emerald Lake Lodge (crmr.com), overlooking the lake in Yoho National Park. In Cranbrook, stay in First Nations–run St Eugene Resort (steugene.ca), while in Nelson, consider the heritage Hume Hotel (humehotel.com), or the Adventure Hotel (adventurehotel.ca).

### When to go

Late May through mid-October is British Columbia's peak season. Expect the best weather in September and early October: warm days, crisp nights and emerging fall colors. Busy July and August are hotter and drier, while May and June are mild, but with more chance of rain. Wildfire risk is highest in summer; Emergency Info BC (emergencyinfobc.gov.bc.ca) can apprise you of any significant blazes. DriveBC (drivebc.ca) provides information about road and weather conditions along BC's highways.

### Further info

Destination British Columbia (destinationbc.ca) provides provincial travel info. Destination Vancouver (destinationvancouver.com), Thompson-Okanagan Tourism (thompsonokanagan.com) and Kootenay-Rockies Tourism (kootenayrockies.com) cover the regions. Parks Canada (parks.canada.ca) lists national-park hiking trails, programs, and campground or parking reservation info; before stopping at Lake Louise, check online for shuttle instructions, since parking is extremely limited.

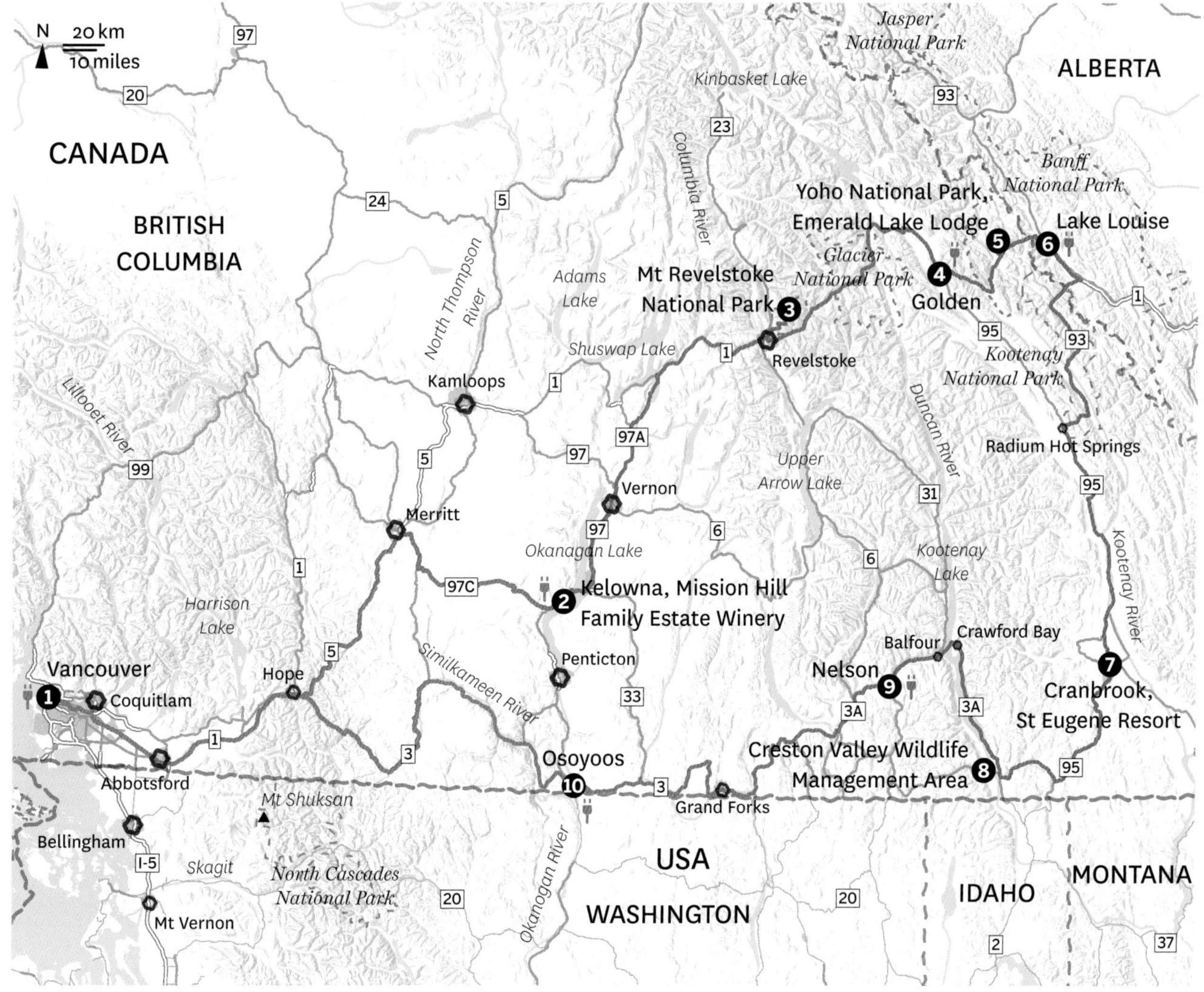


Return to Revelstoke via the Parkway and turn east on Hwy 1, crossing the peaks of Glacier National Park and stopping at the park's Rogers Pass Discovery Centre (which has EV chargers) to watch films about avalanche management or local ecology. Then head on to overnight at Golden. In the morning, take an adrenaline-rush walk over the Golden Skybridge, a series of suspension bridges swinging high above a deep canyon. Then return to Hwy 1, driving east to Yoho National Park, where you can canoe on vividly-colored Emerald Lake, or navigate Yoho Valley Rd's switchbacks to cascading Takakkaw Falls. Recharge at the Field Visitor Center, then overnight at waterside Emerald Lake Lodge.

## KOOTENAY NATIONAL PARK TO NELSON

The next day, make a quick stop to see glacier-topped Rockies surrounding the bluer-than-blue Lake Louise, 30 minutes' drive east, then turn south on Hwy 93 through Kootenay National Park for a hike at Marble Canyon or a soothing soak in Radium Hot Springs' mineral pools. There are EV chargers in Radium and along the highway as you drive south toward Cranbrook; just before town, in a former government-mandated residential school for Indigenous children, several First Nations now operate St Eugene Resort. Tour the Ktunaxa Interpretive Centre here, which illuminates both the site's oppressive history and the Nations' present-day culture.

From Hwy 95 south of Cranbrook, navigate westwards onto Hwy 3, meandering through small mountain communities. Recharge in Creston before hiking the marshlands at Creston Valley Wildlife Management Area, then head north on scenic Hwy 3A, hugging the shores of Kootenay Lake. Catch the free car ferry from Crawford Bay to Balfour, then continue into Nelson. A haven for US citizens avoiding the Vietnam War draft in the 1960s, Nelson retains its counterculture vibe, with vibrant street

art, vegetarian-friendly restaurants, and independent bookstores and shops.

Hwy 3 west leads to Hope, where you pick up Hwy 1 into Vancouver. Break up the drive with a stop – or overnight – in the southern Okanagan Valley, charging your EV while wine-tasting at the Oliver-Osoyoos wineries. Make sure you have a designated driver if you're continuing straight on west; it's still 250 miles (402km) from here to the coast.

## Indigenous tourism

More than 200 distinct First Nations reside in BC, and many communities provide visitor experiences. In Vancouver, tour Stanley Park's rainforest with Talaysay Tours; sample Indigenous cuisine at Salmon n' Bannock restaurant; and stay in art-filled Skwachàys Lodge, Canada's first Indigenous arts and culture hotel. Cross River Education & Retreat Centre, at the end of a remote logging road outside Kootenay National Park, has off-grid cabins and provides Indigenous cultural and outdoor experiences. Near Nelson, soak in mineral pools at Ainsworth Hot Springs Resort, run by the Ktunaxa people; in Osoyoos, tour Nk'Mip Desert Cultural Centre, then sample wines at Nk'Mip Cellars, North America's first Indigenous-owned winery. Also in the Thompson-Okanagan region, learn about Indigenous cultures on a canoeing or hiking tour with Moccasin Trails, or at West Kelowna's Sncewips Heritage Museum. Nearby, at Indigenous-owned Kekuli Café, fuel up with many varieties of bannock (flatbread), from a wild salmon breakfast sandwich to bannock with sweet maple glaze. The Indigenous Tourism Association of BC (indigenousbc.com) has more trip ideas and links.

**Clockwise from top left:** across a stretch of the Golden Skybridge; Stanley Park, Vancouver; taking the car ferry towards Balfour

**Below:** public EV charging station
**Right:** Ucluelet, on the island's western shores

**Distance: 309 miles (498km)**

**Duration: 3 days**

# Vancouver Island

**BRITISH COLUMBIA**

A large island with a comparatively small road network, Vancouver is BC in miniature, with ancient forests, wild sandy beaches and its own wine region, all ripe for exploration by EV.

Victoria is the regal capital of British Columbia and one of the best cities in Canada for access to EV charging points. While you top up for this drive, walk around the Inner Harbor to investigate provincial history at the Royal BC Museum and try one (or both) of the city's British-influenced culinary combos: fish and chips, and tea and scones.

You'll be leaving town on the westernmost extremity of the 4645-mile (7476km) Trans-Canada Hwy (Hwy 1), exchanging Victoria's exurbs for the forested greenery of hiking hotspot Goldstream Provincial Park. After admiring the park's giant evergreens, pull over at the Malahat SkyWalk, 28 miles (45km) north of Victoria, a spiral tower with a 105ft-high (32m) lookout that gives 360-degree views over forest, sea islands and the volcanic hump of Mt Baker in the US.

## FLAVORS TO SAVOR

Beyond Malahat, dense forest gives way to the Cowichan Valley, a patchwork of rolling hills and pastoral farmland with a balmy semi-Mediterranean climate that has given birth to vineyards, a tea plantation and an enthusiastic farm-to-table ethos. Follow Hwy 1 into the harbor city of Nanaimo, 69 miles (111km) north of Victoria; it's

## Plan & prepare

### Tips for EV drivers

Nearly half of Victoria's EV charging stations are free to use. Within the city, EVs are permitted to use HOV lanes irrespective of passenger numbers (search "HOV" at gov.bc.ca). There are plenty of fast chargers on the Island Hwy, Tesla Superchargers in Victoria and Nanaimo and, north of Campbell River, fast chargers in both Port McNeill and Port Hardy. BC's electricity network is powered 90% by hydro – so if you drive an EV in the province, you're effectively running on water power!

### Where to stay

Victoria's Magnolia Hotel & Spa (magnoliahotel.com) has elegant furnishings and an underlying air of refinement. Just north of Qualicum Beach, the extravagantly esoteric Free Spirit Spheres (freespiritspheres.com) comprises three wooden capsules suspended in the trees – compact but deftly designed, they give a unique immersive forest experience. Cumberland's Riding Fool (ridingfool.com) is one of BC's finest hostels, with private rooms and dorms in a handsome woodsy interior, and a bike rental shop.

### When to go

Vancouver Island's climate is relatively benign compared to other parts of BC. Cool summers and mild winters make this EV drive doable year-round. For accessibility to trails and beaches, and a wider range of festivals, come in spring or summer. Victoria has plenty of annual events, including the Victoria Fringe theater festival in late August and the International Buskers Festival in July.

### Further info

The Island Hwy is the unofficial name of Vancouver Island's most scenic south-to-north driving route, including sections of Hwy 1 (Victoria–Nanaimo), Hwy 19A (Qualicum Beach–Cumberland) and Hwy 19 (north of the Comox Valley). The island is easily reached from the BC mainland, with hourly ferries running between Tsawwassen near Vancouver and Swartz Bay, 21 miles (34km) north of Victoria. You can also catch ferries from Nanaimo to either Horseshoe Bay (12.5 miles/20km northwest of Vancouver) or Tsawwassen.

## Repatriated treasure

Well worth the short ferry ride from Port McNeill, Alert Bay is a small, spread-out village on Cormorant Island with an ancient and mythical appeal courtesy of its strong First Nations culture – over half of the population of 450 is Kwakwa̲ka̲'wakw. On the north side of the island, next to the site of the demolished St Michael's Residential School, lies its pièce de résistance: the U'mista Cultural Centre (umista.ca), one of the finest Indigenous-run museums in BC. Housed here is the famous Potlatch Collection, a rich mélange of masks and other ceremonial items that were notoriously confiscated by the Canadian government in the 1920s. Potlatches (traditional Indigenous gift-giving ceremonies) were banned by Canadian authorities in 1885. When the local Kwakwa̲ka̲'wakw tried to stage an "illegal" potlatch on Village Island in 1921, it was promptly broken up: 45 participants were arrested and numerous ceremonial objects impounded. After the law was repealed in 1951, the Kwakwa̲ka̲'wakw began a long process of repatriating their objects from various museums around the world, including London's British Museum and New York's Smithsonian Institute. The U'mista Centre was opened in 1980 to showcase the reassembled treasure.

**Above, from left:** Xwixwi mask at the U'mista Cultural Centre; local treat, the Nanaimo bar **Opposite, from left:** Malahat SkyWalk; the Inside Passage

famed for the Nanaimo bar, one of Canada's favorite snacks, a three-layered slab of wafer, cream and icing that combines coconut, vanilla custard and chocolate. To savor its nuances, the city has come up with a 39-stop Nanaimo bar "trail" allowing you to enjoy the confection in numerous ways – from deep-fried to in a cocktail.

Now head out of Nanaimo on Hwy 19; 20 miles (32km) north of the city, veer onto Hwy 19A, the preferred route for what locals call the "Island Hwy." Qualicum Beach is a small community-focused town of classic seafront motels and a giant bay, where fast-food restaurant franchises are restricted. The nearby Morningstar Farm is famed province-wide for its artisan cheese – you can visit the farm shop and take a self-guided tour.

Continue north on Hwy 19A to Royston, then branch west on Royston Rd to Cumberland, 37.5 miles (60km) north of Qualicum Beach. This former coal-mining settlement reclassified itself as a "village in the forest" in the 1960s, when the mines closed and its population almost evaporated. Cumberland has rebuilt its reputation as a major mountain-biking hub, with a network of over 170 downhill trails, built on forestry land by a local nonprofit with the permission of timber companies.

### HITTING THE NORTH

Back on Hwy 19, forge on to Campbell River, guardian to the island's isolated north. The modern city isn't much to look at, but you can absorb its more illuminating history at the local museum, complete with logging trucks, First Nations masks and fishing paraphernalia.

Further north, Port McNeill, the departure point for Cormorant Island, has a fast charger where you can leave your EV while you ferry over to BC's Indigenous masterpiece, the U'mista Cultural Centre (see left for more on this).

Both your road trip and Hwy 19 end at Port Hardy, a small waterside town with a strong First Nations heritage. Further exploration could start here: this an embarkation point for ferries navigating the narrow channels of the Inside Passage on British Columbia's fjord-indented west coast.

Port Hardy
9
19
Port McNeill
8
30
Nimpkish Lake
CANADA
Lillooet River
19
Nimpkish River
BRITISH COLUMBIA
Salmon River
Campbell River
7
Vancouver Island
Gold River
28
19
Upper Campbell Lake
Cumberland, Riding Fool Hostel
6
Royston
101
99
19A
Qualicum Beach
5
4
Morningstar Farm
Horseshoe Bay
Great Central Lake
4
Sproat Lake
Vancouver
Nanaimo
3
PACIFIC OCEAN
Nanaimo River
Tsawwassen
1
Pacific Rim National Park Reserve
Cowichan Lake
Nitinat Lake
18
Swartz Bay
Malahat SkyWalk
17
2
Victoria, Magnolia Hotel & Spa
1
N
20 km
10 miles
USA
14

**Below:** canoeing on Lake Louise **Right:** the Icefields Parkway in fall

**Distance: 145 miles (233km)**

**Duration: 1-2 days**

# The Icefields Parkway

**ALBERTA**

Alberta's Icefields Parkway truly is one of the most spectacular slices of asphalt in North America, allowing a majestic drive by EV past landscape-shaping glaciers, foraging fauna and grand mountains.

Paralleling North America's Continental Divide for its entire course between Lake Louise and Jasper, the resplendent Icefield Parkway is characterized by rugged good looks and is littered with copious excuses to pull over and contemplate your modest position in the natural pecking order of the Rocky Mountains.

As you charge your EV in Lake Louise, spend a little time admiring the serene, impossibly turquoise lake that stretches out elegantly beneath an amphitheater of finely sculpted mountains, with the Victoria Glacier gleaming from the opposite shore. The lake lies a mere 1.3 miles (2km) from the Parkway's southern terminus: head out of the "village" on the Trans-Canada Hwy in the direction of Golden before taking the first exit north, remembering to purchase your park pass at the Icefields Parkway entrance booth. The speed limit is 56mph (90km/h), ideal for wildlife-spotting and conserving your EV's power.

## LAKES FOR LINGERING

In the hit parade of potential stops, Bow Lake, 23 miles (37km) north of Lake Louise, ranks highly. Ringed by crenelated peaks and wedged beneath the imposing Crowfoot Glacier, the mirror-quality lake is one of the most famed sights in the Canadian Rockies. Early Banff

## Plan & prepare

### Tips for EV drivers

EV chargers can be found in Lake Louise, the Crossing, Jasper and Banff; there are several Tesla Superchargers in Canmore, 50 miles (80km) southeast of Lake Louise. The speed limit of 56mph (90km/h), combined with few road junctions or traffic lights to accelerate away from, will help conserve your battery's charge, though ascents and cold temperatures take a toll. Several Banff hotels have chargers – including the Rimrock, the Moose Hotel, the Banff Springs Hotel and Chateau Lake Louise.

### Where to stay

The Lake Louise Inn (lakelouiseinn.com) is a sprawling resort near the village, with an indoor pool and three restaurants.
In Jasper, the Athabasca (athabascahotel.com) is a reliable, affordable hotel with retro furnishings and its own bar and restaurant, located in the middle of the community. If you're short on battery charge and want to overnight en route, the Crossing Resort (thecrossingresort.com) at Saskatchewan River Crossing has simple motel-style units and a charger.

### When to go

The Icefields Parkway (icefieldsparkway.com) is open year-round, although inclement weather can cause spontaneous closures in winter. Summer is preferable for hiking, wildlife-spotting and maximizing battery range, although the more popular pull-overs can be especially crowded at these times. Don't write off October, which is a good month for stargazing and sees Jasper host its renowned Dark Sky Festival.

### Further info

Parks Canada (parks.canada.ca) maintains superb visitor centers in Lake Louise and Jasper, at either end of the Parkway; it's worth stopping off at either to pick up hiking maps and a special *Summer on the Icefields Parkway* brochure. The road has 14 trailheads, 12 campgrounds, five rustic hostels, four lodges and four eating joints dotted along it. Snacks and meals are available at the Columbia Icefield Discovery Centre dining room.

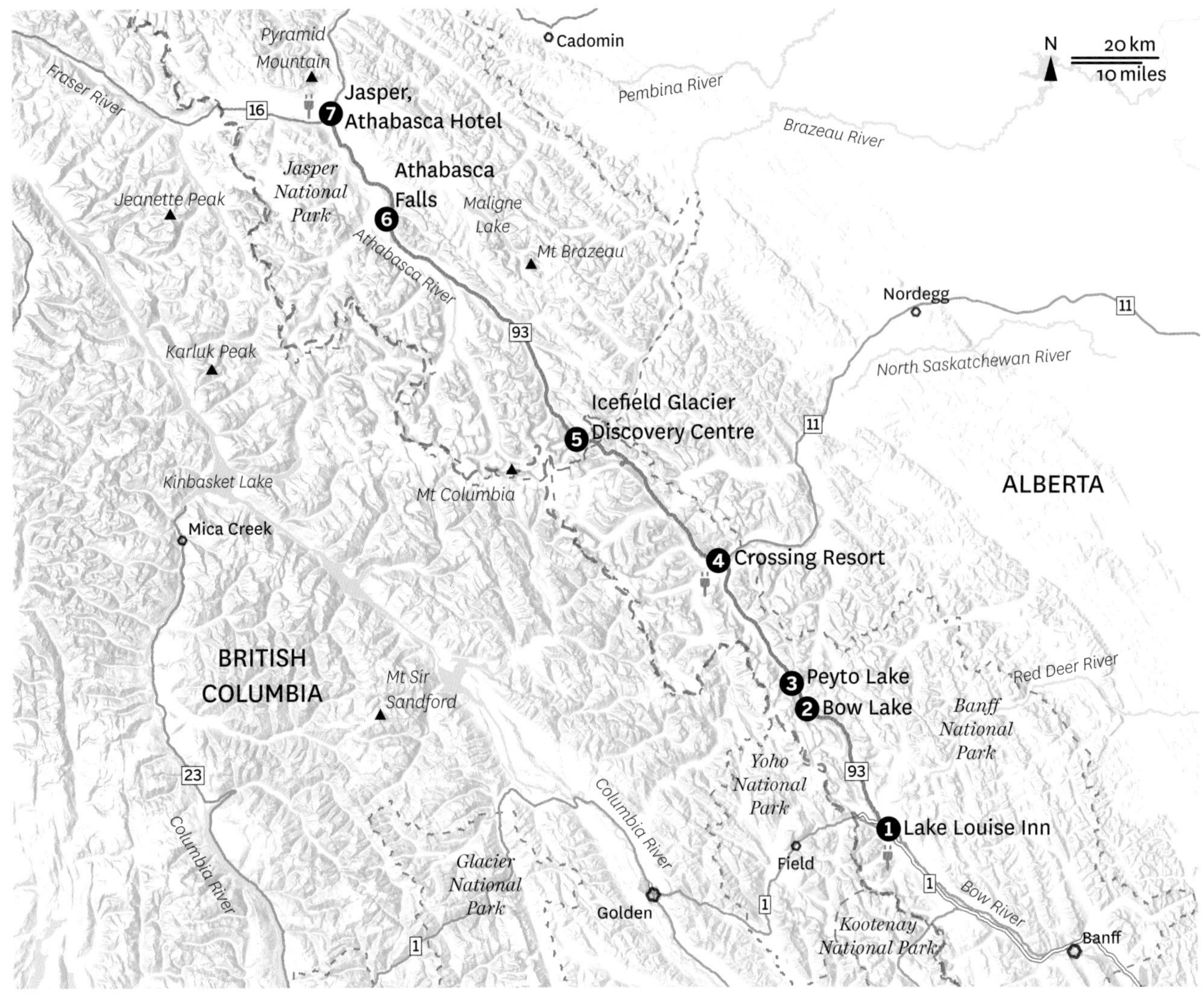


entrepreneur and wilderness outfitter Jimmy Simpson built a pioneering lodge, named Num-Ti-Jah, on the lake's north shore in 1922, over a decade before the construction of the first road. The handsome backwoods structure, now the Lodge at Bow Lake, invites non-guests into its cafe, gallery and gift shop.

Back on the highway, prepare for the short climb to 6800ft (2088m) Bow Pass, where signs usher you toward the rippled apex of Parkway pit stops, Peyto Lake. You'll recognize the glorious sapphire hue of the lake-water from a thousand high-profile publicity shots, but there's nothing like gazing at the genuine article – the lookout point is several hundred feet above. Peyto acquires its remarkable color from sunlight hitting fine particles of glacial sediment floating in the water.

## THE CROSSING & BEYOND

Twenty-two miles (35km) further north, you'll pass the Parkway's only major road intersection (with Hwy 11) at Saskatchewan River Crossing, where 19th-century fur trappers crossed the North Saskatchewan River on their way through the Rockies to British Columbia. Today, just west of the junction, there are several historical signboards; the no-frills motel, restaurant and gas station with chargers here are the only facilities between Lake Louise and the Columbia Icefield, so pause to top up.

From the Crossing, continue north on the Parkway alongside the North Saskatchewan River, passing a 1000ft-high (305m) cliff-face, known as the Weeping Wall, that's covered with a curtain of cascades in summer and becomes a haunting ice sculpture in winter. Soon after, a huge hairpin bend signals the beginning of the ascent to Sunwapta Pass. Stop at the parking area at the top of the bend for fine views back down the valley.

If you only have the energy to go for one hike along the Parkway, opt for the 4-mile (6.4km) out-and-back Parker

## The Wonder Trail

Today, it takes around 2¾ hours to drive the Icefields Parkway in a fully charged EV, if you refrain from stopping en route; some 100 years ago, the journey took a more protracted three weeks, riding on horseback along the so-called Wonder Trail, a rugged route first forged by land surveyors mapping the border between Alberta and British Columbia in the 1880s. With Banff and Jasper both designated national parks (in 1885 and 1907) and developed as tourist stops on the transcontinental railway, a north–south road link through the Rocky Mountains was deemed a priority. The idea became reality in 1931 when Depression-era work gangs were tasked with building a single-lane gravel road between Lake Louise and Jasper, in a massive public works project that took 10 years to complete. Opened in 1941, the original "parkway" served its purpose for 20 years before an increase in car traffic necessitated the building of a two-lane asphalt replacement. Lain mostly over the original route, the modern road cut down journey times substantially and opened headliner sights like the Columbia Icefield to greater numbers. Today over 1.2 million people drive the Parkway each year.

**Clockwise from top left:** looking across Peyto Lake; the Icefields Parkway passes alongside Bow Lake; historic Num-Ti-Jah Lodge, by the shore of Bow Lake

## Joys of Jasper

Compared to Banff, Jasper's townsite is smaller and more understated. Both places act as important wilderness gateways and tourist centers, but Jasper feels more "blue collar" and salt-of-the-earth. This is a working-class railway nexus that never quite jettisoned the shackles of its industrial past, where elk stalk the weed-choked railway yard as rattling trains shunt passengers and freight through a corridor of immense mountains. One of Jasper's great joys is the easy accessibility of the surrounding countryside. Trails for hiking, biking and cross-country skiing emanate directly from town, climbing onto the forested plateau of Pyramid Bench to the west; and east to the Athabasca River Valley with its jumble of lakes and woodland. Other nearby sights include Maligne Canyon, a narrow fissure crossed by six bridges; and the Jasper SkyTram, offering seven-minute rides up to the slopes of Whistlers Mountain.

**From far left:** the Jasper SkyTram; a guided hike on Athabasca Glacier; high-altitude drama builds before the Icefields Parkway



Ridge Trail, short enough to conquer in an afternoon, but leading to one of the most impressive lookouts in Banff: a grandstand view of Mt Saskatchewan, Mt Athabasca and the landscape-altering Saskatchewan Glacier as it slowly bulldozes its way through a valley. When you crest the ridge, you'll be met with a frigid blast of wind and a bombastic panorama of mountains and ice.

## INTO JASPER NATIONAL PARK

Invigorated by the views, return to your EV and head up to Sunwapta Pass, on the boundary of Banff and Jasper National Parks. From here, it's 1.6 miles (2.5km) downhill to the green-roofed Icefield Glacier Discovery Centre, gateway to the Athabasca Glacier.

An outer tentacle of the humongous Columbia Icefield, the Athabasca has retreated about 1.3 miles (2km) since 1844, when it reached the rock moraine on the north side of the road. You can walk from the Icefield Centre along the conjoined Forefield and Toe of the Glacier trails to view its "snout." A more immersive way to get onto the glacier is the Columbia Icefield Adventure tour: a giant all-terrain "snow-coach" grinds a steep track onto the ice, where it stops to allow passengers a 20-minute wander.

Beyond the Icefield, you'll begin the long descent to the Athabasca River valley, following the Parkway north past Tangle Falls, where bears and bighorn sheep are sporadic visitors. Larger Athabasca Falls, on Hwy 93A just off the Parkway, is Jasper's most dramatic waterfall, a deafening combination of sound, spray and water. The thunderous Athabasca River has eroded deeply into the soft limestone rock, carving potholes, canyons and water channels.

From here, it's around 19 miles (30km) further to finish in Jasper Town, hub of its namesake national park, whose long, still palpable history has drawn together Indigenous groups, fur trappers, explorers, railway workers, some of the Canadian Rockies' earliest tourists – and now you.

**Below:** rocky shore in Bruce Peninsula National Park
**Right:** a tugboat passes Flowerpot Island, near Tobermory

**Distance: 700 miles (1127km)**

**Duration: 7-10 days**

# Georgian Bay coastal route

**ONTARIO**

Circle this Northern Ontario lakeshore, where steep cliffs descend to Caribbean-blue waters, shipwrecks await snorkelers and divers, forested hiking trails beckon and Indigenous communities share their cultures.

Beating a retreat from metro Toronto, drive your EV northwest on Hwy 10 toward the Bruce Peninsula, which separates the crystal waters of Georgian Bay from Lake Huron and harbors some of Ontario's most dramatic natural scenery. At the peninsula's southern end, 115 miles (185km) from Toronto, stop at Owen Sound for an introduction to the region's history at the multimedia Grey Roots Museum. Continuing north on Hwy 6, detour to diminutive Lion's Head to hike the Lookout Trail, which climbs up to a cliff-top overlook, or to stretch your legs with a gentler walk by the village's lighthouse.

## LAND & SEA FROM TOBERMORY

At the peninsula's northern tip, Tobermory is the gateway to Bruce Peninsula National Park, where craggy cliffs drop steeply into aqua waters; offshore, you see unusual rock-stacks and numerous shipwrecks within the Fathom Five National Marine Park. Serving both parks, the Visitor Center in Tobermory screens a short film and displays exhibits that provide an intro to the region and its ecosystems. You'll want to book park activities in advance; parking reservations are mandatory for the most popular hikes.

## Plan & prepare

### Tips for EV drivers

Charging facilities are developing around Georgian Bay. On the Bruce Peninsula, you'll find public chargers in Owen Sound, at Bruce County Tourism's Wiarton office and at the Tobermory Community Centre. On Manitoulin, charge at Little Current's post office or Gore Bay's municipal offices. In Killarney, you can charge at Killarney Outfitters, but otherwise, consider recharging in Sudbury. Honey Harbour, where you catch the ferry to Georgian Bay Islands National Park, has an EV charger, with additional chargers in Midland.

### Where to stay

Tobermory's Blue Bay Motel (bluebay-motel.com) has onsite chargers, as does Lion's Head Beach Motel (lionsheadbeachmotel.com). On Manitoulin Island, head for the airy lofts at the Mutchmor (themutchmor.com) in Providence Bay, or First Nations–owned Manitoulin Hotel & Conference Centre (manitoulinhotel.com) in Little Current. Killarney's best option is waterfront Killarney Mountain Lodge (killarney.com). Midland's Quality Inn (choicehotels.com) has EV charging onsite.

### When to go

Explore Georgian Bay from July into October. In these seasonal destinations, most attractions, accommodations and experiences are open only from late May or June through September or October; you'll typically have the best weather and fewest bugs between mid-summer and early fall. The MS *Chi-Cheemaun* ferry connecting the Bruce Peninsula and Manitoulin Island begins operating in May and ends its season in mid-October.

### Further info

Destination Ontario (destinationontario.com) has province-wide travel info. Parks Canada (parks.canada.ca) covers Georgian Bay Islands, Bruce Peninsula and Fathom Five National Parks, including how to reserve parking. Ontario Parks (ontarioparks.com) provides similar information for Killarney Provincial Park. Other useful regional tourism sites include Explore the Bruce (explorethebruce.com), Explore Manitoulin (exploremanitoulin.com) and Experience Simcoe County (experience.simcoe.ca).

## Indigenous experiences on Manitoulin Island

Manitoulin Island is the traditional territory and present-day home of six First Nations: the Wiikwemkoong, Sheguiandah, Aundeck Omni Kaning, M'Chigeeng, Zhiibaahaasing and Sheshegwaning. Wiikwemkoong Tourism (wikytours.com) provides experiences that introduce their Nation's heritage and culture, including a history walk, a guided hike and a culinary adventure where you'll forage for wild plants and prepare a locally-sourced meal. After taking in exhibits at the Ojibwe Cultural Foundation on the M'Chigeeng First Nation, stop in to Lillian's Crafts & Museum, which displays elaborate porcupine quillwork; nearby, the Church of the Immaculate Conception blends Catholic and Indigenous religious traditions. Manitoulin has an Indigenous theater company, too: in Wiikwemikong, Debajehmujig Theatre Group normally performs in July and August. Respectful visitors are also welcome at powwows, cultural celebrations showcasing dance, music and food. These include those staged by the Wiikwemkoong (August), Aundeck Omni Kaning (June) and Sheshegwaning (June). Indigenous Tourism Ontario (indigenousexperience ontario.ca) has info on powwows and other events.

**Clockwise from above:** tipi on Manitoulin Island; shipwreck in Fathom Five National Marine Park; Flowerpot Island rock stack

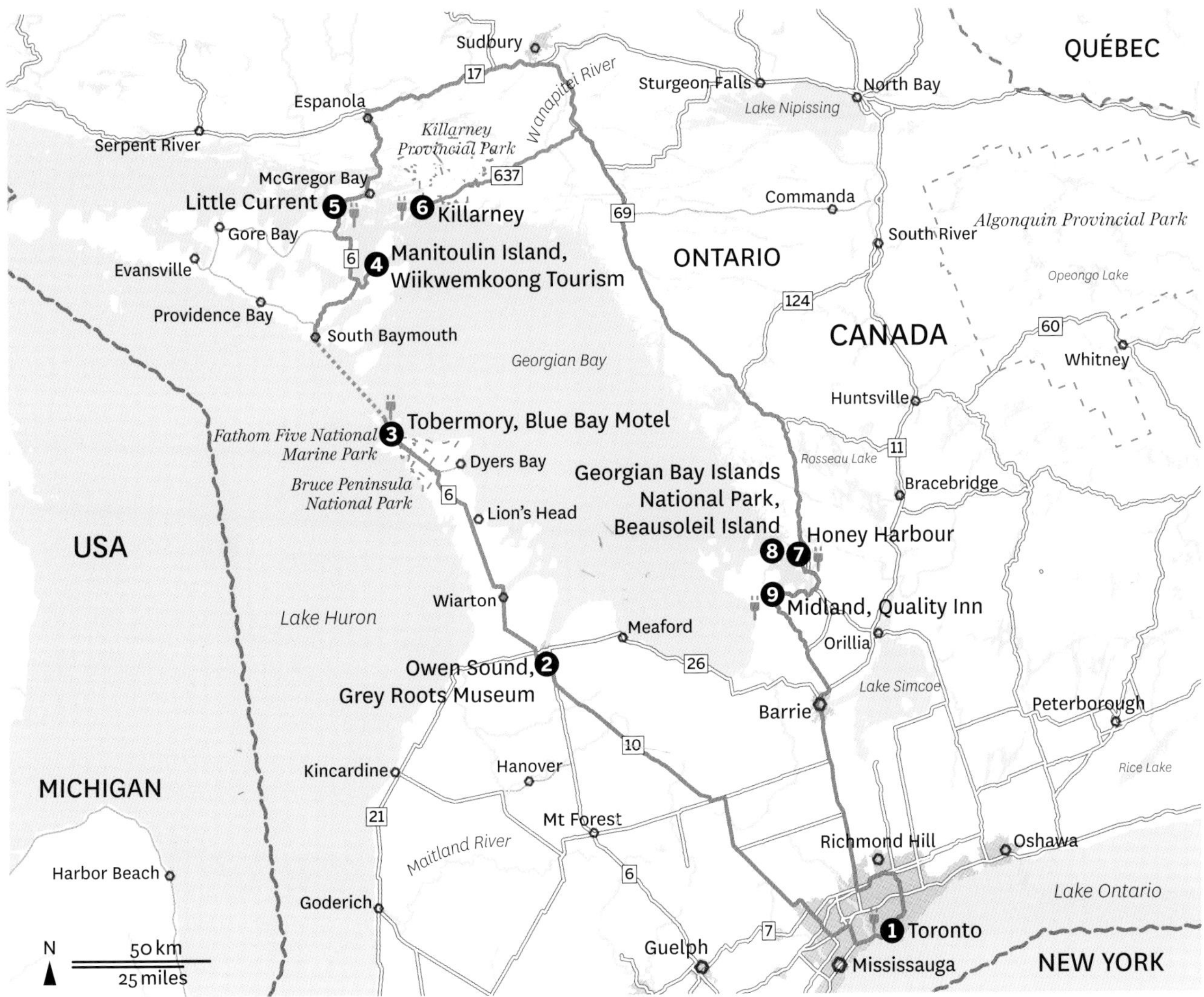


Worthy options include an early morning hike to the Grotto and to Indian Head Cove, where limestone cliffs contrast with the vivid blue waters. Pick up lunch from a local food truck and a gooey butter tart from Little Cove Bakery before a boat tour to Flowerpot Island, named for its top-heavy pillars of wave-eroded rock. After the short hike to view the rock stacks, keep walking to the former lighthouse keepers' house, now a small seasonal museum; behind is a "loo with a view," one of Canada's most scenic outhouses. If you'd rather explore from the water, book a snorkeling or scuba-diving tour that takes you to the bay's surprisingly intact shipwrecks. Back on the mainland, it's a short drive south of town to Singing Sands Beach, on the Lake Huron shore, a peaceful place for a sunset walk.

## THE BIG CANOE TO MANITOULIN

Make sure your EV is fully charged before boarding the two-hour MS *Chi-Cheemaun* ferry to Manitoulin Island; the ferry's name means "Big Canoe" in the Ojibwe language. The world's largest freshwater island, Manitoulin is home to six different First Nations. For an introduction to their culture, reserve a guided hike or cooking workshop with Wiikwemkoong Tourism, and take in Anishinaabe culture and art exhibits at the Ojibwe Cultural Foundation in M'Chigeeng.

Manitoulin also offers plenty to do outdoors: hike the Cup and Saucer Trail for views over the island; walk under the spray at Bridal Veil Falls; stroll the sands at Providence Bay, the island's most scenic beach. Little Current is Manitoulin's largest town, with the greatest choice of services and restaurants; try Bear Restaurant for unique Japanese-Ukrainian cuisine, or the Indigenous-owned North 46. Elsewhere on the island, dig in to excellent local fish at Lake Huron Fish & Chips in Providence Bay, or see what's on the menu at Maja's Garden Bistro in Mindemoya, which often hosts live music.

## The Group of Seven

A group of early 20th-century Canadian landscape painters has become inextricably linked with Northern Ontario's forests, lakes and mountains. Known as the Group of Seven, the original group comprised Franklin Carmichael, Lawren Harris, AY Jackson, Frank Johnston, Arthur Lismer, JEH MacDonald and Frederick Varley. The painters regularly captured Ontario's outdoors, often working in destinations such as Algonquin Park, Killarney and along Georgian Bay. An eighth artist, Tom Thomson, is also considered part of the group, though he died – allegedly under mysterious circumstances – while canoeing in Algonquin Provincial Park before the group was officially formed. Many Ontario museums exhibit work by Group of Seven artists, including Ottawa's National Gallery of Canada and the Art Gallery of Ontario (AGO) in Toronto. Owen Sound's small Tom Thomson Art Gallery shows work by Thomson and other Ontario artists.

**Clockwise from top:** gazing out across Killarney Provincial Park; the historic Little Current Swing Bridge; a selection of paintings by the Group of Seven, at the Art Gallery of Ontario

## TRAILS, LAKES & ISLANDS

Return to the mainland over the historic swing bridge, traveling north on Hwy 6 and then east on Hwy 17, the Trans-Canada Hwy; you're bound for Killarney Provincial Park, 2½ hours' drive from Little Current, where white quartzite mountains and pink-granite shorelines crisscrossed with hiking trails draw outdoor adventurers. For lunch or a charging break en route, detour into Sudbury, the region's largest city; otherwise, press on south along Hwy 69, turning onto Hwy 637; from here, it's 37 miles to Killarney Provincial Park headquarters and another 6 miles (10km) to the tiny town of Killarney.

Killarney's most popular – if strenuous – day hike is the Crack, which climbs steeply through a cascade of boulders to a lookout over the mountains. More moderate routes include the Granite Ridge Trail, which pays off with vistas of Georgian Bay and the surrounding peaks; and the Chikanishing Trail, which crosses the park's signature pink rocks along the shoreline.

Good eating options hereabouts include Killarney's Herbert Fisheries, serving top-rated fish and chips made with locally-caught whitefish; you could also choose one of several restaurants at Killarney Mountain Lodge. Top off the evening with a drink in the Lodge's circular, waterview Carousel Lounge.

When you've had your fill of Killarney's adventures, retrace your route back to Hwy 69 and continue south, where your next outdoor destination is Georgian Bay Islands National Park. Located between Parry Sound and Midland, tiny Honey Harbour is the departure point for the park-run passenger ferry to Beausoleil Island, where most of the park facilities are located, and where you can hike, swim or explore the Georgian Bay Islands' diverse landscape. For a longer stay, you can camp at Beausoleil Island sites or book a rustic cabin.

Otherwise, return to the mainland and spend the night in Midland before pointing your EV south toward journey's end in Toronto.

**Below:** stalls inside ByWard Market, Ottawa
**Right:** Thousand Islands National Park

**Distance: 620 miles (998km)**

**Duration: 6-9 days**

# Ottawa to Lake Ontario

**ONTARIO**

Road-trip by EV across the diverse landscapes of Eastern Ontario from Canada's stately federal capital, heading via the woods of Algonquin Park to Lake Ontario's beaches and out into the Thousand Islands.

Everywhere you look in Ottawa, Canada's national capital, you'll see grand museums and government buildings that highlight the country's heritage and art. Tour Parliament Hill, walk the banks of the Rideau – North America's oldest continuously operating canal – and immerse in as many museums and galleries as you have energy to see. Wander the ByWard Market district, too, full of food vendors, restaurants and bars.

## INTO THE WOODS

Charge your EV in the capital and set out on Hwy 417 for the three-hour drive west to Algonquin Provincial Park. Hwy 60 runs right through Ontario's first provincial park, from the east gate near Whitney through the west gate near Huntsville; there are 15 interpretive walking trails along the way, and miles of rivers and lakes to canoe.

Get oriented at the Algonquin Visitor Centre, which also has displays about the region's natural and human history; nearby Algonquin Logging Museum focuses on the park's complex relationship with the timber industry. Stay at one of three historic park lodges or at numerous campgrounds; outside the park, Huntsville has more accommodations, plus EV chargers.

## Plan & prepare

### Tips for EV drivers

Ottawa, Kingston and Peterborough are well equipped with EV charging stations. Make sure you're fully charged up before venturing into Algonquin Provincial Park; there are chargers in Whitney and Huntsville but (at the time of writing) none along the park's Hwy 60 corridor. There are also EV chargers at some Prince Edward County wineries and at many of the OnRoute (onroute.ca) rest areas along Hwy 401, which extends east from Toronto through Kingston and on toward Montreal.

### Where to stay

Ottawa hotels with EV chargers include Le Germain (germainhotels.com) and Westin Ottawa (marriott.com). In Huntsville, Deerhurst Resort (deerhurstresort.com) and Home2 Suites by Hilton (hilton.com) have chargers, as do the Drake Devonshire (thedrake.ca) and Huff Estates Inn & Winery (huffestates.com) in Prince Edward County. Kingston's elegant Frontenac Club (frontenacclub.com) has an onsite charger; boutique Smith Hotel (thesmithhotel.ca), in a renovated church, is close to downtown chargers.

### When to go

The best months for this road trip are July through early October, when everything is open, the weather is mild and the worst of the late-spring mosquitos and black flies have passed. Fall is especially beautiful, when the trees take on their autumn colors, though you should book ahead for September and October: outdoor destinations such as Algonquin Park draw many leaf-peepers.

### Further info

For regional intel, see Ottawa Tourism (ottawatourism.ca), Peterborough & the Kawarthas Tourism (thekawarthas.ca), Visit the County (visitthecounty.com), Tourism Kingston (visitkingston.ca) and 1000 Islands Tourism (1000islandstourism.com). Parks Canada (parks.canada.ca) covers Thousand Islands National Park; Ontario Parks (ontarioparks.com) oversees provincial parks. Note that in Algonquin Park, distances on Hwy 60 are marked in kilometers. The West Gate is at km marker 0; the East Gate is km marker 56.

## Canada & the canoe

From its significance to everyone from Indigenous peoples to fur-trading settlers to modern-day recreational paddlers, the canoe has always played a major role in Canadian culture and heritage. Peterborough's Canadian Canoe Museum houses the world's largest collection of canoes, kayaks and other paddled watercraft. At the time of writing, relocation was ongoing to a spacious contemporary lakeside building (check if it's open at canoemuseum.ca). The displays will share the canoe's many stories, through multimedia exhibits, talks with local artisans and demonstrations of paddle carving and canoe building. The museum's guided tours in 36ft (11m) voyageur canoes will also be on offer, alongside rentals of canoes, kayaks and stand-up paddleboards on the adjacent lake. Peterborough is also located on the historic 240-mile-long (386km) Trent-Severn Waterway, completed in 1920 to link Lake Ontario and Georgian Bay. The waterway has 42 lock stations that allow boats to navigate its changing elevations – including the Peterborough Lift Lock, which opened back in 1904; today, boats still rise and descend up to 65ft (20m) as the chambers fill and drain. Take a narrated sightseeing cruise through this and other locks or, for a bigger thrill, rent a canoe and paddle through under your own steam.

**Above:** canoeing in Algonquin Provincial Park, colorful in fall
**Opposite from left:** cells inside Kingston Penitentiary; Sandbanks Dunes Beach in Sandbanks Provincial Park

Pick up a pastry at Henrietta's Pine Bakery before heading south of Huntsville along Hwy 35, through woods and along lakes toward Haliburton, where you can wander among the 40-plus contemporary sculptures of Haliburton Sculpture Forest. Charge your EV at the town's information center before continuing south toward Petroglyphs Provincial Park, where the "Teaching Rocks" are Canada's largest known collection of petroglyphs. Indigenous interpreters explain the legends behind the carvings of humans, snakes and other creatures. Another aspect of Canadian culture takes center stage an hour's drive south in Peterborough, site of the Canadian Canoe Museum's new home (see left).

### WINELANDS & ISLANDS

After these adventures, take time to relax in bucolic Prince Edward County, where visitors are drawn by a growing wine-making industry, farm-to-table cuisine and sandy Lake Ontario beaches. Designated driver alongside, taste your way through more than three dozen wineries, cycle the quiet roadways and book a table at locally-focused restaurants such as Stella's Eatery or the Sand and Pearl Oyster Bar. Both are close to the Sandbanks Provincial Park, one of Ontario's busiest beach destinations – reserve a day-pass in advance. Otherwise, restaurants, lodging and other services are concentrated in Wellington, Bloomfield and Picton.

Fifty miles (80km) east, stroll the historic streets of Kingston, Canada's first capital, then check out another unusual attraction. During tours of Kingston Penitentiary, which housed Canada's most notorious criminals between 1835 and 2013, former guards share their experiences of working behind the stone walls. Kingston's diverse restaurants ensure you'll be well fed, from Cambodian Village and Sally's Roti Shop to high-end Chez Piggy.

Then follow Hwy 2 east to Gananoque, gateway to the Thousand Islands. Take a boat cruise around the islands or to 120-room Boldt Castle, constructed by the former owner of New York's Waldorf Astoria Hotel (you'll need your passport if disembarking at the latter, as its Heart Island location is in the US). Nearby, Thousand Islands National Park encompasses 20 St Lawrence River isles and some gorgeous lakeside shoreline. Join a kayak tour or hike the Landon Bay Lookout Trail for great views, before making the 90-minute drive back to Ottawa.

QUÉBEC
Waltham
Low
Campbell's Bay
Sundridge
Algonquin Provincial Park Visitor Centre
Algonquin Park
Masson
Ottawa River
Whitney
60
Wilno
Eganville
Huntsville, Deerhurst Resort
Dwight
Lake of Bays
17
Arnprior
Ottawa
417
11
35
Maynooth
118
Haliburton Sculpture Forest
Bancroft
Denbigh
Carleton Place
416
Kemptville
ONTARIO
Kawartha Highlands Provincial Park
28
CANADA
Smiths Falls
Norland
Catchacoma
Apsley
Big Rideau Lake
Petroglyphs Provincial Park
Kaladar
Newboro
Brockville
St Lawrence River
12
Fenelon Falls
7
15
Charleston Lake
Lake Simcoe
Gananoque, Thousand Islands National Park
Gouverneur
Peterborough, Canadian Canoe Museum
Rice Lake
Belleville
401
Kingston Penitentiary
Antwerp
Trenton
33
Fort Drum
Richmond Hill
Oshawa
Port Hope
I-81
Wellington, Drake Devonshire Hotel
Picton, Sandbanks Provincial Park
Watertown
Black River
NEW YORK
Toronto
Lake Ontario
USA
N
40 km
20 miles

**Below:** Tesla Model X EV parked in the Vieux-Québec district
**Right:** Château Frontenac, Québec City

**Distance: 575 miles (925km)**

**Duration: 5-7 days**

# St Lawrence River loop

**QUÉBEC**

Make use of a handy car ferry to drive your EV alongside, and then over, Québec's mighty waterway, soaking up the region's Gallic charm and looking out for whales en route.

Sixteenth-century mariner Jacques Cartier – the first European to venture inland in North America – called the St Lawrence the "great river of Canada." He wasn't wrong. Rising from Lake Ontario, it runs northeast for almost 750 miles (1200km), past Montréal and Québec City, into the immense Gulf of St Lawrence. Essential to the Indigenous Iroquoians, and then the early explorers, the river remains the lifeblood of Québec province, and still provides an excellent avenue for those wanting to explore: EV drivers will find plentiful scenic roads, a good network of chargers and some useful ferries, meaning no backtracking is required.

## QUÉBEC CITY TO CHARLEVOIX

Québec City doesn't feel especially Canadian. The only remaining walled city in the Americas north of Mexico, its sturdy ramparts, fairytale turrets, pavement cafes and Francophone voices give it a distinctly European vibe. Stay at the Auberge Saint-Antoine, which faces the St Lawrence and is dotted with relics uncovered from the ground below. Then soak up the Gallic atmosphere – stroll Vieux-Québec (Old Town) and the Plains of Abraham, visit the old Citadelle fortress and browse the mouthwatering stalls at the new Grand Marché – before driving on.

## Plan & prepare

### Tips for EV drivers

There's a good network of EV chargers along the St Lawrence River, including fast chargers. These are found at useful spots, including shops, gas stations and visitor centers. Check you have downloaded the latest apps to use the varied brands of chargers in operation at the time of your visit. Some ferries, including the Baie-Comeau–Matane route, offer discounted fares for electric vehicles.

### Where to stay

In downtown Québec City, gorgeous Auberge Saint-Antoine (saint-antoine.com) offers solid green credentials, parking and chargers. Le Germain Charlevoix, Baie-Saint-Paul (germainhotels.com), has a spa, heated outdoor pool and multiple restaurants. Mer et Monde's Bergeronnes campground (vacancesessipit.com) has riverside huts in the Essipit Innu community; there's a charger at nearby Cap-de-Bon-Désir. Near Parc du Bic, charger-equipped Vieux Loup de Mer (vieuxloupdemer.com) has rustic-chic cabins.

### When to go

Summer (June to September) sees the warmest weather, and is best for wild swims, festivals and drinking wine on pop-up patios. This is also peak whale-watching season. Birding is best in spring and autumn when migratory species congregate in the St Lawrence River corridor. Fall colors can be spectacular, usually peaking in October. The Baie-Comeau/Matane ferry runs year-round, though less frequently outside May to September. Winters are frigid, but Québec City's Winter Carnival (February) will give you a warm glow.

### Further info

Road signs in Québec are in French; familiarize yourself with common terms such as *sortie* (exit), *arrêt* (stop) and *centre-ville* (downtown). As well as the Baie-Comeau–Matane service (traversiers.com), ferries cross the St Lawrence between Trois-Pistoles and Les Escoumins (near Cap-de-Bon-Désir; cnbferry.ca), and between Rivière-du-Loup and Saint-Siméon (traverserdl.com). Cars must arrive 45 minutes before the scheduled departure time. Tickets should be booked in advance, especially in high season.

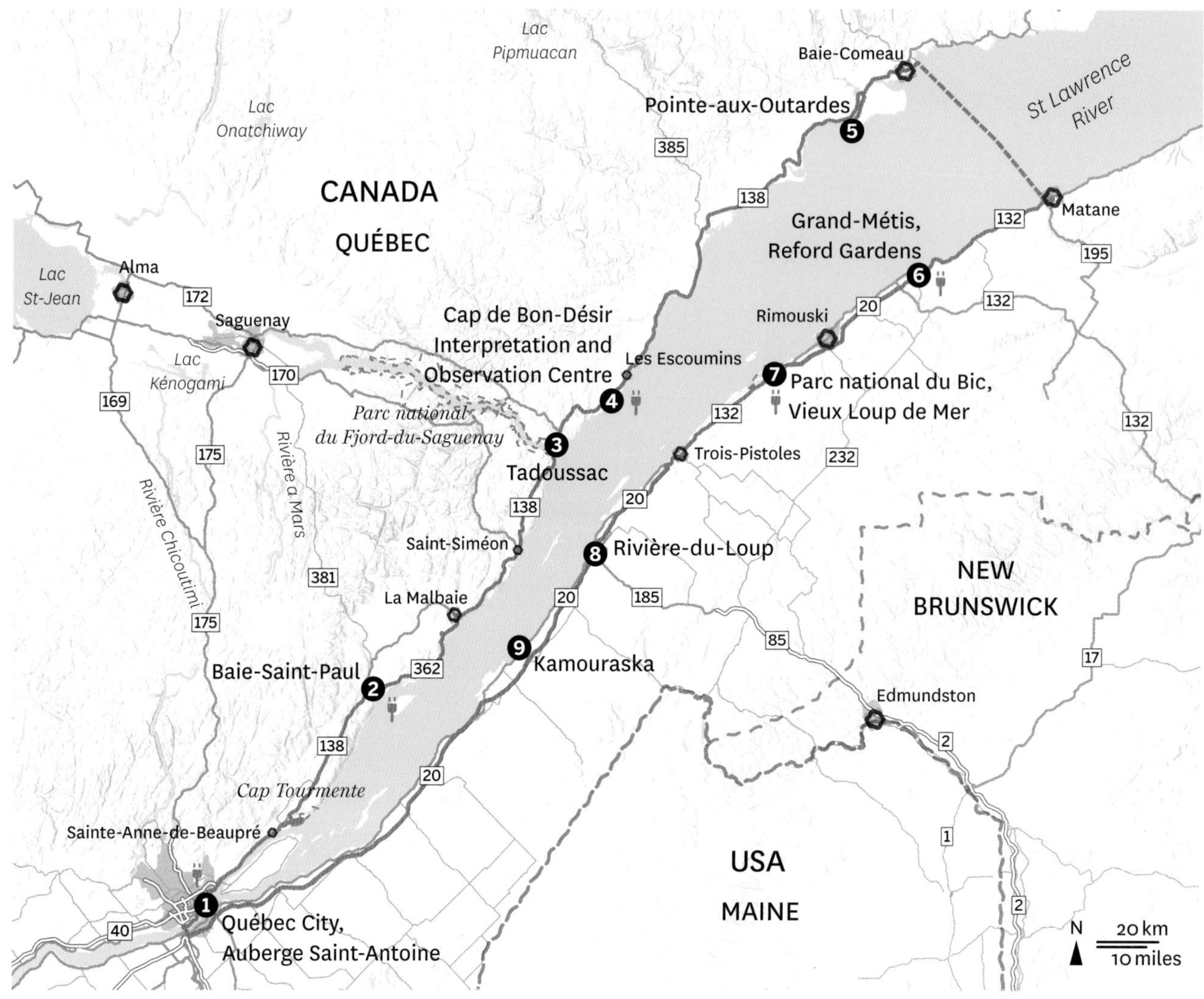




Leave the city via Montmorency Falls, a roaring 272ft (83m) plume only 15 minutes outside the Old Town; get up-close views from the suspension bridge (or the zipline) across it. From here Rte 138 hugs the river's north shore. Detour 28 miles (45km) on, beyond the looming basilica of Sainte-Anne-de-Beaupré, to Cap Tourmente National Wildlife Area, a brilliant place for birds, especially mass gatherings of migrating greater snow geese.

From hereon you're steering your EV into the Charlevoix region, a beautiful Unesco Biosphere of rolling, forested hills and rich culture. Pause in scenically set Baie-Saint-Paul, dotted with art galleries, studios and boutiques. Check in at the classy Le Germain Charlevoix, where you can recharge yourself and your car. Once refreshed, drive onwards to the resort of La Malbaie. Opt for the coastal Rte du Fleuve (Rte 362), which nestles between the Laurentian Mountains and the river, passing the charming villages of Les Éboulements and Saint-Irénée.

## WHALE OF A TIME

Gorgeous Tadoussac – site of Canada's first trading post – is one of the best places in the world to watch whales. From La Malbaie, the town is a 45-mile (72km) drive and a free 10-minute ferry-hop across the mouth of the Saguenay River. Park up and join a boat tour (options range from 12-passenger inflatables to 600-passenger vessels) for good chances of encounters with beluga, blue, humpback, minke and fin. Pay a visit the Marine Mammal Interpretation Centre too, then engage with Tadoussac's Indigenous story (First Nations peoples have occupied the area for nearly 8000 years) and colonial history, including a look at the Petite Chapelle, North America's oldest wooden church.

Keep eyes peeled as you drive along Rte 138 to Cap-de-Bon-Désir: the Interpretation and Observation Centre here (which has EV chargers) is a great place to watch whales from the shore. Nearby is the Mer et Monde

## See the light

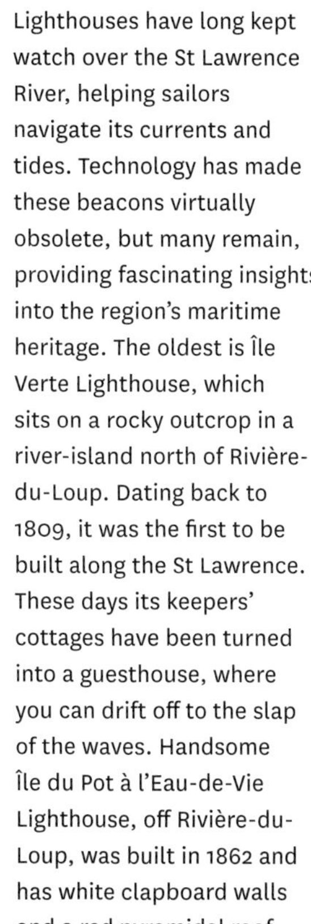

Lighthouses have long kept watch over the St Lawrence River, helping sailors navigate its currents and tides. Technology has made these beacons virtually obsolete, but many remain, providing fascinating insights into the region's maritime heritage. The oldest is Île Verte Lighthouse, which sits on a rocky outcrop in a river-island north of Rivière-du-Loup. Dating back to 1809, it was the first to be built along the St Lawrence. These days its keepers' cottages have been turned into a guesthouse, where you can drift off to the slap of the waves. Handsome Île du Pot à l'Eau-de-Vie Lighthouse, off Rivière-du-Loup, was built in 1862 and has white clapboard walls and a red pyramidal roof, and is only accessible via a series of footbridges and stairs. It was restored by the Duvetnor Society, which runs boat trips across and B&B stays inside. Pointe-au-Père Lighthouse in Rimouski was built in 1909. You can climb the 128 steps for panoramic views and visit the adjacent Empress of Ireland Museum, which tells the story of the sinking of this steamship in 1914, with the loss of 840 lives; many artefacts from the wreck are on display.

**Clockwise from top left:** the powerful Montmorency Falls; Île Verte Lighthouse; Rte 138 with a glimpse of the St Lawrence River beyond; humpback whale displaying its fluke in the St Lawrence

## Saguenay side-trip

Got more time? Then instead of taking the 10-minute ferry across the Saguenay River, head inland on the Route du Fjord. This 146-mile (235km) bonus road trip between Petit-Saguenay and Tadoussac circumnavigates Saguenay Fjord, a glorious, glacier-cut arm off the St Lawrence, protected within a namesake national park. The road gives jaw-dropping views into the steep-sided gorge and passes a scatter of *très belle* villages, not least, lovely L'Anse-Saint-Jean, on the south shore, and Sainte-Rose-du-Nord on the north. It makes a scenic day-drive, but it's way better to spend longer. Paddle out with Fjord en Kayak from L'Anse-Saint-Jean, negotiate the 920ft (280m) rock walls by via ferrata at Rivière-Éternité, learn more at Grande-Baie's Musée du Fjord, and explore First Nations culture and black bear country at Rivière-à-Mars canyon. A highlight is Baie-Sainte-Marguerite, where it's possible to watch beluga whales from the shore.

**From far left:** L'Anse-Saint-Jean; lighthouse at Kamouraska; Reford Gardens

Bergeronnes campsite, where you can rent huts and cabins near the water's edge and book kayaking trips.

Then enjoy the views as you cruise along Rte 138 to reach the Pointe-aux-Outardes Peninsula. Here, over 200 bird species can be spotted in the nature park, and the sandy beaches are good for a dip.

## WILD RETURN

It's only a 30-minute drive from Pointe-aux-Outardes to the city of Baie-Comeau, at the heart of the Manicouagan Uapishka World Biosphere Reserve and home of the enormous Manic-2 and Manic-5 dams. It's also where ferries (daily in high season) cross to Matane, on the St Lawrence River's south shore. Keep an eye out for marine life as you make the 2½-hour crossing.

If you've time, detour 24 miles (39km) away from the river to the Réserve faunique de Matane, a wild expanse of waterways, mountains and hiking trails, home to black bear and moose. Otherwise, follow Rte 132 along the shore south to arrive in Grand-Métis. Here, the magnificent Reford Gardens bloom in exotic defiance of the Québécois weather. Rimouski, 27 miles (43km) on, makes a good base, though Parc national du Bic, 12 miles (19km) more, is lovelier. The idyllic capes, coves and bays of this coast park offer various trails and activities, views to the river isles and glamping accommodation. Or stay at Vieux Loup de Mer's cozy cabins, just outside the park.

Continue on to Rivière-du-Loup, where you could take another whale-watching tour or maybe sailing, paddling, hiking and overnight trips to the wildlife-filled Bas-Saint-Laurent islands. Then pootle down to Kamouraska – officially recognized as one of the most beautiful villages in Québec – to browse the cheesemongers, chocolatiers, craft workshops and boutiques.

From here, Québec City is a two-hour drive. You can complete your loop by EV via either the Pierre Laporte Bridge, the longest main-span suspension bridge in Canada, or the Lévis ferry.

**Below:** tucking in to a dish of poutine
**Right:** umbrellas above Rue du Cul-de-Sac in Québec City

**Distance: 385 miles (620km)**

**Duration: 5 days**

# Montréal to Saguenay

**QUÉBEC**

Discover Québec's long history, experience its rich culture and be bowled over by its biological and geological magnificence on this scenic EV drive along the St Lawrence and Saguenay Rivers.

Start your road trip in Montréal, Québec's cultural and economic capital. Spend a day exploring Vieux-Montréal, cycling along Canal de Lachine and scarfing down poutine (Canada's unofficial national dish of fries, cheese and gravy). The impressive Musée des Beaux-Arts is a required stop for its rich collection of works by Québecois artists. Be sure to climb Mont-Royal for views of downtown Montréal and the St Lawrence River beyond.

## NORTH ALONG THE ST LAWRENCE

Leaving the city, drive northeast, following the western shore of the St Lawrence River and Lac Saint-Pierre for 94 miles (151km) to Trois-Rivières. Dating to 1634, this old mill town is a perfect place to grab some lunch and charge your EV as you wander the historic district. Housed in an old paper mill, Musée Boréalis gives a diverting overview of the city's paper industry.

Continue along Rte 138, the Chemin du Roy (see p284), for another 80 miles (129km) to Québec City, the political capital and historic heart of the region. Founded in 1608, Québec evokes Old Europe with its centuries-old architecture and French-speaking population. The historic quarter is packed with museums and murals,

## Plan & prepare

### Tips for EV drivers

Québec is out in front of the rest of the country (and the neighboring country!) when it comes to EV infrastructure, with more than 3000 public charging stations. Most are in Hydro-Québec's Electric Circuit network (lecircuitelectrique.com). It's also easy to find hotels with onsite charging stations (often free for guests). There has even been a provincial government program that exempts EVs from paying tolls; see Running Electric (roulonselectrique.ca) for details about this and other EV incentive programs.

### Where to stay

The luxurious Honeyrose Hotel (honeyrosemontreal.com) is a stylish choice in downtown Montréal – a throwback to the 1920s with modern amenities. In the heart of Québec City's historic Vieux-Port, Le Germain Québec (germainhotels.com) is a handsome boutique hotel which waives the parking fee for electric vehicles. In Saguenay, OTL Gouverneur Hotel (otlhotelsaguenay.ca) is a snazzy, modern option with a delightful onsite spa – a perfect place to relax after hiking along the fjord. All options have onsite chargers.

### When to go

For warmer weather and whale-watching, the best time to drive from Montréal to Saguenay is between May and October, with peak tourist season in July and August. That said, the cities are lively year-round, and wintertime events (such as Carnaval de Québec in January or February) make them enticing destinations even during the coldest months. Further north, you can swap your hiking boots for skis or snowshoes and experience the magic of Québec in the snow.

### Further info

Bonjour Québec (bonjourquebec.com) is the official website of Québec's tourist board, with many resources for travelers. Note that two highways run between Montréal and Québec City: the newer, faster Autoroute 40 and the historic Rte 138 (the Chemin du Roy). Choose the former if you're in a hurry. But if you have time to spare, the latter is definitely more scenic, especially in the northern stretch between Trois-Rivières and Québec City.

## Chemin du Roy

Traveling north from Montréal to Québec City, you'll notice the route markers at the side of Rte 138, each one picturing a crown adorned with fleurs-de-lis. The signs denote the Chemin du Roy, or the King's Highway (lecheminduroy.com), which is one of the oldest such routes on the continent. In the early 18th century, the St Lawrence River was the primary means of transportation in New France, but in 1706, the Gran Conseil decreed that a new thoroughfare was needed to connect the colony's two main cities. Each landowner along the route was obliged to supply laborers to build the road. These so-called *corvées du roy* constructed the 174-mile (280km) thoroughfare – then the longest road north of the Rio Grande. The *corvées* also manned ferries and barges for river crossings. With the Chemin du Roy came the possibility of public overland transportation. In each village, a local postmaster oversaw a "relay station" where travelers could pick up a carriage or sleigh to the next village. In 1737 it was possible to travel by carriage from Montréal to Québec in 4½ days; nowadays, your EV can drive this same route in about 4½ hours.

**From above left:** the historic small town of Champlain, set on the Chemin du Roy; Tadoussac's harbor and (opposite) craggy shoreline **Opposite:** Tadoussac shoreline

with bistros and boutiques lining the cobblestone streets and the elegant Château Frontenac towering above. Stroll along the Terrasse Dufferin to watch the street performers and marvel at the sweeping views.

The route continues along the St Lawrence River as you motor north in your EV, with several options to stop and stretch your legs (and recharge your car). Beaupré is an excellent option for hiking and fabulous vistas from Mont-Sainte-Anne; charming Baie-Saint-Paul is known for its art galleries and innovative museums – not to mention its claim to fame as the birthplace of the Cirque du Soleil. All together it's 108 miles (174km) from Québec to the tiny town of Baie-Sainte-Catherine. From here, take your EV on a 10-minute ferry ride across the Saguenay River to Tadoussac.

### WEST ALONG THE SAGUENAY

Tadoussac is a picturesque village at the confluence of the St Lawrence and Saguenay Rivers. Visit the Marine Mammal Interpretation Centre to learn about the 13 species of cetaceans that pass through these waters. You can try to spot them from the shore, or take a whale-watching tour to get a closer look. Moving on from Tadoussac, head west along the north shore of the Saguenay River, passing through the Parc national du Fjord-du-Saguenay. Drive about 18 miles (29km) to the Baie-Sainte-Marguerite sector for a short hike and wonderful views over the fjord. Whale sightings are not unusual from the so-called Beluga Lookout, and the scenery is a highlight in any case.

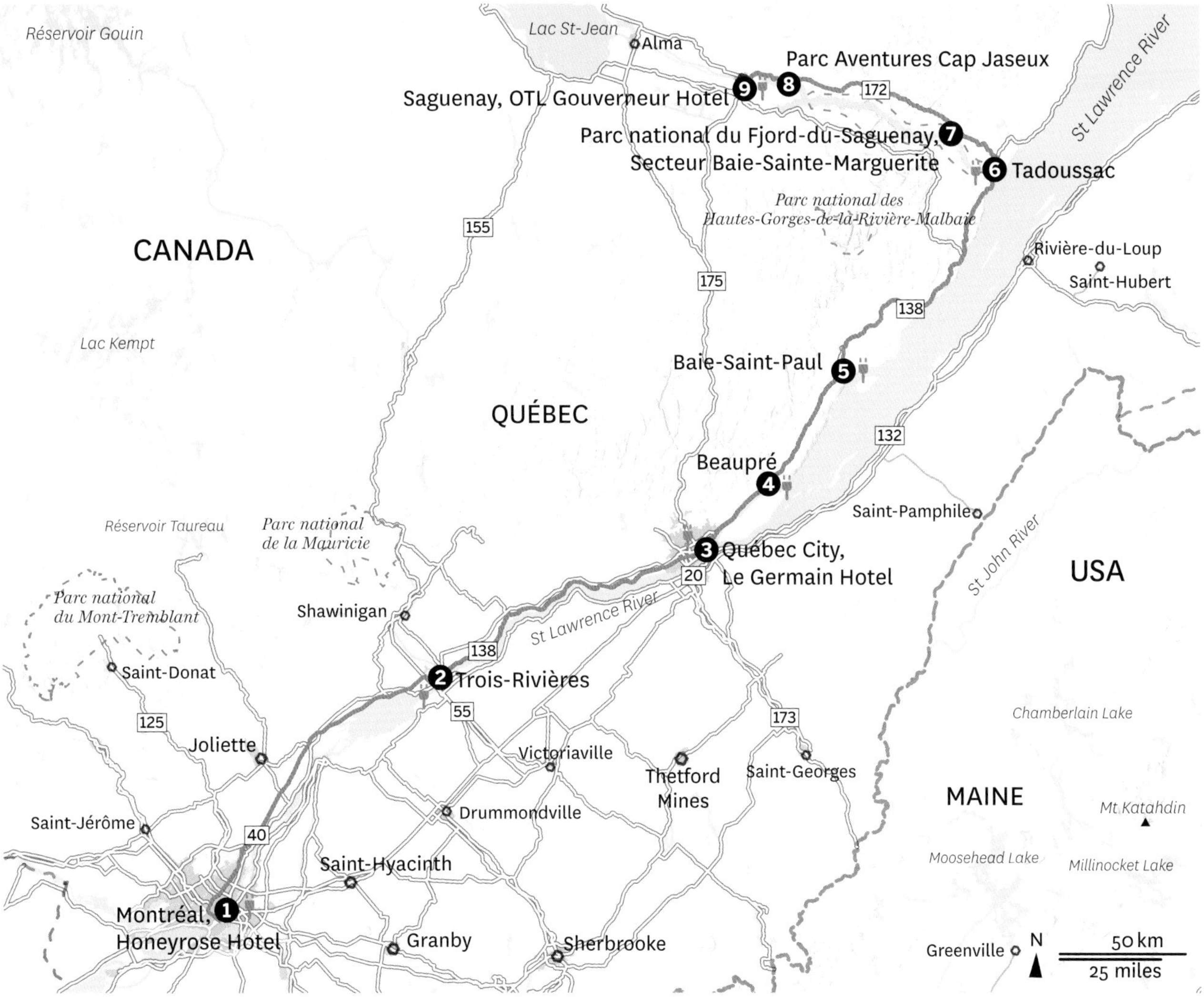

For more outdoor fun in this magnificent setting, make a stop at Parc Aventures Cap Jaseux in Saint-Fulgence. Take your pick from via ferrata climbing or a treetop obstacle course, all with views of the river and towering cliffs. It's another 15 miles (24km) to your final destination at Saguenay, where you can visit the Musée du Fjord to learn about the geology and wildlife of the area you just traversed. Saguenay is also a good base if you want to round off your road trip by exploring deeper into the national park on the south shore of the fjord.

**Below:** path to the beach at Basin Head Provincial Park
**Right:** Charlottetown

**Distance: 332 miles (535km)**

**Duration: 5-7 days**

# Coastal loop from Charlottetown

**PRINCE EDWARD ISLAND**

Drive the rural roadways of Canada's smallest province – setting for the classic *Anne of Green Gables* novels – taking in sandy shores, red cliffs, green fields and foot-stomping ceilidhs.

Start your journey in historic Charlottetown, PEI's compact capital, exploring on foot while you charge up your EV for the drive ahead. At the Confederation Centre of the Arts, tour an exhibition about Charlottetown's role in Canada's birth, and walk through the art gallery to see works by Canadian visual artists. Learn about local history on a Secrets of Charlottetown walking tour, then saunter toward the harbor for a snack at Founders Food Hall or a seafood meal at Water Prince Corner Shop; if staying overnight, enjoy an evening concert at Trailside Music Hall or traditional tunes at Ceilidh in the City.

## LOOPING EAST FROM CHARLOTTETOWN

EV fully charged, head east out of Charlottetown on Hwy 1. For a glimpse of the island's agricultural past, stop at Orwell Corner Historic Village near Vernon Bridge, where interpreters go about their daily lives as if it were the late 1800s. Then detour southwest to Point Prim Lighthouse, the island's oldest, built in 1845. Moving on, continue 23 miles (37km) east, via Hwy 211 and Hwy 326, into Montague, to enjoy the barbecue at Bogside Brewing (there's a nearby charger should you need to top up). Then turn south on Hwy 4 toward

© Darryl Brooks/Shutterstock

## Plan & prepare

### Tips for EV drivers

PEI's EV infrastructure is evolving, with the majority of chargers in Charlottetown, second city Summerside and in Prince Edward Island National Park. You'll find charging stations in the north-central towns of Cavendish, North Rustico, Rustico and Kensington. To the east, Montague currently has the most charging stations; options are limited on the island's rural west side. Fortunately, distances on this compact island are short – even driving PEI end-to-end would mean covering just 160 miles (257km) or so.

### Where to stay

Several Charlottetown hotels, including the Great George (thegreatgeorge.com) and Rodd Charlottetown (roddvacations.com), have EV chargers, as does Rustico's Barachois Inn (barachoisinn.com). In other places, you may need to charge nearby. Options include floating wine barrels at Nellie's Landing (nellieslanding.com) in Murray Harbour; glamping yurts at Nature Space Resort (naturespaceresort.com) near St Peters Harbour; and Kensington's cozy, history-rich Home Place Inn (thehomeplace.ca).

### When to go

July and August are PEI's peak tourism months, when everything is open and the warm, sunny weather draws hordes to the beaches. For a quieter visit, consider June, when the wildflowers bloom; or September and October, when the trees take on their autumn colors and the island celebrates its harvests with the International Shellfish Festival and the Fall Flavours fest. Roadtrippers should avoid the cold, often snowy weather from November through April.

### Further info

Tourism Prince Edward Island (tourismpei.com) is an excellent source of information about things to do, places to stay and where to eat across the island. Parks Canada (parks.canada.ca) has info on campsite bookings and other details about Prince Edward Island National Park; and look for Indigenous cultural offerings at Experience Lennox Island (experiencelennoxisland.com). For local food adventures and tips, see Canada's Food Island (canadasfoodisland.ca).

## Anne of Green Gables

Prince Edward Island's most famous historical resident may well be a fictional red-haired girl – the feisty heroine of the *Anne of Green Gables* novels by Lucy Maud Montgomery. Born on PEI in 1874, Montgomery was raised by her grandparents in Cavendish after her mother died before the future novelist reached her second birthday. Though she trained as a teacher and taught briefly in several of PEI's rural schools, Maud, as she was known, returned to live with her grandmother after her grandfather passed away in 1898. It was in this Cavendish home that Montgomery completed *Anne of Green Gables*, her first novel, in 1905. Numerous publishers rejected the book, but Boston-based LC Page & Co decided to take it on; it became an instant bestseller after its publication in 1908. Following her marriage to Rev Ewen Macdonald in 1911, Montgomery moved to Ontario with her husband; she would remain there for the rest of her life. But Prince Edward Island would always retain a prominent place in her work. Of the 20 books that she authored before her death in 1942, all but one was set on PEI.

**Clockwise from above:** Green Gables Heritage Place in Cavendish – the setting for the *Anne of Green Gables* novels; East Point Lighthouse; a boardwork through wetlands and sand dunes at Greenwich, Prince Edward Island National Park; locally-grown oysters

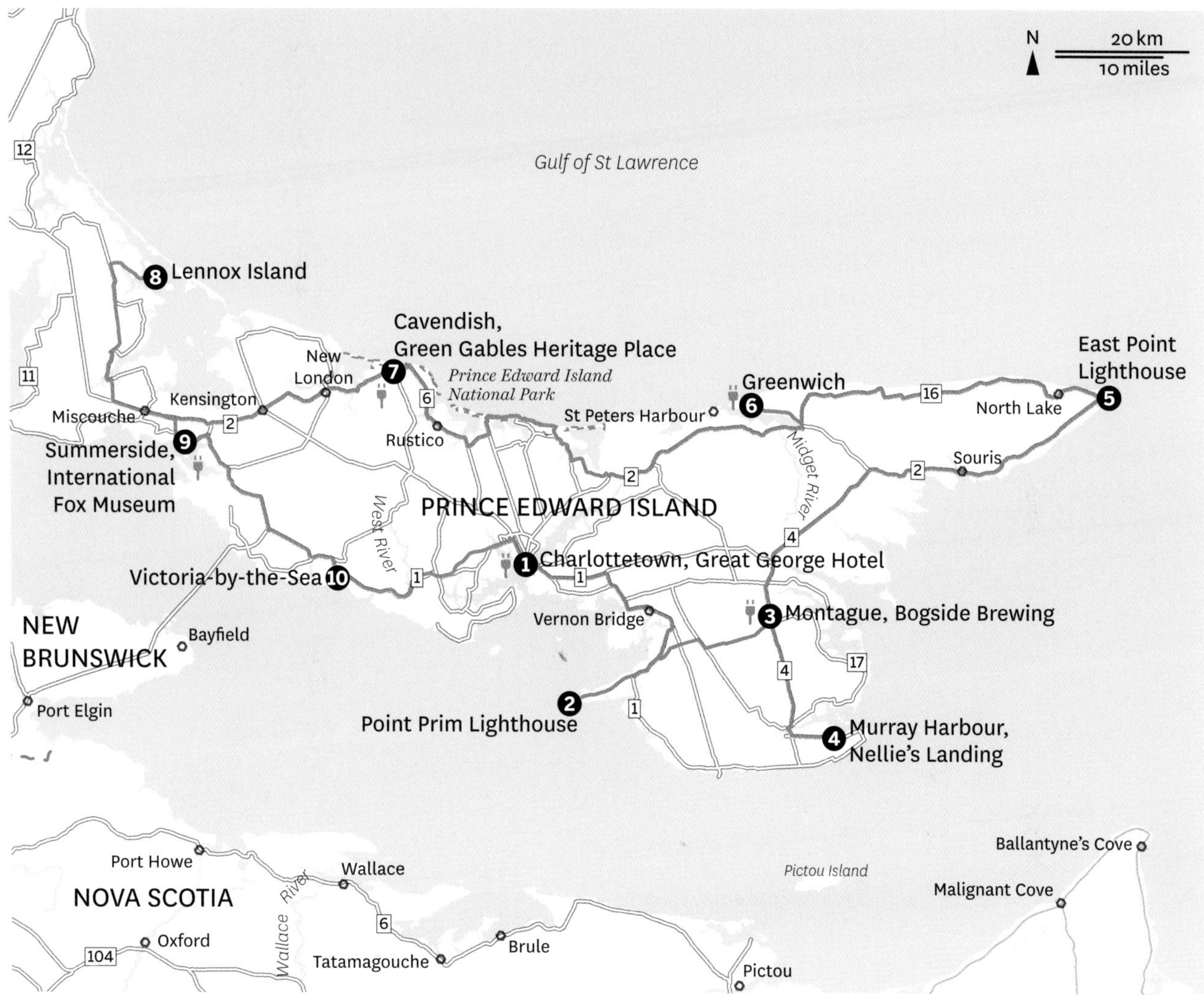




Murray Harbour, where you can overnight in a cozy on-the-water floating wine barrel at Nellie's Landing.

In the morning, head back up to Montague (Lucky Bean Cafe is a fine stop for refreshments) then continue your loop around the island's east end, driving 28 miles (45km) via Hwy 4 and Hwy 2 to Souris for a leg-stretching walk on the beachside boardwalk and the chance to sample unique-to-PEI potato-based candies at Oh Fudge. Continue east, along Hwy 16, to visit Basin Head Provincial Park, where the beach is known for its "singing sands" (the high silica content delivers a squeaking sound as you walk the shore), and on to East Point Lighthouse, which stands guard over the island's northeast tip. Lunch could be a bowl of chowder at nearby North Lake Boathouse Eatery.

Continuing west on Hwy 16, follow the north shore toward Greenwich, at the east end of Prince Edward Island National Park. Plug in your car while you walk the 3-mile (4.8km) Greenwich Dunes Trail across a floating boardwalk and between the park's towering sand dunes. Some 25 minutes' drive further on, your destination for the night is Nature Space Resort near St Peters Harbour; paddle a kayak through the lagoon before settling into your well-appointed yurt in the forest.

## THROUGH PEI NATIONAL PARK

Return to civilization in the morning with breakfast or a walk at Dalvay-by-the-Sea, an 1896 Queen Anne Revival–style manor within the boundaries of PEI National Park. Drive on through the park along Gulf Shore Way, stopping at Brackley Beach for some sun or a swim (there are chargers here, too). At Dunes Studio Gallery & Café just south, wander the fanciful sculpture garden, then pick up Hwy 6 and drive on 10 miles (16km) to North Rustico, where Blue Mussel Café or On the Dock are good choices for a harborside seafood lunch.

## Lobster suppers

Lobster fishing remains important to the PEI's economy, and enjoying a traditional lobster supper is a classic way to experience the island's shellfish bounty. But don't worry if you don't have a lobster-fishing friend to invite you to dinner: several island restaurants offer these substantial lobster meals. In North Rustico, Fisherman's Wharf Lobster Supper (fishermanswharf.ca) starts with a 60ft-long (18m) buffet table, lined with salads, chowders, soups and steamed mussels, plus breads, fruit, cakes and pies. After you help yourself to your first courses, your server brings your lobster; the price you pay depends on the size of the crustacean you choose. Nearby, New Glasgow Lobster Suppers (peilobstersuppers.com) has been serving ample meals since the 1950s. Here, your server delivers salads, soups and mussels, then lobster and your dessert finale. Snap a photo wearing PEI's favorite accessory – a lobster bib.

**Clockwise from top:** vivid field of canola rolls down to the seashore; further brilliant colors on storefronts in the capital of PEI, Charlottetown; fishing boats in North Rustico

In the afternoon, continue on Hwy 6 for about 5 miles (8km) to Cavendish, notable for its association with Lucy Maud Montgomery and her *Anne of Green Gables* novels. At Green Gables Heritage Place (operated by Parks Canada and with EV chargers), exhibits tell you about the author's life; then walk through "Green Gables," the farmhouse that inspired the setting for the novels. Next follow a walking trail through the woods to the Cavendish home in which Montgomery lived for 35 years and wrote many of her books. Moving on, stop for oysters, mussels or lobster at New London's Sou'West Bar & Grill before heading south to overnight in Summerside.

## CLOSING THE LOOP

Just west of Summerside via Hwy 2, visit the Acadian Museum in Miscouche to learn about the heritage and culture of PEI's French-speaking communities. From the museum, it's 28 miles (45km) up to Lennox Island, where Lennox Island First Nation members offer several Indigenous cultural experiences: learn to bake bannock (a biscuit-like bread) in a firepit, make a moose-hide drum, or practice quill-work at a workshop. Stop for a cup of tea and a sandwich at Tyne Valley Teas, then retrace your route back to Summerside. Top up your battery while touring the unusual International Fox Museum, which gives the lowdown on PEI's once-booming fox-farming industry.

From Summerside, it's 23 miles (37km) east on Hwy 1 to the scenic oceanside village of Victoria-by-the-Sea. Kayak near the harbor, then browse the art galleries and sip hot chocolate at Island Chocolates. Dig into fresh oysters or a lobster roll at Landmark Oyster House or the Lobster Barn before wrapping up your trip by driving the 22 miles (35km) east back to Charlottetown. Want one more treat? PEI-based Cows Ice Cream has a convenient shop at their headquarters, which is right on your way.

**Below:** fresh-caught Nova Scotia lobster
**Right:** the route winds towards Peggy's Cove

Distance: 1305 miles (2100km)

Duration: 10-12 days

# Halifax to the Cabot Trail & back

**NOVA SCOTIA**

Circle your EV around Nova Scotia to savor the natural bounty of this magnificent Maritime province: the finest lobster, the most succulent scallops, the sweetest blueberries, the most surprising wine.

Nova Scotia's scenic highways are like a delicious drive-thru. This Maritime Province is renowned for its exquisite lobster but there's plenty more besides, from Digby scallops, caught in the Bay of Fundy, to wild blueberries, Annapolis Valley apples, Scottish-style oatcakes and Acadian rappie (potato and chicken) pie. Buckle up for an electric foodie drive.

## GRAZING AROUND THE COAST

Start in the feel-good provincial capital, Halifax, where you can visit the Citadel, take a Taste Halifax Local Food Tour, hit the live-music bars and finish with a cheeky donair, Nova Scotia's take on a doner kebab.

Then spend a few days heading west on the wonderful Lighthouse Route. It'll take you to ridiculously photogenic Peggy's Cove after 65 miles (105km); gorgeous Lunenburg, 62 miles (101km) further on, is crammed with pretty B&Bs – try Smuggler's Cove Inn – and seafood restaurants. Order the Lunenburger at Grand Banker Bar & Grill, a beef patty topped with lobster.

Next, Fort Point Lighthouse and the seaside section of Kejimkujik National Park are perfect for picnics, while in Liverpool you can sample craft beer at Hell Bay Brewing. Don't miss Captain Kat's Lobster Shack in Barrington,

## Plan & prepare

### Tips for EV drivers

The charging network here is expanding but not extensive. Nova Scotia Power has installed a network of fast-charging stations approximately 40 miles (65km) apart; locations include Sobey's stores in Digby and Liverpool, and the Lynwood Inn in Baddeck. Parks Canada manages chargers at points along the Cabot Trail, which are free to use with a park pass; locations include the Chéticamp Visitor Centre and MacIntosh Brook Trailhead.

### Where to stay

Smuggler's Cove Inn (smugglerscoveinn.ca), in the heart of Lunenburg, has homely rooms and an EV charger for guests. A restored 19th-century sea captain's mansion, Blomidon Inn (blomidon.ns.ca) in Wolfville has characterful rooms; there are EV chargers nearby, further down Main St. Useful if you drink one dram too many, Glenora Inn & Distillery on Cape Breton (glenoradistillery.com) has rooms, cottages and chalets where you can overnight. There's a charger here too.

### When to go

Nova Scotia's weather tends to be less extreme than in some other parts of Canada. That said, winters are still cold and damp, and many tourist businesses close. May and June bring blossom and warming climes. July to August is peak season – expect higher prices, bigger crowds, the most festivals and temperatures of 70°F to 80°F (21°C to 27°C); this is the best time for Fundy whale-watching, too. The Cabot Trail can be magical September through November, when fall colors explode.

### Further info

The Cabot Trail may be driven in either direction. Most people go clockwise, driving on the inland lane; anticlockwise, the views are actually better and traffic lighter but the drop-offs to the coast, directly off the passenger side, can be vertiginous. There are many blind bends and steep climbs and descents – go slowly and carefully. To drive the trail, you'll need to pay the Cape Breton Highlands National Park entrance fee at one of the visitor centers or roadside kiosks.

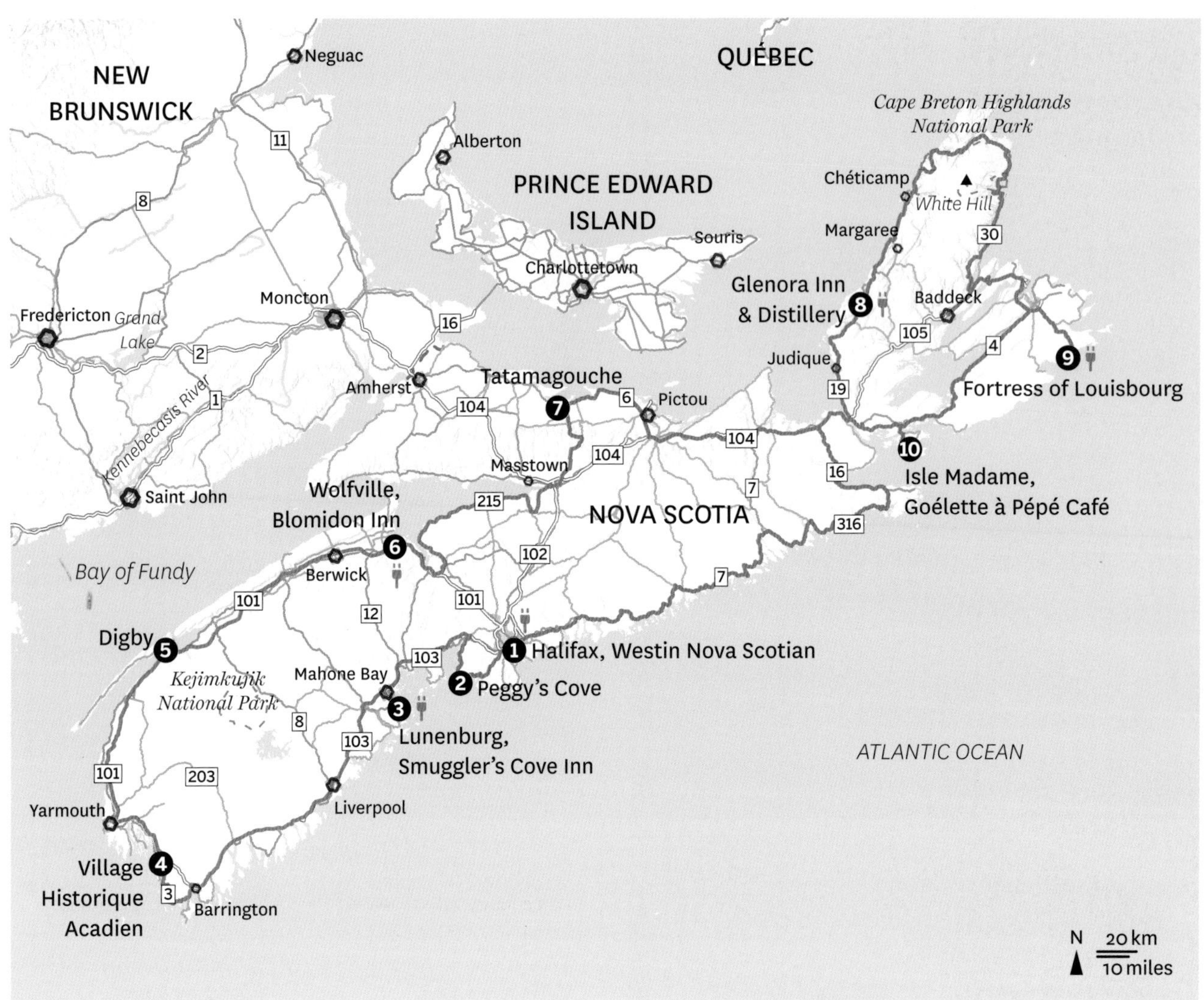


Canada's lobster capital. From hereon Acadian culture becomes more pronounced: visit Le Village Historique Acadien to learn about fishing and farming traditions and try homecooked dishes.

From Yarmouth, drive the Evangeline Trail around the Fundy coast, parking your EV in the Digby area for its eponymous scallops and superb whale-watching. Then meander through the verdant Annapolis Valley, flush with tasty producers. Wolfville's Blomidon Inn, 87 miles (140km) from Digby, provides a characterful overnight.

## TO CAPE BRETON & THE CABOT TRAIL

Moving on, stock up at Masstown Market before taking Rte 311 across to the seaside village of Tatamagouche, home to Appleton Chocolates and the Tatamagouche Brewing Company. Then ride along the sandy Northumberland Strait shore to Cape Breton Island, where things take a Scottish turn. Follow Rte 19 for 20 miles (32km), tracing the coast to Judique's Celtic Music Interpretive Centre (for lunchtime ceilidhs and steaming chowder) and Glenville's Glenora Inn & Distillery, producers of North America's first (Scotch-style) single malt whisky; there are rooms and an EV charger here too.

Perhaps the highlight of this EV odyssey is driving the Cabot Trail, a winding, up-down 186-mile (300km) route between the forested highlands and rugged coast of Cape Breton Highlands National Park – one of the world's great drives. Join the Cabot at Margaree and be wowed at every turn – pulling over regularly to hit one of the park's 26 hiking trails, look for whales or recharge your car. At North River Bridge, stop at the eco-award-winning Chanterelle Inn, where the creative restaurant uses locally-sourced produce.

Leave the Cabot Trail at Baddeck and head to the reconstructed 18th-century Fortress of Louisbourg, offering history, rum tasting, EV charging and

accommodation – you can even bunk in the old prison. Then, it's around 270 miles (435km) back to Halifax via the most direct route. But instead take the Fleur-de-lis Trail, a scenic byway through Acadian country, followed by the Marine Drive along the south coast. Make one last detour to idyllic Isle Madame, to treat yourself to blueberry cheesecake at the Goélette à Pépé Café.

## Wines of Nova Scotia

Grapes have been grown in Nova Scotia since the 17th century, when French settler Louis Hébert planted the first vineyard in Bear River, in the Annapolis Valley, in 1611. However, commercial wineries didn't get going until the 1980s. The province's first wine appellation, Tidal Bay, was launched in 2012; a crisp, aromatic white, it pairs perfectly with the local seafood. These days there are more than 20 wineries in Nova Scotia, and many are open for tours and tastings. Near Wolfville, you can sip and slurp at Grand Pré, also home to the elegant Le Caveau restaurant, or visit Jost Vineyards on the Northumberland shore, the largest and longest-operating winery in the province. Beyond having an eager designated driver, the best plan is to park up in Wolfville (leave your car at the fast-charge point on Main St) and board the Magic Winery Bus (Wednesdays-Sundays; magicwinerybus.ca). This red double-decker will drop you at three or four cellar doors in the Annapolis region, so you can enjoy a tipple or two. A different selection of producers is visited on different days but might include Blomidon Estate, Planters Ridge, Luckett Vineyards and Benjamin Bridge.

**Clockwise from top left:** the lighthouse at Peggy's Cove; sampling local wines, a recent tradition here; hearty Acadian rappie pie

**Below:** Cape Spear Lighthouse National Historic Site
**Right:** track towards Cape Race on the Avalon Peninsula

Distance: 210 miles (338km)

Duration: 2-3 days

# Irish Loop from St John's

**NEWFOUNDLAND**

Where else on Earth can you make an easy, breezy weekend EV drive that comes with huffing whales, drifting icebergs and a joyous soundtrack of traditional music to boot?

Welcome to North America's extreme Atlantic edge. St John's, capital of Newfoundland, is closer to Dublin than Vancouver – and sounds more like it, thanks to the lilting accents and musical traditions, brought over by waves of immigrants from the Emerald Isle. The Irish Loop is a short jaunt around a small corner of this massive island, which is a place of rolling fog, roiling seas, close-knit communities, fresh fish suppers, fiddle players and puffing whales. Hop in your EV for a craic-ing Newfoundland taster.

## CAPITAL & CAPE

With its bright-painted "jellybean" houses and effervescent live-music scene (try the Ship Pub or any bar on George St), St John's is a blast. Stay by the harbor – the DoubleTree by Hilton couldn't be closer – for easy access to nightlife and the coast trails up and around historic Signal Hill. The Irish Loop, which traces the southeast half of the Avalon Peninsula, extends south of St John's. But before starting proper, steer your EV 8 miles (13km) east down Blackhead Rd to reach Cape Spear: stand at the continent's easternmost point, visit the 1836 lighthouse, and look for whales. But no worries if you don't see any cetaceans here. Pick up Rte 10 and

## Plan & prepare

### Tips for EV drivers

For the time being EV charging points aren't widespread but are just frequent enough to allow this route to be covered without stress. St John's has several, including at the public parking garage on Water St and the visitor center parking lot on Signal Hill. Others can be found at Fermeuse (near Ferryland), at St Mary's and at Holyrood, on the return to St John's.

### Where to stay

The DoubleTree by Hilton (hilton.com) in St John's is a smart, harborside hotel with maritime-tinged decor, close to parking lots with EV chargers. The sea-view rooms at the Edge of Avalon Inn (edgeoftheavaloninn.com) in Trepassey sit at the mid-point of the Irish Loop; chargers are nearby. Or try the Keepers Kitchen B&B (thekeeperskitchen.com) in nearby St Shotts, which also offers storytelling and traditional music. The Wilds Resort (thewilds.ca) at Salmonier River has a hotel, villas and golf course.

### When to go

Winters are long, damp, cold and tough in Newfoundland – best avoided. Temperatures are warmest June to August, when highs reach the mid-70°Fs (mid-20°Cs). Icebergs start to drift down the coast from April, with May and June usually the best months; check online (at icebergfinder.com) to track them. The whale-watching season runs from mid-May to September, peaking mid-July to mid-August. Ferryland's Shamrock Festival, a showcase of traditional Irish and Newfoundland music, is held in late July.

### Further info

Newfoundland can be reached by flights into St John's or by ferry from Nova Scotia to either Port aux Basques (a nine-hour drive from St John's) or Argentia (90 minutes). Download the NL 511 app (or visit 511nl.ca) for up-to-date info on driving conditions, construction work, ferries and more. Newfoundland has 120,000 moose; most moose-related vehicle accidents occur between dusk and dawn, so take extra care if you must drive at these times.

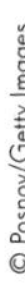

## Irish influx

They call Newfoundland and Labrador the most Irish place outside Ireland. To be sure, there are similarities between their rugged coastlines, verdant hills, amount of precipitation and underlying geology (180 million years ago they were part of the same supercontinent). But it's more about the shared culture. Huge numbers of Irish immigrants came here in the 18th and 19th centuries, drawn by work at the fisheries; by 1840, roughly half Newfoundland's population was of Irish origin. Traveling the Irish Loop you'll hear the lingo, the accents and the music. A welcome stop is Sullivan's Songhouse (sullivanssonghouse.com) in Calvert, an hour's drive south of St John's. Here, on Wednesdays and Saturdays, June through October, Sean Sullivan hosts a traditional "kitchen party" in his family home, which involves a couple of musicians playing old tunes and everyone else singing and toe-tapping along. Newfoundland is a great place to be for St Patrick's Day too; it's a public holiday in the province. Celebrations in St John's aren't confined to 17 March but rather stretched over a week. George St pubs put on live music and are packed with emerald-clad revelers, and Signal Hill is lit up green.

**Clockwise from above:** O'Reilly's pub on George St, St John's; puffin at Witless Bay Ecological Reserve; harbor-side houses, St John's

head for Witless Bay, where masses of humpback and minke, plus millions of seabirds, like to hang out. Boat trips into this ecological reserve leave from spots like Bay Bulls, 22 miles (35km) south of Cape Spear. Keep an eye out for ice, too: massive bergs, drifting down from Greenland, often pass right by this coast.

Further spotting can be done on foot from the East Coast Trail, which runs along this shoreline for 209 miles (336km). Park up to hike a section, perhaps the easy 3.5-mile (5.6km) Caplin Bay Path from Calvert to Ferryland. Calvert's Squid Jigger cafe has a panoramic deck and EV charger. Ferryland, founded in the 1620s, is one of the oldest European settlements in North America; watch archaeologists at work, pick up food to go from Lighthouse Picnics at the old lighthouse and pop into the Southern Shore Folk Arts Council to scope out local festivals and gigs.

### AVALON ENCOUNTERS

Rte 10 rolls scenically on, inland of hazardous Cape Race, wrecker of many ships; it's a wild 12-mile (19km)

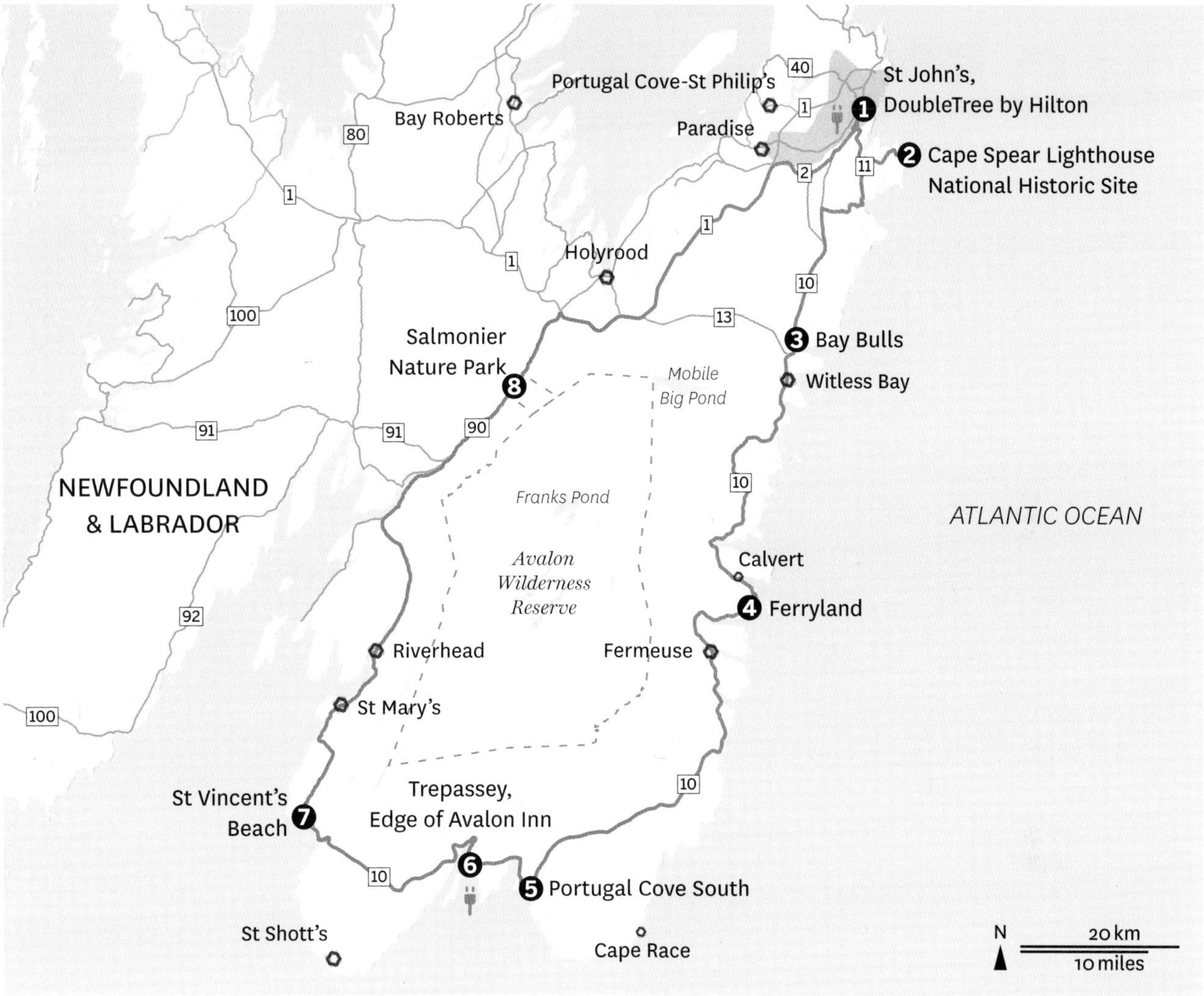
St John's,
1 DoubleTree by Hilton
2 Cape Spear Lighthouse
National Historic Site
Portugal Cove-St Philip's
Bay Roberts
Paradise
Holyrood
Salmonier
Nature Park
8
3 Bay Bulls
Witless Bay
Mobile
Big Pond
Franks Pond
NEWFOUNDLAND
& LABRADOR
ATLANTIC OCEAN
Avalon
Wilderness
Reserve
Calvert
4 Ferryland
Riverhead
Fermeuse
St Mary's
St Vincent's
Beach
7
Trepassey,
Edge of Avalon Inn
6
5 Portugal Cove South
St Shott's
Cape Race
N
20 km
10 miles
40
1
11
2
80
10
13
100
91
90
92

detour from Portugal Cove South to visit the cape's Mistaken Point for fossils, a lonely lighthouse and a former signal station, which received the distress call of the *Titanic*. Otherwise, pull your EV into the old fishing harbor of Trepassey, where there's a little museum, a grocery store with a charger and the welcoming Edge of Avalon Inn.

Rte 10 morphs into Rte 90 around St Vincent's Beach – one of the best shoreline whale-watching spots, well, anywhere, with cetaceans sometimes seen frolicking just a few feet from the sand. Then enjoy your EV's silence as the Irish Loop turns north past Holyrood Pond, bayside St Mary's and Riverhead. The Avalon Wilderness Reserve, flush with wildlife, extends to the east. More accessible is Salmonier Nature Park, where you can get closer to rehabilitated moose, caribou and lynx. The nature-set Wilds Resort at Salmonier River is close by, or toast the close to your trip 40 miles (64km) on, back in St John's.

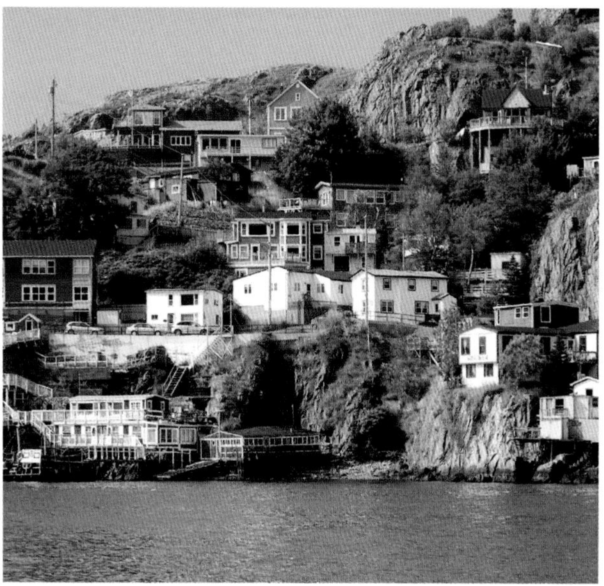

# INDEX

## N

**Electric Vehicle Road Trips USA & Canada**
May 2024
Published by Lonely Planet Global Limited
CRN 554153
www.lonelyplanet.com
10 9 8 7 6 5 4 3 2 1

Printed in China
ISBN 978 18375 8196 2


**Publishing Director** Piers Pickard
**Gift & Illustrated Publisher** Becca Hunt
**Senior Editor** Robin Barton
**Commissioning Editor** Peter Grunert
**Editor** Polly Thomas
**Designer** Kristina Juodenas
**Photo Research** Heike Bohnstengel
**Cartographers** Katerina Pavkova, Bohumil Ptáček, Vojta Bartos
**Print Production** Nigel Longuet

**Writers** Sarah Baxter, Elaine Glusac, Carolyn B Heller, Lauren Keith, Emily Matchar, Etain O'Carroll, Brendan Sainsbury, Mara Vorhees, Clifton Wilkinson

**Data sources**
© Lonely Planet
© OpenStreetMap contributors
NASA/METI/AIST/Japan Space Systems, and US/Japan ASTER Science Team (2019). ASTER Global Digital Elevation Model V003
NASA JPL (2013). NASA Shuttle Radar Topography Mission Global 1 arc second
British Oceanographic Data Centre(2015). The GEBCO_2014 Grid



**STAY IN TOUCH** lonelyplanet.com/contact

Lonely Planet Global Limited

Digital Depot, Roe Lane (off Thomas St), Digital Hub, Dublin 8, D08 TCV4, IRELAND

**Cover images** © f11photo / Shutterstock (front); f11photo / Shutterstock; @ Tobin Akehurst / Shutterstock (back)